BLACK&DECKER®

THE COMPLETE GUIDE TO

WIRING

- **Revised 4th Edition**
  Complies with 2008–2011 NEC
- **Upgrade Your Main Service Panel**
- **Discover the Latest Wiring Products**

Creative Publishing
international

MINNEAPOLIS, MINNESOTA
www.creativepub.com

Creative Publishing international

Copyright © 2008
Creative Publishing international, Inc.
400 First Avenue North, Suite 300
Minneapolis, Minnesota 55401
1-800-328-0590
www.creativepub.com

Printed at R.R.Donnelley

10 9 8 7

Library of Congress Cataloging-in-Publication Data

The complete guide to wiring. -- 4th ed.
    p. cm. -- (Complete guide)
    "Revised 4th Edition Complies with 2008-2010 NEC."
    Includes index.
    Summary: "Covers all of the most common do-it-yourself home wiring
skills and projects, including new circuits, installations and repair.
New projects in this edition include upgrading a service panel to 209
amps and wiring an outbuilding"--Provided by publisher.
    ISBN-13: 978-1-58923-413-0 (soft cover)
    ISBN-10: 1-58923-413-8 (soft cover)
    1. Electric wiring, Interior. I. Title. II. Series.

TK3284.C65 2008
621.319'24--dc22

2008016519

President/CEO: Ken Fund
VP for Sales & Marketing: Kevin Hamric

Home Improvement Group

Publisher: Bryan Trandem
Managing Editor: Tracy Stanley
Senior Editor: Mark Johanson
Editor: Jennifer Gehlhar

Creative Director: Michele Lanci-Altomare
Senior Design Managers: Jon Simpson, Brad Springer
Design Manager: James Kegley

Lead Photographer: Steve Galvin
Photo Coordinator: Joanne Wawra
Shop Manager: Bryan McLain
Shop Assistant: Cesar Fernandez Rodriguez

Production Managers: Linda Halls, Laura Hokkanen

Page Layout Artist: Danielle Smith
Photographer: Andrea Rugg
Shop Help: Scott Boyd, David Hartley

The Complete Guide to Wiring
Created by: The Editors of Creative Publishing international, Inc., in cooperation with Black & Decker.
Black & Decker® is a trademark of The Black & Decker Corporation and is used under license.

NOTICE TO READERS

For safety, use caution, care, and good judgment when following the procedures described in this book. The publisher and Black & Decker cannot assume responsibility for any damage to property or injury to persons as a result of misuse of the information provided.

The techniques shown in this book are general techniques for various applications. In some instances, additional techniques not shown in this book may be required. Always follow manufacturers' instructions included with products, since deviating from the directions may void warranties. The projects in this book vary widely as to skill levels required: some may not be appropriate for all do-it-yourselfers, and some may require professional help.

Consult your local building department for information on building permits, codes, and other laws as they apply to your project.

Contents

The Complete Guide to Wiring

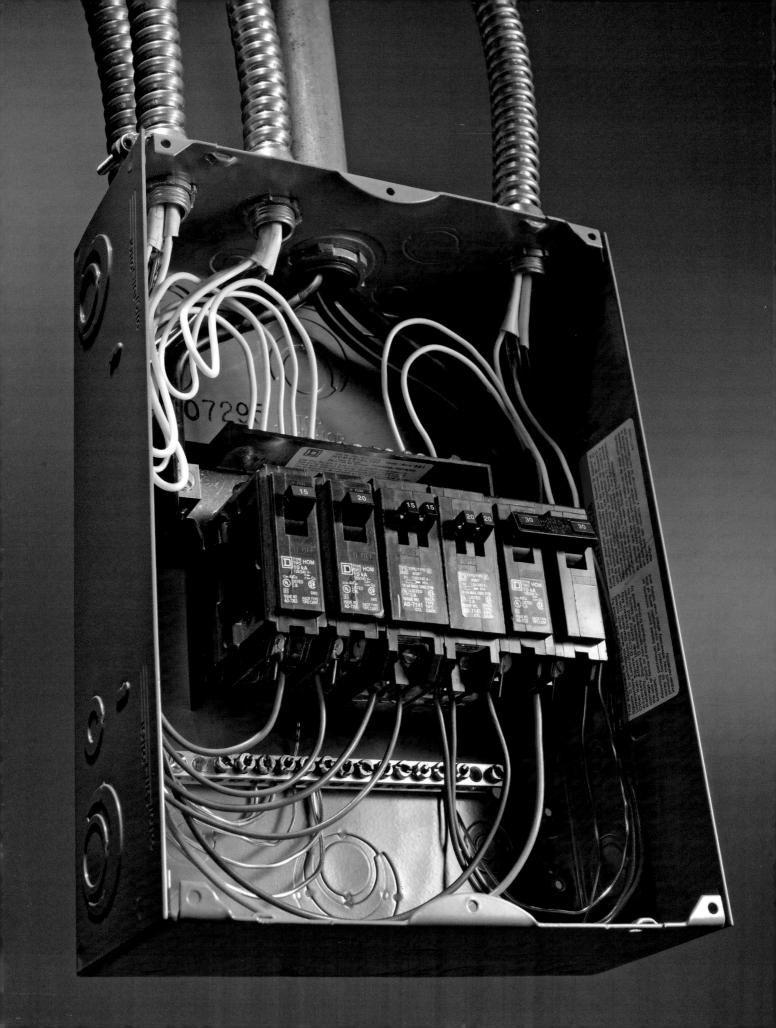

Introduction

When it comes to home wiring for the DIYer, the book you're holding in your hands is one in a million. Now in its 4th edition, Black & Decker's *Complete Guide to Wiring* has sold more than 1 million copies, establishing itself as the best-selling home wiring book in North America. Handy homeowners everywhere have made their choice: if you are looking for reliable, clear, up-to-date information on all aspects of the home electrical system, *Complete Guide to Wiring (4th edition)* is the book for you.

Wiring is an unusual task. It can be deeply satisfying or enormously frustrating. It can be straightforward and simple or devilishly complex. It is a highly useful skill, but it is also highly dangerous. As DIY undertakings go, it is not for the faint of heart. But as your experience grows, you will find that having the ability to manage and maintain your electrical system enables you to respond to all varieties of home emergencies, and to make home improvements that have instant payback.

Updated to conform with the 2008 National Electrical Code (NEC) wiring codes, *The Complete Guide to Wiring* is a comprehensive examination of electricity as it is applied in today's homes. With easy-to-understand definitions, step-by-step instructions, and clear color photos, you will recognize that most electrical work around your home, from basic repairs to advanced wiring projects, is work you can easily accomplish. Even if you hire professionals to replace fixtures or install new circuits, understanding how wiring works and what is required to complete a job will make you a more savvy consumer and help you make the best use of your money.

The pages of this book provide thorough explanations of the home wiring system: wire, cable, and conduit; boxes and panels; switches; and receptacles. You will learn how they work together to create circuits that deliver electrical current safely. You'll see exactly how to handle each of these components using tools that are correct for the job. And you'll also see all of the most common home wiring projects presented for you with step-by-step photos in complete detail. Whether you are replacing a lamp cord or upgrading your main service panel, in this book you will find the information you need to do the job right.

When performing wiring jobs in your home it is critically important to involve your local electrical inspections department from the start. If you are installing new circuits or adding capacity, you need a permit and most likely a physical inspection of your work. Do not avoid this step. Local inspectors are generally very helpful and should be considered valuable resources. Failing to obtain permits or inspections can result in fines. If the wiring is incorrect or of substandard workmanship, major disasters can occur. If at any time during a wiring job you encounter a situation about which you are unsure, stop and get assistance.

Always use the best materials and tools available for the job and do careful, thorough work. Test connections and follow all safety practices and building codes. When you do competent, methodical work, you will feel great pride in your accomplishments and in the self-sufficiency that accompanies them.

BASICS OF WIRING

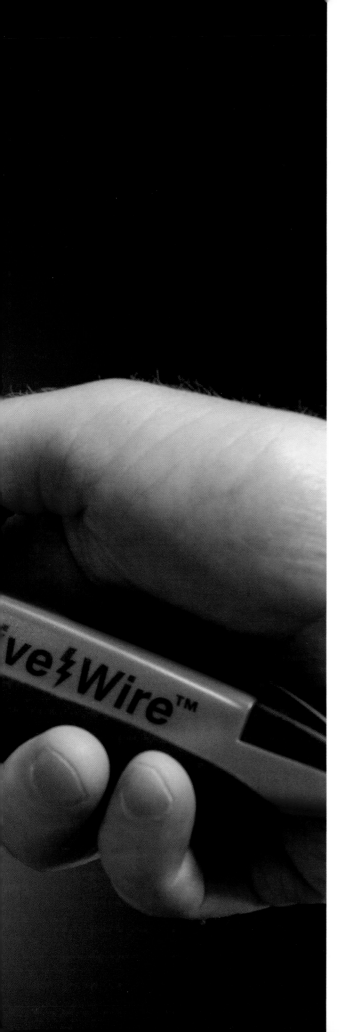

Working Safely with Wiring

The only way you can possibly manage home wiring projects safely is to understand how electricity works and how it is delivered from the street to the outlets in your home.

The most essential quality to appreciate about electricity is that the typical amounts that flow through the wires in your home can be fatal under certain conditions if you contact it directly. Sources estimate that up to 1,000 people are electrocuted accidentally in the U.S. every year. In addition, as many as 500 die in fires from electrical causes. Home wiring can be a very satisfying task for do-it-yourselfers, but if you don't know what you're doing or are in any way uncomfortable with the idea of working around electricity, do not attempt it.

This chapter is intended to explain the fundamental principles behind the electrical circuits that run through our homes. It also includes some very basic tips for working safely with wiring, and it details the essential tools you'll need for the job. For the beginner it should be considered mandatory reading. Even if you have a good idea of electrical principles, take some time to review the material. A refresher course is always useful.

In this chapter:
- How Electricity Works
- Understanding Electrical Circuits
- Grounding & Polarization
- Home Wiring Tools
- Wiring Safety

How Electricity Works

A household electrical system can be compared with a home's plumbing system. Electrical current flows in wires in much the same way that water flows inside pipes. Both electricity and water enter the home, are distributed throughout the house, do their "work," and exit.

In plumbing, water first flows through the pressurized water supply system. In electricity, current first flows along hot wires. Current flowing along hot wires also is pressurized. The pressure of electrical current is called voltage.

Large supply pipes can carry a greater volume of water than small pipes. Likewise, large electrical wires carry more current than small wires. This current-carrying capacity of wires is called amperage.

Water is made available for use through the faucets, spigots, and showerheads in a home. Electricity is made available through receptacles, switches, and fixtures.

Water finally leaves the home through a drain system, which is not pressurized. Similarly, electrical current flows back through neutral wires. The current in neutral wires is not pressurized and is said to be at zero voltage.

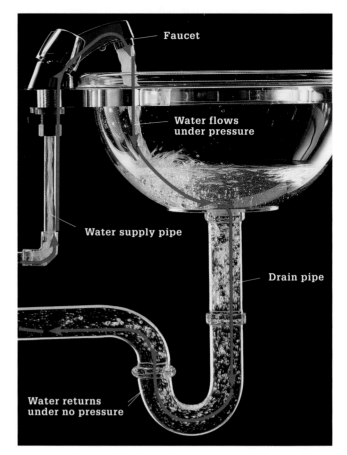

Water and electricity both flow. The main difference is that you can see water (and touching water isn't likely to kill you). Like electricity, water enters a fixture under high pressure and exits under low pressure.

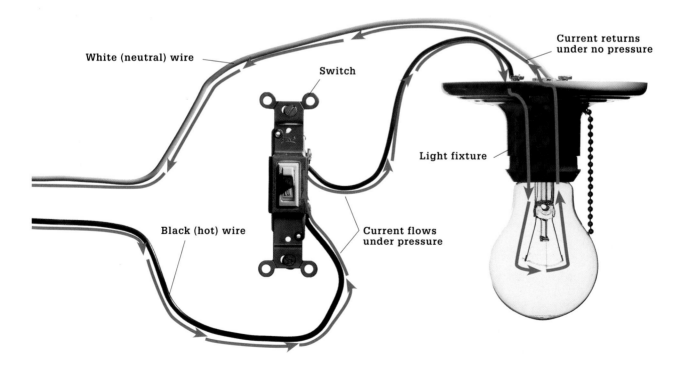

The Delivery System

Electrical power that enters the home is produced by large power plants. Power plants are located in all parts of the country and generate electricity with turbines that are turned by water, wind, or steam. From these plants electricity enters large "step-up" transformers that increase voltage to half a million volts or more.

Electricity flows easily at these large voltages and travels through high-voltage transmission lines to communities that can be hundreds of miles from the power plants. "Step-down" transformers located at substations then reduce the voltage for distribution along street lines. On utility power poles, smaller transformers further reduce the voltage to ordinary 120-volt current for household use.

Lines carrying current to the house either run underground or are strung overhead and attached to a post called a service mast. Most homes built after 1950 have three wires running to the service head: two power lines, each carrying 120 volts of current, and a grounded neutral wire. Power from the two 120-volt lines may be combined at the service panel to supply current to large 240-volt appliances like clothes dryers or electric water heaters.

Incoming power passes through an electric meter that measures power consumption. Power then enters the service panel, where it is distributed to circuits that run throughout the house. The service panel also contains fuses or circuit breakers that shut off power to the individual circuits in the event of a short circuit or an overload. Certain high-wattage appliances, like microwave ovens, are usually plugged into their own individual circuits to prevent overloads.

Voltage ratings determined by power companies and manufacturers have changed over the years. Current rated at 110 volts changed to 115 volts, then 120 volts. Current rated at 220 volts changed to 230 volts, then 240 volts. Similarly, ratings for receptacles, tools, light fixtures, and appliances have changed from 115 volts to 125 volts. These changes do not affect the performance of new devices connected to older wiring. For making electrical calculations, use a rating of 120 volts or 240 volts for your circuits.

Power plants supply electricity to thousands of homes and businesses. Step-up transformers increase the voltage produced at the plant, making the power flow more easily along high-voltage transmission lines.

Substations are located near the communities they serve. A typical substation takes current from high-voltage transmission lines and reduces it for distribution along street lines.

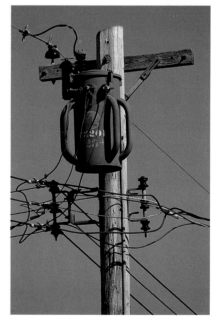

Utility pole transformers reduce the high-voltage current that flows through power lines along neighborhood streets. A utility pole transformer reduces voltage from 10,000 volts to the normal 120-volt current used in households.

Parts of the Electrical System

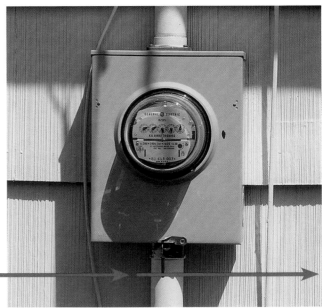

The service mast is the metal pole and weatherhead that create the entry point for electricity into your home. The mast is supplied with three wires carrying 240 volts and originating from the nearest transformer.

The electric meter measures the amount of electrical power consumed. It is usually attached to the side of the house, and connects to the service mast. A thin metal disc inside the meter rotates when power is used. The electric meter belongs to your local power utility company. If you suspect the meter is not functioning properly, contact the power company.

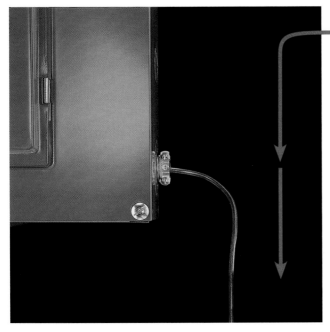

Grounding wire connects the electrical system to the earth through grounding rods or, in older systems, through a cold water pipe. In the event of an overload or short circuit, the grounding wire allows excess electrical power to find its way harmlessly to the earth.

Light fixtures attach directly to a household electrical system. They are usually controlled with wall switches. The two common types of light fixtures are incandescent and fluorescent.

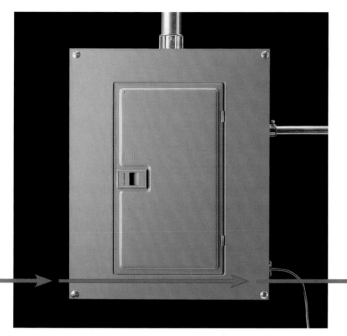

The main service panel, in the form of a fuse box or breaker box, distributes power to individual circuits. Fuses or circuit breakers protect each circuit from short circuits and overloads. Fuses and circuit breakers also are used to shut off power to individual circuits while repairs are made.

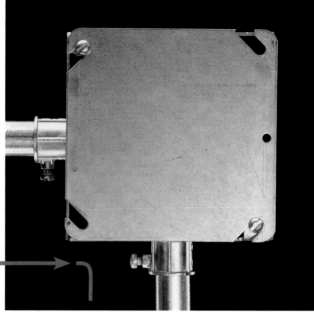

Electrical boxes enclose wire connections. According to the National Electrical Code, all wire splices or connections must be contained entirely in a covered plastic or metal electrical box.

Switches control electrical current passing through hot circuit wires. Switches can be wired to control light fixtures, ceiling fans, appliances, and receptacles.

Receptacles, sometimes called outlets, provide plug-in access to electrical power. A 120-volt, 15-amp receptacle with a grounding hole is the most typical receptacle in wiring systems installed after 1965. Most receptacles have two plug-in locations and are called duplex receptacles.

Glossary of Electrical Terms ▸

Ampere (or amp): Refers to the rate at which electrical power flows to a light, tool, or appliance.

Armored cable: Two or more wires that are grouped together and protected by a flexible metal covering.

Box: A device used to contain wiring connections.

BX: See armored cable (Bx is the older term).

Cable: Two or more wires that are grouped together and protected by a covering or sheath.

Circuit: A continuous loop of electrical current flowing along wires or cables.

Circuit breaker: A safety device that interrupts an electrical circuit in the event of an overload or short circuit.

Conductor: Any material that allows electrical current to flow through it. Copper wire is an especially good conductor.

Conduit: A metal or plastic pipe used to protect wires.

Continuity: An uninterrupted electrical pathway through a circuit or electrical fixture.

Current: The movement of electrons along a conductor.

Duplex receptacle: A receptacle that provides connections for two plugs.

Feed wire: A conductor that carries 120-volt current uninterrupted from the service panel.

Fuse: A safety device, usually found in older homes, that interrupts electrical circuits during an overload or short circuit.

Greenfield: Materials used in flexible metal conduit. See armored cable.

Grounded wire: See neutral wire.

Grounding wire: A wire used in an electrical circuit to conduct current to the earth in the event of a short circuit. The grounding wire often is a bare copper wire.

Hot wire: Any wire that carries voltage. In an electrical circuit, the hot wire usually is covered with black or red insulation.

Insulator: Any material, such as plastic or rubber, that resists the flow of electrical current. Insulating materials protect wires and cables.

Junction box: See box.

Meter: A device used to measure the amount of electrical power being used.

Neutral wire: A wire that returns current at zero voltage to the source of electrical power. Usually covered with white or light gray insulation. Also called the grounded wire.

Outlet: See receptacle.

Overload: A demand for more current than the circuit wires or electrical device was designed to carry. Usually causes a fuse to blow or a circuit breaker to trip.

Pigtail: A short wire used to connect two or more circuit wires to a single screw terminal.

Polarized receptacle: A receptacle designed to keep hot current flowing along black or red wires, and neutral current flowing along white or gray wires.

Power: The result of hot current flowing for a period of time. Use of power makes heat, motion, or light.

Receptacle: A device that provides plug-in access to electrical power.

Romex: A brand name of plastic-sheathed electrical cable that is commonly used for indoor wiring. Commonly known as NM cable.

Screw terminal: A place where a wire connects to a receptacle, switch, or fixture.

Service panel: A metal box usually near the site where electrical power enters the house. In the service panel, electrical current is split into individual circuits. The service panel has circuit breakers or fuses to protect each circuit.

Short circuit: An accidental and improper contact between two current-carrying wires, or between a current-carrying wire and a grounding conductor.

Switch: A device that controls electrical current passing through hot circuit wires. Used to turn lights and appliances on and off.

UL: An abbreviation for Underwriters Laboratories, an organization that tests electrical devices and manufactured products for safety.

Voltage (or volts): A measurement of electricity in terms of pressure.

Wattage (or watt): A measurement of electrical power in terms of total energy consumed. Watts can be calculated by multiplying the voltage times the amps.

Wire connector: A device used to connect two or more wires together. Also called a wire nut.

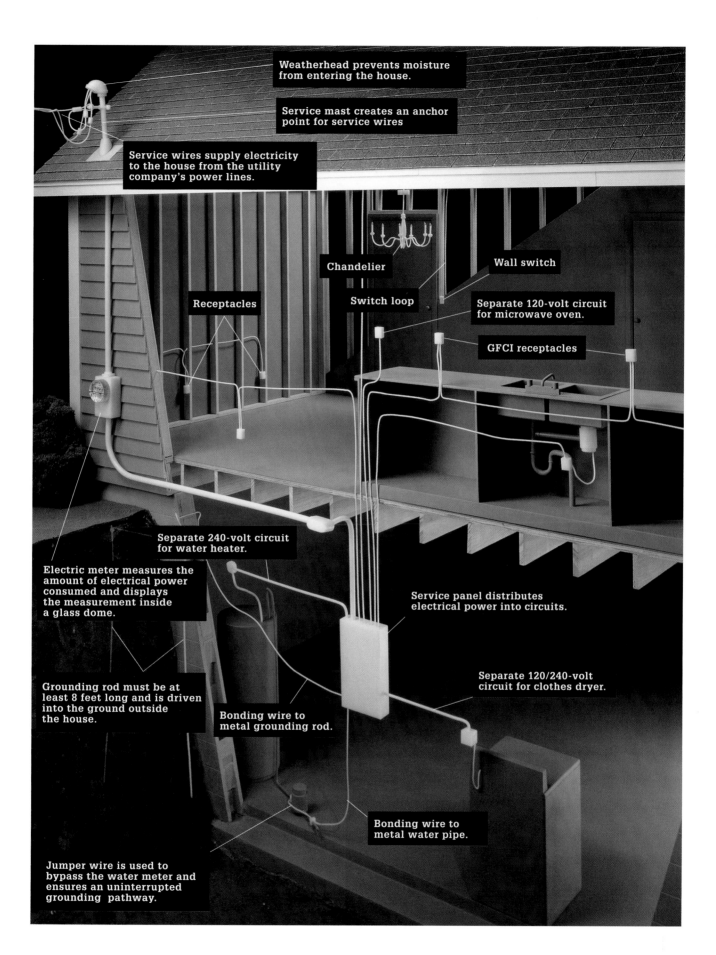

Weatherhead prevents moisture from entering the house.

Service mast creates an anchor point for service wires

Service wires supply electricity to the house from the utility company's power lines.

Chandelier

Wall switch

Switch loop

Receptacles

Separate 120-volt circuit for microwave oven.

GFCI receptacles

Separate 240-volt circuit for water heater.

Electric meter measures the amount of electrical power consumed and displays the measurement inside a glass dome.

Service panel distributes electrical power into circuits.

Grounding rod must be at least 8 feet long and is driven into the ground outside the house.

Bonding wire to metal grounding rod.

Separate 120/240-volt circuit for clothes dryer.

Bonding wire to metal water pipe.

Jumper wire is used to bypass the water meter and ensures an uninterrupted grounding pathway.

Understanding Electrical Circuits

An electrical circuit is a continuous loop. Household circuits carry power from the main service panel, throughout the house, and back to the main service panel. Several switches, receptacles, light fixtures, or appliances may be connected to a single circuit.

Current enters a circuit loop on hot wires and returns along neutral wires. These wires are color coded for easy identification. Hot wires are black or red, and neutral wires are white or light gray. For safety, most circuits include a bare copper or green insulated grounding wire. The grounding wire conducts current in the event of a short circuit or overload, and helps reduce the chance of severe electrical shock. The service panel also has a grounding wire connected to a metal water pipe and metal grounding rod buried underground.

If a circuit carries too much power, it can overload. A fuse or a circuit breaker protects each circuit in case of overloads.

Current returns to the service panel along a neutral circuit wire. Current then becomes part of a main circuit and leaves the house on a large neutral service wire that returns it to the utility pole transformer.

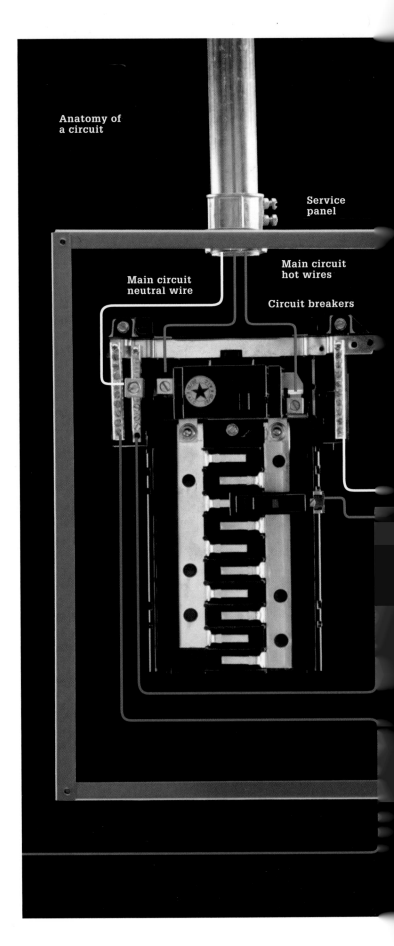

Anatomy of a circuit

Service panel

Main circuit hot wires

Main circuit neutral wire

Circuit breakers

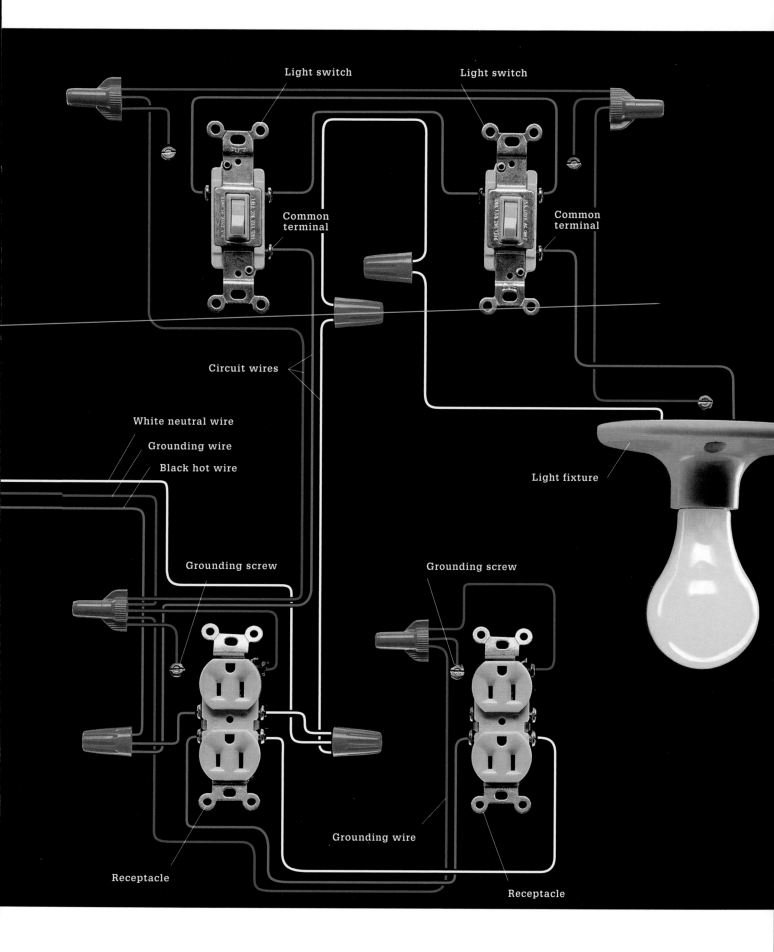

Light switch

Light switch

Common terminal

Common terminal

Circuit wires

White neutral wire

Grounding wire

Black hot wire

Light fixture

Grounding screw

Grounding screw

Receptacle

Grounding wire

Receptacle

Grounding & Polarization

Electricity always seeks to return to its source and complete a continuous circuit. In a household wiring system, this return path is provided by white neutral wires that return current to the main service panel. From the service panel, current returns along a neutral service wire to a power pole transformer.

A grounding wire provides an additional return path for electrical current. The grounding wire is a safety feature. It is designed to conduct electricity if current seeks to return to the service panel along a path other than the neutral wire, a condition known as a short circuit.

A short circuit is a potentially dangerous situation. If an electrical box, tool, or appliance becomes short-circuited and is touched by a person, the electrical current may attempt to return to its source by passing through that person's body.

However, electrical current always seeks to move along the easiest path. A grounding wire provides a safe, easy path for current to follow back to its source. If a person touches an electrical box, tool, or appliance that has a properly installed grounding wire,

any chance of receiving a severe electrical shock is greatly reduced.

In addition, household wiring systems are required to be connected directly to the earth. The earth has a unique ability to absorb the electrons of electrical current. In the event of a short circuit or overload, any excess electricity will find its way along the grounding wire to the earth, where it becomes harmless.

This additional grounding is completed by wiring the household electrical system to a metal cold water pipe and metal grounding rods that are buried in the earth.

After 1920, most American homes included receptacles that accepted polarized plugs. While not a true grounding method, the two-slot polarized plug and receptacle was designed to keep hot current flowing along black or red wires, and neutral current flowing along white or gray wires.

Armored cable and metal conduit, widely installed in homes during the 1940s, provided a true grounding path. When connected to metal junction boxes, it provided a metal pathway back to the service panel.

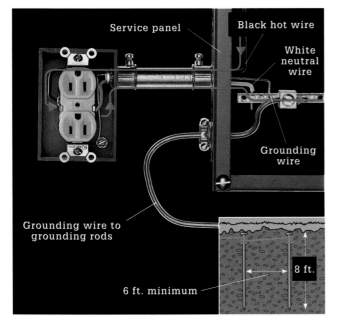

Normal current flow: Current enters the electrical box along a black hot wire, then returns to the service panel along a white neutral wire. Any excess current passes into the earth via a grounding wire attached to grounding rods or a metal water pipe.

Short circuit: Current is detoured by a loose wire in contact with the metal box. The grounding wire picks it up and channels it safely back to the main service panel. There, it returns to its source along a neutral service cable or enters the earth via the grounding system.

Modern cable includes a green insulated or bare copper wire that serves as the grounding path. This grounding wire is connected to all three-slot receptacles and metal boxes to provide a continuous pathway for any short-circuited current. By plugging a three-prong plug into a grounded three-slot receptacle, appliances and tools are protected from short circuits.

Use a receptacle adapter to plug three-prong plugs into two-slot receptacles, but use it only if the receptacle connects to a grounding wire or grounded electrical box. Adapters have short grounding wires or wire loops that attach to the receptacle's coverplate mounting screw. The mounting screw connects the adapter to the grounded metal electrical box.

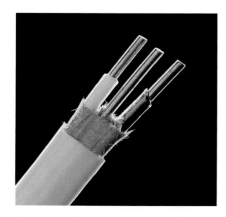

Modern NM (nonmetallic) cable, found in most wiring systems installed after 1965, contains a bare copper wire that provides grounding for receptacle and switch boxes.

Armored cable, sometimes called BX or Greenfield cable, has a metal sheath that serves as the grounding pathway. Short-circuited current flows through the metal sheath back to the service panel.

Polarized receptacles have a long slot and a short slot. Used with a polarized plug, the polarized receptacle keeps electrical current directed for safety.

Three-slot receptacles are required by code for new homes. They are usually connected to a standard two-wire cable with ground.

Receptacle adapter allows three-prong plugs to be inserted into two-slot receptacles. The adapter can be used only with grounded receptacles, and the grounding loop or wire of the adapter must be attached to the coverplate mounting screw of the receptacle.

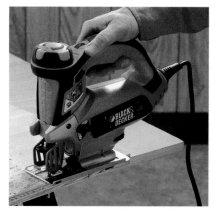

Double-insulated tools have non-conductive plastic bodies to prevent shocks caused by short circuits. Because of these features, double-insulated tools can be used safely with ungrounded receptacles.

Home Wiring Tools

To complete the wiring projects shown in this book, you need a few specialty electrical tools as well as a collection of basic hand tools. As with any tool purchase, invest in good-quality products when you buy tools for electrical work. Keep your tools clean, and sharpen or replace any cutting tools that have dull edges.

The materials used for electrical wiring have changed dramatically in the last 20 years, making it much easier for homeowners to do their own electrical work. The following pages show how to work with the following components for your projects:

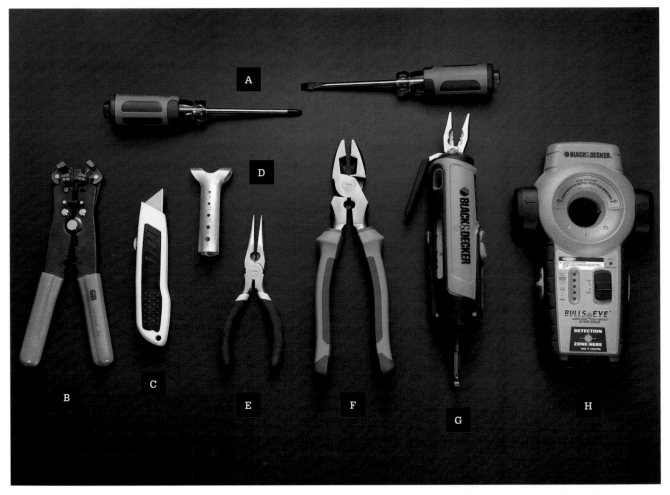

Screwdrivers with insulated handles (A) are used to make wire connections. A combination tool (B) cuts cable and strips insulation from wires. A utility knife (C) trims excess cable sheathing. A cable ripper (D) removes sheathing from NM cables. Needlenose pliers (E) are used to hold and shape wires. Linesman's pliers (F) are used to cut wires. A powered multitool (G) has pliers, wire snipper, cable ripper, screwdriver, and flashlight. A stud finder/laser level (H) helps locate framing members in finished walls; better models also locate wires and plumbing behind walls.

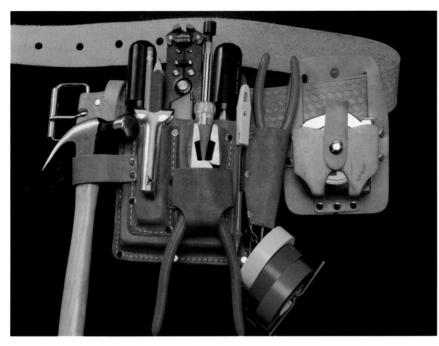

Use a tool belt to keep frequently used tools within easy reach. Electrical tapes in a variety of colors are used for marking wires and for attaching cables to a fish tape.

A fish tape is useful for installing cables in finished wall cavities and for pulling wires through conduit. Products designed for lubrication reduce friction and make it easier to pull cables and wires.

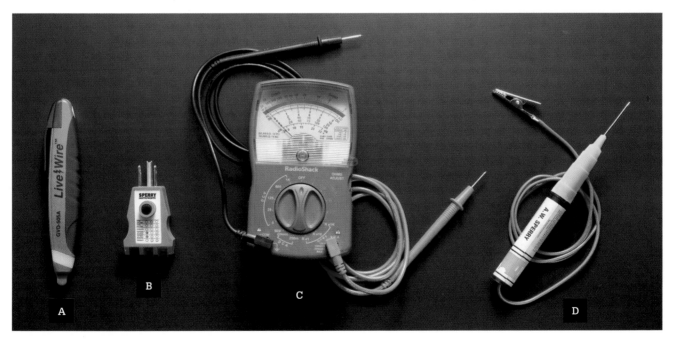

A touchless circuit tester (A) is convenient and safe for quickly checking wires for power. A plug-in tester (B) checks receptacles for polarity, grounding, and circuit protection. An auto-ranging multimeter (C) takes precise measurements of the amount of current on a line. A continuity tester (D) determines if an electrical circuit can be made between two points.

Wiring Safety

Safety should be the primary concern of anyone working with electricity. Although most household electrical repairs are simple and straightforward, always use caution and good judgment when working with electrical wiring or devices. Common sense can prevent accidents.

The basic rule of electrical safety is: Always turn off power to the area or device you are working on. At the main service panel, remove the fuse or shut off the circuit breaker that controls the circuit you are servicing.

Then check to make sure the power is off by testing for power with a current tester. Restore power only when the repair or replacement project is complete.

Follow the safety tips shown on these pages. Never attempt an electrical project beyond your skill or confidence level. Never attempt to repair or replace your main service panel or service entrance head. These are jobs for a qualified electrician and require that the power company shuts off power to your house.

Shut power OFF at the main service panel or the main fuse box before beginning any work.

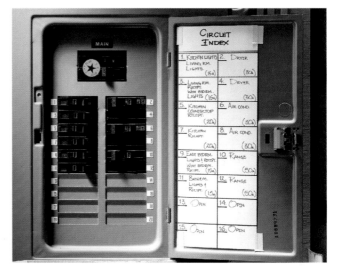

Create a circuit index and affix it to the inside of the door to your main service panel. Update it as needed.

Confirm power is OFF by testing at the outlet, switch, or fixture with a current tester.

Use only UL-approved electrical parts or devices. These devices have been tested for safety by Underwriters Laboratories.

Wear rubber-soled shoes while working on electrical projects. On damp floors, stand on a rubber mat or dry wooden boards.

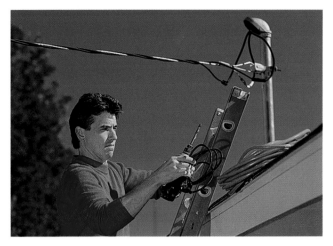

Use fiberglass or wood ladders when making routine household repairs near the service mast.

Extension cords are for temporary use only. Cords must be rated for the intended usage.

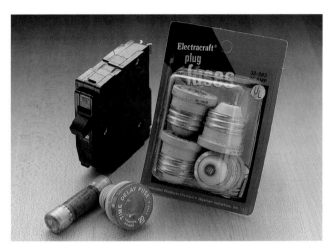

Breakers and fuses must be compatible with the panel manufacturer and match the circuit capacity.

Never alter the prongs of a plug to fit a receptacle. If possible, install a new grounded receptacle.

Do not penetrate walls or ceilings without first shutting off electrical power to the circuits that may be hidden.

Wire, Cable & Conduit

Wire and cable comprise the electrical infrastructure in your home. Selecting the appropriate size and type and handling it correctly is absolutely necessary to a successful wiring project that will pass inspection.

Copper wire is the primary conductor of electricity in any home. The electricity itself travels on the outer surfaces of the wire, so insulation is normally added to the wires to protect against shock and fires. The insulated wires are frequently grouped together and bound up in rugged plastic sheathing according to gauge and function. Multiple wires housed in shared sheathing form a cable. In some cases, the conductors are further isolated and grouped in metal or plastic tubes known as conduit. Conduit (also known as raceway) is used primarily in situations where the cables or wires are exposed, such as open garage walls.

This chapter introduces all of the many varieties of wire, cable, and conduit used in home construction, and explains which types to use where. It also will demonstrate the essential skills used to run new cable, install conduit, strip sheathing, make wire connections, and more.

In this chapter:

- Wire & Cable
- NM Cable
- Conduit
- Raceway Wiring

Wire & Cable

Wires are made of copper, aluminum, or aluminum covered with a thin layer of copper. Solid copper wires are the best conductors of electricity and are the most widely used. Aluminum and copper-covered aluminum wires require special installation techniques.

A group of two or more wires enclosed in a metal, rubber, or plastic sheath is called a cable (photo, opposite page). The sheath protects the wires from damage. Metal conduit also protects wires, but it is not considered a cable.

Individual wires are covered with rubber or plastic vinyl insulation. An exception is a bare copper grounding wire, which does not need an insulation cover. The insulation is color coded (chart, left) to identify the wire as a hot wire, a neutral wire, or a grounding wire.

In most wiring systems installed after 1965, the wires and cables are insulated with plastic vinyl. This type of insulation is very durable and can last as long as the house itself.

Before 1965, wires and cables were insulated with rubber. Rubber insulation has a life expectancy of about 25 years. Old insulation that is cracked or damaged can be reinforced temporarily by wrapping the wire with plastic electrical tape. However, old wiring with cracked or damaged insulation should be inspected by a qualified electrician to make sure it is safe.

Wires must be large enough for the amperage rating of the circuit (chart, right). A wire that is too small can become dangerously hot. Wire sizes are categorized according to the American Wire Gauge (AWG) system. To check the size of a wire, use the wire stripper openings of a combination tool (page 30) as a guide.

Wire Color Chart ▶

Wire color		Function
	White	Neutral wire carrying current at zero voltage.
	Black	Hot wire carrying current at full voltage.
	Red	Hot wire carrying current at full voltage.
	White, black markings	Hot wire carrying current at full voltage.
	Green	Serves as a grounding pathway.
	Bare copper	Serves as a grounding pathway.

Individual wires are color-coded to identify their function. In some circuit installations, the white wire serves as a hot wire that carries voltage. If so, this white wire may be labeled with black tape or paint to identify it as a hot wire.

Wire Size Chart ▶

Wire gauge		Wire capacity & use
	#6	60 amps, 240 volts; central air conditioner, electric furnace.
	#8	40 amps, 240 volts; electric range, central air conditioner.
	#10	30 amps, 240 volts; window air conditioner, clothes dryer.
	#12	20 amps, 120 volts; light fixtures, receptacles, microwave oven.
	#14	15 amps, 120 volts; light fixtures, receptacles.
	#16	Light-duty extension cords.
	#18 to 22	Thermostats, doorbells, security systems.

Wire sizes (shown actual size) are categorized by the American Wire Gauge system. The larger the wire size, the smaller the AWG number.

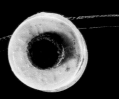

Knob and tube wiring, so called because of the shape of its porcelain insulating brackets, was common before 1940. Wires are covered with a layer of rubberized cloth fabric, but have no additional protection.

Flexible armored cable, sometimes called Greenfield was used from the 1920s to the 1940s. It was an improvement over knob and tube wiring because it provided a shield for the wires. Armored cable is grounded through the metal coils: there is no separate ground wire.

Metal conduit was installed from the 1940s until 1970. The metal walls of the conduit provide the grounding path: no separate grounding wire is present. Conduit is still recommended by codes for some installations, like a basement or garage.

Early NM (nonmetallic) cable was used from 1930 until 1965. It features a rubberized fabric sheathing that protects individual wires. NM cable greatly simplified installations because separate wires no longer had to be pulled by hand through a conduit or armored cable. Early NM cable had no grounding wire.

Modern NM (nonmetallic) cable came into use in 1965. It includes a bare copper grounding wire. Wire insulation and outer sheathing are both made of plastic vinyl. Modern NM cable is inexpensive and easy to install.

UF (underground feeder) cable has wires embedded in a solid-core plastic vinyl sheathing and includes a bare copper grounding wire. It is designed for installations in damp conditions, such as buried circuits.

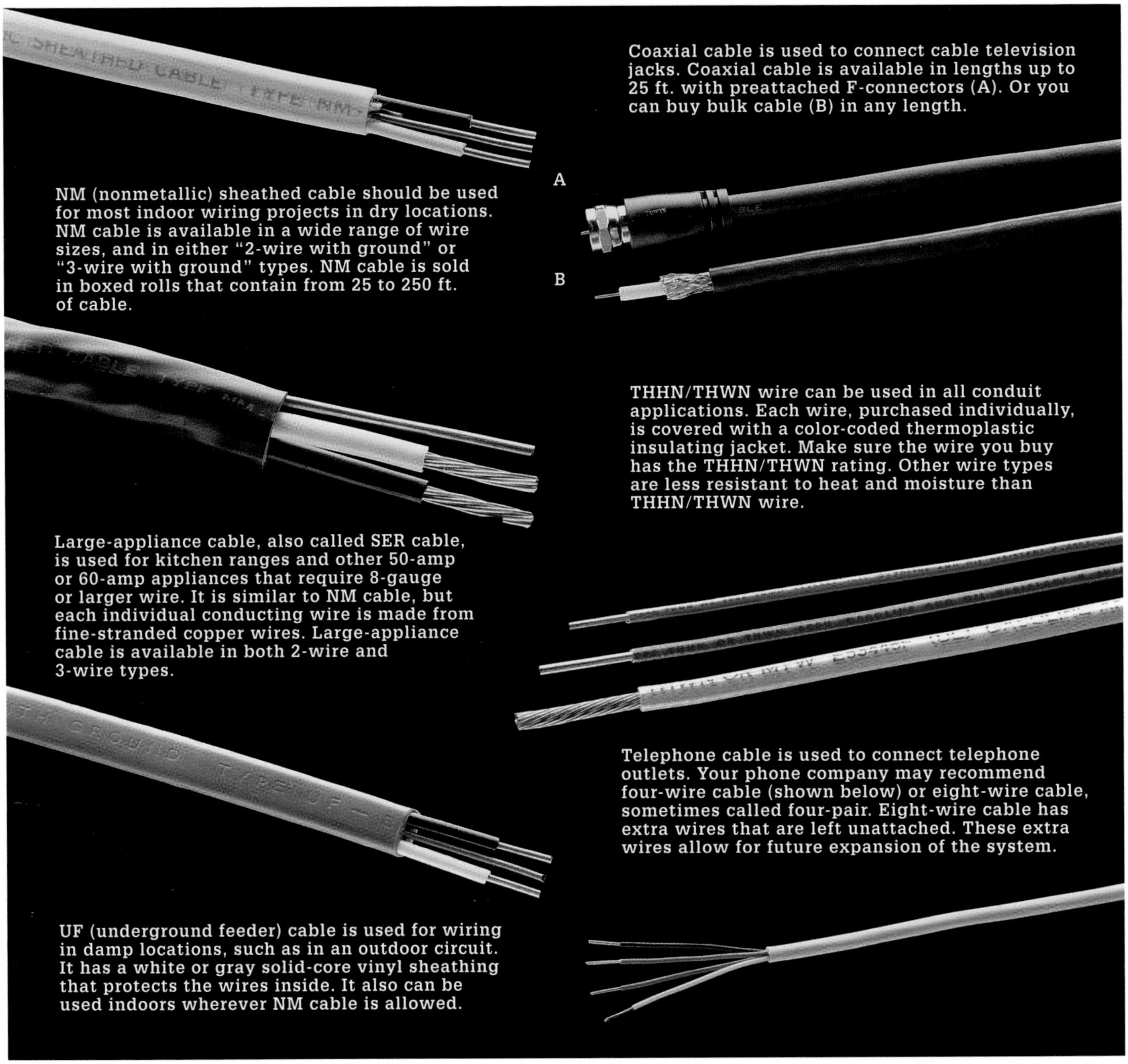

Coaxial cable is used to connect cable television jacks. Coaxial cable is available in lengths up to 25 ft. with preattached F-connectors (A). Or you can buy bulk cable (B) in any length.

A

B

NM (nonmetallic) sheathed cable should be used for most indoor wiring projects in dry locations. NM cable is available in a wide range of wire sizes, and in either "2-wire with ground" or "3-wire with ground" types. NM cable is sold in boxed rolls that contain from 25 to 250 ft. of cable.

THHN/THWN wire can be used in all conduit applications. Each wire, purchased individually, is covered with a color-coded thermoplastic insulating jacket. Make sure the wire you buy has the THHN/THWN rating. Other wire types are less resistant to heat and moisture than THHN/THWN wire.

Large-appliance cable, also called SER cable, is used for kitchen ranges and other 50-amp or 60-amp appliances that require 8-gauge or larger wire. It is similar to NM cable, but each individual conducting wire is made from fine-stranded copper wires. Large-appliance cable is available in both 2-wire and 3-wire types.

Telephone cable is used to connect telephone outlets. Your phone company may recommend four-wire cable (shown below) or eight-wire cable, sometimes called four-pair. Eight-wire cable has extra wires that are left unattached. These extra wires allow for future expansion of the system.

UF (underground feeder) cable is used for wiring in damp locations, such as in an outdoor circuit. It has a white or gray solid-core vinyl sheathing that protects the wires inside. It also can be used indoors wherever NM cable is allowed.

Tips for Working With Wire ▸

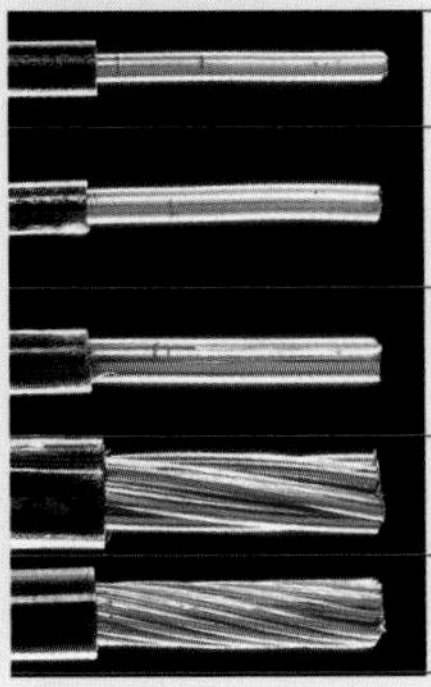

Wire gauge		Ampacity	Maximum wattage load
	14-gauge	15 amps	1440 watts (120 volts)
	12-gauge	20 amps	1920 watts (120 volts) 3840 watts (240 volts)
	10-gauge	30 amps	2880 watts (120 volts) 5760 watts (240 volts)
	8-gauge	40 amps	7680 watts (240 volts)
	6-gauge	50 amps	9600 watts (240 volts)

Wire **"ampacity"** is a measurement of how much current a wire can carry safely. Ampacity varies according to the size of the wires, as shown at left. When installing a new circuit, choose wire with an ampacity rating matching the circuit size. For dedicated appliance circuits, check the wattage rating of the appliance and make sure it does not exceed the maximum wattage load of the circuit.

Reading NM (Nonmetallic) Cable

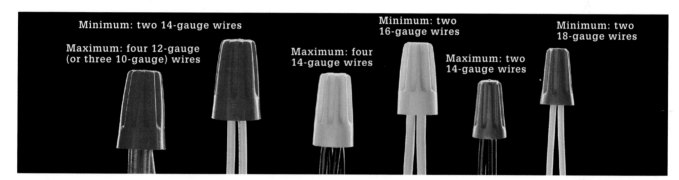

Number of insulated wires — 14-2 G NON METALLIC SHEATHED CABLE TYPE NM-B 600V

Cable type (nonmetallic) **Paper**

Wire gauge **Maximum voltage rating (600 volts)**

NM (nonmetallic) cable is labeled with the number of insulated wires it contains. The bare grounding wire is not counted. For example, a cable marked 14/2 G (or 14/2 WITH GROUND) contains two insulated 14-gauge wires, plus a bare copper grounding wire. Cable marked 14/3 WITH GROUND has three 14-gauge wires plus a grounding wire. NM cable also is stamped with a maximum voltage rating, as determined by Underwriters Laboratories (UL).

Reading Unsheathed, Individual Wire

Maximum voltage rating (600 volts)

Wire material

Wire gauge **Corrosion resistance code**

Unsheathed, individual wires are used for conduit and raceway installations. Wire insulation is coded with letters to indicate resistance to moisture, heat, and gas or oil. Code requires certain letter combinations for certain applications. T indicates thermoplastic insulation. H stands for heat resistance and two Hs indicate high resistance (up to 194° F). W denotes wire suitable for wet locations. Wire coded with an N is impervious to damage from oil or gas.

Maximum: four 12-gauge (or three 10-gauge) wires

Minimum: two 14-gauge wires

Maximum: four 14-gauge wires

Minimum: two 16-gauge wires

Maximum: two 14-gauge wires

Minimum: two 18-gauge wires

Use wire connectors rated for the wires you are connecting. Wire connectors are color-coded by size, but the coding scheme varies according to manufacturer. The wire connectors shown above come from one major manufacturer. To ensure safe connections, each connector is rated for both minimum and maximum wire capacity. These connectors can be used to connect both conducting wires and grounding wires. Green wire connectors are used only for grounding wires.

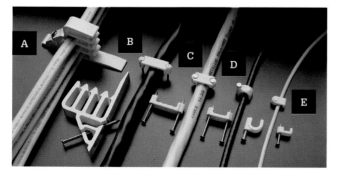

Use plastic cable staples to fasten cables. Choose staples sized to match the cables. Stack-It® staples (A) hold up to four 2-wire cables; ¾" staples (B) for 12/2, 12/3, and all 10-gauge cables; ½" staples (C) for 14/2, 14/3, or 12/2 cables; coaxial staples (D) for anchoring television cables; bell wire staples (E) for attaching telephone cables.

Push-in connectors are a relatively new product for joining wires. Instead of twisting the bare wire ends together, you strip off about ¾" of insulation and insert them into a hole in the connector. The connectors come with two to four holes sized for various gauge wires. These connectors are perfect for inexperienced DIYers because they do not pull apart like a sloppy twisted connection can.

How to Strip NM Sheathing & Insulation

1

Measure and mark the cable 8 to 10" from end. Slide the cable ripper onto the cable, and squeeze tool firmly to force cutting point through plastic sheathing.

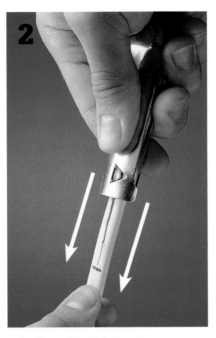

2

Grip the cable tightly with one hand, and pull the cable ripper toward the end of the cable to cut open the plastic sheathing.

3

Peel back the plastic sheathing and the paper wrapping from the individual wires.

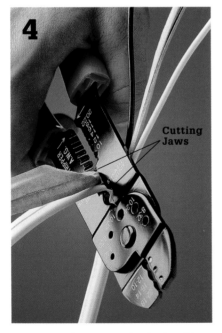

4

Cut away the excess plastic sheathing and paper wrapping, using the cutting jaws of a combination tool.

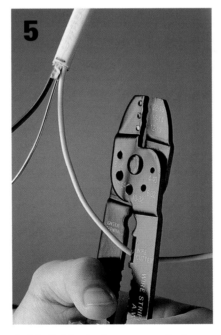

5

Cut individual wires as needed using the cutting jaws of the combination tool.

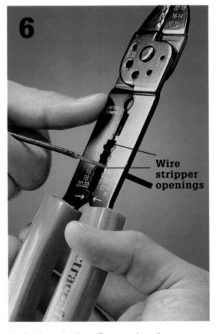

6

Strip insulation for each wire, using the stripper openings. Choose the opening that matches the gauge of the wire, and take care not to nick or scratch the ends of the wires.

How to Connect Wires to Screw Terminals

Strip about ¾" of insulation from each wire using a combination tool. Choose the stripper opening that matches the gauge of the wire, then clamp the wire in the tool. Pull the wire firmly to remove plastic insulation.

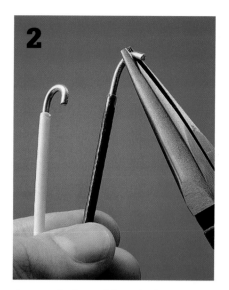

Form a C-shaped loop in the end of each wire using a needlenose pliers. The wire should have no scratches or nicks.

Hook each wire around the screw terminal so it forms a clockwise loop. Tighten screw firmly. Insulation should just touch head of screw. Never place the ends of two wires under a single screw terminal. Instead, use a pigtail wire (page 33).

How to Connect Wires with Push-ins

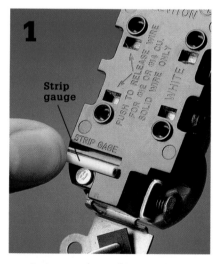

Mark the amount of insulation to be stripped from each wire using the strip gauge on the back of the switch or receptacle. Strip the wires using a combination tool (step 1, above). Never use push-in fittings with aluminum wiring.

Insert the bare copper wires firmly into the push-in fittings on the back of the switch or receptacle. When inserted, wires should have no bare copper exposed. *Note: Although push-in fittings are convenient, most experts believe screw terminal connections (above) are more dependable.*

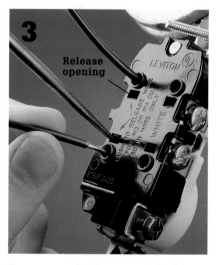

Remove a wire from a push-in fitting by inserting a small nail or screwdriver in the release opening next to the wire. Wire will pull out easily.

How to Join Wires with a Wire Connector

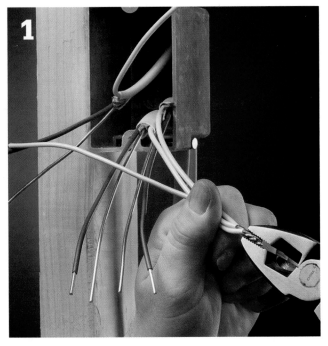

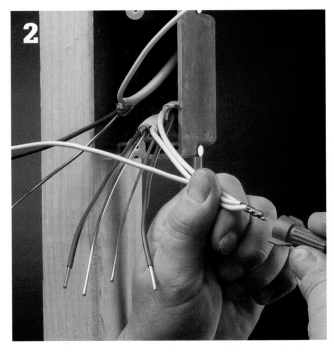

Ensure power is off and test for power. Grasp the wires to be joined in the jaws of a pair of linesman's pliers. The ends of the wires should be flush and they should be parallel and touching. Rotate the pliers clockwise two or three turns to twist the wire ends together.

Twist a wire connector over the ends of the wires. Make sure the connector is the right size (see page 29). Hand-twist the connector as far onto the wires as you can. There should be no bare wire exposed beneath the collar of the connector. Do not overtighten the connector.

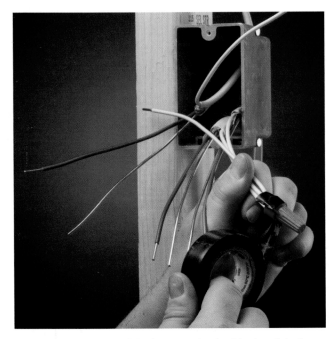

Option: Reinforce the joint by wrapping it with electrician's tape. By code, you cannot bind the wire joint with tape only, but it can be used as insurance. Few professional electricians use tape for purposes other than tagging wires for identification.

Option: Strip ¾" of insulation off the ends of the wires to be joined, and insert each wire into a push-in connector. Gently tug on each wire to make sure it is secure.

How to Pigtail Wires

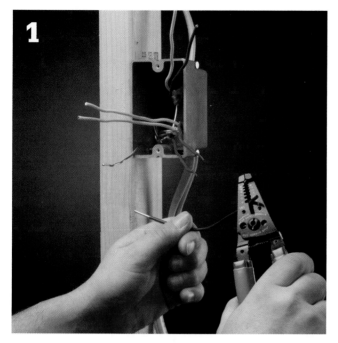

Cut a 6" length from a piece of insulated wire the same gauge and color as the wires it will be joining. Strip ¾" of insulation from each end of the insulated wire. *Note: Pigtailing is done mainly to avoid connecting multiple wires to one terminal, which is a code violation.*

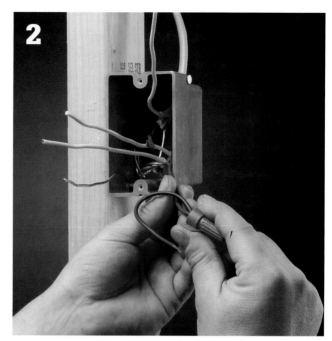

Join one end of the pigtail to the wires that will share the connection using a wire nut (see previous page).

Alternative: If you are pigtailing to a grounding screw or grounding clip in a metal box, you may find it easier to attach one end of the wire to the grounding screw before you attach the other end to the other wires.

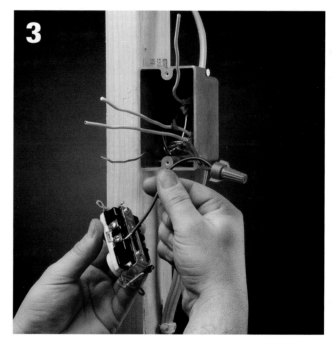

Connect the pigtail to the appropriate terminal on the receptacle or switch. Fold the wires neatly and press the fitting into the box.

NM Cable

NM cable is used for all indoor wiring projects except those requiring conduit. Cut and install the cable after all electrical boxes have been mounted. Refer to your wiring plan to make sure each length of cable is correct for the circuit size and configuration.

Cable runs are difficult to measure exactly, so leave plenty of extra wire when cutting each length. Cable splices inside walls are not allowed by code. When inserting cables into a circuit breaker panel, make sure the power is shut off.

After all cables are installed, call your electrical inspector to arrange for the rough-in inspection. Do not install wallboard or attach light fixtures and other devices until this inspection is done.

Tools & Materials ▸

Drill	Fish tape
Bits	NM cable
Tape measure	Cable clamps
Cable ripper	Cable staples
Combination tool	Masking tape
Screwdrivers	Grounding pigtails
Needlenose pliers	Wire connectors
Hammer	

Pulling cables through studs is easier if you drill smooth, straight holes at the same height. Prevent kinks by straightening the cable before pulling it through the studs. Use plastic grommets to protect cables on steel studs (inset).

Framing member	Maximum hole size	Maximum notch size
2 × 4 loadbearing stud	1⁷⁄₁₆" diameter	⁷⁄₈" deep
2 × 4 non-loadbearing stud	2½" diameter	1⁷⁄₁₆" deep
2 × 6 loadbearing stud	2¼" diameter	1⅜" deep
2 × 6 non-loadbearing stud	3⁵⁄₁₆" diameter	2³⁄₁₆" deep
2 × 6 joists	1½" diameter	⁷⁄₈" deep
2 × 8 joists	2⅜" diameter	1¼" deep
2 × 10 joists	3¹⁄₁₆" diameter	1½" deep
2 × 12 joists	3¾" diameter	1⅞" deep

This framing member chart shows the maximum sizes for holes and notches that can be cut into studs and joists when running cables. When boring holes, there must be at least 1¼" of wood between the edge of a stud and the hole, and at least 2" between the edge of a joist and the hole. Joists can be notched only in the end ⅓ of the overall span; never in the middle ⅓ of the joist.

How to Install NM Cable

Drill ⅝" holes in framing members for the cable runs. This is done easily with a right-angle drill, available at rental centers. Holes should be set back at least 1¼" from the front face of the framing members.

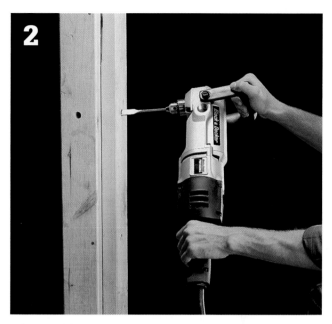

Where cables will turn corners (step 6, page 36), drill intersecting holes in adjoining faces of studs. Measure and cut all cables, allowing 2 ft. extra at ends entering the breaker panel and 1 foot for ends entering the electrical box.

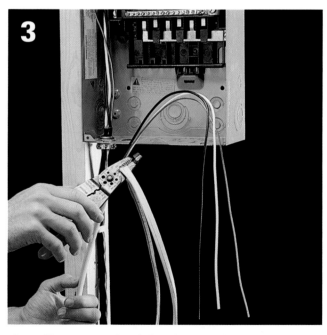

Shut off power to circuit breaker panel. Use a cable ripper to strip cable, leaving at least ¼" of sheathing to enter the circuit breaker panel. Clip away the excess sheathing.

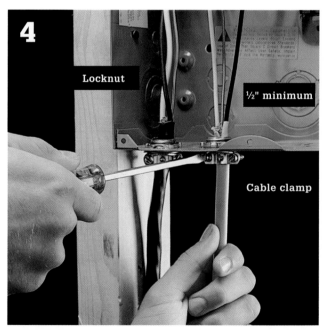

Locknut

½" minimum

Cable clamp

Open a knockout in the circuit breaker panel using a hammer and screwdriver. Insert a cable clamp into the knockout, and secure it with a locknut. Insert the cable through the clamp so that at least ½" of sheathing extends inside the circuit breaker panel. Tighten the mounting screws on the clamp so the cable is gripped securely but not so tightly that the sheathing is crushed.

(continued)

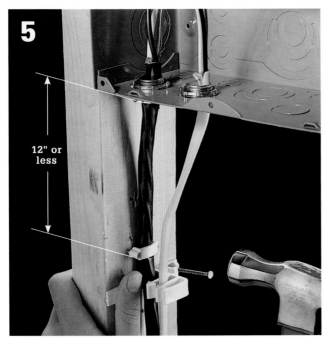

Anchor the cable to the center of a framing member within 12" of the circuit breaker panel using a cable staple. Stack-It® staples work well where two or more cables must be anchored to the same side of a stud. Run the cable to the first electrical box. Where the cable runs along the sides of framing members, anchor it with cable staples no more than 4 ft. apart.

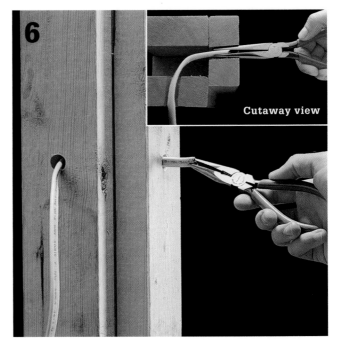

Cutaway view

At corners, form a slight L-shaped bend in the end of the cable and insert it into one hole. Retrieve the cable through the other hole using needlenose pliers (inset).

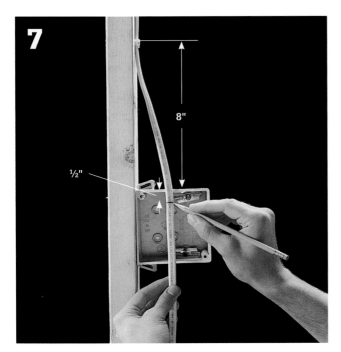

Staple the cable to a framing member 8" from the box. Hold the cable taut against the front of the box, and mark a point on the sheathing ½" past the box edge. Remove sheathing from the marked line to the end using a cable ripper, and clip away excess sheathing with a combination tool. Insert the cable through the knockout in the box.

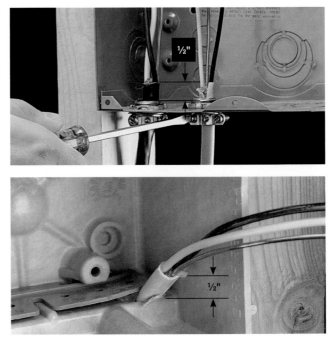

Variation: Different types of boxes have different clamping devices. Make sure cable sheathing extends ½" past the edge of the clamp to ensure that the cable is secure and that the wire won't be damaged by the edges of the clamp.

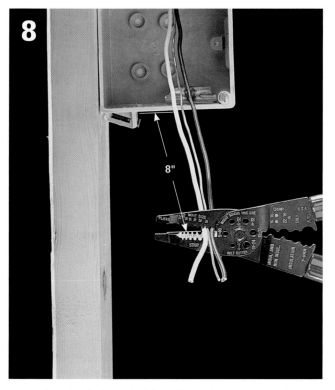

As each cable is installed in a box, clip back each wire so that 8" of workable wire extends past the front edge of the box.

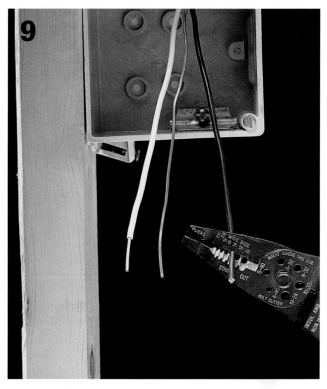

Strip ¾" of insulation from each circuit wire in the box using a combination tool. Take care not to nick the copper.

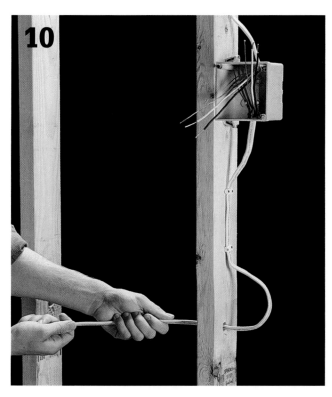

Continue the circuit by running cable between each pair of electrical boxes, leaving an extra 1 ft. of cable at each end.

At metal boxes and recessed fixtures, open knockouts, and attach cables with cable clamps. From inside fixture, strip away all but ¼" of sheathing. Clip back wires so there is 8" of workable length, then strip ¾" of insulation from each wire.

(continued)

For a surface-mounted fixture like a baseboard heater or fluorescent light fixture, staple the cable to a stud near the fixture location, leaving plenty of excess cable. Mark the floor so the cable will be easy to find after the walls are finished.

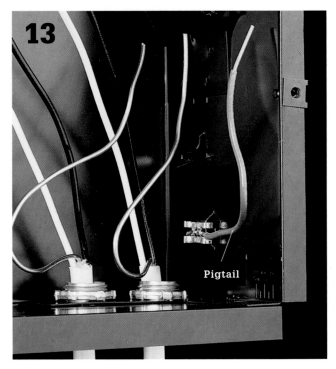

At each recessed fixture and metal electrical box, connect one end of a grounding pigtail to the metal frame using a grounding clip attached to the frame (shown above) or a green grounding screw.

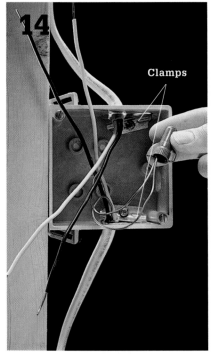

At each electrical box and recessed fixture, join grounding wires together with a wire connector. If the box has internal clamps, tighten the clamps over the cables.

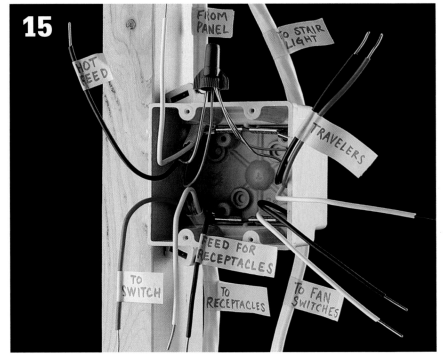

Label the cables entering each box to indicate their destinations. In boxes with complex wiring configurations, also tag the individual wires to make final hookups easier. After all cables are installed, your rough-in work is ready to be reviewed by the electrical inspector.

How to Run NM Cable Inside a Finished Wall

From the unfinished space below the finished wall, look for a reference point, like a soil stack, plumbing pipes, or electrical cables, that indicates the location of the wall above. Choose a location for the new cable that does not interfere with existing utilities. Drill a 1" hole up into the stud cavity.

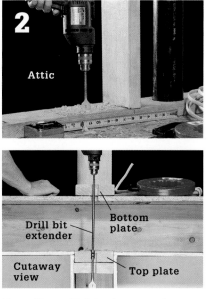

From the unfinished space above the finished wall, find the top of the stud cavity by measuring from the same fixed reference point used in step 1. Drill a 1" hole down through the top plate and into the stud cavity using a drill bit extender.

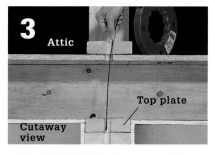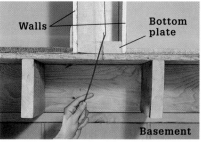

Extend a fish tape down through the top plate, twisting the tape until it reaches the bottom of the stud cavity. From the unfinished space below the wall, use a piece of stiff wire with a hook on one end to retrieve the fish tape through the drilled hole in the bottom plate.

Trim back 2" of sheathing from the end of the NM cable, then insert the wires through the loop at the tip of the fish tape.

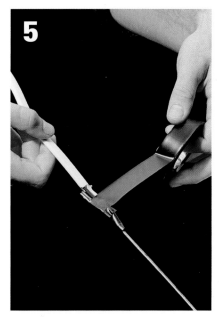

Bend the wires against the cable, then use electrical tape to bind them tightly. Apply cable-pulling lubricant to the taped end of the fish tape.

From above the finished wall, pull steadily on the fish tape to draw the cable up through the stud cavity. This job will be easier if you have a helper feed the cable from below as you pull.

Running Cable Inside Finished Walls

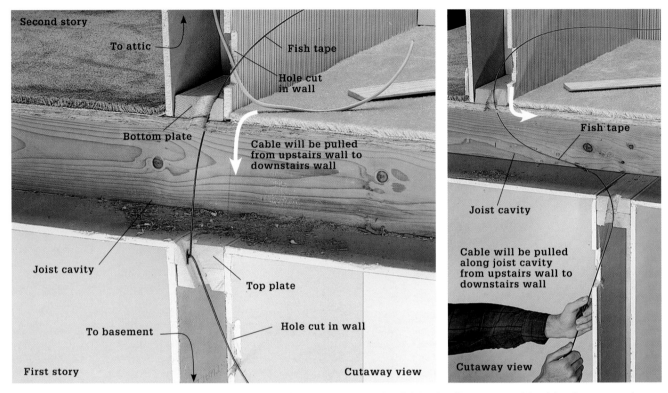

Second story
To attic
Fish tape
Hole cut in wall
Bottom plate
Cable will be pulled from upstairs wall to downstairs wall
Joist cavity
Top plate
To basement
Hole cut in wall
First story
Cutaway view

Fish tape
Joist cavity
Cable will be pulled along joist cavity from upstairs wall to downstairs wall
Cutaway view
Cutaway view

If there is no access space above and below a wall, cut openings in the finished walls to run a cable. This often occurs in two-story homes when a cable is extended from an upstairs wall to a downstairs wall. Cut small openings in the wall near the top and bottom plates, then drill an angled 1" hole through each plate. Extend a fish tape into the joist cavity between the walls and use it to pull the cable from one wall to the next. If the walls line up one over the other (left), you can retrieve the fish tape using a piece of stiff wire. If walls do not line up (right), use a second fish tape. After running the cable, repair the holes in the walls with patching plaster or wallboard scraps and taping compound.

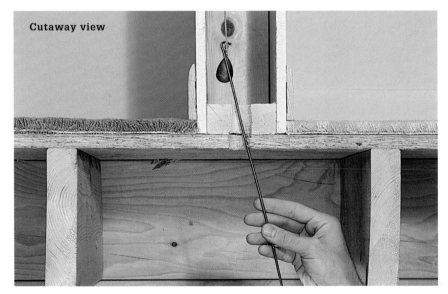

Cutaway view

If you don't have a fish tape, use a length of sturdy string and a lead weight or heavy washer. Drop the line into the stud cavity from above, then use a piece of stiff wire to hook the line from below.

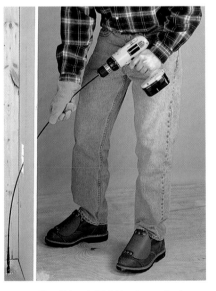

Use a flexible drill bit, also called a bell-hanger's bit, to bore holes through framing in finished walls.

How to Install NM Cable in Finished Ceilings

If you don't have access to a ceiling from above, you can run cable for a new ceiling fixture from an existing receptacle in the room up the wall and into the ceiling without disturbing much of the ceiling. To begin, run cable from the receptacle to the stud channel that aligns with the ceiling joists on which you want to install a fixture. Be sure to plan a location for the new switch. Remove short strips of drywall from the wall and ceiling. Make a notch in the center of the top plates, and protect the notch with metal nail stops. Use a fish tape to pull the new cable up through the wall cavity and the notch in top plates. Next, use the fish tape to pull the cable through the ceiling to the fixture hole. After having your work inspected, replace the drywall and install the fixture and switch.

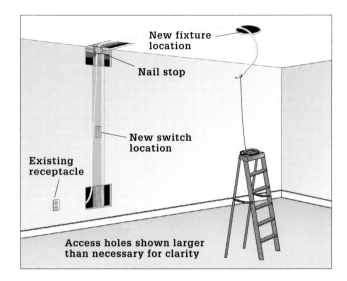

1

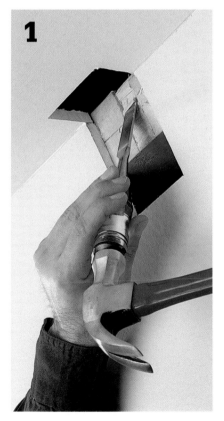

Plan a route for running cable between electrical boxes (see illustration above). Remove drywall on the wall and ceiling surface. Where cable must cross framing members, cut a small access opening in the wall and ceiling surface; then cut a notch into the framing with a wood chisel.

2

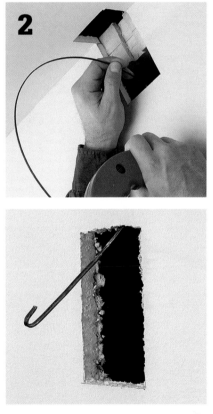

Fish a cable from the existing receptacle locationup to the notch at the top of the wall. Protect the notch with a metal nail stop. Fish the cable through the ceiling to the location of the new ceiling fixture.

3

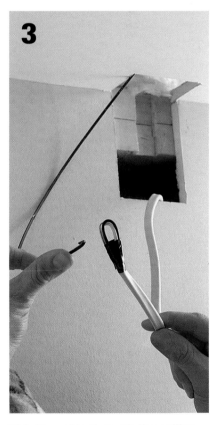

Fish the cable through the ceiling to the location of the new ceiling fixture.

Conduit

Electrical wiring that runs in exposed locations must be protected by rigid tubing called conduit. For example, conduit is used for wiring that runs across masonry walls in a basement laundry and for exposed outdoor wiring. THHN/THWN wire (page 28) normally is installed inside conduit, although UF or NM cable can also be installed in conduit.

There are several types of conduit available, so check with your electrical inspector to find out which type meets code requirements in your area. Conduit installed outdoors must be rated for exterior use. Metal conduit should be used only with metal boxes, never with plastic boxes.

At one time, conduit could only be fitted by using elaborate bending techniques and special tools. Now, however, a variety of shaped fittings are available to let a homeowner join conduit easily.

Electrical Grounding in Metal Conduit

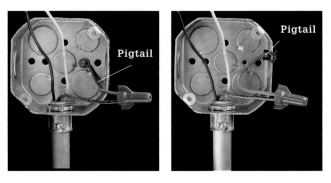

Install a green insulated grounding wire for any circuit that runs through metal conduit. Although code allows the metal conduit to serve as the grounding conductor, most electricians install a green insulated wire as a more dependable means of grounding the system. The grounding wires must be connected to metal boxes with a pigtail and grounding screw (left) or grounding clip (right).

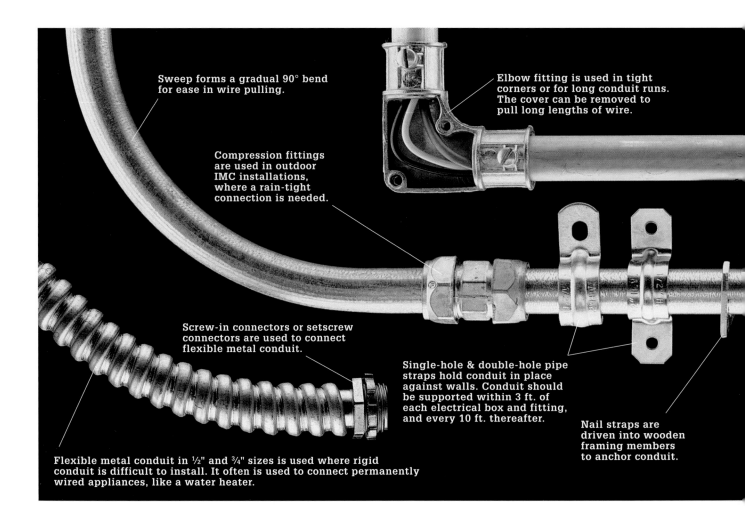

Sweep forms a gradual 90° bend for ease in wire pulling.

Compression fittings are used in outdoor IMC installations, where a rain-tight connection is needed.

Elbow fitting is used in tight corners or for long conduit runs. The cover can be removed to pull long lengths of wire.

Screw-in connectors or setscrew connectors are used to connect flexible metal conduit.

Single-hole & double-hole pipe straps hold conduit in place against walls. Conduit should be supported within 3 ft. of each electrical box and fitting, and every 10 ft. thereafter.

Nail straps are driven into wooden framing members to anchor conduit.

Flexible metal conduit in ½" and ¾" sizes is used where rigid conduit is difficult to install. It often is used to connect permanently wired appliances, like a water heater.

Fill Capacity

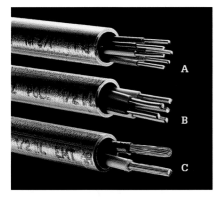

Conduit ½" in diameter can hold up to six 14-gauge or 12-gauge THHN/THWN wires (A), five 10-gauge wires (B), or two 8-gauge wires (C). Use ¾" conduit for greater capacity.

Metal Conduit

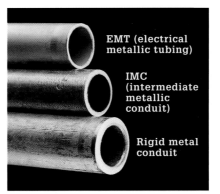

EMT (electrical metallic tubing)

IMC (intermediate metallic conduit)

Rigid metal conduit

EMT is lightweight and easy to install but should not be used where it can be damaged. IMC has thicker galvanized walls and is a good choice for exposed outdoor use. Rigid metal conduit provides the greatest protection for wires, but it is more expensive and requires threaded fittings.

Plastic Conduit

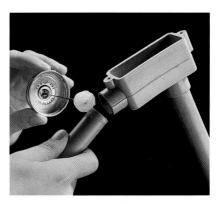

Plastic PVC conduit is allowed by many local codes. It is assembled with solvent glue and PVC fittings that resemble those for metal conduit. When wiring with PVC conduit, always run a green grounding wire.

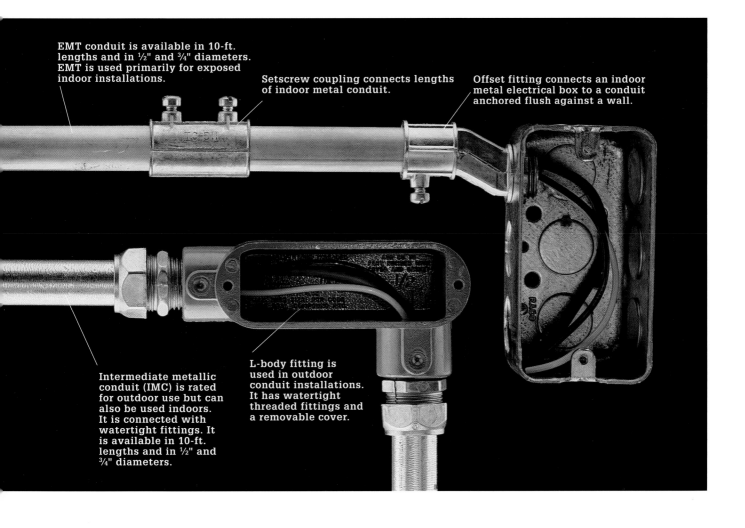

EMT conduit is available in 10-ft. lengths and in ½" and ¾" diameters. EMT is used primarily for exposed indoor installations.

Setscrew coupling connects lengths of indoor metal conduit.

Offset fitting connects an indoor metal electrical box to a conduit anchored flush against a wall.

Intermediate metallic conduit (IMC) is rated for outdoor use but can also be used indoors. It is connected with watertight fittings. It is available in 10-ft. lengths and in ½" and ¾" diameters.

L-body fitting is used in outdoor conduit installations. It has watertight threaded fittings and a removable cover.

Working with Conduit

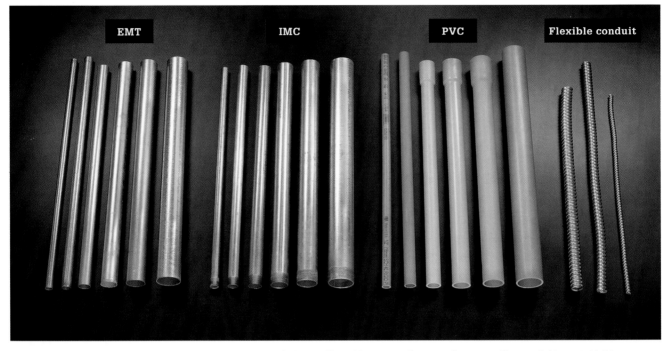

Conduit types used most in homes are EMT (electrical metallic tubing), IMC (intermediate metallic conduit), RNC (rigid nonmetallic conduit), and flexible metal conduit. The most common diameters by far are ½" and ¾", but larger sizes are stocked at most building centers.

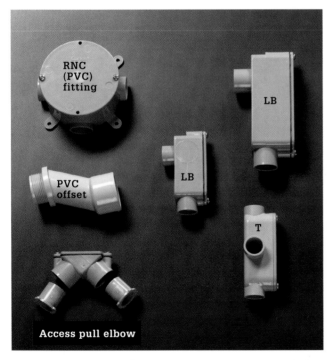

Nonmetallic conduit fittings typically are solvent welded to nonmetallic conduit, as opposed to metal conduit, which can be threaded and screwed into threaded fittings or attached with setscrews or compression fittings.

A thin-wall conduit bender is used to bend sweeps into EMT or IMC conduit.

How to Make Nonmetallic Conduit Connections

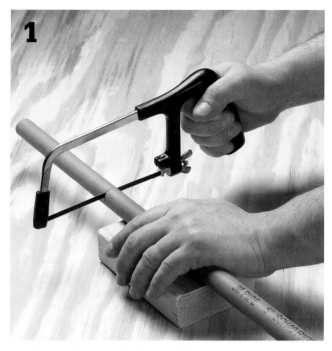

Cut the rigid nonmetallic conduit (RNC) to length with a fine-tooth saw, such as a hacksaw. For larger diameter (1½" and above), use a power miter box with a fine-tooth or plastic cutting blade.

Deburr the cut edges with a utility knife or fine sandpaper such as emery paper. Wipe the cut ends with a dry rag. Also wipe the coupling or fitting to clean it.

Apply a coat of PVC cement to the end of the conduit. Wear latex gloves to protect your hands. The cement should be applied past the point on the conduit where it enters the fitting or coupling.

Insert the conduit into the fitting or coupling and spin it a quarter turn to help spread the cement. Allow the joint to set undisturbed for 10 minutes.

How to Install Conduit & Wires on a Concrete Wall

Measure from the floor to position electrical boxes on the wall, and mark location for mounting screws. Boxes for receptacles in an unfinished basement or other damp area are mounted at least 2 ft. from the floor. Laundry receptacles usually are mounted at 48".

Drill pilot holes with a masonry bit, then mount the box against a masonry wall with masonry anchors. Or use masonry anchors and panhead screws.

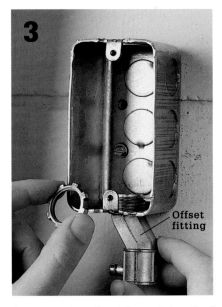

Open one knockout for each length of conduit that will be attached to the box. Attach an offset fitting to each knockout using a locknut.

Offset fitting

Measure the first length of conduit and cut it with a hacksaw. Remove any rough inside edges with a pipe reamer or a round file. Attach the conduit to the offset fitting on the box, and tighten the setscrew.

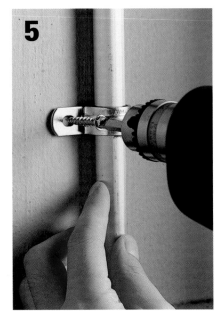

Anchor the conduit against the wall with pipe straps and masonry anchors. Conduit should be anchored within 3 ft. of each box and fitting, and every 10 ft. thereafter.

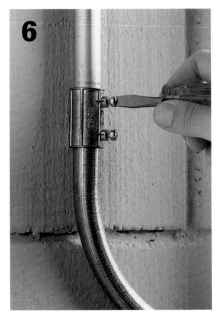

Make conduit bends by attaching a sweep fitting using a setscrew fitting or compression fitting. Continue conduit run by attaching additional lengths using setscrew or compression fittings.

Use an elbow fitting in conduit runs that have many bends, or in runs that require very long wires. The cover on the elbow fitting can be removed to make it easier to extend a fish tape and pull wires.

At the service breaker panel, turn the power off, then remove the cover and test for power. Open a knockout in the panel, then attach a setscrew fitting, and install the last length of conduit.

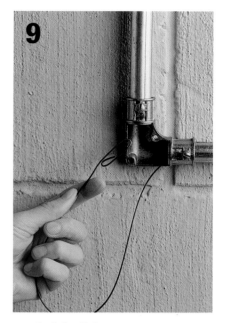

Unwind the fish tape and extend it through the conduit from the circuit breaker panel outward. Remove the cover on an elbow fitting when extending the fish tape around tight corners.

Trim back 2" of outer insulation from the end of the wires, then insert the wires through the loop at the tip of the fish tape.

Retrieve the wires through the conduit by pulling on the fish tape with steady pressure. *Note: Use extreme care when using a metal fish tape inside a circuit breaker panel, even when the power is turned off.*

Clip off the taped ends of the wires. Leave at least 2 ft. of wire at the service panel and 8" at each electrical box.

Raceway Wiring

Raceways are essentially decorative conduit. Often called surface-mounted wiring, a raceway is a track of flattened metal or plastic tubing that attaches to a wall and houses cable for a circuit. The systems include matching elbows, T-connectors, and various other fittings and boxes that are also surface-mounted. The main advantage to a raceway system is that you can add a new fixture onto a circuit without cutting into your walls.

Although they are extremely convenient and can even contribute to a room's decor when used thoughtfully, raceway systems do have some limitations. They are not allowed for some specific applications (such as damp areas like bathrooms) in many areas, so check with the local building authorities before beginning a project. And, the boxes that house the switches and receptacles tend to be very shallow and more difficult to work with than ordinary boxes.

In some cases, you may choose to run an entirely new circuit with raceway components (at least starting at the point where the feeder wire reaches the room from the service panel). But more often, a raceway circuit ties into an existing receptacle or switch. If you are tying into a standard switch box for power, make sure the load wire for the new raceway circuit is connected to the hot wire in the switch box before it is connected to the switch (otherwise, the raceway circuit will be off whenever the switch is off).

Raceway wiring systems are surface-mounted networks of electrical boxes and hollow metal tracks that allow you to expand an existing wiring circuit without cutting into your walls.

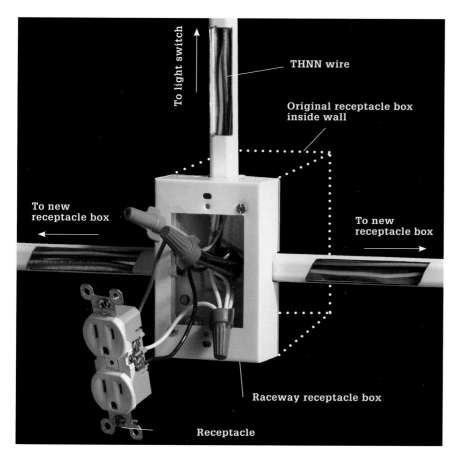

The raceway receptacle box is mounted directly to the original electrical box (usually for a receptacle) and raceway tracks are attached to it. The tracks house THNN wires that run from the raceway box to new receptacles and light switches.

Parts of a Raceway System

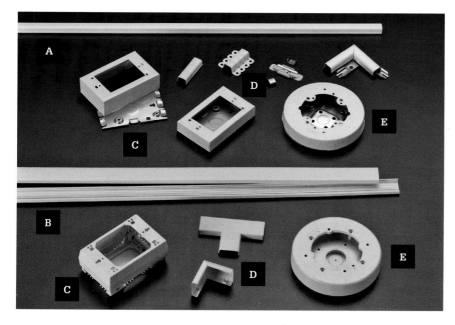

Raceway systems employ two-part tracks that are mounted directly to the wall surface to house cable. Lighter-duty plastic raceways (A), used frequently in office buildings, are made of snap-together plastic components. For home wiring, look for a heavier metal-component system (B). Both systems include box extenders for tying in to a receptacle (C), elbows, T-connectors, and couplings (D), and boxes for fixtures (E).

How to Install Raceway Wiring

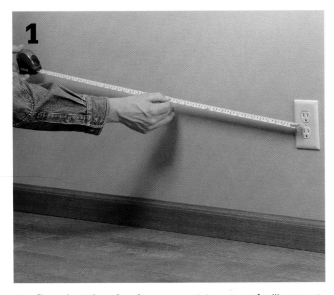

Confirm that the circuit you want to expand will support a new receptacle or light (see pages 136 to 141). Mark the planned location of the new receptacle or switch on the wall and measure to the nearest existing receptacle. Purchase enough raceway to cover this distance plus about 10 percent extra. Buy a surface-mounted starter box, new receptacle box, and fittings for your project (the raceway product packaging usually provides guidance for shopping).

Shut off the power to the switch. Remove the cover plate from the receptacle by unscrewing the screw that holds the plate to the electrical box. Set the screws and the plate aside. With the cover plate off, you will be able to see the receptacle and the electrical box it is attached to.

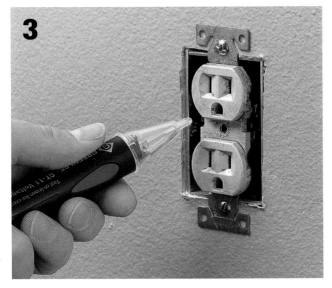

Before you remove the old receptacle, use a voltage sensor to double-check that the circuit is dead. Hold your voltage sensor's probe within ½" of the wires on each side of the receptacle. If the sensor beeps or lights up, then the receptacle is still live, and you'll need to trip the correct breaker to disconnect power to the receptacle. If the sensor does not beep or light up, the receptacle is dead and you can proceed safely.

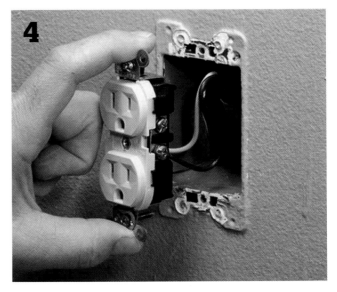

Remove the receptacle from the box by unscrewing the two long screws that hold it to the box. Once the screws are out, gently pull the receptacle away from the box. Depending on how your receptacle has been wired, you may find two insulated wires and a bare copper wire or four insulated wires and a bare wire. Detach these wires and set the receptacle aside.

Your starter box includes a box and a mounting plate with a hole in its center. Pull all the wires you just disconnected through the hole, taking care not to scrape them on the edges of the hole. Screw the mounting plate to the existing receptacle box with the included mounting screws.

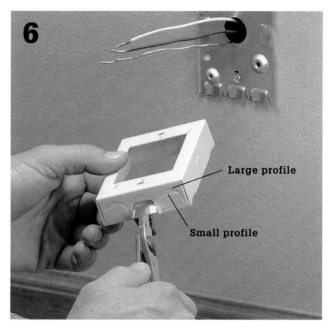

Remove a knockout from the starter box to create an opening for the raceway track using pliers. Often, the prepunched knockouts have two profile options—make sure the knockout you remove matches the profile of your track.

Large profile

Small profile

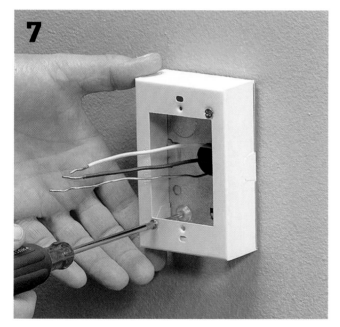

Hold the box portion of the starter box over the mounting plate on the existing receptacle. Drive the mounting screws through the holes in the box and into the threaded openings in the mounting plate.

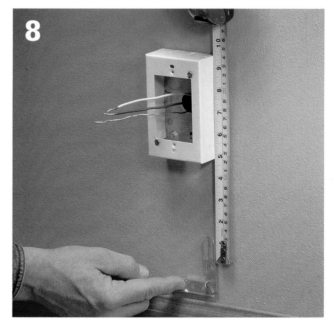

Set the mounting bracket for an elbow connector ¼" above the baseboard (having the track run along the baseboard edge looks better than running it in a straight line out of the starter box). Measure from the knockout in the starter box to the top of the bracket and cut a piece of raceway ½" longer than this measurement.

(continued)

Tool Tip ▶

Metal raceway can be cut like metal conduit. Secure the track or conduit in a vise or clamping work support and cut with a hacksaw. For best results, use long, slow strokes and don't bear down too hard on the saw.

9

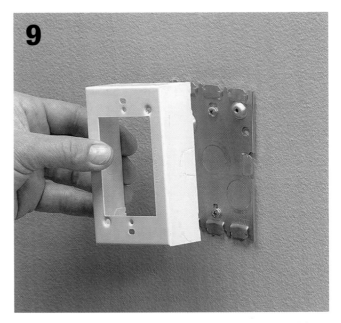

At the new receptacle location, transfer the height of the top of the starter box and mark a reference line. If possible, locate the box so at least one screw hole in the mounting plate falls over a wall stud. Position the mounting plate for the receptacle box up against the reference line and secure it with screws driven through the mounting plate holes. If the plate is not located over a wall stud, use wall anchors (see below right).

10

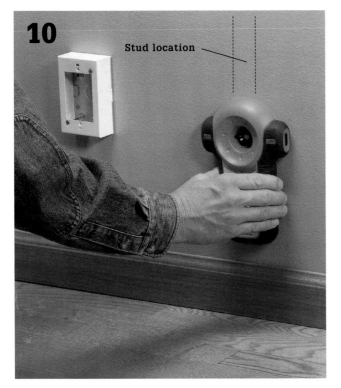

Stud location

Use a stud finder to locate and mark all of the wall framing members between the old receptacle and the new one. There is usually a 1½"-wide stud every 16" behind the wall.

Here's How ▶

Here's how to install wall anchors. Mark screw locations on the wall, then drill ¼" holes through the wall at the marks. Tap a plastic wall anchor into the hole with a hammer so the underside of the top flange is flush against the surface of the wall. When a screw is driven into the wall anchor sleeve, the sleeve will expand in the hole and hold the screw securely.

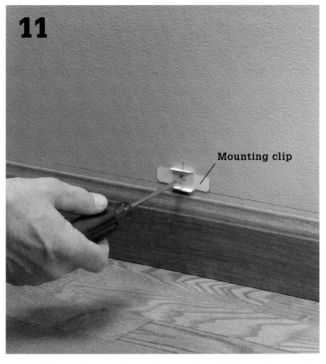

11

Mounting clip

At stud locations mark a reference line ¼" above the top of the baseboard. Attach mounting clips for the raceway track at these marks.

12

Install mounting clips ½" or so below the knockouts on both the starter box and the new receptacle box. The clips should line up with the knockouts.

13

At the starter box slide one end of the short piece of raceway into the knockout so that about ⅛" extends into the box. Snap the raceway into the clip below the knockout. Repeat this same procedure at the new receptacle box. Slip a bushing (included with installation kit) over the ends of the tracks where they enter the box.

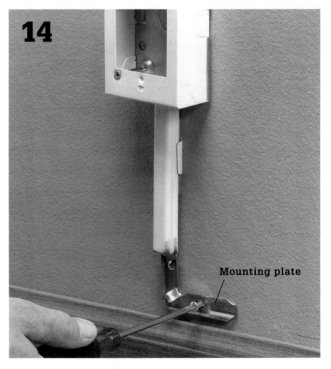

14

Mounting plate

The elbow piece will have two parts, a mounting plate and a cap. Install the mounting plates directly below the pieces of track entering the receptacle boxes.

(continued)

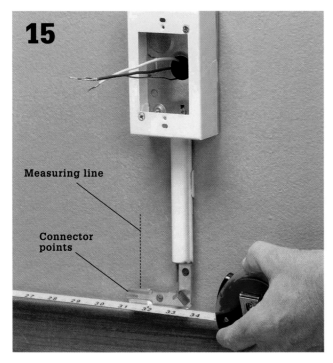

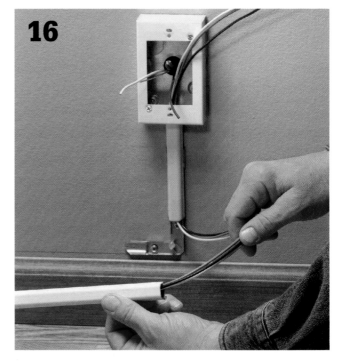

Measure and cut the long piece of raceway that fits between the two receptacles. Measure the distance between the ends of the horizontal parts of the elbows, and cut a length of raceway to that length. Be sure to measure all the way to the base of the clip, not just to the tips of the connector points.

Cut black, white, and green THNN wire about 2-ft. longer than the length of each wiring run. Snake the end of each wire into the starter box, through the knockout, and into the vertical raceway. Then snake the wire all the way through the long piece of raceway so about 12 to 16" comes out on each end.

What If...? ▸

What if I need to go around a corner? Use corner pieces to guide raceway around corners. Corners are available for inside or outside corners and consist of a mounting plate and a cap piece. Inside corners may be used at wall/ceiling junctures.

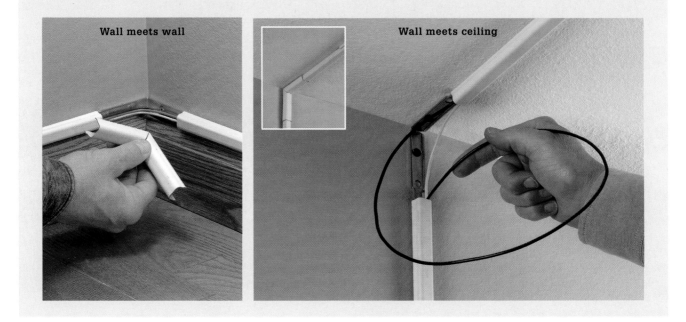

What if I need a piece of raceway track that's longer than the longest piece available at the hardware store (usually 5 ft.)? You can use straight connector pieces to join two lengths of raceway. Much like an elbow piece, they have a mounting plate and a cover that snaps over the wiring.

Snap the long piece of raceway into the mounting clips. Line up one end of the raceway with the end of an elbow and begin pressing the raceway into the clips until it is snapped into all of the clips. At the new receptacle location, snake the ends of the wires up through the vertical piece of raceway and into the new receptacle box. There should be about 6" of wire coming out at each box.

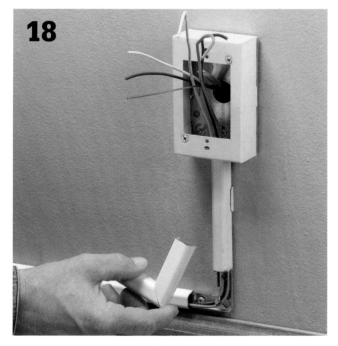

Finish the raceway by snapping the elbow cover pieces into place over the mounting plates, one at the starter box and another at the new receptacle location. You may need to rap the plate with a rubber mallet to get enough force to snap it on. Make sure all of the wire fits completely within the cover pieces.

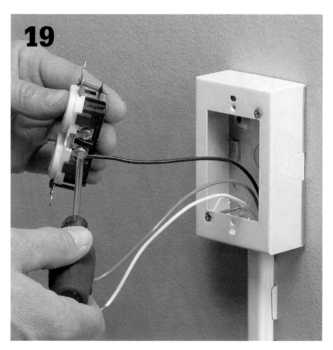

Now you can wire the receptacles. Begin at the new receptacle location. Wrap the end of the black wire around the bottom gold screw on the side of the receptacle. Tighten the screw so it's snug.

(continued)

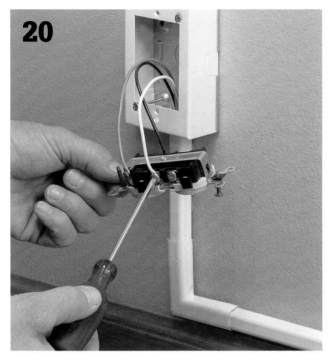

20

Wrap the end of the white wire around the silver screw opposite the gold one you just used. Tighten the screw so it's snug. Connect the green wire to the green-colored screw on the bottom of the receptacle.

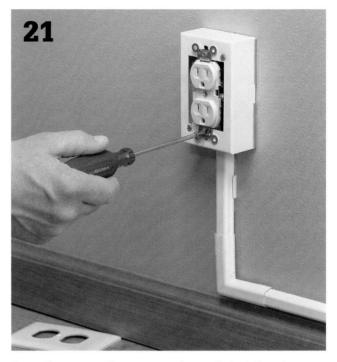

21

Once the connections are made, gently tuck the wires and the receptacle into the box so the holes in the top and bottom of the receptacle align with the holes in the box. Use a screwdriver to drive the two long mounting screws that hold the receptacle to the box. Attach the cover plate.

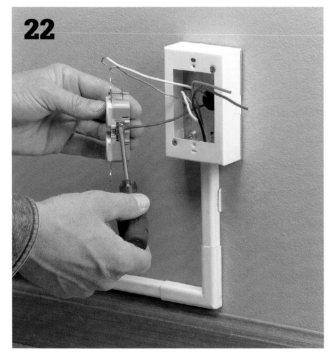

22

Now you can reinstall the old receptacle (or a replacement) at the starter box. First, make sure the power is still off with your voltage tester. Wrap the end of the black wire around the top gold screw on the side of the receptacle. Tighten the screw.

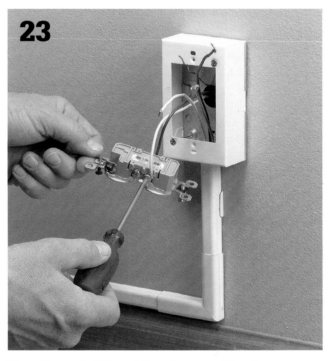

23

Wrap the end of the white wire around the silver screw opposite the gold one you just used. Tighten the screw.

24 Original receptacle

Black wire lead to new receptacle

Connect the old receptacle to the new one. Take the black wire that goes into the raceway and wrap the end of the wire around the bottom gold screw on the side of the receptacle. Tighten the screw.

25 Black wire lead to new receptacle

White wire lead to new receptacle

Wrap the end of the old white wire around the silver screw opposite the copper one you just used. Tighten the screw.

26

Finally, cut a piece of green wire about 6" long and strip ¾" from both ends (this is called a pigtail wire). Join one end of the pigtail with the ends of the bare and green wires in the box using a wire connector. Wrap the other end of the pigtail around the green screw on the receptacle.

27

Once the connections are made, tuck the wires and the receptacle into the box so the holes in the top and bottom of the receptacle align with the holes in the box. Use a screwdriver to drive the two long mounting screws that hold the receptacle to the box. Install the cover plate. You can now restore the power and test your new receptacle.

Boxes & Panels

All wiring connections must be housed within a box that is locatable and accessible. The box may be as simple as a small handy box for making a splice, or as complex as a 200-amp main service panel. It is typically rectangular, square, round, or octagonal, but be aware that the boxes are shaped as they are for specific reasons, so make sure you are using the right one for the job.

Installing a box that is too small is an extremely common wiring mistake that is easy to understand: small boxes cost less. But they are not one-size fits all. The smallest common boxes, called handy boxes, may be used only for a single device (such as a switch or receptacle) with no more than three conductors. Be sure to refer to a box fill chart (see page 60) to learn which size and shape box is required for your job.

Electrical panels function like other electrical boxes insofar as they house connections, but they also house breakers or fuses and other parts that transmit power from the service entry to the individual circuits. Subpanels are smaller electrical panels that perform the same function but are supplied by the main service panel so they can distribute power into multiple circuits in a remote spot.

In this chapter:
- Electrical Boxes
- Installing Boxes
- Electrical Panels

Electrical Boxes

The National Electrical Code requires that wire connections and cable splices be contained inside an approved metal or plastic box. This shields framing members and other flammable materials from electrical sparks.

Electrical boxes come in several shapes. Rectangular and square boxes are used for switches and receptacles. Rectangular (2 × 3") boxes are used for single switches or duplex receptacles. Square (4 × 4") boxes are used any time it is convenient for two switches or receptacles to be wired, or "ganged," in one box, an arrangement common in kitchens or entry hallways. Octagonal electrical boxes contain wire connections for ceiling fixtures.

All electrical boxes are available in different depths. A box must be deep enough so a switch or receptacle can be removed or installed easily without crimping and damaging the circuit wires. Replace an undersized box with a larger box using the Electrical Box Chart (right) as a guide. The NEC also says that all electrical boxes must remain accessible. Never cover an electrical box with drywall, paneling, or wallcoverings.

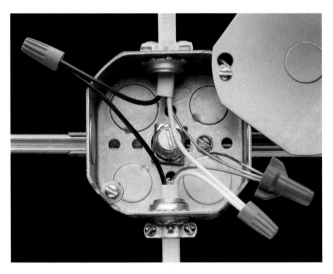

Octagonal boxes usually contain wire connections for ceiling fixtures. Cables are inserted into the box through knockout openings and are held with cable clamps. Because the ceiling fixture attaches directly to the box, the box should be anchored firmly to a framing member. Often, it is nailed directly to a ceiling joist. However, metal braces are available that allow a box to be mounted between joists or studs. A properly installed octagonal box can support a ceiling fixture weighing up to 35 pounds. Any box must be covered with a tightly fitting cover plate, and the box must not have open knockouts.

Electrical Box Fill Chart ▶

Box size and shape	Maximum number of conductors permitted (see Notes below)			
	18 AWG	16 AWG	14 AWG	12 AWG
Junction boxes				
4 × 1¼" R or O	8	7	6	5
4 × 1½" R or O	10	8	7	6
4 × 2⅛" R or O	14	12	10	9
4 × 1¼" S	12	10	9	8
4 × 1½" S	14	12	10	9
4 × 2⅛" S	20	17	15	13
4¹¹⁄₁₆ × 1¼" S	17	14	12	11
4¹¹⁄₁₆ × 1½" S	19	16	14	13
4¹¹⁄₁₆ × 2⅛" S	28	24	21	18
Device boxes				
3 × 2 × 1½"	5	4	3	3
3 × 2 × 2"	6	5	5	4
3 × 2 × 2¼"	7	6	5	4
3 × 2 × 2½"	8	7	6	5
3 × 2 × 2¾"	9	8	7	6
3 × 2 × 3½"	12	10	9	8
4 × 2⅛ × 1½"	6	5	5	4
4 × 2⅛ × 1⅞"	8	7	6	5
4 × 2⅛ × 2⅛"	9	8	7	6

Notes:

- R = Round; O = Octagonal; S = Square or rectangular
- Each hot or neutral wire entering the box is counted as one conductor.
- Grounding wires are counted as one conductor in total—do not count each one individually.
- Raceway fittings and external cable clamps do not count. Internal cable connectors and straps count as either half or one conductor, depending on type.
- Devices (switches and receptacles mainly) each count as two conductors.
- Straps (yokes) from mounting devices each count as two conductors.
- When calculating total conductors, any nonwire components should be assigned the gauge of the largest wire in the box.
- For wire gauges not shown here, contact your local electrical inspections office.

Common Electrical Boxes

Rectangular boxes are used with wall switches and duplex receptacles. Single-size rectangular boxes (shown above) may have detachable sides that allow them to be ganged together to form double-size boxes.

Square 4 × 4" boxes are large enough for most wiring applications. They are used for cable splices and ganged receptacles or switches. To install one switch or receptacle in a square box, use an adapter cover.

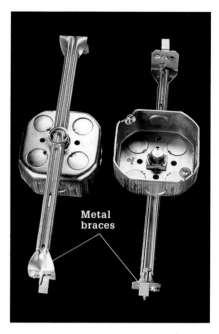

Braced octagonal boxes fit between ceiling joists. The metal braces extend to fit any joist spacing and are nailed or screwed to framing members.

Outdoor boxes have sealed seams and foam gaskets to guard a switch or receptacle against moisture. Corrosion-resistant coatings protect all metal parts. Code compliant models include a watertight hood.

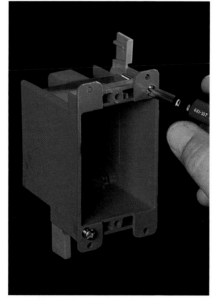

Retrofit boxes upgrade older boxes to larger sizes. One type (above) has built-in clamps that tighten against the inside of a wall and hold the box in place.

Plastic boxes are common in new construction. They can be used only with NM (nonmetallic) cable. The box may include preattached nails for anchoring it to framing members. Wall switches must have grounding screws if installed in plastic boxes.

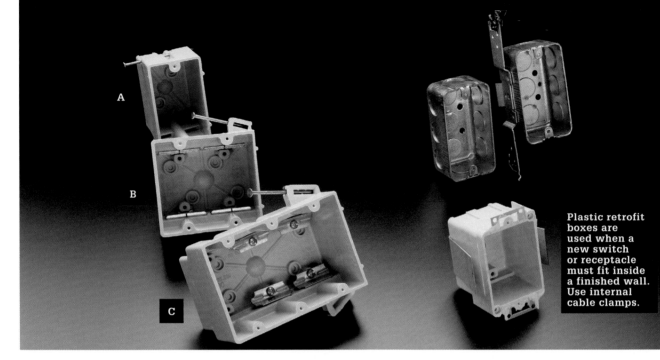

3½"-deep plastic boxes with preattached mounting nails are used for any wiring project protected by finished walls. Common styles include single-gang (A), double-gang (B), and triple-gang (C). Double-gang and triple-gang boxes require internal cable clamps.

Metal boxes should be used for exposed indoor wiring, such as conduit installations in an unfinished basement. Metal boxes, also can be used for wiring that will be covered by finished walls.

Plastic retrofit boxes are used when a new switch or receptacle must fit inside a finished wall. Use internal cable clamps.

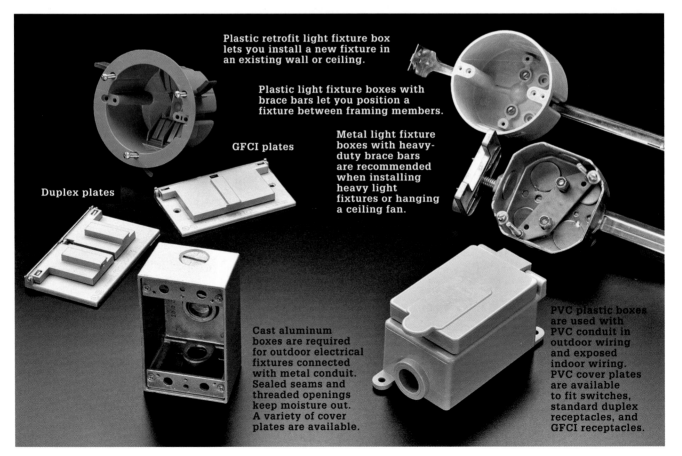

Plastic retrofit light fixture box lets you install a new fixture in an existing wall or ceiling.

Plastic light fixture boxes with brace bars let you position a fixture between framing members.

Duplex plates

GFCI plates

Metal light fixture boxes with heavy-duty brace bars are recommended when installing heavy light fixtures or hanging a ceiling fan.

Cast aluminum boxes are required for outdoor electrical fixtures connected with metal conduit. Sealed seams and threaded openings keep moisture out. A variety of cover plates are available.

PVC plastic boxes are used with PVC conduit in outdoor wiring and exposed indoor wiring. PVC cover plates are available to fit switches, standard duplex receptacles, and GFCI receptacles.

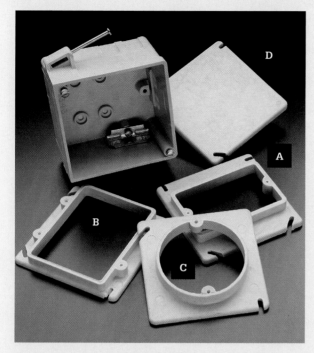

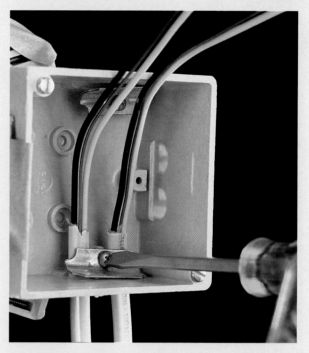

High-quality nonmetallic boxes are rigid and don't contort easily. A variety of adapter plates are available, including single-gang (A), double-gang (B), light fixture (C), and junction box cover plate (D). Adapter plates come in several thicknesses to match different wall constructions.

Boxes larger than 2 × 4" and all retrofit boxes must have internal cable clamps. After installing cables in the box, tighten the cable clamps over the cables so they are gripped firmly, but not so tightly that the cable sheathing is crushed.

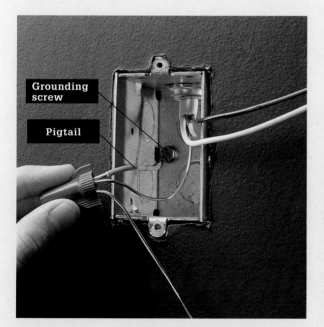

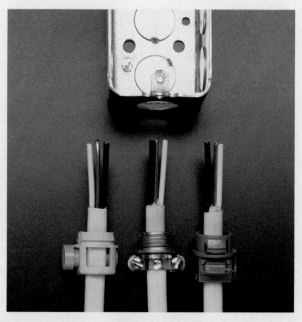

Metal boxes must be grounded to the circuit grounding system. Connect the circuit grounding wires to the box with a green insulated pigtail wire and wire connector (as shown) or with a grounding clip (page 38).

Cables entering a metal box must be clamped. A variety of clamps are available, including plastic clamps (A, C) and threaded metal clamps (B).

Nonmetallic Boxes

Nonmetallic electrical boxes have taken over much of the do-it-yourself market. Most are sold prefitted with installation hardware—from metal wings to 10d common nails attached at the perfect angle for a nail-in box. The bulk of the nonmetallic boxes sold today are inexpensive blue PVC. You can also purchase heavier-duty fiberglass or thermoset plastic models that provide a nonmetallic option for installing heavier fixtures such as ceiling fans and chandeliers.

In addition to cost and availability, nonmetallic boxes hold a big advantage over metal boxes in that their resistance to conducting electricity will prevent a sparking short circuit if a hot wire contacts the box. Nonmetallic boxes generally are not approved for exposed areas, where they may be susceptible to damage. Their lack of rigidity also allows them to compress or distort, which can reduce the interior capacity beyond code minimums or make outlets difficult to attach.

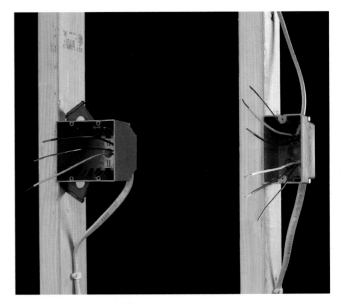

Low cost is the primary reason that blue PVC nail-in boxes are so popular. Not only are they inexpensive, they also feature built-in cable clamps so you may not need to buy extra hardware to install them. The standard PVC nail-in box is prefitted with a pair of 10d common nails for attaching to exposed wall studs. These boxes, often called handy boxes, are too small to be of much use (see fill chart, page 60).

Nonmetallic boxes for home use include: Single-gang, double-gang, triple gang, and quad boxes (A); thermoset and fiberglass boxes for heavier duty (B); round fixture boxes (C) for ceiling installation (nail-in and with integral metal bracket).

Working With Nonmetallic Boxes

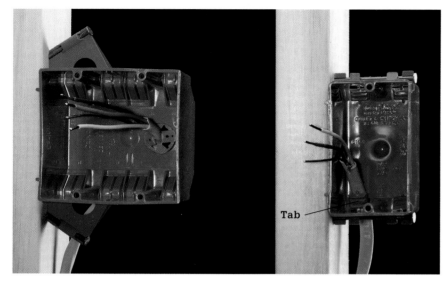

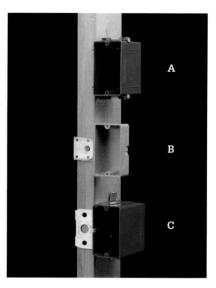

Do not break off the tabs that cover cable entry holes in plastic boxes. These are not knockouts as you would find in metal boxes. In single-gang boxes (right), the pressure from the tab is sufficient to secure the cable as long as it enters with sheathing intact and is stapled no more than 8" from the box. On larger boxes (left), you will find traditional knockouts intended to be used with plastic cable clamps that resemble metal cable clamps. Use these for heavier gauge cable and cable with more than three wires.

Nail-in boxes (A) are prefitted with 10d nails that are attached perpendicular to the face of single-gang boxes and at an inward angle for better gripping power on larger boxes. Side-mount boxes (B) feature a nailing plate that is attached to the front of the stud to automatically create the correct setback; adjustable side-mount boxes (C) are installed the same way but can be moved on the bracket.

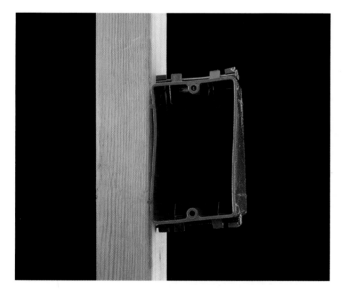

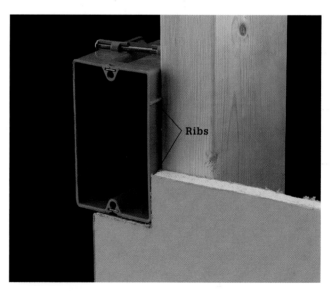

Distortion can occur in nonmetallic boxes when nails or other fasteners are overdriven or installed at improper angles, or when the semiflexible boxes are compressed into improperly sized or shaped openings. This can reduce the box capacity and prevent devices and faceplates from fitting.

Integral ribs cast into many nonmetallic boxes are used to register the box against the wall studs so the front edges of the box will be flush with the wall surface after drywall is installed. Most are set for ½" drywall, but if your wall will be a different thickness you may be able to find a box with corresponding ribs. Otherwise, use a piece of the wallcovering material as a reference.

Installing Boxes

Install electrical boxes for receptacles, switches, and fixtures only after your wiring project plan has been approved by your inspector. Use your wiring plan as a guide, and follow electrical code height and spacing guidelines when laying out box positions.

Always use the deepest electrical boxes that are practical for your installation. Using deep boxes ensures that you will meet code regulations regarding box volume and makes it easier to make the wire connections.

Some electrical fixtures, like recessed light fixtures, electric heaters, and exhaust fans, have built-in wire connection boxes. Install the frames for these fixtures at the same time you are installing the other electrical boxes.

Electrical boxes in adjacent rooms should be positioned close together when they share a common wall and are controlled by the same circuit. This simplifies the cable installations and also reduces the amount of cable needed.

Fixtures That Do Not Need Electrical Boxes

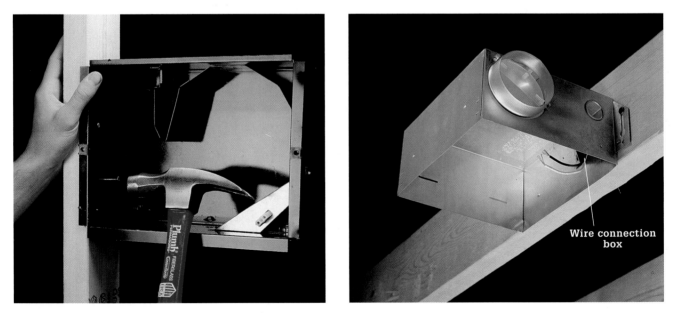

Wire connection box

Recessed fixtures that fit inside wall cavities have built-in wire connection boxes and require no additional electrical boxes. Common recessed fixtures include electric blower-heaters (left), bathroom vent fans (right), and recessed light fixtures. Install the frames for these fixtures at the same time you are installing the other electrical boxes along the circuit. Surface-mounted fixtures like electric baseboard heaters (pages 234 to 237) and under-cabinet fluorescent lights (pages 206 to 209), also have built-in wire connection boxes. These fixtures are not installed until it is time to make the final hookups.

How to Install Electrical Boxes for Receptacles

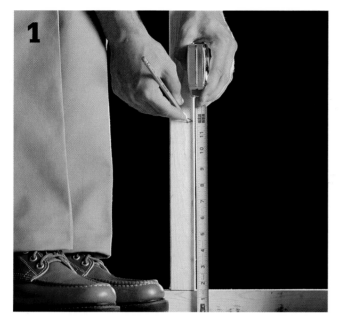

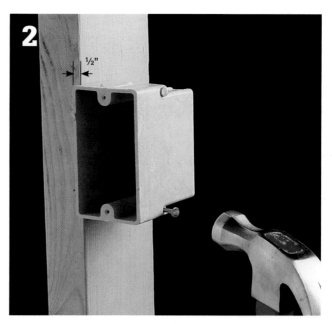

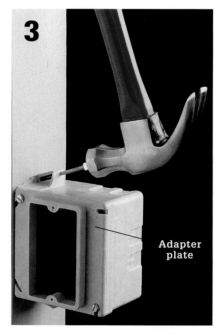

Mark the location of each box on studs. Standard receptacle boxes should be centered 12" above floor level. GFCI receptacle boxes in a bathroom should be mounted so they will be about 10" above the finished countertop.

Position each box against a stud so the front face will be flush with the finished wall. For example, if you will be installing ½" wallboard, position the box so it extends ½" past the face of the stud. Anchor the box by driving the mounting nails into the stud.

Adapter plate

If installing square boxes, attach the adapter plates before positioning the boxes. Use adapter plates that match the thickness of the finished wall. Anchor the box by driving the mounting nails into the stud.

Open one knockout for each cable that will enter the box using a hammer and screwdriver.

Break off any sharp edges that might damage vinyl cable sheathing by rotating a screwdriver in the knockout.

How to Install Boxes for Light Fixtures

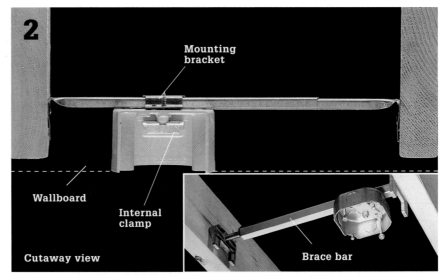

Position the light fixture box for a vanity light above the frame opening for a mirror or medicine cabinet. Place the box for a ceiling light fixture in the center of the room. Position each box against a framing member so the front face will be flush with the finished wall or ceiling, then anchor the box by driving the mounting nails into the framing.

To position a light fixture between joists, attach an electrical box to an adjustable brace bar. Nail the ends of the brace bar to joists so the face of the box will be flush with the finished ceiling surface. Slide the box along the brace bar to the desired position, then tighten the mounting screws. Use internal cable clamps when using a box with a brace bar. Note: For ceiling fans and heavy fixtures, use a metal box and a heavy-duty brace bar rated for heavy loads (inset photo).

How to Install Boxes for Switches

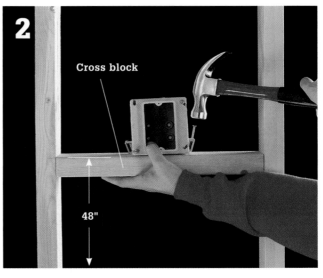

Install switch boxes at accessible locations, usually on the latch side of a door, with the center of the box 48" from the floor. The box for a thermostat is mounted at 48" to 60". Position each box against the side of a stud so the front face will be flush with the finished wall, and drive the mounting nails into the stud.

To install a switch box between studs, first install a cross block between studs, with the top edge 46" above the floor. Position the box on the cross block so the front face will be flush with the finished wall, and drive the mounting nails into the cross block.

How to Locate Electrical Boxes

Heights of electrical boxes vary depending on use. In the kitchen shown here, boxes above the countertop are 45" above the floor, in the center of 18" backsplashes that extend from the countertop to the cabinets. All boxes for wall switches also are installed at this height. The center of the box for the microwave receptacle is 72" off the floor. The centers of the boxes for the range and food disposer receptacles are 12" off the floor, but the center of the box for the dishwasher receptacle is 6" off the floor.

Typical Wallcovering Thickness

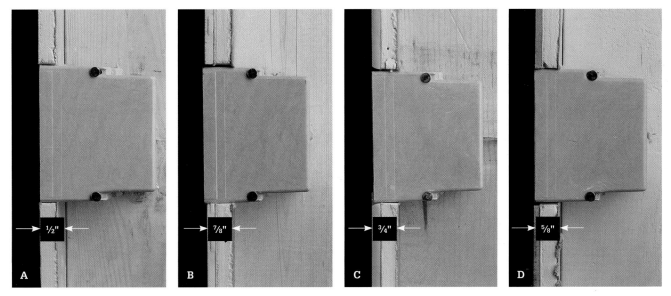

Consider the thickness of finished walls when mounting electrical boxes against framing members. Code requires that the front face of boxes be flush with the finished wall surface, so how you install boxes will vary depending on the type of wall finish that will be used. For example, if the walls will be finished with ½" wallboard (A), attach the boxes so the front faces extend ½" past the front of the framing members. With ceramic tile and wall board (B), extend the boxes ⅞" past the framing members. With ¼" Corian® over wallboard (C), boxes should extend ¾"; and with wallboard and laminate (D), boxes extend ⅝".

Ceiling Boxes

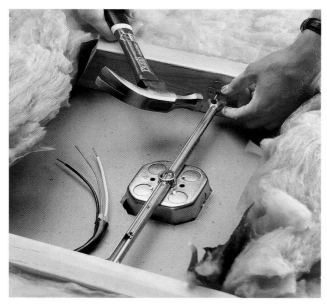

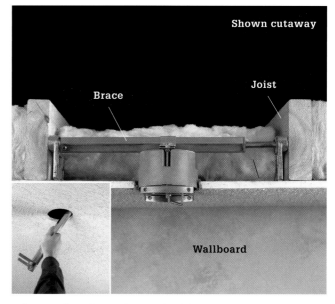

Ceiling boxes for lights are generally round or octagonal in shape to fit typical lamp mounting plates. The easiest way to install one is by nailing the brace to open ceiling joists from above. If the ceiling is insulated, pull the insulation away from the box if the fixture you're installing is not rated IC for insulation contact.

A heavy-duty brace is required for anchoring boxes that will support heavy chandeliers and ceiling fans. A remodeling brace like the one seen here is designed to install through a small cutout in the ceiling (inset photo).

How to Install a Junction Box

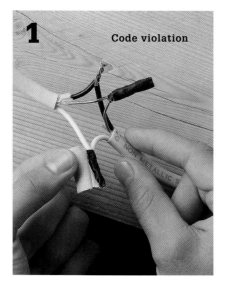

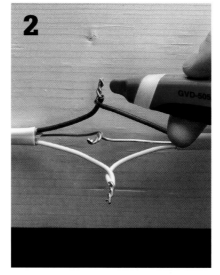

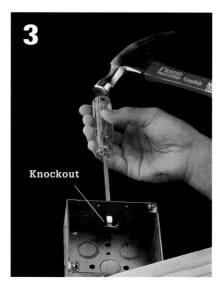

Turn off power to circuit wires at the main service panel. Carefully remove any tape or wire connectors from the exposed splice. Avoid contact with the bare wire ends until the wires have been tested for power.

Test for power. The tester should not glow. If it does, the wires are still hot. Shut off power to correct circuit at the main service panel. Disconnect the illegally spliced wires.

Open one knockout for each cable that will enter the box using a hammer and screwdriver. Any unopened knockouts should remain sealed.

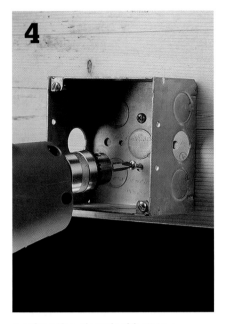

Anchor the electrical box to a wooden framing member using screws or nails.

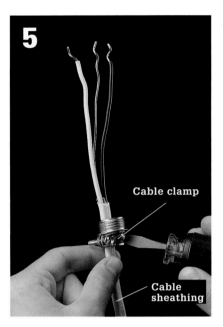

Thread each cable end through a cable clamp. Tighten the clamp with a screwdriver. See if there is any slack in the cables so you can gain a little extra cable to work with.

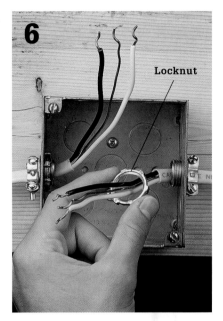

Insert the cables into the electrical box, and screw a locknut onto each cable clamp.

Tighten the locknuts by pushing against the lugs with the blade of a screwdriver.

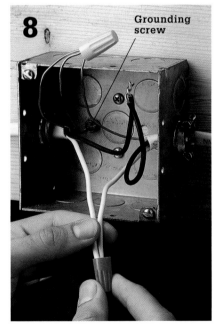

Use wire connectors to reconnect the wires. Pigtail the copper grounding wires to the green grounding screw in the back of the box.

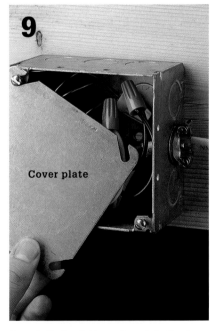

Carefully tuck the wires into the box, and attach the cover plate. Turn on the power to the circuit at the main service panel. Make sure the box remains accessible and is not concealed by finished walls or ceilings.

Installing Pop-in Retrofit Boxes

Attaching an electrical box to a wall stud during new construction is relatively easy (pages 66 to 69). The task becomes complicated, however, when you're working in finished walls during remodeling or repair. In most cases, it's best to use an electronic stud finder, make a large cutout in the wall, and attach a new box directly to a framing member or bracing (and then replace and refinish the wall materials). But there are occasions when this isn't possible or practical and you just need to retrofit an electrical box without making a large hole in the wall. You also may find that an older switch or receptacle box is too shallow to accommodate a new dimmer or GFCI safely. These situations call for a pop-in retrofit box (sometimes called an "old work" box).

A pop-in box typically has wings, tabs, or brackets that are drawn tight against the wall surface on the wall cavity side, holding the box in place. It can be made either of metal or plastic.

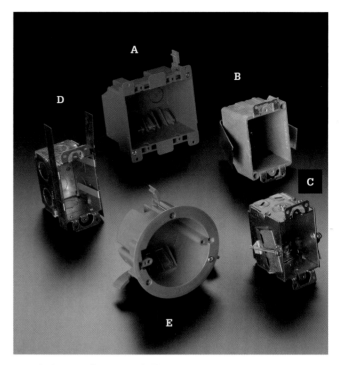

Pop-in boxes for remodeling come in variety of styles. For walls, they include plastic retrofit boxes with flip-out wings (A), metal or plastic boxes with compression tabs or brackets (B), metal retrofit boxes with flip-out wings (C), and metal boxes with bendable brackets, also known as F-straps, (D). For ceilings, plastic fixture boxes with flip-out wings (E) are available.

Tools & Materials ▶

Screwdriver   Template (if provided)
Pencil   Plastic or metal
Wallboard saw   pop-in box

How to Replace an Electrical Box

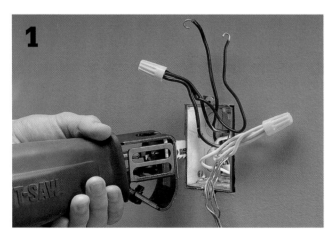

To install a dimmer switch or GFCI receptacle, you may have to replace an old, overcrowded box. Shut off power and remove the old switch or receptacle. Identify the location of nails holding the box to the framing member and cut the nails with a hacksaw or reciprocating saw with a metal blade inserted between the box and the stud.

Bind the cable ends together and attach string in case they fall into the wall cavity when the old box is removed. Disconnect the cable clamps and slide the old box out. Install a new pop-in box (see next page).

How to Install a Pop-in Box

1

Use a template to trace a cutout for the box at the intended location. If no template is provided, press the pop-in box against the wall surface and trace its front edges (but not the tabs on the top and bottom).

2

Puncture the wallboard with the tip of a wallboard saw or by drilling a small hole inside the lines, and make the cutout for the box.

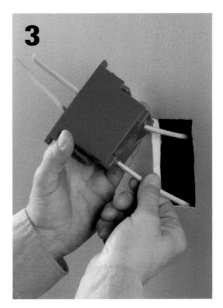

3

Pull NM cable through a knockout in the box (no cable clamp is required with a plastic box, just be sure not to break the pressure tab that holds the cable in place).

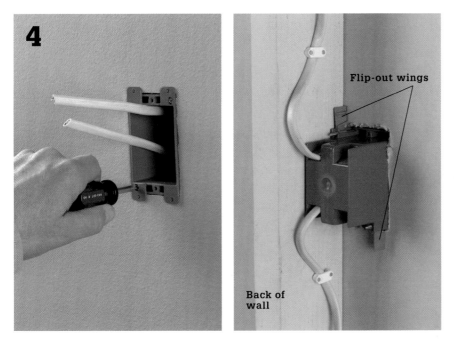

4

Flip-out wings

Back of wall

Insert the box into the cutout so the tabs are flush against the wall surface. Tighten the screws that cause the flip-out wings to pivot (right) until the box is held firmly in place. Connect the switch or receptacle that the box will house.

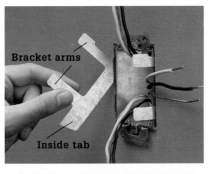

Bracket arms

Inside tab

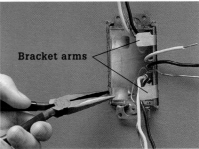

Bracket arms

Variation: Feed cable into the new box and secure it in the opening after clamping the cables. With this pop-in box, bracket arms are inserted at the sides of the box (top) and then bent around the front edges to secure the box in the opening (bottom).

Electrical Panels

Every home has a main service panel that distributes electrical current to the individual circuits. The main service panel usually is found in the basement, garage, or utility area, and can be identified by its metal casing. Before making any repair to your electrical system, you must shut off power to the correct circuit at the main service panel. The service panel should be indexed (page 22) so circuits can be identified easily.

Service panels vary in appearance, depending on the age of the system. Very old wiring may operate on 30-amp service that has only two circuits. New homes can have 200-amp service with 30 or more circuits. Find the size of the service by reading the amperage rating printed on the main fuse block or main circuit breaker.

Regardless of age, all service panels have fuses or circuit breakers (pages 78 to 81) that control each circuit and protect them from overloads. In general, older service panels use fuses, while newer service panels use circuit breakers.

In addition to the main service panel, your electrical system may have a subpanel that controls some of the circuits in the home. A subpanel has its own circuit breakers or fuses and is installed to control circuits that have been added to an existing wiring system.

The subpanel resembles the main service panel but is usually smaller. It may be located near the main panel, or it may be found near the areas served by the new circuits. Garages and basements that have been updated often have their own subpanels. If your home has a subpanel, make sure that its circuits are indexed correctly.

When handling fuses or circuit breakers, make sure the area around the service panel is dry. Never remove the protective cover on the service panel. After turning off a circuit to make electrical repairs, remember to always test the circuit for power before touching any wires.

The main service panel is the heart of your wiring system. As our demand for household energy has increased, the panels have also grown in capacity. Today, a 200-amp panel is considered the minimum for new construction.

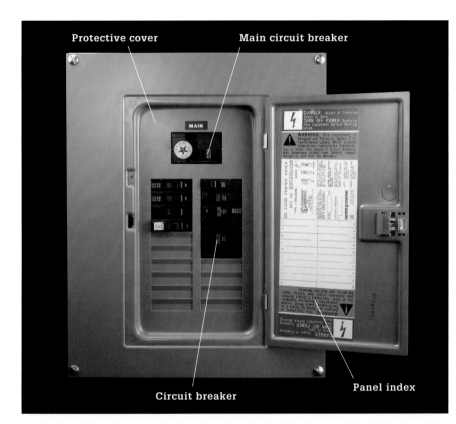

Protective cover
Main circuit breaker
Circuit breaker
Panel index

A circuit breaker panel providing 100 amps or more of power is common in wiring systems installed during the 1960s and later. A circuit breaker panel is housed in a gray metal cabinet that contains two rows of individual circuit breakers. The size of the service can be identified by reading the amperage rating of the main circuit breaker, which is located at the top or bottom of the main service panel.

A 100-amp service panel is now the minimum standard for all new housing. It is considered adequate for a medium-sized house with no more than three major electric appliances. However, larger houses with more electrical appliances require a service panel that provides 150 amps or more.

To shut off power to individual circuits in a circuit breaker panel, flip the lever on the appropriate circuit breaker to the OFF position. To shut off the power to the entire house, turn the main circuit breaker to the OFF position.

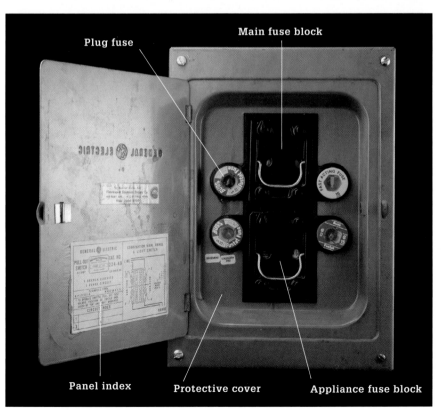

Plug fuse
Main fuse block
Panel index
Protective cover
Appliance fuse block

A 60-amp fuse panel often is found in wiring systems installed between 1950 and 1965. It usually is housed in a gray metal cabinet that contains four individual plug fuses, plus one or two pull-out fuse blocks that hold cartridge fuses. This type of panel is regarded as adequate for a small, 1,100-square-foot house that has no more than one 240-volt appliance. Many homeowners update 60-amp service to 100 amps or more so that additional lighting and appliance circuits can be added to the system. Home loan programs also may require that 60-amp service be updated before a home can qualify for financing.

To shut off power to a circuit, carefully unscrew the plug fuse, touching only its insulated rim. To shut off power to the entire house, hold the handle of the main fuse block and pull sharply to remove it. Major appliance circuits are controlled with another cartridge fuse block. Shut off the appliance circuit by pulling out this fuse block.

Circuit Breaker Panels

The circuit breaker panel is the electrical distribution center for your home. It divides the current into branch circuits that are carried throughout the house. Each branch circuit is controlled by a circuit breaker that protects the wires from dangerous current overloads. When installing new circuits, the last step is to connect the wires to new circuit breakers at the panel. Working inside a circuit breaker panel is not dangerous if you follow basic safety procedures. Always shut off the main circuit breaker and test for power before touching any parts inside the panel, and never touch the service wire lugs. If unsure of your own skills, hire an electrician to make the final circuit connections. (If you have an older electrical service with fuses instead of circuit breakers, always have an electrician make these final hookups.)

If the main circuit breaker panel does not have enough open slots to hold new circuit breakers, install a subpanel (pages 184 to 187). This job is well within the skill level of an experienced do-it-yourselfer,

Slimline circuit breakers require half as much space as standard single-pole breakers. Slimlines can be used to make room for added circuits.

Grounding bus bar has terminals for linking grounding wires to the main grounding conductor. It is bonded to the neutral bus bar.

Service wire lugs: DO NOT TOUCH

120-volt branch circuits

Main circuit breaker panel distributes the power entering the home into branch circuits.

Neutral service wire carries current back to the power source after it has passed through the home.

Two hot service wires provide 120 volts of power to the main circuit breaker. These wires are always HOT.

Main circuit breaker protects the hot service wires from overloads and transfers power to two hot bus bars.

Double-pole breaker wired for a 120/240 circuit transfers power from the two hot bus bars to red and black hot wires in a three-wire cable.

Neutral bus bar has setscrew terminals for linking all neutral circuit wires to the neutral service wire.

Subpanel feeder breaker is a double-pole breaker, usually 30 to 50 amps. It is wired in the same way as a 120/240-volt circuit.

Two hot bus bars run through the center of the panel, supplying power to the circuit breakers. Each carries 120 volts.

Grounding conductor leads to metal grounding rods driven into the earth.

120/240-volt branch circuit

although you can also hire an electrician to install the subpanel.

Before installing any new wiring, evaluate your electrical service to make sure it provides enough current to support both the existing wiring and any new circuits. If your service does not provide enough power, have an electrician upgrade it to a higher amp rating. During the upgrade, the electrician will install a new circuit breaker panel with enough extra breaker slots for the new circuits you want to install.

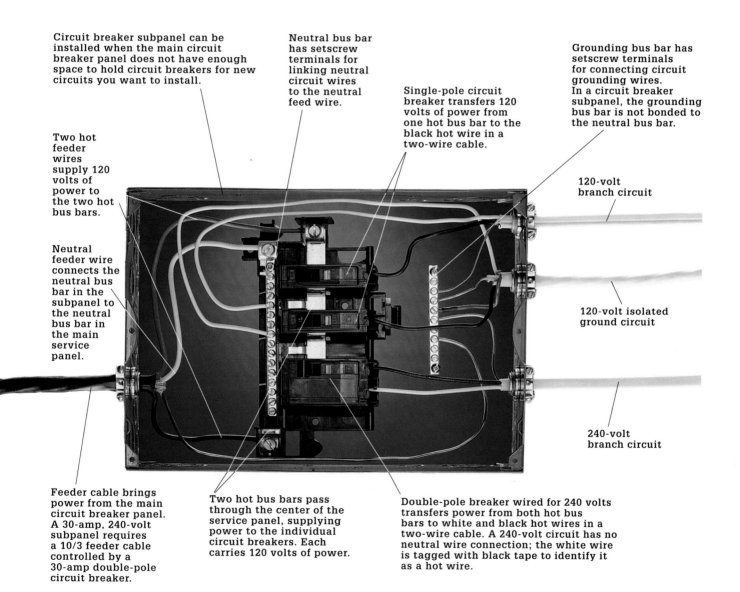

Circuit breaker subpanel can be installed when the main circuit breaker panel does not have enough space to hold circuit breakers for new circuits you want to install.

Two hot feeder wires supply 120 volts of power to the two hot bus bars.

Neutral feeder wire connects the neutral bus bar in the subpanel to the neutral bus bar in the main service panel.

Neutral bus bar has setscrew terminals for linking neutral circuit wires to the neutral feed wire.

Single-pole circuit breaker transfers 120 volts of power from one hot bus bar to the black hot wire in a two-wire cable.

Grounding bus bar has setscrew terminals for connecting circuit grounding wires. In a circuit breaker subpanel, the grounding bus bar is not bonded to the neutral bus bar.

120-volt branch circuit

120-volt isolated ground circuit

240-volt branch circuit

Feeder cable brings power from the main circuit breaker panel. A 30-amp, 240-volt subpanel requires a 10/3 feeder cable controlled by a 30-amp double-pole circuit breaker.

Two hot bus bars pass through the center of the service panel, supplying power to the individual circuit breakers. Each carries 120 volts of power.

Double-pole breaker wired for 240 volts transfers power from both hot bus bars to white and black hot wires in a two-wire cable. A 240-volt circuit has no neutral wire connection; the white wire is tagged with black tape to identify it as a hot wire.

Fuses & Circuit Breakers

Fuses and circuit breakers are safety devices designed to protect the electrical system from short circuits and overloads. Fuses and circuit breakers are located in the main service panel.

Most service panels installed before 1965 rely on fuses to control and protect individual circuits. Screw-in plug fuses protect 120-volt circuits that power lights and receptacles. Cartridge fuses protect 240-volt appliance circuits and the main shutoff of the service panel.

Inside each fuse is a current-carrying metal alloy ribbon. If a circuit is overloaded, the metal ribbon melts and stops the flow of power. A fuse must match the amperage rating of the circuit. Never replace a fuse with one that has a larger amperage rating.

In most service panels installed after 1965, circuit breakers protect and control individual circuits. Single-pole circuit breakers protect 120-volt circuits, and double-pole circuit breakers protect 240-volt circuits. Amperage ratings for circuit breakers range from 15 to 100 amps.

Each circuit breaker has a permanent metal strip that heats up and bends when voltage passes through it. If a circuit is overloaded, the metal strip inside the breaker bends enough to "trip" the switch and stop the flow of power. If a circuit breaker trips frequently even though the power demand is small, the mechanism inside the breaker may be worn out. Worn circuit breakers should be replaced by an electrician.

When a fuse blows or a circuit breaker trips, it is usually because there are too many light fixtures and plug-in appliances drawing power through the circuit. Move some of the plug-in appliances to another circuit, then replace the fuse or reset the breaker. If the fuse blows or the breaker trips again immediately, there may be a short circuit in the system. Call a licensed electrician if you suspect a short circuit.

Tools & Materials ▸

Fuse puller and continuity tester
   (for cartridge fuses only)
Replacement fuse

Circuit breakers are found in the majority of panels installed since the 1940s. Single-pole breakers control 120-volt circuits. Double-pole breakers rated for 20 to 60 amps control 240-volt circuits. Ground-fault circuit interrupter (GFCI) and arc-fault circuit interrupter (AFCI) breakers provide protection from shocks and fire-causing arcs for the entire circuit.

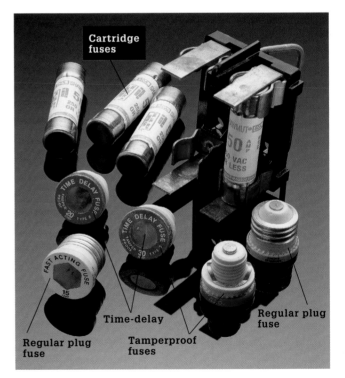

Fuses are used in older service panels. Plug fuses usually control 120-volt circuits rated for 15, 20, or 30 amps. Tamper-proof plug fuses have threads that fit only matching sockets, making it impossible to install a wrong-sized fuse. Time-delay fuses absorb temporary heavy power loads without blowing. Cartridge fuses control 240-volt circuits and range from 30 to 100 amps.

How to Identify & Replace a Blown Plug Fuse

Locate the blown fuse at the main service panel. If the metal ribbon inside is cleanly melted (right), the circuit was overloaded. If window is discolored (left), there was a short circuit.

Unscrew the fuse, being careful to touch only the insulated rim of the fuse. Replace it with a fuse that has the same amperage rating.

How to Remove, Test & Replace a Cartridge Fuse

Remove cartridge fuses by gripping the handle of the fuse block and pulling sharply.

Remove the individual cartridge fuses from the block using a fuse puller.

Test each fuse using a continuity tester. If the tester glows, the fuse is good. If not, install a new fuse with the same amperage rating.

How to Reset a Circuit Breaker

Open the service panel and locate the tripped breaker. The lever on the tripped breaker will be either in the OFF position, or in a position between ON and OFF.

Reset the tripped circuit breaker by pressing the circuit breaker lever all the way to the OFF position, then pressing it to the ON position.

Test AFCI and GFCI circuit breakers by pushing the TEST button. The breaker should trip to the OFF position. If not, the breaker is faulty and must be replaced by an electrician.

Connecting Circuit Breakers

The last step in a wiring project is connecting circuits at the breaker panel. After this is done, the work is ready for the final inspection.

Circuits are connected at the main breaker panel, if it has enough open slots, or at a circuit breaker subpanel (pages 184 to 187). When working at a subpanel, make sure the feeder breaker at the main panel has been turned off, and test for power (photo, right) before touching any parts in the subpanel.

Make sure the circuit breaker amperage does not exceed the ampacity of the circuit wires you are connecting to it. Also be aware that circuit breaker styles and installation techniques vary according to manufacturer. Use breakers designed for your type of panel.

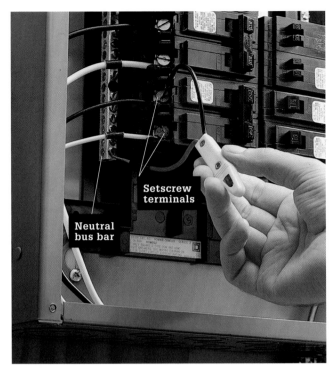

Test for current before touching any parts inside a circuit breaker panel. With main breaker turned off but all other breakers turned on, touch one probe of a neon tester to the neutral bus bar, and touch other probe to each setscrew on one of the double-pole breakers (not the main breaker). If tester does not light for either setscrew, it is safe to work in the panel.

Tools & Materials ▸

Screwdriver	Circuit tester
Hammer	Pliers
Pencil	Cable clamps
Combination tool	Single- and double-pole
Cable ripper	circuit breakers

How to Connect Circuit Breakers

Shut off the main circuit breaker in the main circuit breaker panel (if you are working in a subpanel, shut off the feeder breaker in the main panel). Remove the panel cover plate, taking care not to touch the parts inside the panel. Test for power (photo, top).

Open a knockout in the side of the circuit breaker panel using a screwdriver and hammer. Attach a cable clamp to the knockout.

Hold cable across the front of the panel near the knockout, and mark sheathing about ½" inside the edge of the panel. Strip the cable from marked line to end using a cable ripper. (There should be 18 to 24" of excess cable.) Insert the cable through the clamp and into the service panel, then tighten the clamp.

Bend the bare copper grounding wire around the inside edge of the panel to an open setscrew terminal on the grounding bus bar. Insert the wire into the opening on the bus bar, and tighten the setscrew. Fold excess wire around the inside edge of the panel.

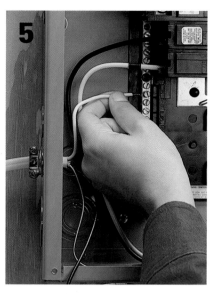

For 120-volt circuits, bend the white circuit wire around the outside of the panel to an open setscrew terminal on the neutral bus bar. Clip away excess wire, then strip ½" of insulation from the wire using a combination tool. Insert the wire into the terminal opening, and tighten the setscrew.

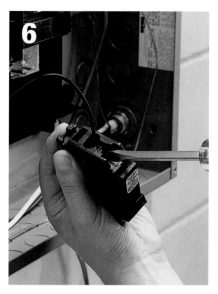

Strip ½" of insulation from the end of the black circuit wire. Insert the wire into the setscrew terminal on a new single-pole circuit breaker, and tighten the setscrew.

Slide one end of the circuit breaker onto the guide hook, then press it firmly against the bus bar until it snaps into place. (Breaker installation may vary, depending on the manufacturer.) Fold excess black wire around the inside edge of the panel.

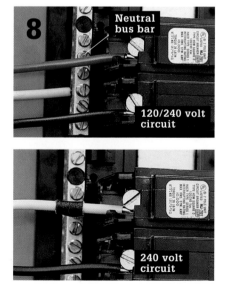

120/240-volt circuits (top): Connect red and black wires to double-pole breaker. Connect white wire to neutral bus bar, and grounding wire to grounding bus bar. For 240-volt circuits (bottom), attach white and black wires to double-pole breaker, tagging white wire with black tape. There is no neutral bus bar connection on this circuit.

Remove the appropriate breaker knockout on the panel cover plate to make room for the new circuit breaker. A single-pole breaker requires one knockout, while a double-pole breaker requires two knockouts. Reattach the cover plate, and label the new circuit on the panel index.

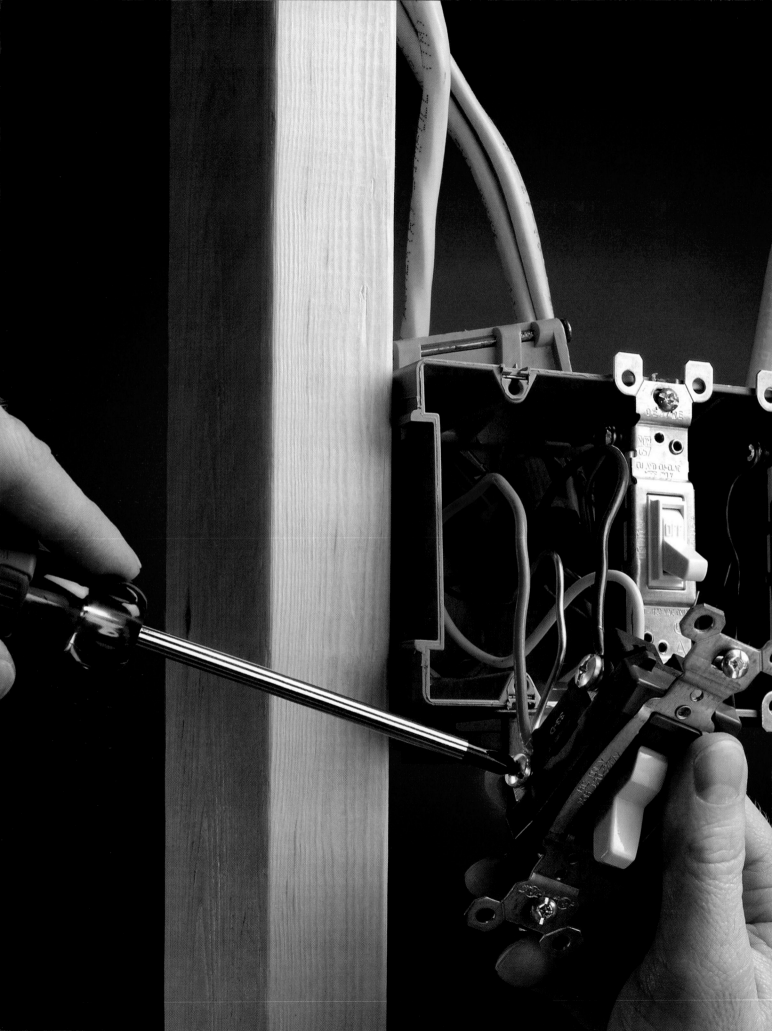

Switches

Among wiring devices, switches fail with surprising frequency. If you've carefully wired a new circuit or a fixture and you know you got it right, but when you turn on the power it doesn't work, you should direct your attention to any switches in the line. Even brand-new switches can fail to function correctly. This is why most professional electricians will pay the extra couple of dollars to buy a quality switch out of the gate. It is also why most of them routinely test each switch for continuity before installing it (see pages 98 to 101).

The most basic switches for home wiring are single-pole switches, which control only one fixture and have only two screw (or push-in) terminals (not counting the grounding screw). Next, three-way switches and four-way switches have more installation possibilities and control circuits that are more complicated to wire. Dimmer switches, isolated ground switches, and motion-sensor switches are some of the other switch options.

Use caution when you handle switches. The wires are usually attached to screw terminals on the sides of the fitting, which makes them very easy to contact if you grab the switch. Always shut off the power to the switch before removing the switch cover plate. Also shut off the power at the service panel if you will be working downline from the switch—never count on a switch that is open to function as a breaker.

In this chapter:

- Wall Switches
- Types of Switches
- Specialty Switches
- Testing Switches

Wall Switches

An average wall switch is turned on and off more than 1,000 times each year. Because switches receive constant use, wire connections can loosen and switch parts gradually wear out. If a switch no longer operates smoothly, it must be repaired or replaced.

The methods for repairing or replacing a switch vary slightly, depending on the switch type and its location along an electrical circuit. When working on a switch, use the photographs on pages 86 to 97 to identify your switch type and its wiring configuration. Individual switch styles may vary from manufacturer to manufacturer, but the basic switch types are universal.

It is possible to replace most ordinary wall switches with a specialty switch, like a timer switch or an electronic switch. When installing a specialty switch, make sure it is compatible with the wiring configuration of the switch box.

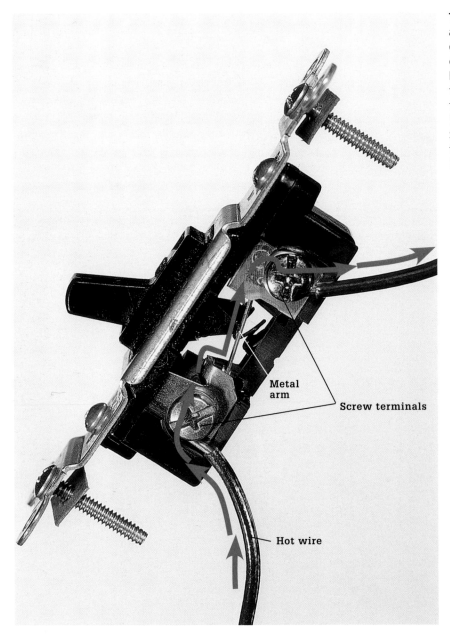

Typical wall switch has a movable metal arm that opens and closes the electrical circuit. When the switch is ON, the arm completes the circuit and power flows between the screw terminals and through the black hot wire to the light fixture. When the switch is OFF, the arm lifts away to interrupt the circuit, and no power flows. Switch problems can occur if the screw terminals are not tight or if the metal arm inside the switch wears out.

Metal arm

Screw terminals

Hot wire

Rotary snap switches are found in many installations completed between 1900 and 1920. The handle is twisted clockwise to turn light on and off. The switch is enclosed in a ceramic housing.

Push-button switches were widely used from 1920 until about 1940. Many switches of this type are still in operation. Reproductions of this switch type are available for restoration projects.

Toggle switches were introduced in the 1930s. This early design has a switch mechanism that is mounted in a ceramic housing sealed with a layer of insulating paper.

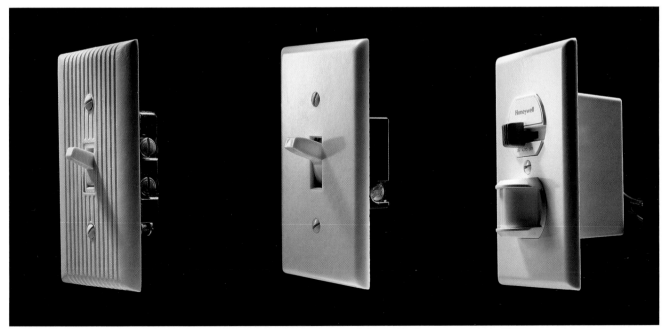

Toggle switches were improved during the 1950s and are now the most commonly used type. This switch type was the first to use a sealed plastic housing that protects the inner switch mechanism from dust and moisture.

Mercury switches became common in the early 1960s. They conduct electrical current by means of a sealed vial of mercury. No longer manufactured for home use, old mercury switches are considered a hazardous waste.

Electronic motion-sensor switches have an infrared eye that senses movement and automatically turns on lights when a person enters a room. Motion-sensor switches can provide added security against intruders.

Types of Wall Switches

Wall switches are available in three general types. To repair or replace a switch, it is important to identify its type.

Single-pole switches are used to control a set of lights from one location. Three-way switches are used to control a set of lights from two different locations and are always installed in pairs. Four-way switches are used in combination with a pair of three-way switches to control a set of lights from three or more locations.

Identify switch types by counting the screw terminals. Single-pole switches have two screw terminals, three-way switches have three screw terminals, and four-way switches have four. Most switches include a grounding screw terminal, which is identified by its green color.

When replacing a switch, choose a new switch that has the same number of screw terminals as the old one. The location of the screws on the switch body varies depending on the manufacturer, but these differences will not affect the switch operation.

Whenever possible, connect switches using the screw terminals rather than push-in fittings. Some specialty switches (pages 94 to 97) have wire leads instead of screw terminals. They are connected to circuit wires with wire connectors.

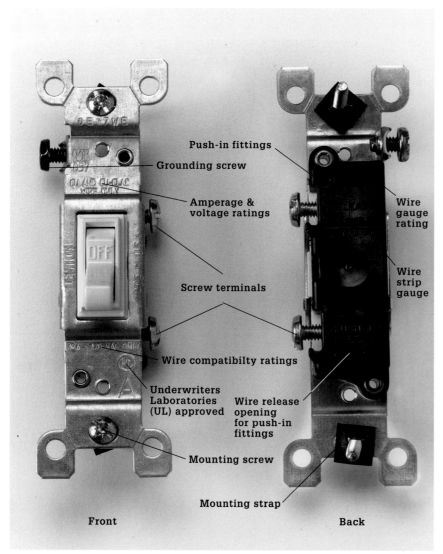

Front   **Back**

Push-in fittings

Grounding screw

Amperage & voltage ratings

Screw terminals

Wire compatibilty ratings

Underwriters Laboratories (UL) approved

Wire release opening for push-in fittings

Mounting screw

Mounting strap

Wire gauge rating

Wire strip gauge

A wall switch is connected to circuit wires with screw terminals or with push-in fittings on the back of the switch. A switch may have a stamped strip gauge that indicates how much insulation must be stripped from the circuit wires to make the connections.

The switch body is attached to a metal mounting strap that allows it to be mounted in an electrical box. Several rating stamps are found on the strap and on the back of the switch. The abbreviation UL or UND. LAB. INC. LIST means that the switch meets the safety standards of the Underwriters Laboratories. Switches also are stamped with maximum voltage and amperage ratings. Standard wall switches are rated 15A or 125V. Voltage ratings of 110, 120, and 125 are considered to be identical for purposes of identification.

For standard wall switch installations, choose a switch that has a wire gauge rating of #12 or #14. For wire systems with solid-core copper wiring, use only switches marked COPPER or CU. For aluminum wiring, use only switches marked CO/ALR. Switches marked AL/CU can no longer be used with aluminum wiring, according to the National Electrical Code.

Single-Pole Wall Switches

A single-pole switch is the most common type of wall switch. It has ON-OFF markings on the switch lever and is used to control a set of lights, an appliance, or a receptacle from a single location. A single-pole switch has two screw terminals and a grounding screw. When installing a single-pole switch, check to make sure the ON marking shows when the switch lever is in the up position.

In a correctly wired single-pole switch, a hot circuit wire is attached to each screw terminal. However, the color and number of wires inside the switch box will vary, depending on the location of the switch along the electrical circuit.

If two cables enter the box, then the switch lies in the middle of the circuit. In this installation, both of the hot wires attached to the switch are black.

If only one cable enters the box, then the switch lies at the end of the circuit. In this installation (sometimes called a switch loop), one of the hot wires is black, but the other hot wire usually is white. A white hot wire sometimes is coded with black tape or paint.

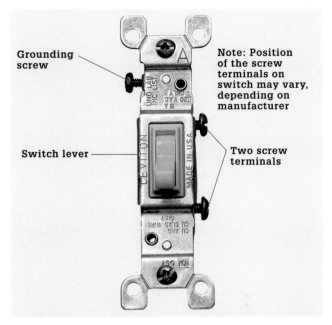

A single-pole switch is essentially an interruption in the black power supply wire that is opened or closed with the toggle. Single-pole switches are the simplest of all home wiring switches.

Typical Single-Pole Switch Installations

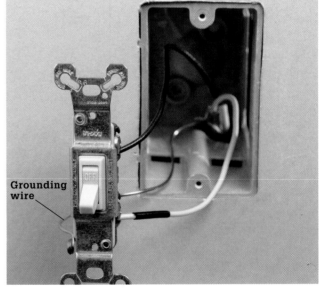

Two cables enter the box when a switch is located in the middle of a circuit. Each cable has a white and a black insulated wire, plus a bare copper grounding wire. The black wires are hot and are connected to the screw terminals on the switch. The white wires are neutral and are joined together with a wire connector. Grounding wires are pigtailed to the switch.

One cable enters the box when a switch is located at the end of a circuit. The cable has a white and a black insulated wire, plus a bare copper grounding wire. In this installation, both of the insulated wires are hot. The white wire may be labeled with black tape or paint to identify it as a hot wire. The grounding wire is connected to the switch grounding screw.

Three-way Wall Switches

Three-way switches have three screw terminals and do not have ON-OFF markings. Three-way switches are always installed in pairs and are used to control a set of lights from two locations.

One of the screw terminals on a three-way switch is darker than the others. This screw is the common screw terminal. The position of the common screw terminal on the switch body may vary, depending on the manufacturer. Before disconnecting a three-way switch, always label the wire that is connected to the common screw terminal. It must be reconnected to the common screw terminal on the new switch.

The two lighter-colored screw terminals on a three-way switch are called the traveler screw terminals. The traveler terminals are interchangeable, so there is no need to label the wires attached to them.

Because three-way switches are installed in pairs, it sometimes is difficult to determine which of the switches is causing a problem. The switch that receives greater use is more likely to fail, but you may need to inspect both switches to find the source of the problem.

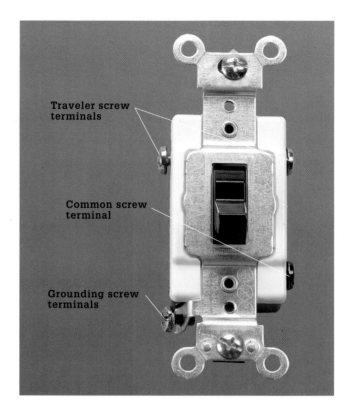

Traveler screw terminals

Common screw terminal

Grounding screw terminals

Typical Three-way Switch Installations

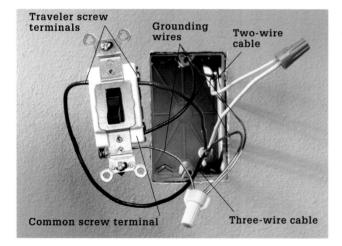

Traveler screw terminals

Grounding wires

Two-wire cable

Common screw terminal

Three-wire cable

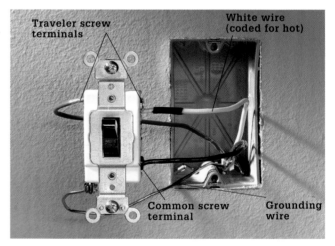

Traveler screw terminals

White wire (coded for hot)

Common screw terminal

Grounding wire

Two cables enter the box if the switch lies in the middle of a circuit. One cable has two wires, plus a bare copper grounding wire; the other cable has three wires, plus a ground. The black wire from the two-wire cable is connected to the dark common screw terminal. The red and black wires from the three-wire cable are connected to the traveler screw terminals. The white neutral wires are joined together with a wire connector, and the grounding wires are pigtailed to the grounded metal box.

One cable enters the box if the switch lies at the end of the circuit. The cable has a black wire, red wire, and white wire, plus a bare copper grounding wire. The black wire must be connected to the common screw terminal, which is darker than the other two screw terminals. The white and red wires are connected to the two traveler screw terminals. The white wire is taped to indicate that it is hot. The bare copper grounding wire is connected to the grounded metal box.

How to Fix or Replace a Three-way Wall Switch

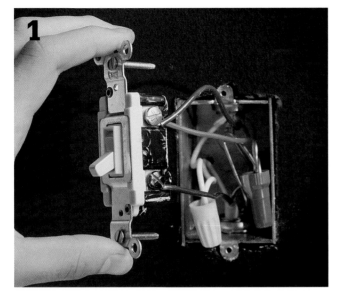

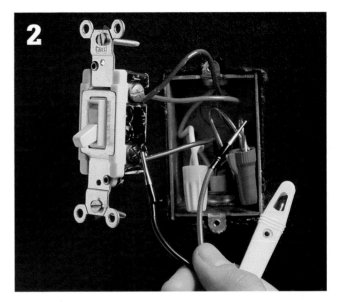

Turn off the power to the switch at the main service panel, then remove the switch cover plate and mounting screws. Holding the mounting strap carefully, pull the switch from the box. Be careful not to touch the bare wires or screw terminals until they have been tested for power.

Test for power by touching one probe of the circuit tester to the grounded metal box or to the bare copper grounding wire, and touching the other probe to each screw terminal. Tester should not glow. If it does, there is still power entering the box. Return to the service panel, and turn off the correct circuit.

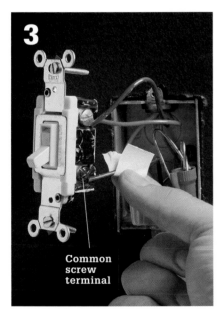

Locate the dark common screw terminal, and use masking tape to label the "common" wire attached to it. Disconnect wires and remove switch. Test switch for continuity. If it tests faulty, buy a replacement. Inspect wires for nicks and scratches. If necessary, clip damaged wires and strip them.

Connect the common wire to the dark common screw terminal on the switch. On most three-way switches, the common screw terminal is black. Or it may be labeled with the word COMMON stamped on the back of the switch. If the switch has a grounding screw, connect it to the circuit grounding wires with a pigtail.

Connect the remaining two circuit wires to the screw terminals. These wires are interchangeable and can be connected to either screw terminal. Carefully tuck the wires into the box. Remount the switch, and attach the cover plate. Turn on the power at the main service panel.

Four-way Wall Switches

Four-way switches have four screw terminals and do not have ON-OFF markings. Four-way switches are always installed between a pair of three-way switches. This switch combination makes it possible to control a set of lights from three or more locations. Four-way switches are common in homes where large rooms contain multiple living areas, such as a kitchen opening into a dining room. Switch problems in a four-way installation can be caused by loose connections or worn parts in a four-way switch or in one of the three-way switches (facing page).

In a typical installation, there will be a pair of three-way cables that enter the box for the four-way switch. With most switches, the white and red wires from one cable should be attached to the bottom or top pair of screw terminals, and the white and red wires from the other cable should be attached to the remaining pair of screw terminals. However, not all switches are configured the same way, and wiring configurations in the box may vary, so always study the wiring diagram that comes with the switch.

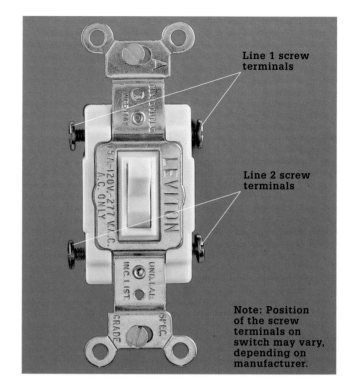

Line 1 screw terminals

Line 2 screw terminals

Note: Position of the screw terminals on switch may vary, depending on manufacturer.

Typical Four-way Switch Installation

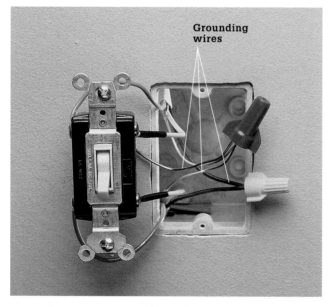

Grounding wires

Four wires are connected to a four-way switch. The red and white wires from one cable are attached to the top pair of screw terminals, while the red and white wires from the other cable are attached to the bottom screw terminals.

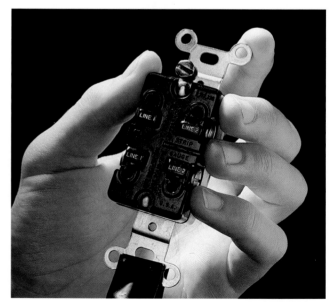

Switch variation: Some four-way switches have a wiring guide stamped on the back to help simplify installation. For the switch shown above, one pair of color-matched circuit wires will be connected to the screw terminals marked LINE 1, while the other pair of wires will be attached to the screw terminals marked LINE 2.

How to Fix or Replace a Four-way Wall Switch

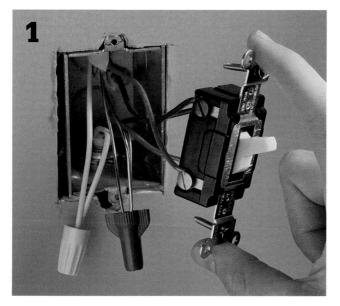

1

Turn off the power to the switch at the main service panel, then remove the switch cover plate and mounting screws. Holding the mounting strap carefully, pull the switch from the box. Be careful not to touch any bare wires or screw terminals until they have been tested for power.

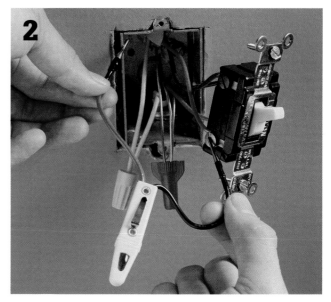

2

Test for power by touching one probe of the neon circuit tester to the grounded metal box or bare copper grounding wire, and touching the other probe to each of the screw terminals. Tester should not glow. If it does, there is still power entering the box. Return to the service panel, and turn off the correct circuit.

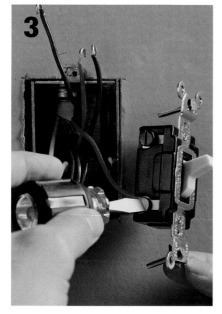

3

Disconnect the wires and inspect them for nicks and scratches. If necessary, clip damaged wires and strip them. Test the switch for continuity (pages 98 to 101). Buy a replacement if the switch tests faulty.

4

Connect two wires from one incoming cable to the top set of screw terminals.

5

Attach remaining wires to the other set of screw terminals. Pigtail the grounding wires to the grounding screw. Carefully tuck the wires inside the switch box, then remount the switch and cover plate. Turn on power at main service panel.

Double Switches

A double switch has two switch levers in a single housing. It is used to control two light fixtures or appliances from the same switch box.

In most installations, both halves of the switch are powered by the same circuit. In these single-circuit installations, three wires are connected to the double switch. One wire, called the feed wire, supplies power to both halves of the switch. The other wires carry power out to the individual light fixtures or appliances.

In rare installations, each half of the switch is powered by a separate circuit. In these separate-circuit installations, four wires are connected to the switch, and the metal connecting tab joining two of the screw terminals is removed (photo below).

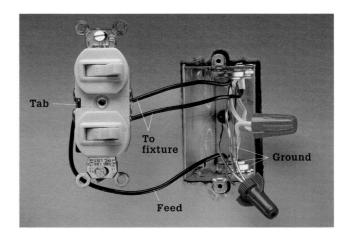

Single-circuit wiring: Three black wires are attached to the switch. The black feed wire bringing power into the box is connected to the side of the switch that has a connecting tab. The wires carrying power out to the light fixtures or appliances are connected to the side of the switch that does not have a connecting tab. The white neutral wires are connected together with a wire connector.

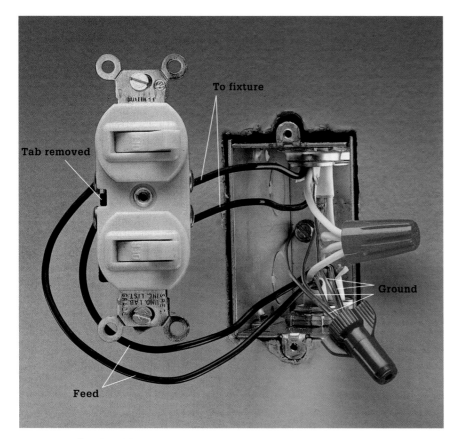

Separate-circuit wiring: Four black wires are attached to the switch. Feed wires from the power source are attached to the side of the switch that has a connecting tab, and the connecting tab is removed (photo, right). Wires carrying power from the switch to light fixtures or appliances are connected to the side of the switch that does not have a connecting tab. White neutral wires are connected together with a wire connector.

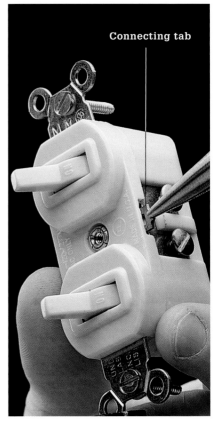

Remove the connecting tab on a double switch when wired in a separate-circuit installation. The tab can be removed with needlenose pliers or a screwdriver.

Pilot-light Switches

A pilot-light switch has a built-in bulb that glows when power flows through the switch to a light fixture or appliance. Pilot-light switches often are installed for convenience if a light fixture or appliance cannot be seen from the switch location. Basement lights, garage lights, and attic exhaust fans frequently are controlled by pilot-light switches.

A pilot-light switch requires a neutral wire connection. A switch box that contains a single two-wire cable has only hot wires and cannot be fitted with a pilot-light switch.

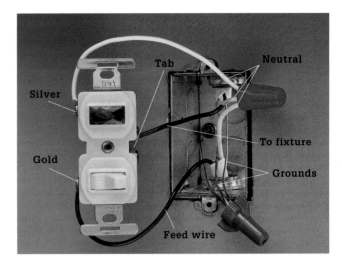

Pilot-light switch wiring: Three wires are connected to the switch. One black wire is the feed wire that brings power into the box. It is connected to the brass (gold) screw terminal on the side of the switch that does not have a connecting tab. The white neutral wires are pigtailed to the silver screw terminal. Black wire carrying power out to light fixture or appliance is connected to screw terminal on side of the switch that has a connecting tab.

Switch/Receptacles

A switch/receptacle combines a grounded receptacle with a single-pole wall switch. In a room that does not have enough wall receptacles, electrical service can be improved by replacing a single-pole switch with a switch/receptacle.

A switch/receptacle requires a neutral wire connection. A switch box that contains a single two-wire cable has only hot wires and cannot be fitted with a switch/receptacle.

A switch/receptacle can be installed in one of two ways. In the most common installations, the receptacle is hot even when the switch is off (photo, right).

In rare installations, a switch/receptacle is wired so the receptacle is hot only when the switch is on. In this installation, the hot wires are reversed, so that the feed wire is attached to the brass screw terminal on the side of the switch that does not have a connecting tab.

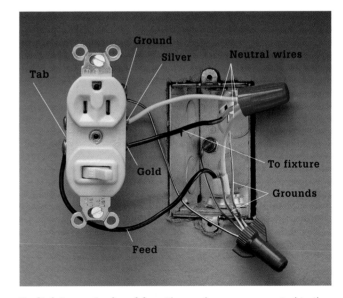

Switch/receptacle wiring: Three wires are connected to the switch/receptacle. One of the hot wires is the feed wire that brings power into the box. It is connected to the side of the switch that has a connecting tab. The other hot wire carries power out to the light fixture or appliance. It is connected to the brass screw terminal on the side that does not have a connecting tab. The white neutral wire is pigtailed to the silver screw terminal. The grounding wires must be pigtailed to the green grounding screw on the switch/receptacle and to the grounded metal box.

Specialty Switches

Your house may have several types of specialty switches. Dimmer switches (pages 96 to 97) are used frequently to control light intensity in dining and recreation areas. Timer switches and time-delay switches (below) are used to control light fixtures and exhaust fans automatically. Electronic switches (facing page) provide added convenience and home security, and they are easy to install. Electronic switches are durable, and they rarely need repair.

Most specialty switches have preattached wire leads instead of screw terminals and are connected to circuit wires with wire connectors. Some motor-driven timer switches require a neutral wire connection and cannot be installed in switch boxes that have only one cable with two hot wires.

If a specialty switch is not operating correctly, you may be able to test it with a continuity tester. Timer switches and time-delay switches can be tested for continuity, but dimmer switches cannot be tested. With electronic switches, the manual switch can be tested for continuity, but the automatic features cannot be tested.

Timer Switches

Timer switches have an electrically powered control dial that can be set to turn lights on and off automatically once each day. They are commonly used to control outdoor light fixtures.

Timer switches have three preattached wire leads. The black wire lead is connected to the hot feed wire that brings power into the box, and the red lead is connected to the wire carrying power out to the light fixture. The remaining wire lead is the neutral lead. It must be connected to any neutral circuit wires. A switch box that contains only one cable has no neutral wires, so it cannot be fitted with a timer switch.

After a power failure, the dial on a timer switch must be reset to the proper time.

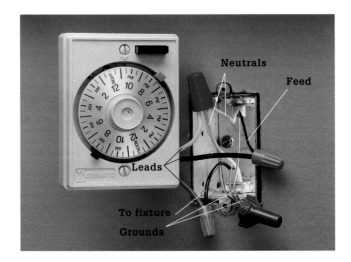

Time-delay Switches

A time-delay switch has a spring-driven dial that is wound by hand. The dial can be set to turn off a light fixture after a delay ranging from 1 to 60 minutes. Time-delay switches often are used for exhaust fans, bathroom vent fans, and heat lamps.

The black wire leads on the switch are connected to the hot circuit wires. If the switch box contains white neutral wires, these are connected with a wire connector. The bare copper grounding wires are pigtailed to the grounded metal box.

A time-delay switch needs no neutral wire connection, so it can be fitted in a switch box that contains either one or two cables.

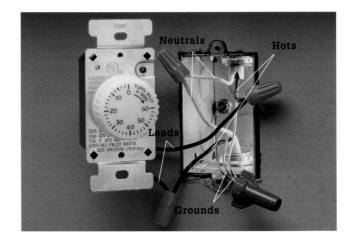

Automatic Switches

An automatic switch uses a narrow infrared beam to detect movement. When a hand passes within a few inches of the beam, an electronic signal turns the switch on or off. Some automatic switches have a manual dimming feature.

Automatic switches can be installed wherever a standard single-pole switch is used. Automatic switches are especially convenient for children and persons with disabilities.

Automatic switches require no neutral wire connections. For this reason, an automatic switch can be installed in a switch box containing either one or two cables. The wire leads on the switch are connected to hot circuit wires with wire connectors.

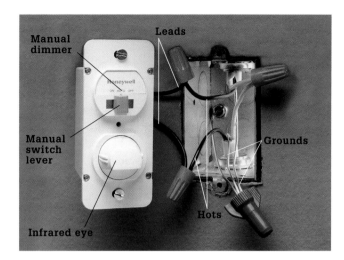

Motion-sensor Security Switches

A motion-sensor switch uses a wide-angle infrared beam to detect movement over a large area and turns on a light fixture automatically. A time-delay feature turns off lights after movement stops.

Most motion-sensor switches have an override feature that allows the switch to be operated manually. Better switches include an adjustable sensitivity control and a variable time-delay shutoff control.

Motion-sensor switches require no neutral wire connections. They can be installed in switch boxes containing either one or two cables. The wire leads on the switch are connected to hot circuit wires.

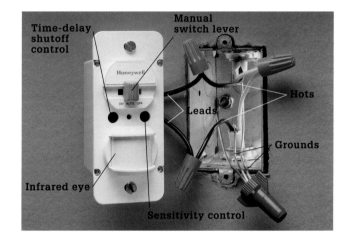

Programmable Switches

Programmable switches have digital controls and can provide four on-off cycles each day. They frequently are used to provide security when a homeowner is absent from the house. Law enforcement experts say that programmed lighting is a proven crime deterrent. For best protection, programmable switches should be set to a random on-off pattern.

Programmable switches require no neutral wire connections. They can be installed in switch boxes containing either one or two cables. The wire leads on the switch are connected to hot circuit wires with wire connectors.

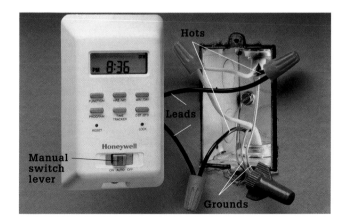

Dimmer Switches

A dimmer switch makes it possible to vary the brightness of a light fixture. Dimmers are often installed in dining rooms, recreation areas, or bedrooms.

Any standard single-pole switch can be replaced with a dimmer, as long as the switch box is of adequate size. Dimmer switches have larger bodies than standard switches. They also generate a small amount of heat that must dissipate. For these reasons, dimmers should not be installed in undersized electrical boxes or in boxes that are crowded with circuit wires. Always follow the manufacturer's specifications for installation.

In lighting configurations that use three-way switches (pages 88 to 89), replace the standard switches with special three-way dimmers. If replacing both the switches with dimmers, buy a packaged pair of three-way dimmers designed to work together.

Dimmer switches are available in several styles (photo, right). All types have wire leads instead of screw terminals, and they are connected to circuit wires using wire connectors. Some types have a green grounding lead that should be connected to the grounded metal box or to the bare copper grounding wires.

Tools & Materials ▸

Screwdriver
Circuit tester
Needlenose pliers
Wire connectors
Masking tape

Toggle-type dimmer resembles standard switches. Toggle dimmers are available in both single-pole and three-way designs.

Dial-type dimmer is the most common style. Rotating the dial changes the light intensity.

Slide-action dimmer has an illuminated face that makes the switch easy to locate in the dark.

Automatic dimmer has an electronic sensor that adjusts the light fixture to compensate for the changing levels of natural light. An automatic dimmer also can be operated manually.

How to Install a Dimmer Switch

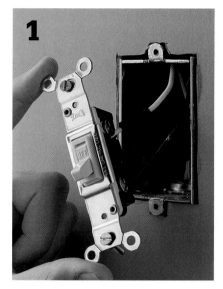

Turn off power to switch at the main service panel, then remove the cover plate and mounting screws. Holding the mounting straps carefully, pull switch from the box. Be careful not to touch bare wires or screw terminals until they have been tested for power.

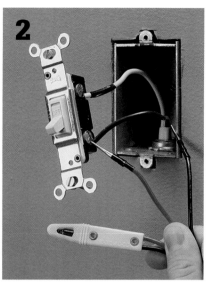

Test for power by touching one probe of neon circuit tester to the grounded metal box or to the bare copper grounding wires, and touching other probe to each screw terminal. Tester should not glow. If it does, there is still power entering the box. Return to the service panel and turn off the correct circuit.

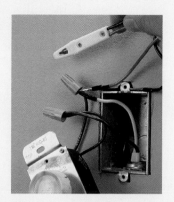

Disconnect the circuit wires and remove the switch. Straighten the circuit wires, and clip the ends, leaving about ½" of the bare wire end exposed.

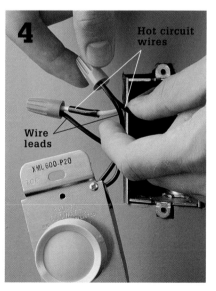

Connect the wire leads on the dimmer switch to the circuit wires using wire connectors. The switch leads are interchangeable and can be attached to either of the two circuit wires.

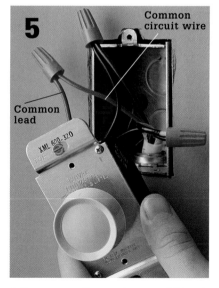

A three-way dimmer has an additional wire lead. This "common" lead is connected to the common circuit wire. When replacing a standard three-way switch with a dimmer, the common circuit wire is attached to the darkest screw terminal on the old switch.

Testing Switches

A switch that does not work properly may have worn or broken internal parts. Test switches with a battery-operated continuity tester. The continuity tester detects any break in the metal pathway inside the switch. Replace the switch if the continuity tester shows the switch to be faulty.

Never use a continuity tester on wires that might carry live current. Always shut off the power and disconnect the switch before testing for continuity.

Some specialty switches, like dimmers, cannot be tested for continuity. Electronic switches can be tested for manual operation using a continuity tester, but the automatic operation of these switches cannot be tested.

How to Test a Single-Pole Wall Switch

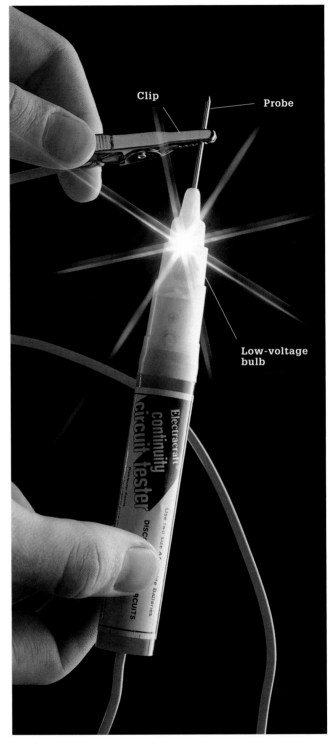

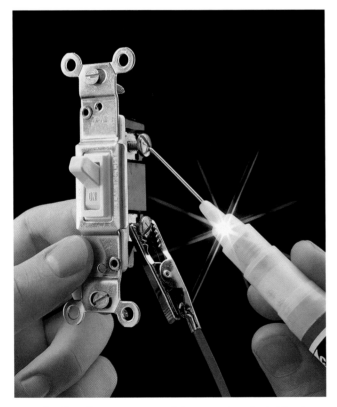

Attach clip of tester to one of the screw terminals. Touch the tester probe to the other screw terminal. Flip switch lever from ON to OFF. If switch is good, tester glows when lever is ON, but not when OFF.

Continuity tester uses battery-generated current to test the metal pathways running through switches and other electrical fixtures. Always "test" the tester before use. Touch the tester clip to the metal probe. The tester should glow. If not, then the battery or lightbulb is dead and must be replaced.

How to Test a Three-way Wall Switch

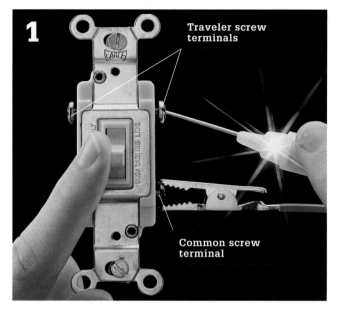

1 Traveler screw terminals

Common screw terminal

Attach tester clip to the dark common screw terminal. Touch the tester probe to one of the traveler screw terminals, and flip switch lever back and forth. If switch is good, the tester should glow when the lever is in one position, but not both.

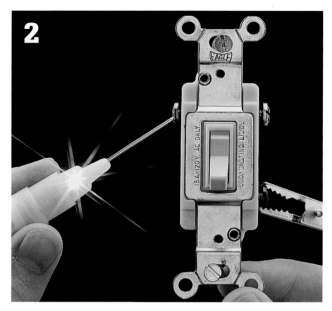

2

Touch probe to the other traveler screw terminal, and flip the switch lever back and forth. If switch is good, the tester will glow only when the switch lever is in the position opposite from the positive test in step 1.

How to Test a Four-way Wall Switch

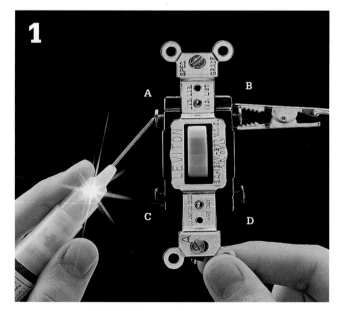

1 A   B   C   D

Test switch by touching probe and clip of continuity tester to each pair of screw terminals (A-B, C-D, A-D, B-C, A-C, B-D). The test should show continuous pathways between two different pairs of screw terminals. Flip lever to opposite position, and repeat test. Test should show continuous pathways between two different pairs of screw terminals.

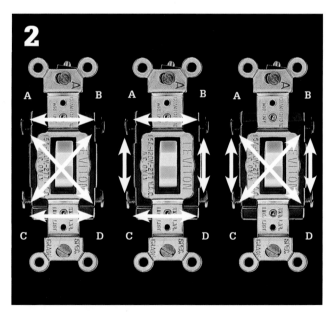

2

If switch is good, test will show a total of four continuous pathways between screw terminals—two pathways for each lever position. If not, then switch is faulty and must be replaced. (The arrangement of the pathways may differ, depending on the switch manufacturer. The photo above shows the three possible pathway arrangements.)

How to Test a Pilot-Light Switch

Test pilot light by flipping the switch lever to the ON position. Check to see if the light fixture or appliance is working. If the pilot light does not glow even though the switch operates the light fixture or appliance, then the pilot light is defective and the unit must be replaced.

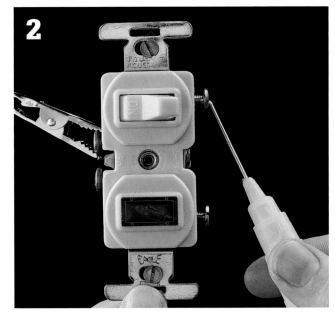

Test the switch by disconnecting the unit. With the switch lever in the ON position, attach the tester clip to the top screw terminal on one side of the switch. Touch tester probe to top screw terminal on opposite side of the switch. If switch is good, tester will glow when switch is ON, but not when OFF.

How to Test a Timer Switch

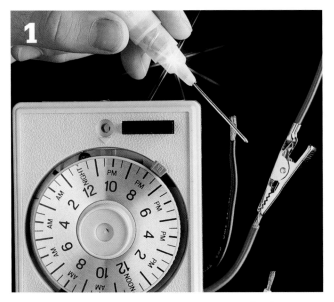

Attach the tester clip to the red wire lead on the timer switch, and touch the tester probe to the black hot lead. Rotate the timer dial clockwise until the ON tab passes the arrow marker. Tester should glow. If it does not, the switch is faulty and must be replaced.

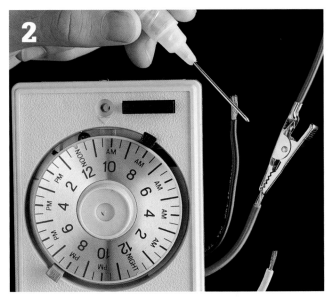

Rotate the dial clockwise until the OFF tab passes the arrow marker. Tester should not glow. If it does, the switch is faulty and must be replaced.

How to Test a Switch/Receptacle

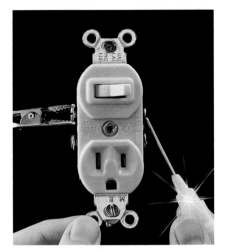

Attach tester clip to one of the top screw terminals. Touch the tester probe to the top screw terminal on the opposite side. Flip the switch lever from ON to OFF position. If the switch is working correctly, the tester will glow when the switch lever is ON, but not when OFF.

How to Test a Double Switch

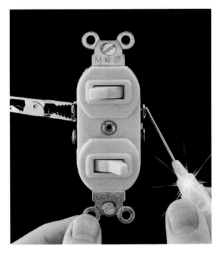

Test each half of switch by attaching the tester clip to one screw terminal and touching the probe to the opposite side. Flip switch lever from ON to OFF position. If switch is good, tester glows when the switch lever is ON, but not when OFF. Repeat test with the remaining pair of screw terminals. If either half tests faulty, replace the unit.

How to Test a Time-Delay Switch

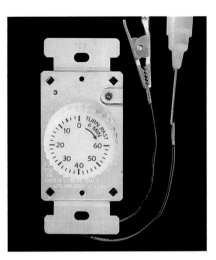

Attach tester clip to one of the wire leads, and touch the tester probe to the other lead. Set the timer for a few minutes. If switch is working correctly, the tester will glow until the time expires.

How to Test Manual Operation of Electronic Switches

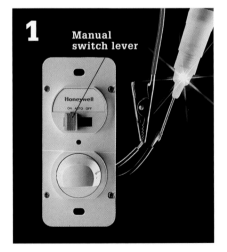

Automatic switch: Attach the tester clip to a black wire lead, and touch the tester probe to the other black lead. Flip the manual switch lever from ON to OFF position. If switch is working correctly, tester will glow when the switch lever is ON, but not when OFF.

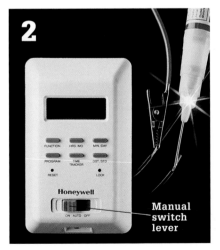

Programmable switch: Attach the tester clip to a wire lead, and touch the tester probe to the other lead. Flip the manual switch lever from ON to OFF position. If the switch is working correctly, the tester will glow when the switch lever is ON, but not when OFF.

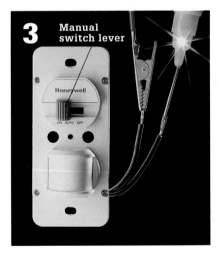

Motion-sensor switch: Attach the tester clip to a wire lead, and touch the tester probe to the other lead. Flip the manual switch lever from ON to OFF position. If the switch is working correctly, the tester will glow when the switch lever is ON, but not when OFF.

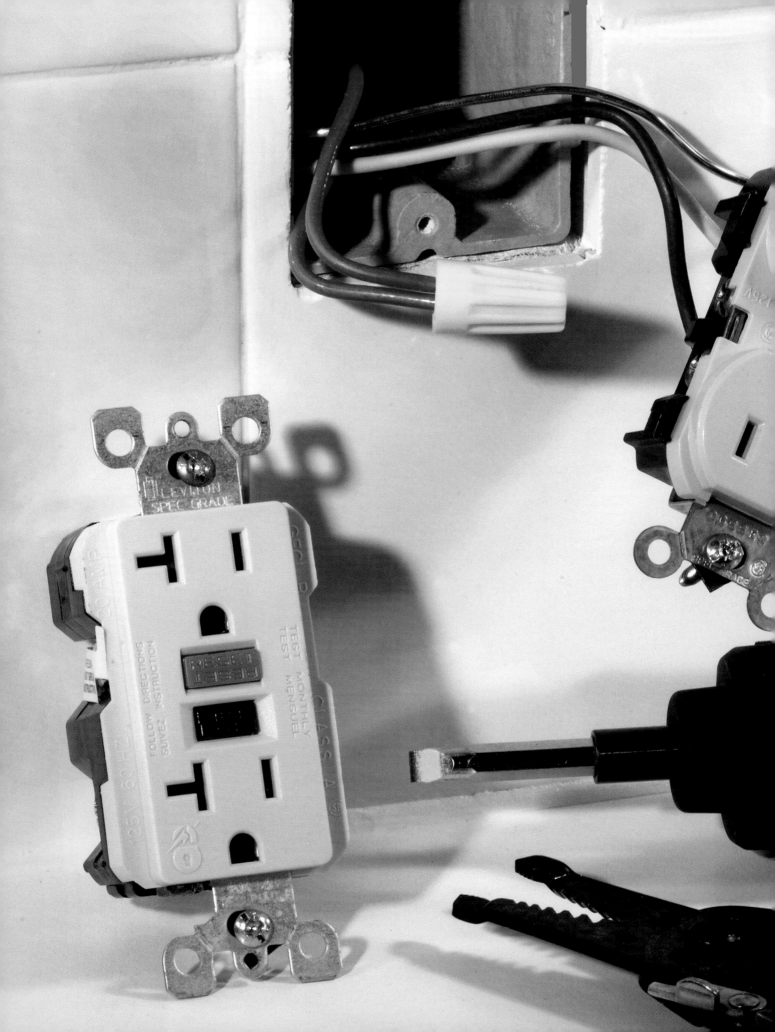

Receptacles

Whether you call them outlets, plug-ins, or receptacles, these important devices represent the point where the rubber meets the road in your home wiring system. From the basic 15-amp, 120-volt duplex receptacle to the burly 50-amp, 240-volt appliance receptacle, the many outlets in your home do pretty much the same thing: transmit power to a load.

Learning the essential differences between receptacles does not take long. Amperage is the main variable, as each receptacle must match the amperage and voltage of the circuit in which it is installed. A 15-amp circuit should be wired with 15-amp receptacles; a 20-amp circuit, such as a small appliance circuit in a kitchen, needs 20-amp receptacles (identified by the horizontal slot that Ts into each tall polarized slot). Receptacles for 240-volt service have unique slot configurations so you can't accidentally plug in an appliance that's not rated for the amperage in the circuit. Some receptacles can be wired using the push-in wire holes, but only if you are using 14-gauge copper wire; otherwise, they're all connected at screw terminals. Some receptacles provide built-in, ground-fault circuit protection, tripping the circuit breaker if there is a short circuit or power surge. These are easy to identify by reset and test buttons.

One last bit of information about receptacles: like switches, they vary quite a bit in quality. Paying the extra couple of dollars for a well made, durable device is worth the money.

In this chapter:

- Types of Receptacles
- Receptacle Wiring
- GFCI Receptacles
- Isolated-Ground Receptacles
- Testing Receptacles

Types of Receptacles

Several different types of receptacles are found in the typical home. Each has a unique arrangement of slots that accepts only a certain kind of plug, and each is designed for a specific job.

Household receptacles provide two types of voltage: normal and high voltage. Although voltage ratings have changed slightly over the years, normal receptacles should be rated for 110, 115, 120, or 125 volts. For purposes of replacement, these ratings are considered identical. High-voltage receptacles are rated at 220, 240, or 250 volts. These ratings are considered identical.

When replacing a receptacle, check the amperage rating of the circuit at the main service panel, and buy a receptacle with the correct amperage rating.

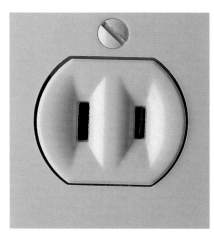

15 amps, 120 volts. Polarized two-slot receptacle is common in homes built before 1960. Slots are different sizes to accept polarized plugs.

15 amps, 120 volts. Three-slot grounded receptacle has two different sized slots and a U-shaped hole for grounding. It is required in all new wiring installations.

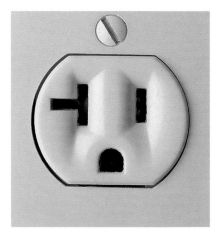

20 amps, 120 volts. This three-slot grounded receptacle features a special T-shaped slot. It is installed for use with large appliances or portable tools that require 20 amps of current.

15 amps, 250 volts. This receptacle is used primarily for window air conditioners. It is available as a single unit or as half of a duplex receptacle with the other half wired for 120 volts.

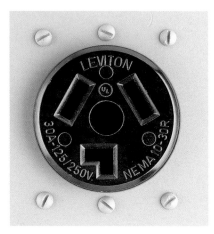

30 amps, 125/250 volts. This receptacle is used for clothes dryers. It provides high-voltage current for heating coils and 125-volt current to run lights and timers.

50 amps, 125/250 volts. This receptacle is used for ranges. The high-voltage current powers heating coils, and the 125-volt current runs clocks and lights.

Older Receptacles

Older receptacles may look different from more modern types, but most will stay in good working order. Follow these simple guidelines for evaluating or replacing older receptacles:

- Never replace an older receptacle with one of a different voltage or higher amperage rating.

- Any two-slot, unpolarized receptacle should be replaced with a two-slot polarized receptacle.
- If no means of grounding is available at the receptacle box, install a GFCI (pages 114 to 117).
- If in doubt, contact an electrician.
- Never alter the prongs of a plug to fit an older receptacle. Altering the prongs may remove the grounding or polarizing features of the plug.

The earliest receptacles were modifications of the screw-in light bulb. This receptacle was used in the early 1900s.

Unpolarized receptacles have same-length slots. Modern plugs may not fit these receptacles. Never modify the prongs of a polarized plug to fit the slots of an unpolarized receptacle.

Surface-mounted receptacles were popular in the 1940s and 1950s for their ease of installation. Wiring ran behind hollowed-out base moldings. These receptacles are usually ungrounded.

Ceramic duplex receptacles were manufactured in the 1930s. They are polarized but ungrounded, and they are wired for 120 volts.

Twist-lock receptacles are designed to be used with plugs that are inserted and rotated. A small tab on the end of one of the prongs prevents the plug from being pulled from the receptacle.

This ceramic duplex receptacle has a unique hourglass shape. It is rated for 250 volts but only 5 amps and would not be allowed by today's electrical codes.

High-Voltage Receptacles

High-voltage receptacles provide current to large appliances like clothes dryers, ranges, water heaters, and air conditioners. The slot configuration of a high-voltage receptacle (page 104) will not accept a plug rated for 120 volts.

A high-voltage receptacle can be wired in one of two ways. In a standard high-voltage receptacle, voltage is brought to the receptacle with two hot wires, each carrying a maximum of 120 volts. No white neutral wire is necessary, but a grounding wire should be attached to the receptacle and to the metal receptacle box. Conduit can also act as a ground from the metal receptacle box back to the service panel.

A clothes dryer or range also may require normal current (a maximum of 120 volts) to run lights, timers and clocks. If so, a white neutral wire will be attached to the receptacle. The appliance itself will split the incoming current into a 120-volt circuit and a 240-volt circuit.

It is important to identify and tag all wires on the existing receptacle so that the new receptacle will be properly wired.

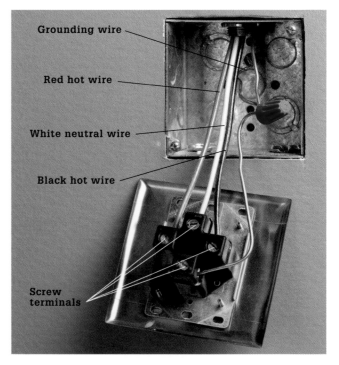

A receptacle rated for 120/240 volts has two incoming hot wires, each carrying 120 volts, a white neutral wire, and a bare copper grounding wire. Connections are made with setscrew terminals at the back of the receptacle.

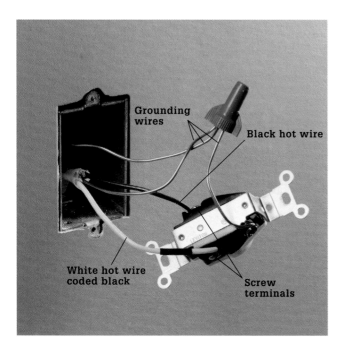

Standard receptacle rated for 240 volts has two incoming hot wires and no neutral wire. A grounding wire is pigtailed to the receptacle and to the metal receptacle box.

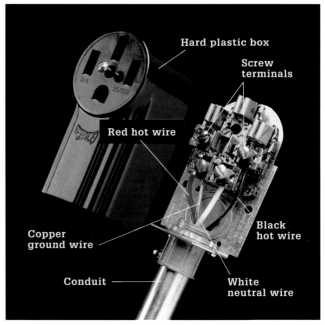

Surface-mounted receptacle rated for 240 volts has a hard plastic box that can be installed on concrete or block walls. Surface-mounted receptacles are often found in basements and utility rooms.

Childproofing

Childproof your receptacles or adapt them for special uses by adding receptacle accessories. Before installing an accessory, be sure to read the manufacturer's instructions.

Homeowners with small children should add inexpensive caps or covers to guard against accidental electric shocks.

Plastic caps do not conduct electricity and are virtually impossible for small children to remove. A receptacle cover attaches directly to the receptacle and fits over plugs, preventing the cords from being removed. For more information on childproofing, see pages 190 to 193.

Standard receptacles present a real shock hazard to small children. Fortunately, there are many products that make receptacles safer without making them less convenient.

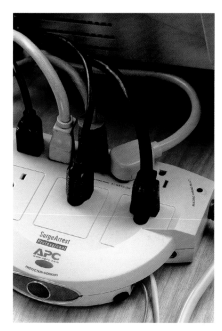

Protect electronic equipment, such as a home computer or stereo, with a surge protector. The surge protector prevents any damage to sensitive wiring or circuitry caused by sudden drops or surges in power.

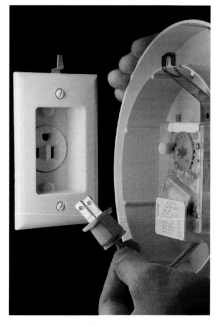

A recessed wall receptacle permits a plug-in clock to be hung flush against a wall surface.

Snap protective caps over sockets to prevent children from having access to the slots.

Duplex Receptacles

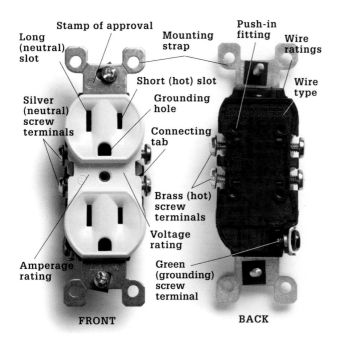

Long (neutral) slot · Stamp of approval · Mounting strap · Push-in fitting · Wire ratings · Short (hot) slot · Grounding hole · Wire type · Silver (neutral) screw terminals · Connecting tab · Brass (hot) screw terminals · Voltage rating · Amperage rating · Green (grounding) screw terminal

FRONT   BACK

The standard duplex receptacle has two halves for receiving plugs. Each half has a long (neutral) slot, a short (hot) slot, and a U-shaped grounding hole. The slots fit the wide prong, narrow prong, and grounding prong of a three-prong plug. This ensures that the connection between receptacle and plug will be polarized and grounded for safety.

Wires are attached to the receptacle at screw terminals or push-in fittings. A connecting tab between the screw terminals allows a variety of different wiring configurations. Receptacles also include mounting straps for attaching to electrical boxes.

Stamps of approval from testing agencies are found on the front and back of the receptacle. Look for the symbol UL or UND. LAB. INC. LIST to make sure the receptacle meets the strict standards of Underwriters Laboratories.

The receptacle is marked with ratings for maximum volts and amps. The common receptacle is marked 15A, 125V. Receptacles marked CU or COPPER are used with solid copper wire. Those marked CU-CLAD ONLY are used with copper-coated aluminum wire. Only receptacles marked CO/ALR may be used with solid aluminum wiring (page 334). Receptacles marked AL/CU no longer may be used with aluminum wire, according to code.

The polarized receptacle became standard in the 1920s. The different sized slots direct current flow for safety.

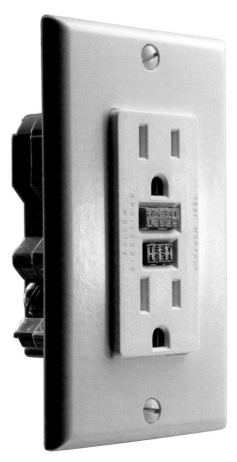

The ground-fault circuit-interrupter, or GFCI receptacle, is a modern safety device. When it detects slight changes in current, it instantly shuts off power.

Common Receptacle Problems

Household receptacles, also called outlets, have no moving parts to wear out and usually last for many years without servicing. Most problems associated with receptacles are actually caused by faulty lamps and appliances, or their plugs and cords. However, the constant plugging in and removal of appliance cords can wear out the metal contacts inside a receptacle. Any receptacle that does not hold plugs firmly should be replaced. In addition, older receptacles made of hard plastic may harden and crack with age. They must be replaced when this happens.

A loose wire connection with the receptacle box is another possible problem. A loose connection can spark (called arcing), trip a circuit breaker, or cause heat to build up in the receptacle box, creating a potential fire hazard.

Wires can come loose for a number of reasons. Everyday vibrations caused by walking across floors, or from nearby street traffic, may cause a connection to shake loose. In addition, because wires heat and cool with normal use, the ends of the wires will expand and contract slightly. This movement also may cause the wires to come loose from the screw terminal connections.

Not all receptacles are created equally. When replacing, make sure to buy one with the same amp rating as the old one. Inadvertently installing a 20-amp receptacle in replacement of a 15-amp receptacle is a very common error.

Problem	Repair
Circuit breaker trips repeatedly, or fuse burns out immediately after being replaced.	1. Repair or replace worn or damaged lamp or appliance cord. 2. Move lamps or appliances to other circuits to prevent overloads. 3. Tighten any loose wire connections. 4. Clean dirty or oxidized wire ends.
Lamp or appliance does not work.	1. Make sure lamp or appliance is plugged in. 2. Replace burned-out bulbs. 3. Repair or replace worn or damaged lamp or appliance cord. 4. Tighten any loose wire connections. 5. Clean dirty or oxidized wire ends. 6. Repair or replace any faulty receptacle.
Receptacle does not hold plugs firmly.	1. Repair or replace worn or damaged plugs. 2. Replace faulty receptacle.
Receptacle is warm to the touch, buzzes, or sparks when plugs are inserted or removed.	1. Move lamps or appliances to other circuits to prevent overloads. 2. Tighten any loose wire connections. 3. Clean dirty or oxidized wire ends. 4. Replace faulty receptacle.

Receptacle Wiring

A 120-volt duplex receptacle can be wired to the electrical system in a number of ways. The most common are shown on these pages.

Wiring configurations may vary slightly from these photographs, depending on the kind of receptacles used, the type of cable, or the technique of the electrician who installed the wiring. To make dependable repairs or replacements, use masking tape and label each wire according to its location on the terminals of the existing receptacle.

Receptacles are wired as either end-of-run or middle-of-run. These two basic configurations are easily identified by counting the number of cables entering the receptacle box. End-of-run wiring has only one cable, indicating that the circuit ends. Middle-of-run wiring has two cables, indicating that the circuit continues on to other receptacles, switches, or fixtures.

A split-circuit receptacle is shown on the next page. Each half of a split-circuit receptacle is wired to a separate circuit. This allows two appliances of high wattage to be plugged into the same receptacle without blowing a fuse or tripping a breaker. This wiring configuration is similar to a receptacle that is controlled by a wall switch. Code requires a switch-controlled receptacle in any room that does not have a built-in light fixture operated by a wall switch.

Split-circuit and switch-controlled receptacles are connected to two hot wires, so use caution during repairs or replacements. Make sure the connecting tab between the hot screw terminals is removed.

Two-slot receptacles are common in older homes. There is no grounding wire attached to the receptacle, but the box may be grounded with armored cable or conduit.

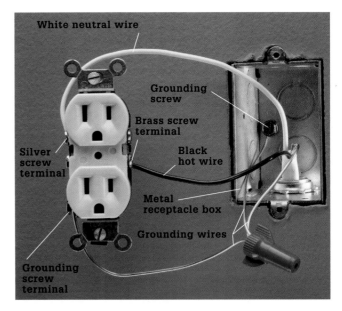

Single cable entering the box indicates end-of-run wiring. The black hot wire is attached to a brass screw terminal, and the white neutral wire is connected to a silver screw terminal. If the box is metal, the grounding wire is pigtailed to the grounding screws of the receptacle and the box. In a plastic box, the grounding wire is attached directly to the grounding screw terminal of the receptacle.

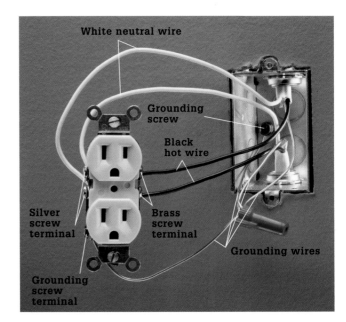

Two cables entering the box indicate middle-of-run wiring. Black hot wires are connected to brass screw terminals, and white neutral wires to silver screw terminals. The grounding wire is pigtailed to the grounding screws of the receptacle and the box.

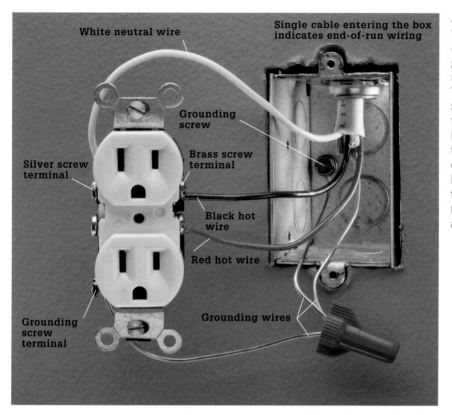

White neutral wire

Single cable entering the box indicates end-of-run wiring

Grounding screw

Brass screw terminal

Silver screw terminal

Black hot wire

Red hot wire

Grounding screw terminal

Grounding wires

A split-circuit receptacle is attached to a black hot wire, a red hot wire, a white neutral wire, and a bare grounding wire. The wiring is similar to a switch-controlled receptacle. The hot wires are attached to the brass screw terminals, and the connecting tab or fin between the brass terminals is removed. The white wire is attached to a silver screw terminal, and the connecting tab on the neutral side remains intact. The grounding wire is pigtailed to the grounding screw terminal of the receptacle and to the grounding screw attached to the box.

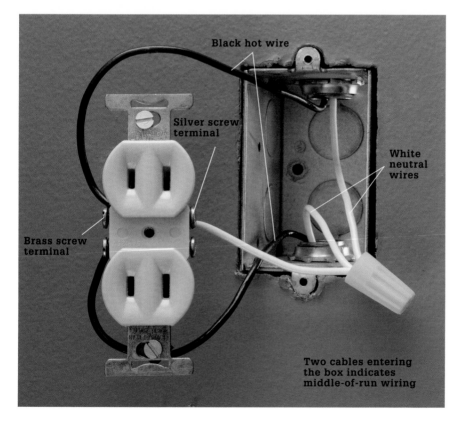

Black hot wire

Silver screw terminal

White neutral wires

Brass screw terminal

Two cables entering the box indicates middle-of-run wiring

A two-slot receptacle is often found in older homes. The black hot wires are connected to the brass screw terminals, and the white neutral wires are pigtailed to a silver screw terminal. Two-slot receptacles may be replaced with three-slot types, but only if a means of grounding exists at the receptacle box. In some municipalities, you may replace a two-slot receptacle with a GFCI receptacle as long as the receptacle has a sticker that reads "No equipment ground."

How to Install a New Receptacle

Position the new pop-in box on the wall and trace around it. Consider the location of hidden utilities within the wall before you cut.

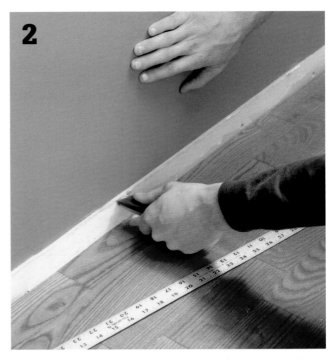

Remove baseboard between new and existing receptacle. Cut away the drywall about 1" below the baseboard with a jigsaw, wallboard saw, or utility knife.

Drill a ⅝" hole in the center of each stud along the opening between the two receptacles. A drill bit extender or a flexible drill bit will allow you a better angle and make drilling the holes easier.

Run the branch cable through the holes from the new location to the existing receptacle. Staple the cable to the stud below the box. Install a metal nail plate on the front edge of each stud that the cable routes through.

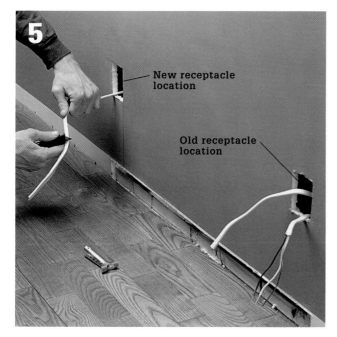

Turn off the power at the main panel and test for power.
Remove the old receptacle and its box, and pull the new branch cable up through the hole. Remove sheathing and insulation from both ends of the new cable.

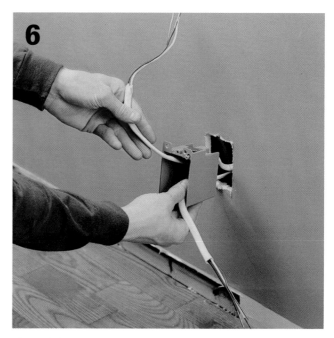

Thread the new and old cables into a pop-in box large enough to contain the added wires and clamp the cables. Fit the box into the old hole and attach it.

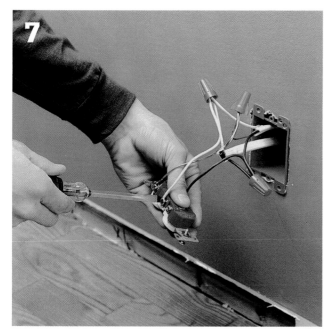

Reconnect the old receptacle by connecting its neutral, hot, and grounding screws to the new branch cable and the old cable from the panel with pigtails.

Pull the cable through another pop-in box for the new receptacle. Secure the cable and install the box. Connect the new receptacle to the new branch cable. Insert the receptacle into the box and attach the receptacle and cover plate with screws. Patch the opening with ½"-thick wood strips or drywall. Reattach the baseboard to the studs.

GFCI Receptacles

The ground-fault circuit-interrupter (GFCI) receptacle protects against electrical shock caused by a faulty appliance, or a worn cord or plug. It senses small changes in current flow and can shut off power in as little as 1/40 of a second.

GFCIs are now required in bathrooms, kitchens, garages, crawl spaces, unfinished basements, and outdoor receptacle locations. Consult your local codes for any requirements regarding the installation of GFCI receptacles. Most GFCIs use standard screw terminal connections, but some have wire leads and are attached with wire connectors. Because the body of a GFCI receptacle is larger than a standard receptacle, small crowded electrical boxes may need to be replaced with more spacious boxes.

The GFCI receptacle may be wired to protect only itself (single location), or it can be wired to protect all receptacles, switches, and light fixtures from the GFCI "forward" to the end of the circuit (multiple locations).

Because the GFCI is so sensitive, it is most effective when wired to protect a single location. The more receptacles any one GFCI protects, the more susceptible it is to "phantom tripping," shutting off power because of tiny, normal fluctuations in current flow.

Circuit tester   Wire connectors
Screwdriver   Masking tape

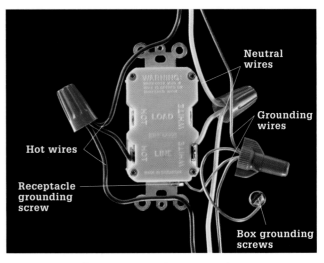

A GFCI wired for single-location protection (shown from the back) has hot and neutral wires connected only to the screw terminals marked LINE. A GFCI connected for single-location protection may be wired as either an end-of-run or middle-of-run configuration (page 110).

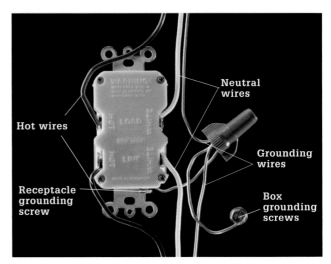

A GFCI wired for multiple-location protection (shown from the back) has one set of hot and neutral wires connected to the LINE pair of screw terminals, and the other set connected to the LOAD pair of screw terminals. A GFCI receptacle connected for multiple-location protection may be wired only as a middle-of-run configuration.

How to Install a GFCI for Single-Location Protection

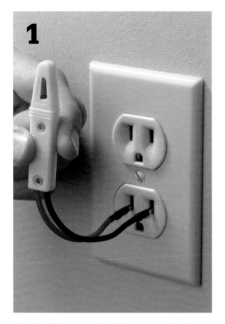

Shut off power to the receptacle at the main service panel. Test for power with a neon circuit tester. Be sure to check both halves of the receptacle.

Remove cover plate. Loosen mounting screws, and gently pull receptacle from the box. Do not touch wires. Confirm power is off with a circuit tester.

Disconnect all white neutral wires from the silver screw terminals of the old receptacle.

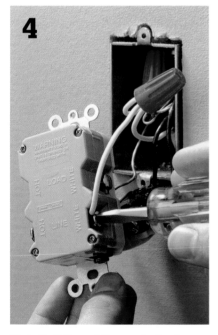

Pigtail all the white neutral wires together, and connect the pigtail to the terminal marked WHITE LINE on the GFCI (see photo on opposite page).

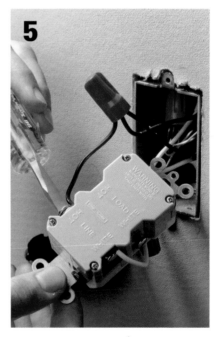

Disconnect all black hot wires from the brass screw terminals of the old receptacle. Pigtail these wires together, and connect them to the terminal marked HOT LINE on the GFCI.

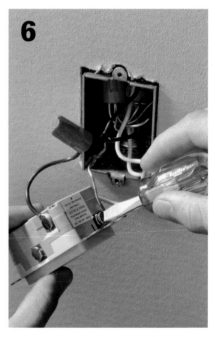

If a grounding wire is available, connect it to the green grounding screw terminal of the GFCI. Mount the GFCI in the receptacle box, and reattach the cover plate. Restore power, and test the GFCI according to the manufacturer's instructions.

How to Install a GFCI for Multiple-Location Protection

Use a map of your house circuits to determine a location for your GFCI. Indicate all receptacles that will be protected by the GFCI installation.

Turn off power to the correct circuit at the main service panel. Test all the receptacles in the circuit with a neon circuit tester to make sure the power is off. Always check both halves of each duplex receptacle.

Remove the cover plate from the receptacle that will be replaced with the GFCI. Loosen the mounting screws and gently pull the receptacle from its box. Take care not to touch any bare wires. Confirm the power is off with a neon circuit tester.

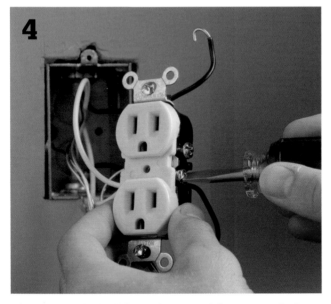

Disconnect all black hot wires. Carefully separate the hot wires and position them so that the bare ends do not touch anything. Restore power to the circuit at the main service panel. Determine which black wire is the feed wire by testing for hot wires. The feed wire brings power to the receptacle from the service panel. Use caution: This is a live wire test, during which the power is turned on temporarily.

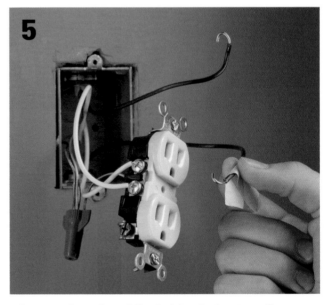

When you have found the hot feed wire, turn off power at the main service panel. Identify the feed wire by marking it with masking tape.

6

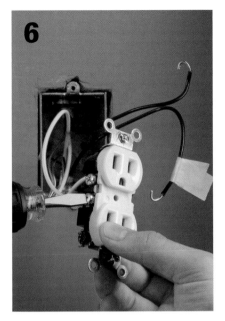

Disconnect the white neutral wires from the old receptacle. Identify the white feed wire and label it with masking tape. The white feed wire will be the one that shares the same cable as the black feed wire.

7

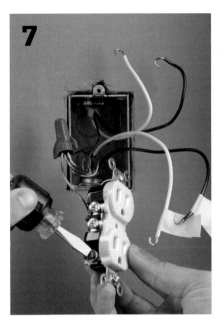

Disconnect the grounding wire from the grounding screw terminal of the old receptacle. Remove the old receptacle. Connect the grounding wire to the grounding screw terminal of the GFCI.

8

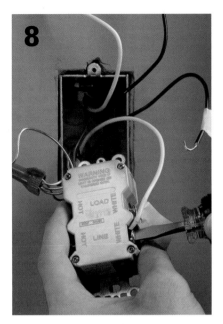

Connect the white feed wire to the terminal marked WHITE LINE on the GFCI. Connect the black feed wire to the terminal marked HOT LINE on the GFCI.

9

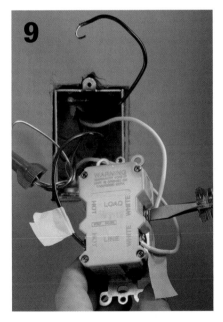

Connect the other white neutral wire to the terminal marked WHITE LOAD on the GFCI.

10

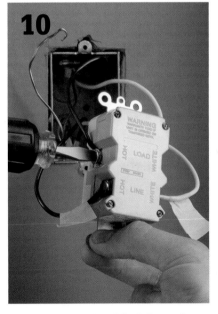

Connect the other black hot wire to the terminal marked HOT LOAD on the GFCI.

11

Carefully tuck all wires into the receptacle box. Mount the GFCI in the box and attach the cover plate. Turn on power to the circuit at the main service panel. Test the GFCI according to the manufacturer's instructions.

Isolated-Ground Receptacles

An isolated-ground circuit is simply a receptacle wired so that it does not share a common grounding path with the rest of the electrical system. The wire connected to the grounding screw on the isolated-ground receptacle leads directly back to the grounding bar at the panel. The receptacle (typically orange in color) is isolated such that it does not ground through the box itself, so it is imperative that the isolated grounding wire be properly connected.

An isolated-ground circuit provides protection beyond standard surge suppression for computer equipment, and it also significantly reduces the potential for electromagnetic noise from the common grounding path. This noise may interfere with the proper function of sensitive audio and video equipment by causing an audible hum or poor picture quality. If you have a high-end home theater, isolated-ground receptacles are a good idea to ensure maximum picture and sound quality.

Typically, to install an isolated-ground receptacle, a new circuit is run from a 15-amp breaker (see circuit map 16, page 162). To create an isolated grounding path, the circuit is wired with three-wire cable. The bare grounding wire terminates at the box's grounding screw, and the red wire (coded green at its end) provides the dedicated path back to the panel's grounding or neutral bar.

Tools & Materials ▸

Hammer	Combination tool
Screwdriver	14/3 NM cable
Fish tape	Isolated-ground
Circuit tester	receptacle
Stud finder	Single-pole breaker

How to Replace an Existing Receptacle with an Isolated-Ground Receptacle

Isolated-ground receptacles provide extra protection for computers, and they isolate audio-video equipment from interference-causing electrical noise.

Turn off the power to the old receptacle at the service panel. Remove the cover and test that power is off. If the receptacle is at the end of a run, disconnect it and trace the cable back to the next box in the circuit. Disconnect the cable between the old receptacle and the upstream device, and remove the cable. If the box is in the middle of the run (as shown), disconnect the receptacle and join the circuit wires so they pass uninterrupted through the box. Push the connectors to the back of the box. You may need to install a deeper box.

Run 14/3 NM cable for the new circuit from the service panel to the receptacle box. Leave 10" of cable at the receptacle end. Clamp the cable in the box. Strip sheathing and insulation from the cable. Ground the bare copper wire to the grounding screw on the box.

Code the red wire with green tape and connect it to the grounding screw on the isolated-ground receptacle. Connect the white wire to the silver neutral terminal on the receptacle, and connect the black wire to the brass hot terminal. Push the wires into the box and attach the receptacle to the box. Install the cover plate.

At the service panel, switch off the main breaker. Remove the cover. Test that the power is off by touching one probe of a tester to the neutral bar and the other probe to each breaker's setscrew. Remove a knockout from the side of the panel and thread the end of the 14/3 NM into the panel. Secure it with a clamp.

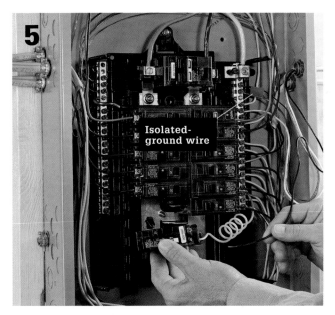

Connect the white wire from the cable to the neutral bar. Connect the bare copper wire to the grounding bar. Connect the red wire (coded green on the end) to the grounding bar or neutral bar (shown), whichever is the shortest path. Connect the black wire to a new 15-amp breaker. Snap the breaker into an open space on the panel. Restore power and test the circuit. Replace the panel cover.

Testing Receptacles

For testing receptacles and other devices for power, grounding, and polarity, neon circuit testers are inexpensive and easy to use. But they are less sensitive than auto-ranging multimeters. In some cases, neon testers won't detect the presence of lower voltage in a circuit. This can lead you to believe that a circuit is shut off when it is not—a dangerous mistake. The small probes on a neon circuit tester also force you to get too close to live terminals and wires. For a quick check and confirmation, a neon circuit tester (or a plug-in tester) is adequate. But for the most reliable readings, buy and learn to use a multimeter.

The best multimeters are auto-ranging models with a digital readout. Unlike manual multimeters, auto-ranging models do not require you to preset the voltage range to get an accurate reading. Unlike neon testers, multimeters may be used for a host of additional diagnostic functions such as testing fuses, measuring battery voltage, testing internal wiring in appliances, and checking light fixtures to determine if they're functional.

Tools & Materials ▸

Multimeter
Neon circuit tester

Plug-in tester
Screwdriver

Metal probes

How to Use a Plug-in Tester

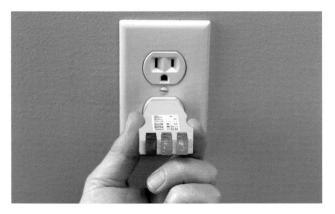

Use a plug-in tester to test a three-slot receptacle. With the power on, insert the tester into the suspect outlet. The face of the tester has three colored lights that will light up in different combinations, according to the outlet's problem. A reference chart is provided with the tester, and many have a chart on the tester itself.

How to Test Quickly for Power

Use a circuit tester to verify that power is not flowing to a receptacle. Using either a no-touch sensor or a probe-style circuit tester, test the receptacle for current before you remove the cover plate. Once the plate is removed, double-check at the terminals to make sure there is no current.

How to Test a Receptacle for Power

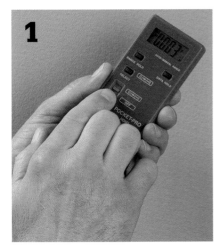

1

Set the selector dial for alternating-current voltage. Plug the black probe lead into the common jack on the multimeter (labeled COM). Plug the red probe lead into the V-labeled jack.

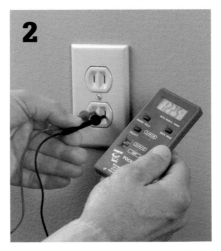

2

Insert the test ends of the probe into the receptacle slots. It does not make a difference which probe goes into which slot as long as they're in the same receptacle. If power is present and flowing normally, you will see a voltage reading on the readout screen.

3

If the multimeter reads 0 or gives a very low reading (less than 1 or 2 volts), power is not present in the receptacle and it is safe to remove the cover plate and work on the fixture (although it's always a good idea to confirm your reading by touching the probes directly to the screw terminals on the receptacles).

How to Test for Hot Wires

How to Test a Two-Slot Receptacle for Grounding

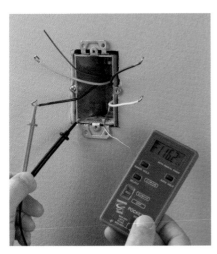

When a receptacle or switch is in the middle of a circuit, it is difficult to tell which wires are carrying current. Use a multimeter to check. With power off, remove the receptacle and separate the wires. Restore power. Touch one probe to the bare ground or the grounded metal box and touch the other probe to the end of each wire. The wire that shows current on the meter is hot.

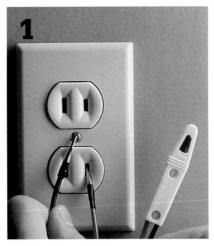

1

Confirm that the receptacle has power. Place one probe of a neon tester or multimeter in the short (hot) slot and the other on the cover plate screw (screw must be unpainted). If the tester shows current, the receptacle is grounded. If the tester doesn't show current, proceed to step 2.

2

Place one probe in the long (neutral) slot and the other on the cover plate screw. If the tester shows current, the hot and neutral wires are reversed. If not, the box is ungrounded.

CADET
Manufacturing Company
Vancouver, WA
Model: BTF2
Volts: 125-240 · USA
Amps: 17 Amp-Canada

Use only on series baseboard
heater F.

Dec. 07

WIRING PROJECTS

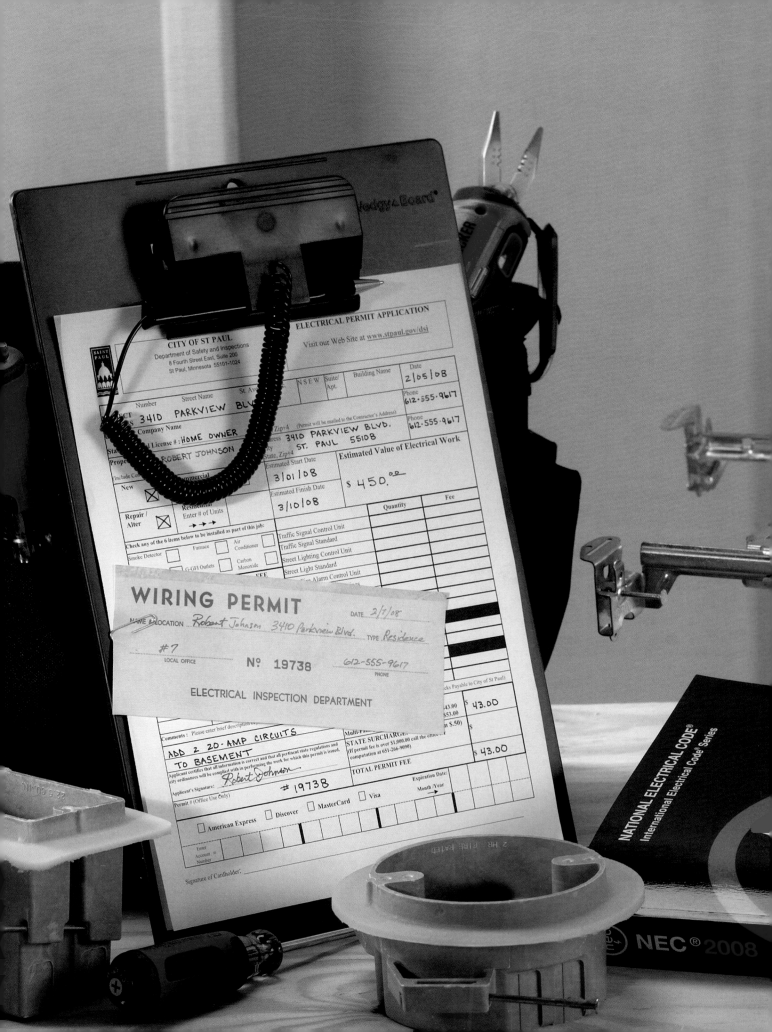

ELECTRICAL PERMIT APPLICATION

CITY OF ST PAUL
Department of Safety and Inspections
8 Fourth Street East, Suite 200
St Paul, Minnesota 55101-1024

Visit our Web Site at www.stpaul.gov/dsi

| | Number | Street Name | St. Av | N S E W | Suite/Apt. | Building Name | Date 2|05|08 |

PROJECT 3410 PARKVIEW BLVD

Company Name: Phone 612-555-9617

State al License #: HOME OWNER   Zip+4 (Permit will be mailed to the Contractor's Address)   Address 3410 PARKVIEW BLVD.   Phone 612-555-9617

Property ROBERT JOHNSON   State, Zip+4   City ST. PAUL 55108

Include Co   Estimated Start Date 3/01/08   Estimated Value of Electrical Work

New ☒   Commercial $ 450.00

Repair / Alter ☒   Residential Enter # of Units → 2 →   Estimated Finish Date 3/10/08

| | | Quantity | Fee |

Check any of the 6 items below to be installed as part of this job:

Furnace ☐   Air Conditioner ☐   Traffic Signal Control Unit

Smoke Detector ☐   Traffic Signal Standard

G-GFI Outlets ☐   Carbon Monoxide ☐   Street Lighting Control Unit
Street Light Standard
Fire Alarm Control Unit

WIRING PERMIT   DATE 2/7/08

NAME & LOCATION Robert Johnson 3410 Parkview Blvd.   TYPE Residence

#7
LOCAL OFFICE   N° 19738   612-555-9617   PHONE

ELECTRICAL INSPECTION DEPARTMENT

Comments: Please enter brief description

ADD 2 20-AMP CIRCUITS
TO BASEMENT

Applicant certifies that all information is correct and that all pertinent state regulations and city ordinances will be complied with in performing the work for which this permit is issued.

Robert Johnson

Applicant's Signature: # 19738

Permit # (Office Use Only)

☐ American Express   ☐ Discover   ☐ MasterCard   ☐ Visa

Enter Account # Number

Signature of Cardholder:

cks Payable to City of St Paul)
43.00 $ 43.00
53.00 $
n $.50) $

Multi-Fa

STATE SURCHARGE
(If permit fee is over $1,000.00 call the office
computation at 651-266-9090) $ 43.00

TOTAL PERMIT FEE

Expiration Date:
Month /Year →

NATIONAL ELECTRICAL CODE®
International Electrical Code® Series

NEC® 2008

Preliminary Work

Some very important parts of any electrical project occur well before you ever make a box cutout or strip a wire. In addition to the most elementary tasks of figuring out what needs to happen and how its done, there are required procedural steps you'll need to take as well as some basic household planning you'll need to do.

To form an overview of what you want to accomplish and how to get it done, you'll need to begin by assessing the condition of your wiring system as it exists. This involves a little investigative work and a little math. You'll find plenty of information on both in this chapter.

Once you've made an evaluation of what you've got to work with, it's time to start the planning in earnest. Naturally, the amount of planning required depends largely on the scale of the project. If you are wiring a room addition or an extensive remodel, the wiring plan should be established and approved well in advance of the start of the project. In fact, without an approved wiring plan you will be unable to obtain a valid building permit. Even for small-scale projects, such as adding a new light circuit, you need a permit, and to get the permit you need a plan. You typically do not need a permit for simple one-for-replacements of devices such as switches and receptacles, but it still pays to plan. For example, if you are replacing a light switch, you should plan ahead and do the job during the daytime to take advantage of the natural light while you work.

In this chapter:
- Planning Your Project
- Case Study: Attic Conversion
- Case Study: Kitchen Remodel

Planning Your Project

Careful planning of a wiring project ensures you will have plenty of power for present and future needs. Whether you are adding circuits in a room addition, wiring a remodeled kitchen, or adding an outdoor circuit, consider all possible ways the space might be used, and plan for enough electrical service to meet peak needs.

For example, when wiring a room addition, remember that the way a room is used can change. In a room used as a spare bedroom, a single 15-amp circuit provides plenty of power, but if you ever choose to convert the same room to a family recreation space, you will need additional circuits.

When wiring a remodeled kitchen, it is a good idea to install circuits for an electric oven and countertop range, even if you do not have these electric appliances. Installing these circuits now makes it easy to convert from gas to electric appliances at a later date.

A large wiring project adds a considerable load to your main electrical service. In about 25 percent of all homes, some type of service upgrade is needed before new wiring can be installed. For example, many homeowners will need to replace an older 60-amp electrical service with a new service rated for 100 amps or more. This is a job for a licensed electrician but is well worth the investment. In other cases, the existing main service provides adequate power, but the main circuit breaker panel is too full to hold any new circuit breakers. In this case it is necessary to install a circuit breaker subpanel to provide room for hooking up added circuits. Installing a subpanel is a job most homeowners can do themselves (pages 184 to 187).

This chapter gives an easy five-step method for determining your electrical needs and planning new circuits.

Five Steps for Planning a Wiring Project

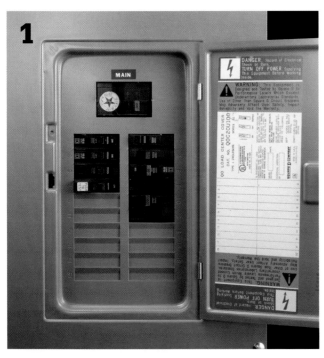

Examine your main service (page 128). The amp rating of the electrical service and the size of the circuit breaker panel will help you determine if a service upgrade is needed.

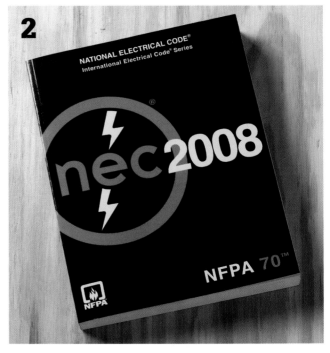

Learn about codes (pages 129 to 133). The National Electrical Code (NEC), and local electrical codes and building codes, provide guidelines for determining how much power and how many circuits your home needs. Your local electrical inspector can tell you which regulations apply to your job.

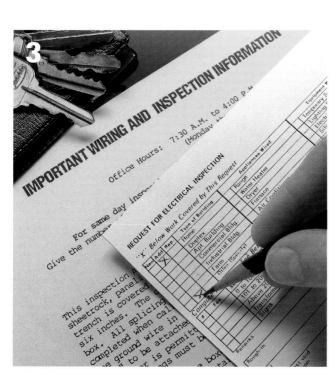

Prepare for inspections (pages 134 to 135). Remember that your work must be reviewed by your local electrical inspector. When planning your wiring project, always follow the inspector's guidelines for quality workmanship.

Evaluate electrical loads (pages 136 to 141). New circuits put an added load on your electrical service. Make sure that total load of the existing wiring and the planned new circuits does not exceed the main service capacity.

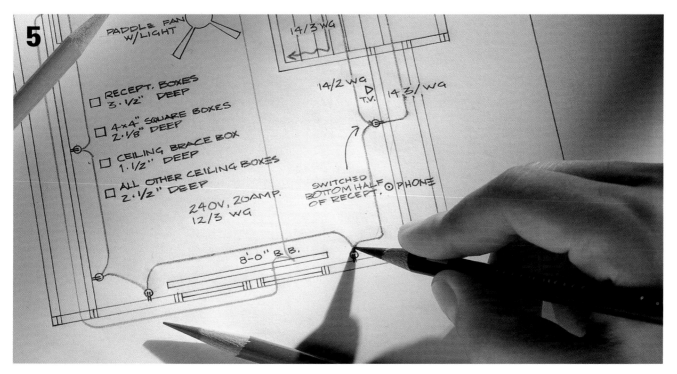

Draw a wiring diagram and get a permit (pages 142 to 143). This wiring plan will help you organize your work.

Examine Your Main Service Panel

The first step in planning a new wiring project is to look in your main circuit breaker panel and find the size of the service by reading the amperage rating on the main circuit breaker. As you plan new circuits and evaluate electrical loads, knowing the size of the main service helps you determine if you need a service upgrade.

Also look for open circuit breaker slots in the panel. The number of open slots will determine if you need to add a circuit breaker subpanel.

Find the service size by opening the main service panel and reading the amp rating printed on the main circuit breaker. In most cases, 100-amp service provides enough power to handle the added loads of projects like the ones shown in this book. A service rated for 60 amps or less may need to be upgraded.

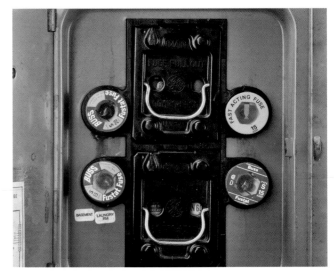

Older service panels use fuses instead of circuit breakers. Have an electrician replace this type of panel with a circuit breaker panel that provides enough power and enough open breaker slots for the new circuits you are planning.

Look for open circuit breaker slots in the main circuit breaker panel or in a circuit breaker subpanel, if your home already has one. You will need one open slot for each 120-volt circuit you plan to install and two slots for each 240-volt circuit. If your main circuit breaker panel has no open breaker slots, install a subpanel (pages 184 to 187) to provide room for connecting new circuits.

Learn About Codes

To ensure public safety, your community requires that you get a permit to install new wiring and have the completed work reviewed by an appointed inspector. Electrical inspectors use the National Electrical Code (NEC) as the primary authority for evaluating wiring, but they also follow the local Building Code and Electrical Code standards.

As you begin planning new circuits, call or visit your local electrical inspector and discuss the project with him. The inspector can tell you which of the national and local code requirements apply to your job, and may give you a packet of information summarizing these regulations. Later, when you apply to the inspector for a work permit, he will expect you to understand the local guidelines as well as a few basic National Electrical Code requirements.

The National Electrical Code is a set of standards that provides minimum safety requirements for wiring installations. It is revised every three years. The national code requirements for the projects shown in this book are thoroughly explained on the following pages. For more information, you can find copies of the current NEC, as well as a number of excellent handbooks based on the NEC, at libraries and bookstores.

In addition to being the final authority of code requirements, inspectors are electrical professionals with years of experience. Although they have busy schedules, most inspectors are happy to answer questions and help you design well-planned circuits.

Basic Electrical Code Requirements

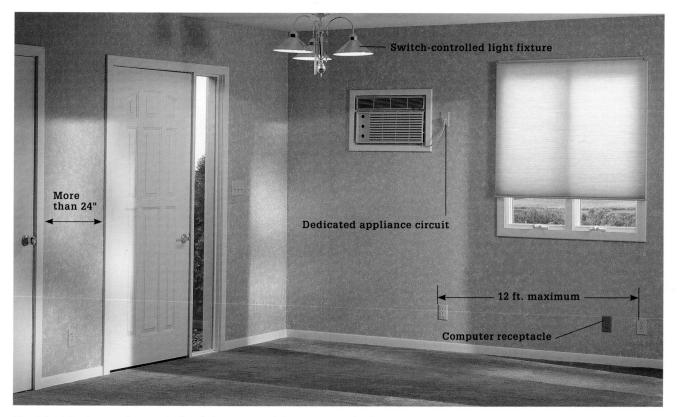

Electrical Code requirements for living areas: Living areas need at least one 15-amp or 20-amp basic lighting/receptacle circuit for each 600 sq. ft. of living space and should have a dedicated circuit for each type of permanent appliance, like an air conditioner, computer, or a group of baseboard heaters and within 6 ft. of any door opening. Receptacles on basic lighting/receptacle circuits should be spaced no more than 12 ft. apart. Many electricians and electrical inspectors recommend even closer spacing. Any wall more than 24" wide also needs a receptacle. Every room should have a wall switch at the point of entry to control either a ceiling light or plug-in lamp. Kitchens and bathrooms must have a ceiling-mounted light fixture.

Selected NEC Standards & Tips

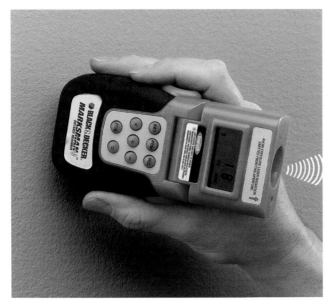

Measure the living areas of your home, excluding closets and unfinished spaces. A sonic measuring tool gives room dimensions quickly and contains a built-in calculator for figuring floor area. You will need a minimum of one basic lighting/receptacle circuit for every 600 sq. ft. of living space. The total square footage also helps you determine heating and cooling needs for new room additions.

Three-way switches

Stairways with six steps or more must have lighting that illuminates each step. The light fixture must be controlled by three-way switches at the top and bottom landings.

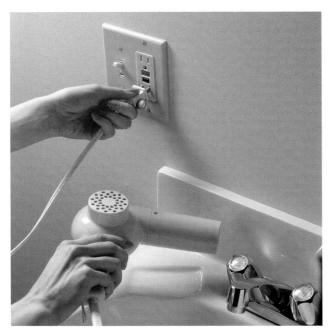

Kitchen and bathroom receptacles must be protected by a ground-fault circuit-interrupter (GFCI). Also, all outdoor receptacles and general-use receptacles in an unfinished basement or crawl space and garages must be protected by a GFCI.

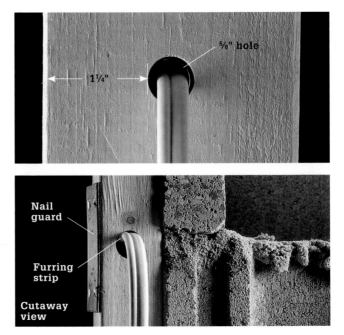

⅝" hole

1¼"

Nail guard

Furring strip

Cutaway view

Cables must be protected against damage by nails and screws by at least 1¼" of wood (top). When cables pass through 2 × 2 furring strips (bottom), protect the cables with metal nail guards.

What Inspectors Look For

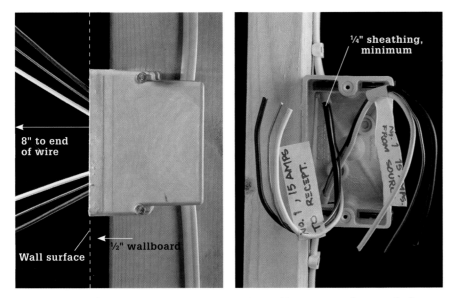

Electrical box faces should extend past the front of framing members so the boxes will be flush with finished walls (left). Inspectors will check to see that all boxes are large enough for the wires they contain. Cables should be cut and stripped back so that 8" of usable length extends past the front of the box, and so that at least ¼" of sheathing reaches into the box (right). Label all cables to show which circuits they serve: inspectors recognize this as a mark of careful work. The labels also simplify the final hookups after the wallboard is installed.

Install an isolated-ground circuit and receptacle if recommended by your inspector. An isolated-ground circuit protects sensitive electronic equipment against tiny current fluctuations and interference. Electronics also should be protected by either a plug-in surge protector or a whole-house surge arrestor.

Heating & Air Conditioning Chart ▸
(compiled from manufacturers' literature)

Room addition living area	Recommended total heating rating	Recommended circuit size	Recommended air-conditioner rating	Recommended circuit size
100 sq. ft.	900 watts	15-amp (240 volts)	5,000 BTU	15-amp (120 volts)
150 sq. ft.	1,350 watts		6,000 BTU	
200 sq. ft.	1,800 watts		7,000 BTU	
300 sq. ft.	2,700 watts		9,000 BTU	
400 sq. ft.	3,600 watts	20-amp (240 volts)	10,500 BTU	
500 sq. ft.	4,500 watts	30-amp (240 volts)	11,500 BTU	20-amp (120 volts)
800 sq. ft.	7,200 watts	two 20-amp	17,000 BTU	15-amp (240 volts)
1,000 sq. ft.	9,000 watts	two 30-amp	21,000 BTU	20-amp (240 volts)

Electric heating and air conditioning for a new room addition will be checked by an inspector. Determine your heating and air-conditioning needs by finding the total area of the living space. Choose electric heating units with a combined wattage rating close to the chart recommendation above. Choose an air conditioner with a BTU rating close to the chart recommendation for your room size. *Note: These recommendations are for homes in moderately cool climates, sometimes referred to as Zone 4 regions. Cities in Zone 4 include Denver, Chicago, and Boston. In more severe climates, check with your electrical inspector or energy agency to learn how to find heating and air-conditioning needs.*

Evaluate Electrical Loads

Before drawing a plan and applying for a work permit, make sure your home's electrical service provides enough power to handle the added load of the new circuits. In a safe wiring system, the current drawn by fixtures and appliances never exceeds the main service capacity.

To evaluate electrical loads, use the work sheet on page 141 or whatever evaluation method is recommended by your electrical inspector. Include the load for all existing wiring as well as that for proposed new wiring when making your evaluation.

Most of the light fixtures and plug-in appliances in your home are evaluated as part of general allowances for basic lighting/receptacle circuits and small-appliance circuits. However, appliances that are permanently installed require their own dedicated circuits. The electrical loads for these appliances are added in separately when evaluating wiring.

If your evaluation shows that the load exceeds the main service capacity, you must have an electrician upgrade the main service before you can install new wiring. An electrical service upgrade is a worthwhile investment that improves the value of your home and provides plenty of power for present and future wiring projects.

Amperage ▸

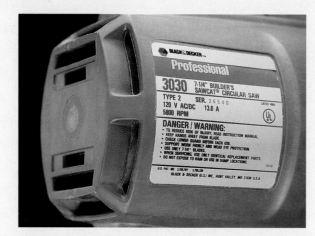

Amperage rating can be used to find the wattage of an appliance. Multiply the amperage by the voltage of the circuit. For example, a 13-amp, 120-volt circular saw is rated for 1,560 watts.

Amps × Volts	Total capacity	Safe capacity
15 A × 120 V =	1,800 watts	1,440 watts
20 A × 120 V =	2,400 watts	1,920 watts
25 A × 120 V =	3,000 watts	2,400 watts
30 A × 120 V =	3,600 watts	2,880 watts
20 A × 240 V =	4,800 watts	3,840 watts
30 A × 240 V =	7,200 watts	5,760 watts

Calculating Loads

Add 1,500 watts for each small appliance circuit required by the local electrical code. In most communities, three such circuits are required—two in the kitchen and one for the laundry—for a total of 4,500 watts. No further calculations are needed for appliances that plug into small-appliance or basic lighting/receptacle circuits.

If the nameplate gives the rating in kilowatts, find the watts by multiplying kilowatts times 1,000. If an appliance lists only amps, find watts by multiplying the amps times the voltage—either 120 or 240 volts.

Air-conditioning and heating appliances are not used at the same time, so figure in only the larger of these two numbers when evaluating your home's electrical load.

Outdoor receptacles and fixtures are not included in basic lighting calculations. When evaluating electrical loads, add in the nameplate wattage rating for each outdoor light fixture, and add in 180 watts for each outdoor receptacle. Receptacles and light fixtures in garages also are considered to be outdoor fixtures when evaluating loads.

Locating Wattage

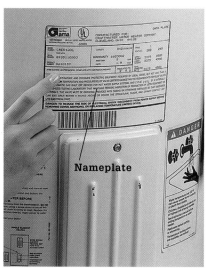

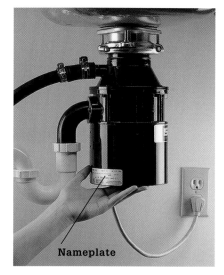

Light bulb wattage ratings are printed on the top of the bulb. If a light fixture has more than one bulb, remember to add the wattages of all the bulbs to find the total wattage of the fixture.

Electric water heaters are permanent appliances that require their own dedicated 30-amp, 240-volt circuits. Most water heaters are rated between 3,500 and 4,500 watts. If the nameplate lists several wattage ratings, use the one labeled "Total Connected Wattage" when figuring electrical loads.

Food disposers are considered permanent appliances and require their own dedicated 15-amp, 120-volt circuits. Most disposers are rated between 500 and 900 watts.

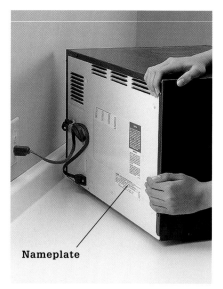

Dishwashers installed permanently under a countertop need dedicated 15-amp, 120-volt circuits. Dishwasher ratings are usually between 1,000 and 1,500 watts. Portable dishwashers are regarded as part of small appliance circuits and are not added in when figuring loads.

Electric ranges can be rated for as little as 3,000 watts or as much as 12,000 watts. They require dedicated 120/240-volt circuits. Find the exact wattage rating by reading the nameplate found inside the oven door or on the back of the unit.

Microwave ovens are regarded by many local codes as permanent appliances. If your inspector asks you to install a separate 20-amp, 120-volt circuit for the microwave oven, add in its wattage rating when calculating loads. The nameplate is found on the back of the cabinet or inside the front door. Most microwave ovens are rated between 500 and 1,200 watts.

Freezers are permanent appliances that require dedicated 15-amp, 120-volt circuits. Freezer ratings are usually between 240 and 480 watts. But combination refrigerator-freezers rated for 1,000 watts or less are plugged into small appliance circuits and do not need their own dedicated circuits. The nameplate for a freezer is found inside the door or on the back of the unit, just below the door seal.

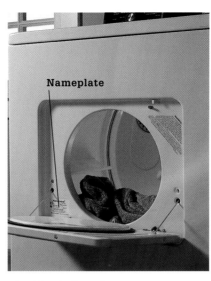

Electric clothes dryers are permanent appliances that need dedicated 30-amp, 120/240-volt circuits. The wattage rating, usually between 4,500 and 5,500 watts, is printed on the nameplate inside the dryer door. Washing machines and gas-heat clothes dryers with electric tumbler motors do not need dedicated circuits. They plug into the 20-amp small-appliance circuit in the laundry room.

Forced-air furnaces have electric fans and are considered permanent appliances. They require dedicated 15-amp, 120-volt circuits. Include the fan wattage rating, printed on a nameplate inside the control panel, when figuring wattage loads for heating.

A central air conditioner requires a dedicated 240-volt circuit. Its wattage rating, usually between 2,300 and 5,500 watts, is printed on a metal plate near the electrical hookup panel.

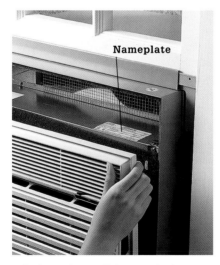

Window air conditioners, both 120-volt and 240-volt types, are permanent appliances that require dedicated 15-amp or 20-amp circuits. The wattage rating, which can range from 500 to 2,000 watts, is found on the nameplate located inside the front grill. Make sure to include all window air conditioners in your evaluation.

Electric room heaters that are permanently installed require a dedicated circuit and must be figured into the load calculations. Use the maximum wattage rating printed inside the cover. In general, 240-volt baseboard-type heaters are rated for 180 to 250 watts for each linear foot.

(continued)

Sample Circuit Evaluation

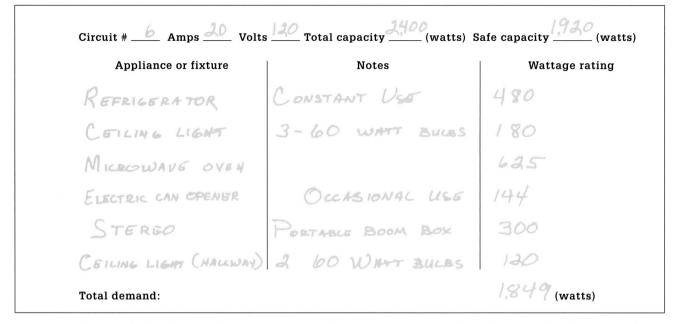

Circuit # __6__ Amps __20__ Volts __120__ Total capacity __2400__ (watts) Safe capacity __1,920__ (watts)

Appliance or fixture	Notes	Wattage rating
Refrigerator	Constant Use	480
Ceiling light	3-60 watt bulbs	180
Microwave oven		625
Electric can opener	Occasional use	144
Stereo	Portable Boom Box	300
Ceiling light (hallway)	2 60 watt bulbs	120
Total demand:		1,849 (watts)

Photocopy this sample circuit evaluation to keep a record of the power demand of each circuit. The words and numbers printed in blue will not reproduce on photocopies. In this sample kitchen circuit, the demand on the circuit is very close to the safe capacity. Adding another appliance, such as an electric frying pan, could overload the circuit and cause a fuse to blow or a circuit breaker to trip.

Typical Wattage Ratings (120-volt Circuit Except Where Noted) ▶

Appliance	Amps	Watts	Appliance	Amps	Watts
Air conditioner (central)	13 to 36 (240-v)	3,120 to 8,640	Garbage disposer	3.5 to 7.5	420 to 900
Air conditioner (window)	6 to 13	720 to 1,560	Hair dryer	5 to 10	600 to 1,200
Blender	2 to 4	240 to 480	Heater (portable)	7 to 12	840 to 1,440
Broiler	12.5	1,500	Microwave oven	4 to 10	480 to 1,200
Can opener	1.2	144	Range (oven/stove)	5.5 to 10.8 (240-v)	1,320 to 2,600
Circular saw	10 to 12	1,200 to 1,440	Refrigerator	2 to 4	240 to 600
Coffeemaker	4 to 8	480 to 960	Router	8	960
Clothes dryer	16.5 to 34 (240-v)	3,960 to 8,160	Sander (portable)	2 to 5	240 to 600
Clothes iron	9	1,080	Saw (table)	7 to 10	840 to 1,200
Computer	4 to 7	480 to 840	Sewing machine	1	120
Dishwasher	8.5 to 12.5	1,020 to 1,500	Stereo	2.5 to 4	300 to 480
Drill (portable)	2 to 4	240 to 480	Television	2.5	300
DVD player	2.5 to 4	300 to 480	Toaster	9	1,080
Fan (ceiling)	3.5	420	Trash compactor	4 to 8	480 to 960
Fan (portable)	2	240	Vacuum cleaner	6 to 11	720 to 1,320
Freezer	2 to 4	240 to 600	Waffle iron	7.5	900
Frying pan	9	1,080	Washing machine	12.5	1,500
Furnace, forced-air gas	6.5 to 13	780 to 1,560	Water heater (elec.)	15.8 to 21 (240-v)	3,800 to 5,040

How to Evaluate Electrical Loads (photocopy this work sheet as a guide)

1.	Find the basic lighting/receptacle load by multiplying the square footage of all living areas (including any room additions) times 3 watts.	Existing space: _1,100_ sq. ft. New additions: _400_ sq. ft. _1,500_ total sq. ft. × 3 watts =	_4,500_ watts
2.	Add 1,500 watts for each kitchen small-appliance circuit and for the laundry circuit.	_3_ circuits × 1,500 watts =	_4,500_ watts
3.	Add ratings for permanent electrical appliances, including range, food disposer, dishwasher, freezer, water heater, and clothes dryer.	RANGE 12.3 K.W.=12,300 WATTS	12,300 watts
		DRYER 5,000	5,000 watts
		DISHWASHER 1,200	1,200 watts
		FREEZER 550	550 watts
		FOOD DISPOSER 800	800 watts
	Find total wattages for the furnace and heating units, and for air conditioners. Add in only the larger of these numbers.	Furnace heat: _1,200_ watts Space heaters: _5,450_ watts Total heating = _6,650_ watts Central air conditioner: _3,500_ watts Window air conditioners: _1,100_ watts Total cooling = _4,600_ watts	watts _6,650_ watts
4.	For outdoor fixtures (including those in garages) find the nameplate wattage ratings.	Total fixture watts =	_650_ watts
	Multiply the number of outdoor receptacles (including those in garages) times 180 watts.	_3_ receptacles × 180 watts =	_540_ watts
5.	Total the wattages to find the gross load.		_36,690_ wattw
6.	Figure the first 10,000 watts of the gross load at 100%.	100% × 10,000 = 10,000	10,000 watts
7.	Subtract 10,000 watts from the gross load, then figure the remaining load at 40%.	_36,690_ watts − 10,000 = _26,690_ wat _26,690_ watts × .40 =	_10,676_ watts
8.	Add steps 6 and 7 to estimate the true electrical load.		_20,676_ watts
9.	Convert the estimated true electrical load to amps by dividing by 230.	_20,676_ watts ÷ 230 =	_89.9_ amps
10.	Compare the load with the amp rating of your home's electrical service, printed on the main circuit breaker. If the load is less than the main circuit breaker rating, the system is safe. If the load exceeds the main circuit breaker rating, your service should be upgraded.	OK ☑ Upgrade ☐	

Draw a Diagram & Obtain a Permit

Drawing a wiring diagram is the last step in planning a circuit installation. A detailed wiring diagram helps you get a work permit, makes it easy to create a list of materials, and serves as a guide for laying out circuits and installing cables and fixtures. Use the circuit maps on pages 152 to 169 as a guide for planning wiring configurations and cable runs. Bring the diagram and materials list when you visit electrical inspectors to apply for a work permit.

Never install new wiring without following your community's permit and inspection procedure. A work permit is not expensive, and it ensures that your work will be reviewed by a qualified inspector to guarantee its safety. If you install new wiring without the proper permit, an accident or fire traced to faulty wiring could cause your insurance company to discontinue your policy and can hurt the resale value of your home.

When electrical inspectors look over your wiring diagram, they will ask questions to see if you have a basic understanding of the electrical code and fundamental wiring skills. Some inspectors ask these questions informally, while others give a short written test. Inspectors may allow you to do some, but not all, of the work. For example, they may ask that all final circuit connections at the circuit breaker panel be made by a licensed electrician, while allowing you to do all other work.

A few communities allow you to install wiring only when supervised by an electrician. This means you can still install your own wiring but must hire an electrician to apply for the work permit and to check your work before inspectors review it. The electrician is held responsible for the quality of the job.

Remember that it is the inspectors' responsibility to help you do a safe and professional job. Feel free to call them with questions about wiring techniques or materials.

A detailed wiring diagram and a list of materials is required before electrical inspectors will issue a work permit. If blueprints exist for the space you are remodeling, start your electrical diagram by tracing the wall outlines from the blueprint. Use standard electrical symbols (next page) to clearly show all the receptacles, switches, light fixtures, and permanent appliances. Make a copy of the symbol key, and attach it to the wiring diagram for the inspectors' convenience. Show each cable run, and label its wire size and circuit amperage.

How to Draw a Wiring Plan

Draw a scaled diagram of the space you will be wiring, showing walls, doors, windows, plumbing pipes and fixtures, and heating and cooling ducts. Find the floor space by multiplying room length by width, and indicate this on the diagram. Do not include closets or storage areas when figuring space.

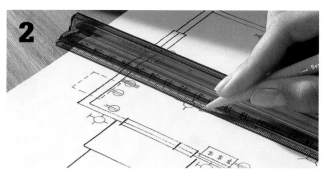

Mark the location of all switches, receptacles, light fixtures, and permanent appliances using the electrical symbols shown below. Where you locate these devices along the cable run determines how they are wired. Use the circuit maps on pages 152 to 169 as a guide for drawing wiring diagrams.

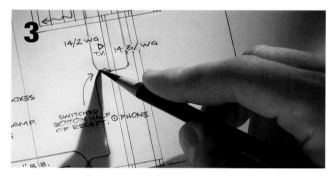

Draw in cable runs between devices. Indicate cable size and type, and the amperage of the circuits. Use a different-colored pencil for each circuit.

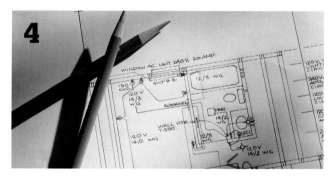

Identify the wattages for light fixtures and permanent appliances, and the type and size of each electrical box. On another sheet of paper, make a detailed list of all materials you will use.

Electrical Symbol Key ▸
(copy this key and attach it to your wiring plan)

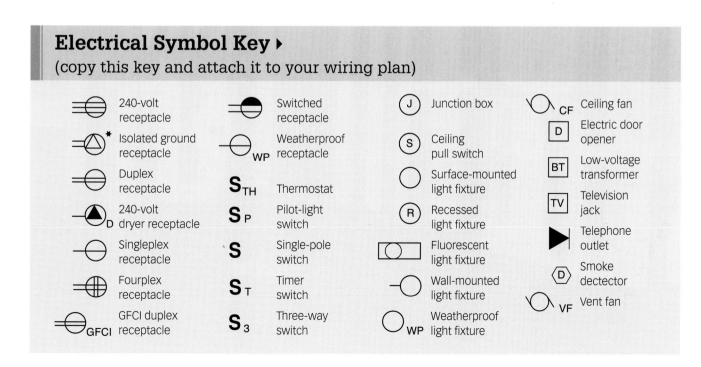

240-volt receptacle	Switched receptacle	Junction box
Isolated ground receptacle	Weatherproof receptacle WP	Ceiling pull switch
Duplex receptacle	S TH Thermostat	Surface-mounted light fixture
240-volt dryer receptacle D	S P Pilot-light switch	Recessed light fixture
Singleplex receptacle	S Single-pole switch	Fluorescent light fixture
Fourplex receptacle	S T Timer switch	Wall-mounted light fixture
GFCI duplex receptacle GFCI	S 3 Three-way switch	Weatherproof WP light fixture
		Ceiling fan CF
		Electric door opener D
		Low-voltage transformer BT
		Television jack TV
		Telephone outlet
		Smoke dectector D
		Vent fan VF

Case Study: Attic Conversion

The photo below shows the circuits you would likely want to install in a large room addition. This example shows the framing and wiring of an unfinished attic converted to an office or entertainment room with a bathroom. This room includes a subpanel and five new circuits plus telephone and cable-TV lines.

A wiring project of this sort is a potentially complicated undertaking that can be made simpler by breaking the project into convenient steps, and finishing one step before moving on to the next. Turn to pages 146 to 147 to see this project represented as a wiring diagram.

Individual Circuits

■ **#1: Bathroom circuit.** This 15-amp, 120-volt circuit supplies power to bathroom fixtures and to fixtures in the adjacent closet. All general-use receptacles in a bathroom must be protected by a GFCI and a separate 20-amp circuit.

■ **#2: Computer circuit.** A 15-amp, 120-volt dedicated circuit with an extra isolated grounding wire that protects computer equipment.

Circuit breaker subpanel receives power through a 10-gauge, three-wire feeder cable connected to a 30-amp, 240-volt circuit breaker at the main circuit breaker panel.

14/2 cable
Circuit breaker subpanel
Vent fan
Vanity light fixture
GFCI receptacle
12/2 cable
12/2 cable
Time & light fixture switch
14/3 cable
Blower heater
10/3 cable

Larger room additions may require a 60-amp or a 100-amp feeder circuit breaker.

■ **#3: Air-conditioner circuit.** A 20-amp, 240-volt dedicated circuit. In cooler climates, or in a smaller room, you may need an air conditioner and circuit rated for only 120 volts.

■ **#4: Basic lighting/receptacle circuit.** This 15-amp, 120-volt circuit supplies power to most of the fixtures in the bedroom and study areas.

■ **#5: Heater circuit.** This 20-amp, 240-volt circuit supplies power to the bathroom blower-heater and to the baseboard heaters. Depending on the size of your room and the wattage

rating of the baseboard heaters, you may need a 30-amp, 240-volt heating circuit.

Telephone outlet is wired with 22-gauge four-wire phone cable. If your home phone system has two or more separate lines, you may need to run a cable with eight wires, commonly called four-pair cable.

Cable television jack is wired with coaxial cable running from an existing television junction in the utility area.

14/3 cable

14/3 cable

Phone cable

Coaxial cable

These cables continue through the foreground wall to complete the circuits. This wall has been removed for clarity.

12/2 cable

14/2 cable

Diagram View

The diagram below shows the layout of the five circuits and the locations of their receptacles, switches, fixtures, and devices as shown in the photo on the previous pages. The circuits and receptacles are based on the needs of a 400-sq.-ft. space. An inspector will want to see a diagram like this one before issuing a permit. After you've received approval for your addition, the wiring diagram will serve as your guide as you complete your project.

■ **Circuit #1:** A 15-amp, 120-volt circuit serving the bathroom and closet area. Includes: 14/2 NM cable, double-gang box, timer switch, single-pole switch, 4 × 4" box with single-gang adapter plate, two plastic light fixture boxes, vanity light fixture, closet light fixture, 15-amp single-pole circuit breaker.

■ **Circuit #2:** A 15-amp, 120-volt computer circuit. Includes: 14/3 NM cable, single-gang box, 15-amp isolated-ground receptacle, 15-amp single-pole circuit breaker.

■ **Circuit #3:** A 20-amp, 240-volt air-conditioner circuit. Includes: 12/2 NM cable; single-gang box; 20-amp,

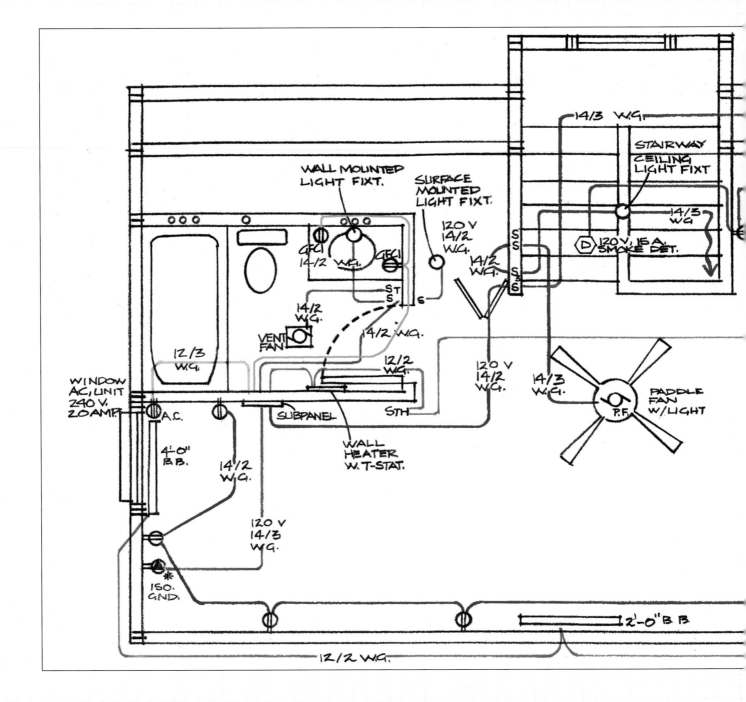

240-volt receptacle (duplex or singleplex style); 20-amp double-pole circuit.

Circuit #4: A 15-amp, 120-volt basic lighting/receptacle circuit serving most of the fixtures in the bedroom and study areas. Includes: 14/2 and 14/3 NM cable, two double-gang boxes, fan speed-control switch, dimmer switch, single-pole switch, two three-way switches, two plastic light fixture boxes, light fixture for stairway, smoke detector, metal light fixture box with brace bar, ceiling fan with light fixture, 10 single-gang boxes, 4 × 4" box with single-gang adapter plate, 10 duplex receptacles (15-amp), 15-amp single-pole circuit breaker.

Circuit #5: A 20-amp, 240-volt circuit that supplies power to three baseboard heaters controlled by a wall thermostat, and to a bathroom blower-heater controlled by a built-in thermostat. Includes: 12/2 NM cable, 750-watt blower heater, single-gang box, line-voltage thermostat, three baseboard heaters, 20-amp double-pole circuit breaker.

TV **Cable television jack:** Coaxial cable with F-connectors, signal splitter, cable television outlet with mounting brackets.

Circuit #6: A 20-amp, 120-volt, GFCI-protected small appliance circuit for the bathroom. Includes GFCI breaker, 14/2 NM cable, boxes and 20-amp receptacles.

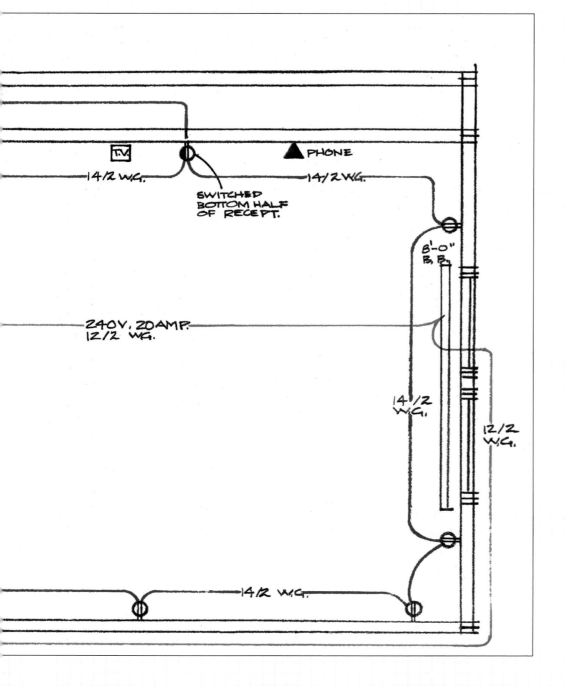

Case Study: Kitchen Remodel

14/2 cable

12/3 cable

12/2 cable

6/3 cable

14/2 cable

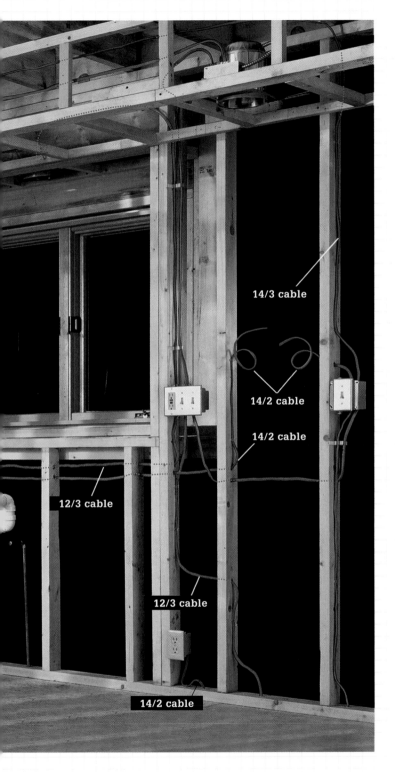

14/3 cable

14/2 cable

14/2 cable

12/3 cable

12/3 cable

14/2 cable

The photo at left shows the circuits you would probably want to install in a total kitchen remodel. Kitchens require a wide range of electrical services, from simple 15-amp lighting circuits to 120/240, 60-amp appliance circuits. This kitchen example has seven circuits, including separate dedicated circuits for a dishwasher and food disposer. Some codes allow the disposer and dishwasher to share a single circuit.

All rough carpentry and plumbing should be in place before beginning any electrical work. As always, divide a project of this scale into manageable steps, and finish one step before moving on. Turn to pages 150 to 151 to see this project represented as a wiring diagram.

Individual Circuits

■ **#1 & #2: Small-appliance circuits.** Two 20-amp, 120-volt circuits supply power to countertop and eating areas for small appliances. All general-use receptacles must be on these circuits. One 12/3 cable fed by a 20-amp double-pole breaker wires both circuits. These circuits share one electrical box with the disposer circuit (#5), and another with the basic lighting circuit (#7).

■ **#3: Range circuit.** A 50-amp, 120/240-volt dedicated circuit supplies power to the range/ oven appliance. It is wired with 6/3 cable.

□ **#4: Microwave circuit.** A dedicated 20-amp, 120-volt circuit supplies power to the microwave. It is wired with 12/2 cable. Microwaves that use less than 300 watts can be installed on a 15-amp circuit or plugged into the small-appliance circuits.

■ **#5: Food disposer/dishwasher circuit.** A dedicated 15-amp, 120-volt circuit supplies power to the disposer. It is wired with 14/2 cable. Some local codes allow disposer to be on the same circuit as the dishwasher.

■ **#6: Basic lighting circuit.** A 15-amp, 120-volt circuit powers the ceiling fixture, recessed fixtures, and undercabinet task lights. 14/2 and 14/3 cables connect the fixtures and switches in the circuit. Each task light has a self-contained switch.

Diagram View

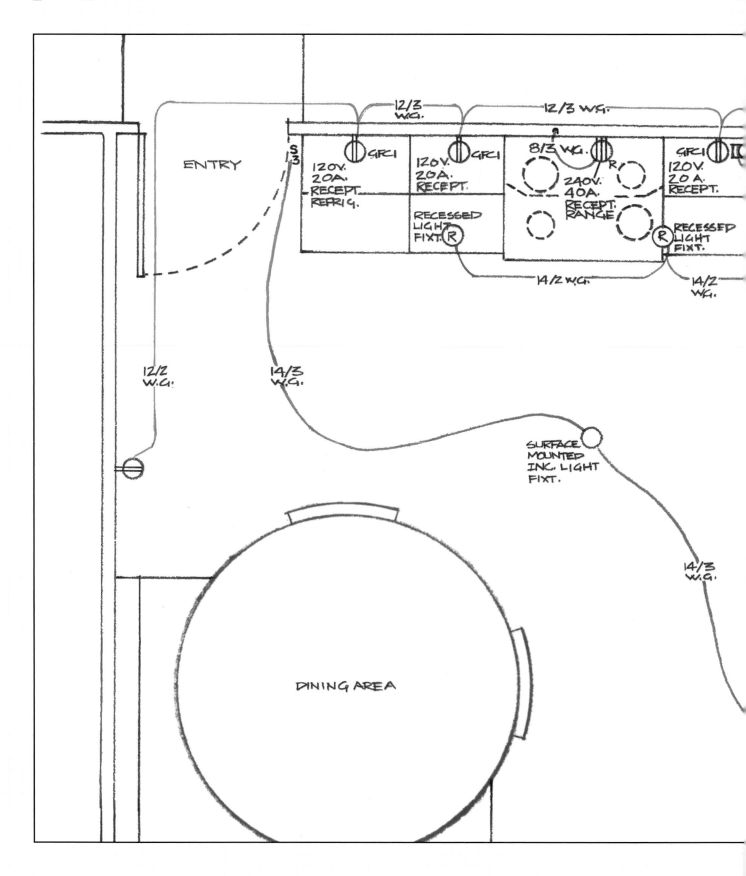

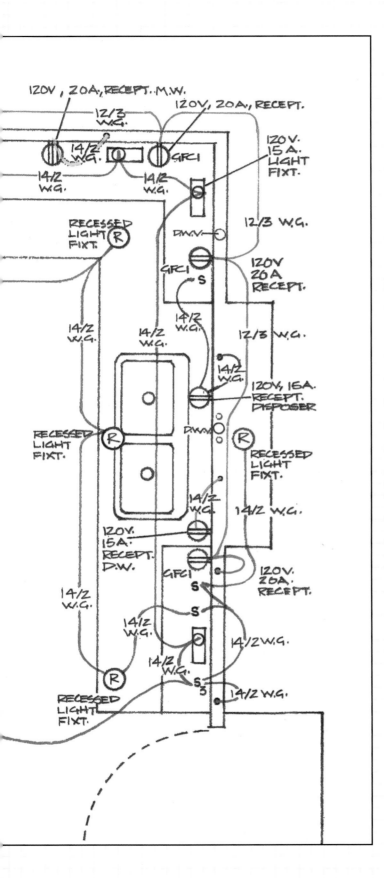

The diagram at left shows the layout of the seven circuits and the locations of their receptacles, switches, fixtures, and devices as shown in the photo on the previous pages. The circuits and receptacles are based on the needs of a 175-sq.-ft. space kitchen. An inspector will want to see a diagram like this one before issuing a permit. After you've received approval for your addition, the wiring diagram will serve as your guide as you complete your project.

■ **Circuits #1 & #2:** Two 20-amp, 120-volt small-appliance circuits wired with one cable. All general-use receptacles must be on these circuits, and they must be GFCI units. Includes: seven GFCI receptacles rated for 20 amps, five electrical boxes that are 4 × 4", and 12/3 cable. One GFCI shares a double-gang box with circuit #5, and another GFCI shares a triple-gang box with circuit #7.

■ **Circuit #3:** A 50-amp, 120/240-volt dedicated circuit for the range. Includes: a 4 × 4" box; a 120/240-volt, 50-amp range receptacle; and 6/3 NM cable.

■ **Circuit #4:** A 20-amp, 120-volt dedicated circuit for the microwave. Includes: a 20-amp duplex receptacle, a single-gang box, and 12/2 NM cable.

■ **Circuit #5:** A 15-amp, 120-volt dedicated circuit for the food disposer. Includes: a 15-amp duplex receptacle, a single-pole switch (installed in a double-gang box with a GFCI receptacle from the small-appliance circuits), one single-gang box, and 14/2 cable.

■ **Circuit #6:** A 15-amp, 120-volt dedicated circuit for the dishwasher. Includes: a 15-amp duplex receptacle, one single-gang box, and 14/2 cable.

■ **Circuit #7:** A 15-amp, 120-volt basic lighting circuit serving all of the lighting needs in the kitchen. Includes: two single-pole switches, two three-way switches, single-gang box, 4 × 4" box, triple-gang box (shared with one of the GFCI receptacles from the small-appliance circuits), plastic light fixture box with brace, ceiling light fixture, four fluorescent undercabinet light fixtures, six recessed light fixtures, 14/2 and 14/3 cables.

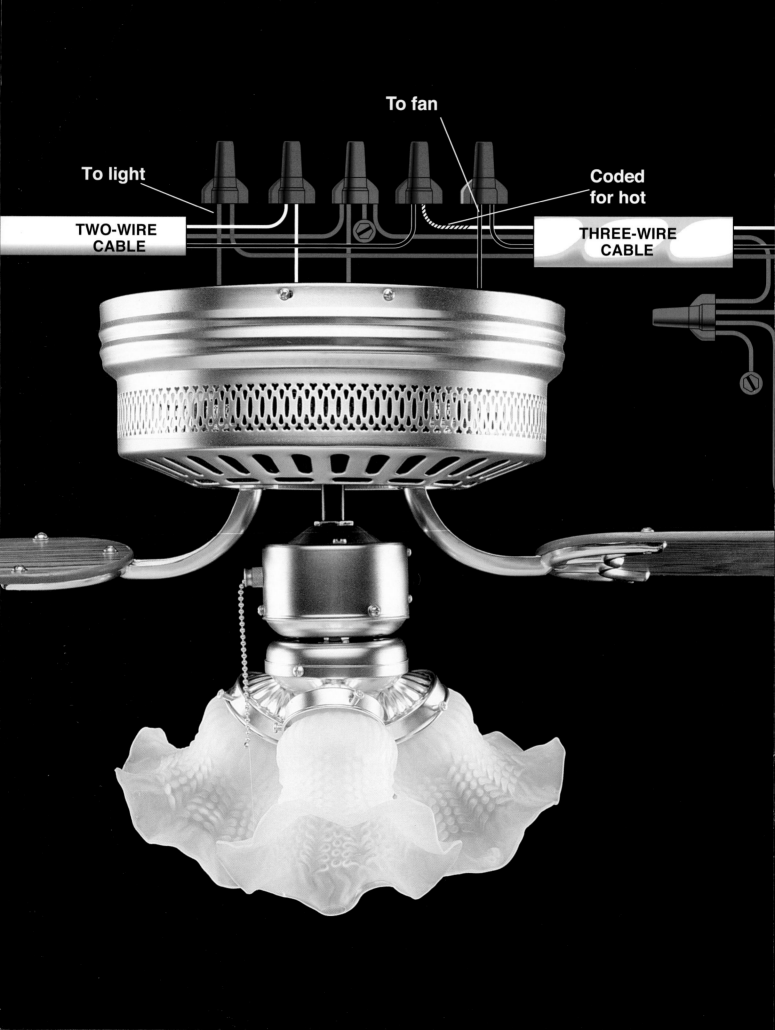

To fan

To light

Coded for hot

TWO-WIRE CABLE

THREE-WIRE CABLE

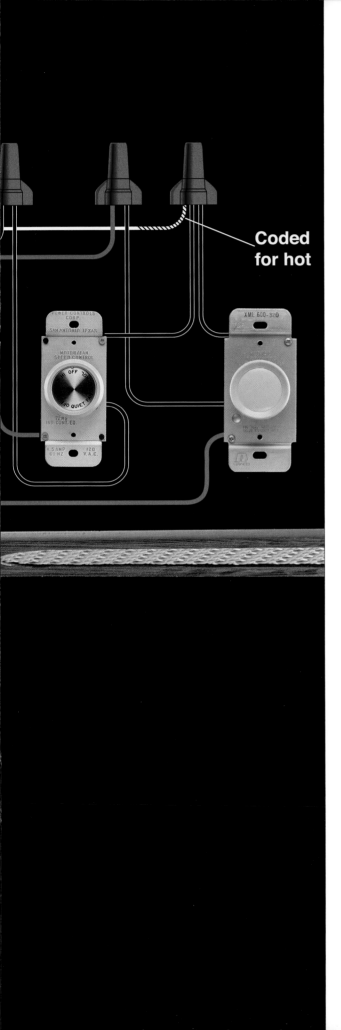

Coded
for hot

Circuit Maps

The arrangement of switches and appliances along an electrical circuit differs for every project. This means that the configuration of wires inside an electrical box can vary greatly, even when fixtures are identical.

The circuit maps on the following pages show the most common wiring variations for typical electrical devices. Most new wiring you install will match one or more of the maps shown. Find the maps that match your situation and use them to plan your circuit layouts.

The 120-volt circuits shown on the following pages are wired for 15 amps using 14-gauge wire and receptacles rated at 15 amps. If you are installing a 20-amp circuit, substitute 12-gauge cables and use receptacles rated for 20 amps.

In configurations where a white wire serves as a hot wire instead of a neutral, both ends of the wire are coded with black tape to identify it as hot. In addition, each of the circuit maps shows a box grounding screw. This grounding screw is required in all metal boxes, but plastic electrical boxes do not need to be grounded.

Note: For clarity, all grounding conductors in the circuit maps are colored green. In practice, the grounding wires inside sheathed cables usually are bare copper.

In this chapter:

- Common Household Circuits

Common Household Circuits

1. 120-VOLT DUPLEX RECEPTACLES WIRED IN SEQUENCE

Use this layout to link any number of duplex receptacles in a basic lighting/receptacle circuit. The last receptacle in the cable run is connected like the receptacle shown at the right side of the circuit map below. All other receptacles are wired like the receptacle shown on the left side. Requires two-wire cables.

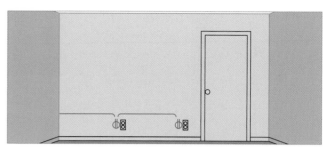

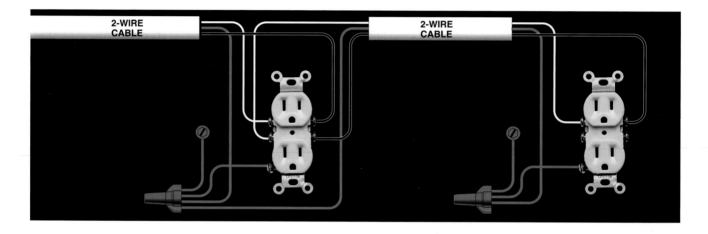

2. GFCI RECEPTACLES (SINGLE-LOCATION PROTECTION)

Use this layout when receptacles are within 6 ft. of a water source, like those in kitchens and bathrooms. To prevent nuisance tripping caused by normal power surges, GFCIs should be connected only at the line screw terminal so they protect a single location not the fixtures on the load side of the circuit. Requires two-wire cables. Where a GFCI must protect other fixtures, use circuit map 3.

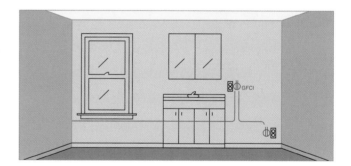

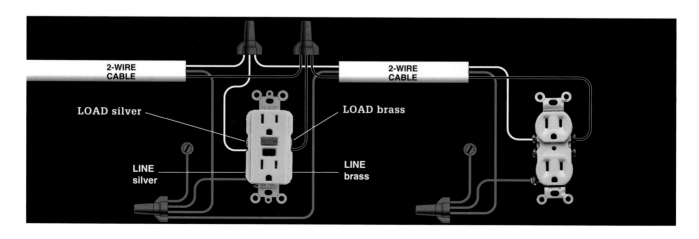

3. GFCI RECEPTACLE, SWITCH & LIGHT FIXTURE (WIRED FOR MULTIPLE-LOCATION PROTECTION)

In some locations, such as an outdoor circuit, it is a good idea to connect a GFCI receptacle so it also provides shock protection to the wires and fixtures that continue to the end of the circuit. Wires from the power source are connected to the line screw terminals; outgoing wires are connected to load screws. Requires two-wire cables.

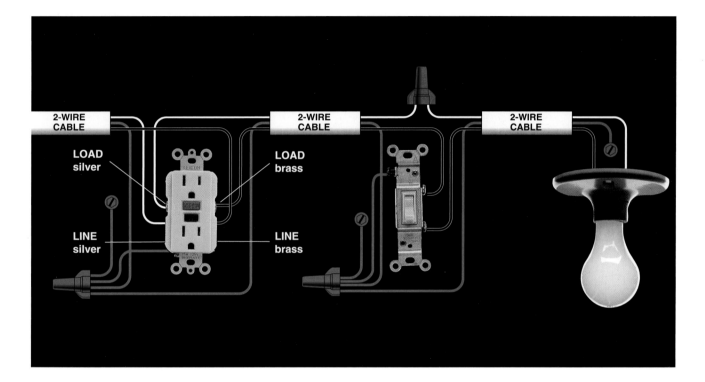

4. SINGLE-POLE SWITCH & LIGHT FIXTURE (LIGHT FIXTURE AT END OF CABLE RUN)

Use this layout for light fixtures in basic lighting/receptacle circuits throughout the home. It is often used as an extension to a series of receptacles (circuit map 1). Requires two-wire cables.

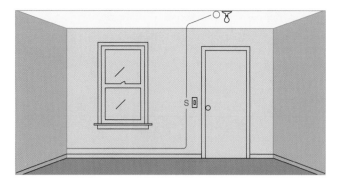

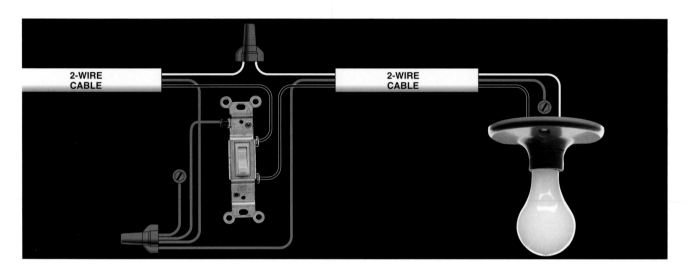

5. SINGLE-POLE SWITCH & LIGHT FIXTURE (SWITCH AT END OF CABLE RUN)

Use this layout, sometimes called a switch loop, where it is more practical to locate a switch at the end of the cable run. In the last length of cable, both insulated wires are hot; the white wire is tagged with black tape at both ends to indicate it is hot. Requires two-wire cables.

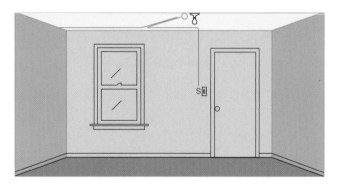

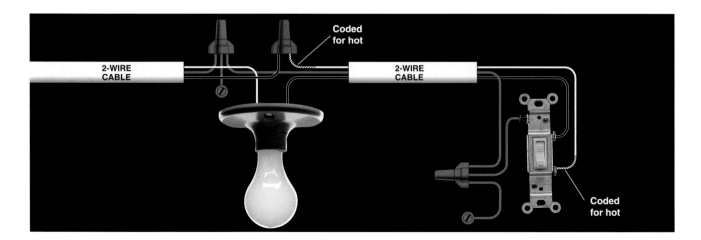

6. SINGLE-POLE SWITCH & TWO LIGHT FIXTURES (SWITCH BETWEEN LIGHT FIXTURES, LIGHT AT START OF CABLE RUN)

Use this layout when you need to control two fixtures from one single-pole switch and the switch is between the two lights in the cable run. Power feeds to one of the lights. Requires two-wire and three-wire cables.

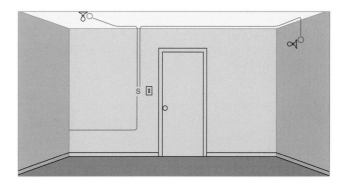

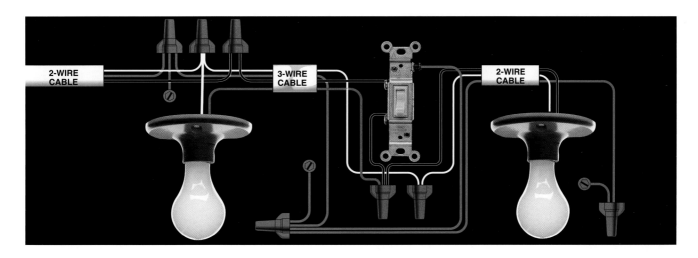

7. SINGLE-POLE SWITCH & LIGHT FIXTURE, DUPLEX RECEPTACLE (SWITCH AT START OF CABLE RUN)

Use this layout to continue a circuit past a switched light fixture to one or more duplex receptacles. To add multiple receptacles to the circuit, see circuit map 1. Requires two-wire and three-wire cables.

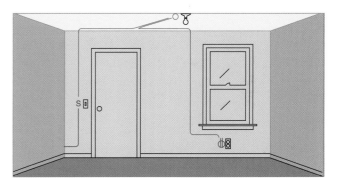

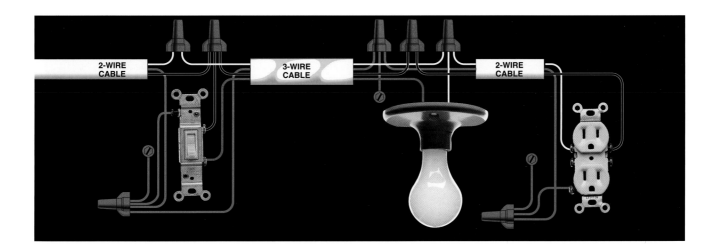

8. SWITCH-CONTROLLED SPLIT RECEPTACLE, DUPLEX RECEPTACLE (SWITCH AT START OF CABLE RUN)

This layout lets you use a wall switch to control a lamp plugged into a wall receptacle. This configuration is required by code for any room that does not have a switch-controlled ceiling fixture. Only the bottom half of the first receptacle is controlled by the wall switch; the top half of the receptacle and all additional receptacles on the circuit are always hot. Requires two-wire and three-wire cables.

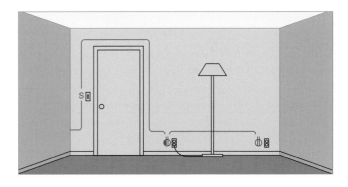

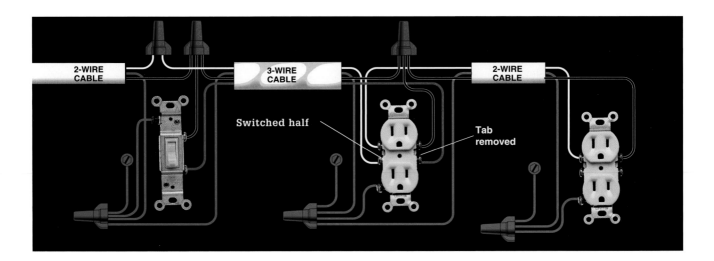

9. SWITCH-CONTROLLED SPLIT RECEPTACLE (SWITCH AT END OF CABLE RUN)

Use this switch loop layout to control a split receptacle (see circuit map 7) from an end-of-run circuit location. The bottom half of the receptacle is controlled by the wall switch, while the top half is always hot. White circuit wire attached to the switch is tagged with black tape to indicate it is hot. Requires two-wire cable.

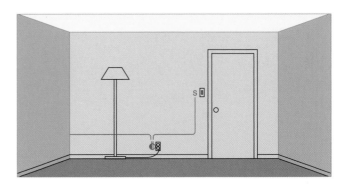

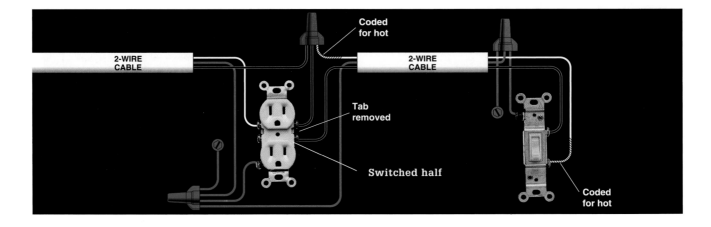

10. SWITCH-CONTROLLED SPLIT RECEPTACLE, DUPLEX RECEPTACLE (SPLIT RECEPTACLE AT START OF RUN)

Use this variation of circuit map 7 where it is more practical to locate a switch-controlled receptacle at the start of a cable run. Only the bottom half of the first receptacle is controlled by the wall switch; the top half of the receptacle, and all other receptacles on the circuit, are always hot. Requires two-wire cables.

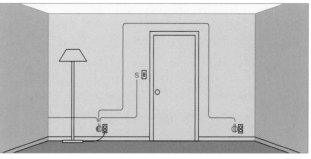

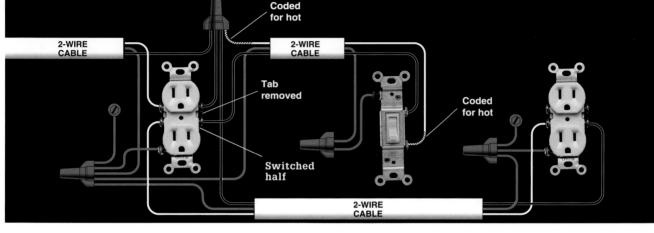

11. DOUBLE RECEPTACLE CIRCUIT WITH SHARED NEUTRAL WIRE (RECEPTACLES ALTERNATE CIRCUITS)

This layout features two 120-volt circuits wired with one three-wire cable connected to a double-pole circuit breaker. The black hot wire powers one circuit; the red wire powers the other. The white wire is a shared neutral that serves both circuits. When wired with 12/2 and 12/3 cable and receptacles rated for 20 amps, this layout can be used for the two small-appliance circuits required in a kitchen.

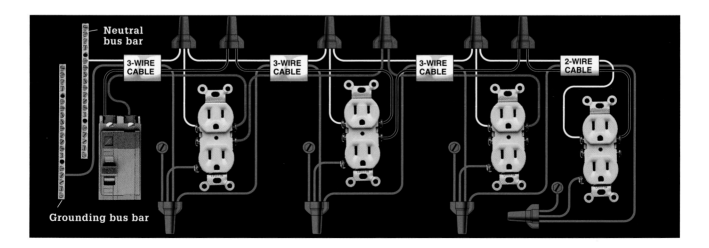

12. DOUBLE RECEPTACLE SMALL-APPLIANCE CIRCUIT WITH GFCIs & SHARED NEUTRAL WIRE

Use this layout variation of circuit map 10 to wire a double receptacle circuit when code requires that some of the receptacles be GFCIs. The GFCIs should be wired for single-location protection (see circuit map 2). Requires three-wire and two-wire cables.

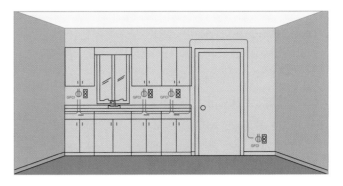

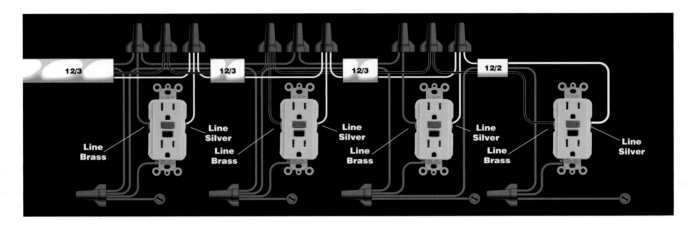

13. DOUBLE RECEPTACLE SMALL APPLIANCE CIRCUIT WITH GFCIs & SEPARATE NEUTRAL WIRES

If the room layout or local codes do not allow for a shared neutral wire, use this layout instead. The GFCIs should be wired for single-location protection (see circuit map 2). Requires two-wire cable.

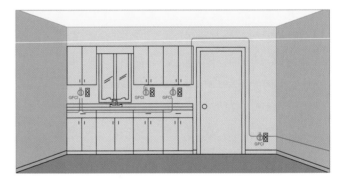

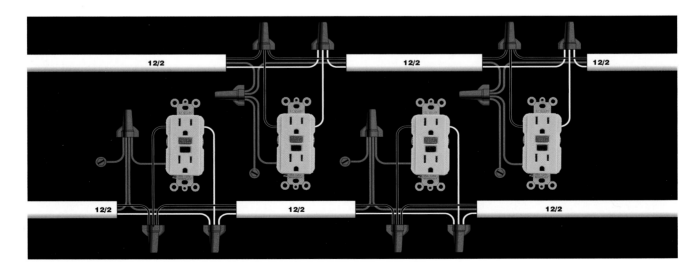

14. 120/240-VOLT RANGE RECEPTACLE

This layout is for a 50- or 60-amp, 120/240-volt dedicated appliance circuit wired with 6/3 cable, as required by code for a large kitchen range. The black and red circuit wires, connected to a double-pole circuit breaker in the circuit breaker panel, each bring 120 volts of power to the setscrew terminals on the receptacle. The white circuit wire attached to the neutral bus bar in the circuit breaker panel is connected to the neutral setscrew terminal on the receptacle.

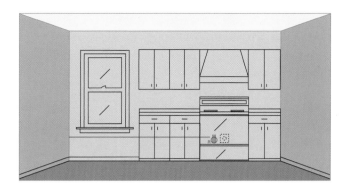

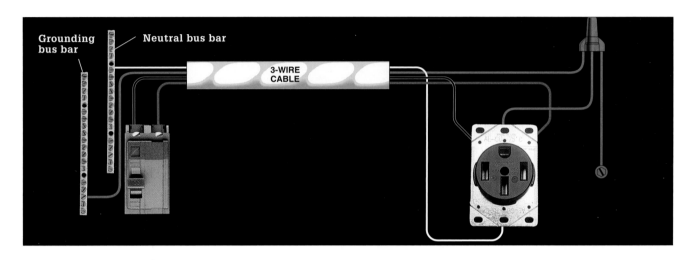

15. 240-VOLT BASEBOARD HEATERS, THERMOSTAT

This layout is typical for a series of 240-volt baseboard heaters controlled by a wall thermostat. Except for the last heater in the circuit, all heaters are wired as shown below. The last heater is connected to only one cable. The size of the circuit and cables are determined by finding the total wattage of all heaters. Requires two-wire cable.

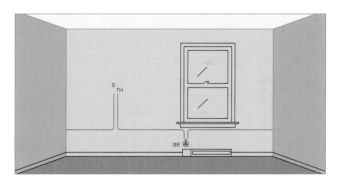

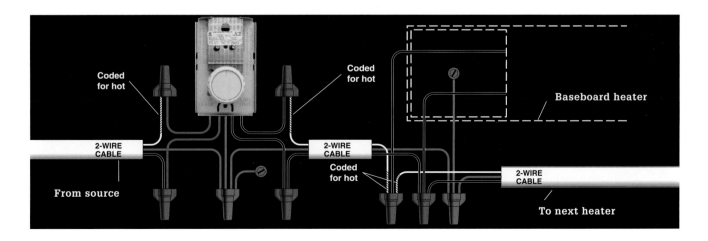

16. DEDICATED 120-VOLT COMPUTER CIRCUIT, ISOLATED-GROUND RECEPTACLE

This 15-amp isolated-ground circuit provides extra protection against surges and interference that can harm electronics. It uses 14/3 cable with the red wire serving as an extra grounding conductor. The red wire is tagged with green tape for identification. It is connected to the grounding screw on an isolated-ground receptacle and runs back to the grounding bus bar in the circuit breaker panel without touching any other house wiring.

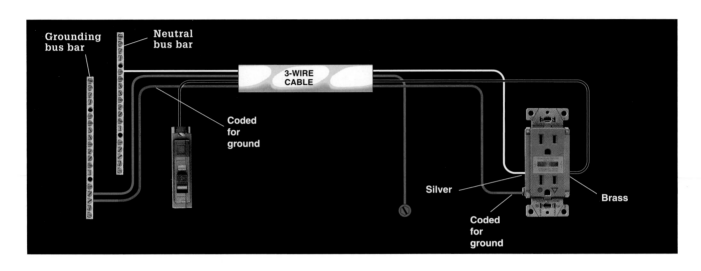

17. 240-VOLT APPLIANCE RECEPTACLE

This layout represents a 20-amp, 240-volt dedicated appliance circuit wired with 12/2 cable, as required by code for a large window air conditioner. Receptacles are available in both singleplex (shown) and duplex styles. The black and the white circuit wires connected to a double-pole breaker each bring 120 volts of power to the receptacle. The white wire is tagged with black tape to indicate it is hot.

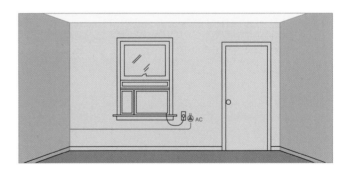

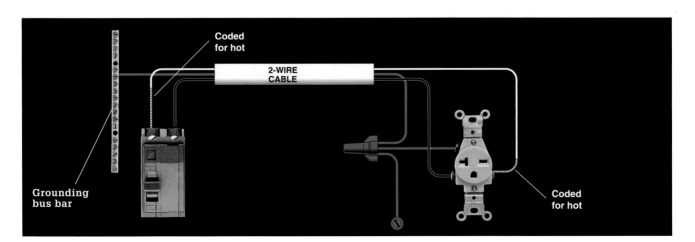

18. GANGED SINGLE-POLE SWITCHES CONTROLLING SEPARATE LIGHT FIXTURES

This layout lets you place two switches controlled by the same 120-volt circuit in one double-gang electrical box. A single feed cable provides power to both switches. A similar layout with two feed cables can be used to place switches from different circuits in the same box. Requires two-wire cable.

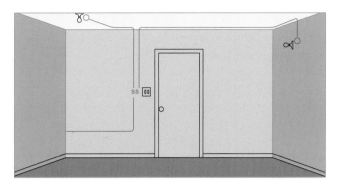

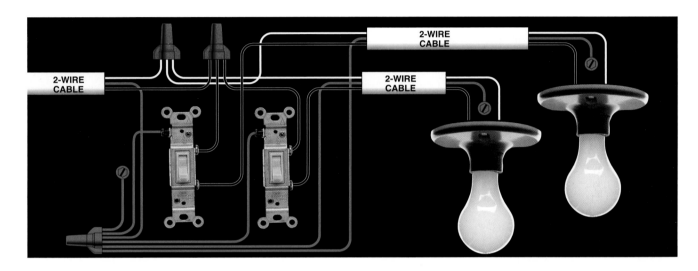

19. GANGED SWITCHES CONTROLLING A LIGHT FIXTURE AND A VENT FAN

This layout lets you place two switches controlled by the same 120-volt circuit in one double-gang electrical box. A single feed cable provides power to both switches. A standard switch controls the light fixture and a time-delay switch controls the vent fan.

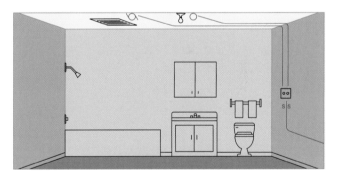

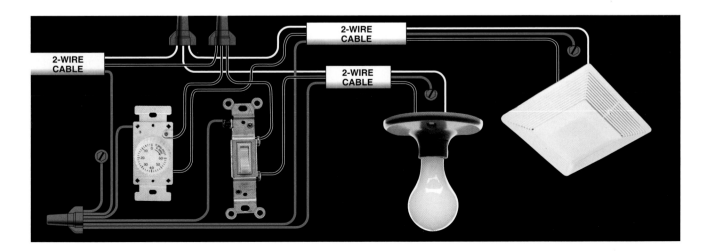

20. THREE-WAY SWITCHES & LIGHT FIXTURE (FIXTURE BETWEEN SWITCHES)

This layout for three-way switches lets you control a light fixture from two locations. Each switch has one common screw terminal and two traveler screws. Circuit wires attached to the traveler screws run between the two switches, and hot wires attached to the common screws bring current from the power source and carry it to the light fixture. Requires two-wire and three-wire cables.

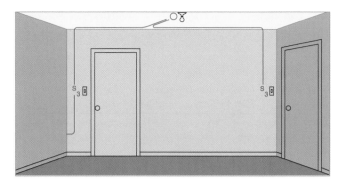

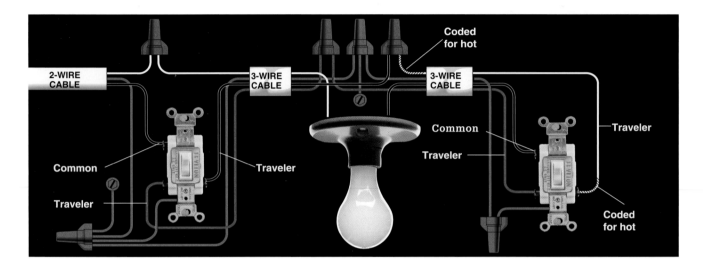

21. THREE-WAY SWITCHES & LIGHT FIXTURE (FIXTURE AT START OF CABLE RUN)

Use this layout variation of circuit map 19 where it is more convenient to locate the fixture ahead of the three-way switches in the cable run. Requires two-wire and three-wire cables.

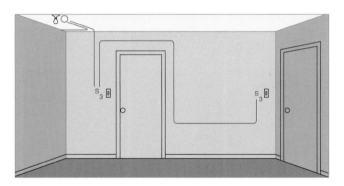

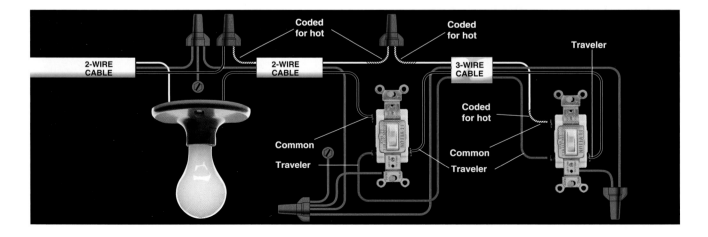

22. THREE-WAY SWITCHES & LIGHT FIXTURE (FIXTURE AT END OF CABLE RUN)

This variation of the three-way switch layout (circuit map 20) is used where it is more practical to locate the fixture at the end of the cable run. Requires two-wire and three-wire cables.

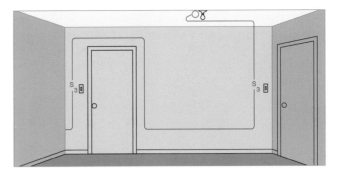

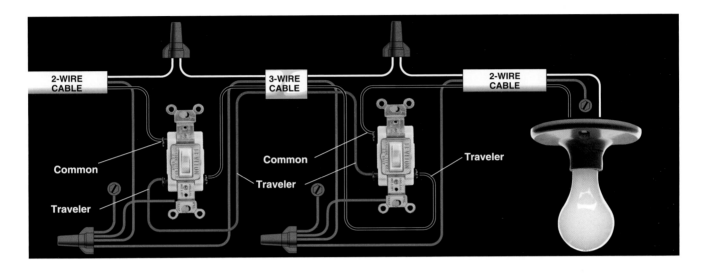

23. THREE-WAY SWITCHES & LIGHT FIXTURE WITH DUPLEX RECEPTACLE

Use this layout to add a receptacle to a three-way switch configuration (circuit map 21). Requires two-wire and three-wire cables.

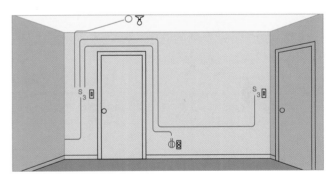

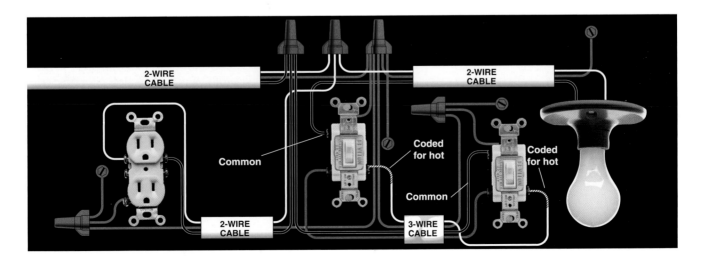

24. THREE-WAY SWITCHES & MULTIPLE LIGHT FIXTURES (FIXTURES BETWEEN SWITCHES)

This is a variation of circuit map 20. Use it to place multiple light fixtures between two three-way switches where power comes in at one of the switches. Requires two- and three-wire cable.

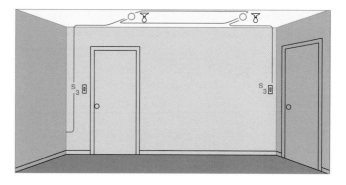

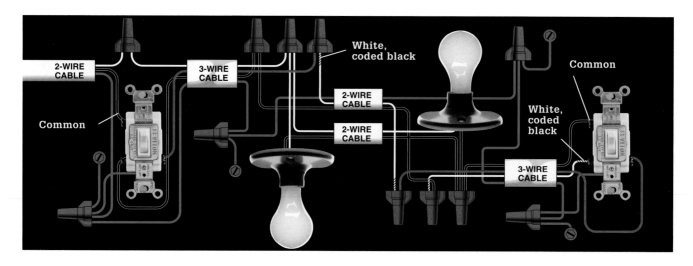

25. THREE-WAY SWITCHES & MULTIPLE LIGHT FIXTURES (FIXTURES AT BEGINNING OF RUN)

This is a variation of circuit map 21. Use it to place multiple light fixtures at the beginning of a run controlled by two three-way switches. Power comes in at the first fixture. Requires two- and three-wire cable.

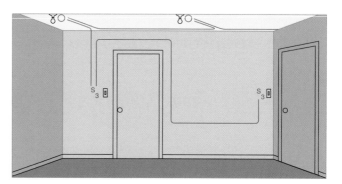

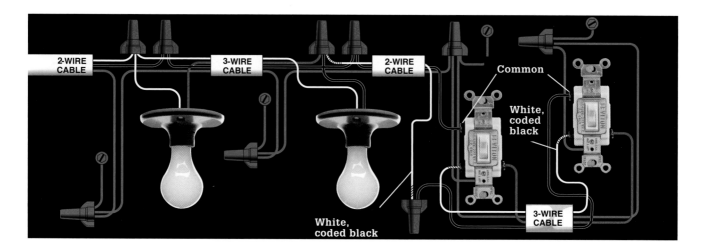

26. FOUR-WAY SWITCH & LIGHT FIXTURE (FIXTURE AT START OF CABLE RUN)

This layout lets you control a light fixture from three locations. The end switches are three-way and the middle is four-way. A pair of three-wire cables enter the box of the four-way switch. The white and red wires from one cable attach to the top pair of screw terminals (line 1) and the white and red wires from the other cable attaches to the bottom screw terminals (line 2). Requires two three-way switches and one four-way switch and two-wire and three-wire cables.

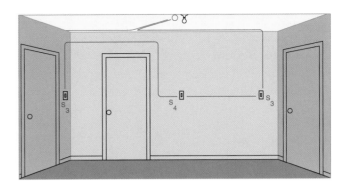

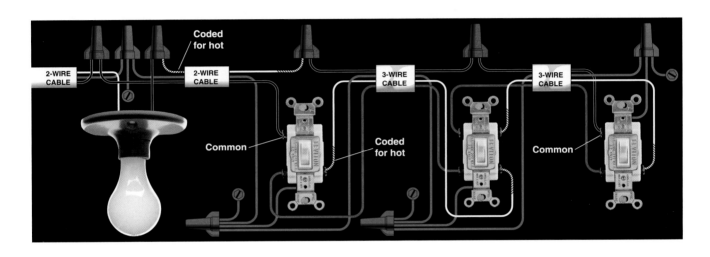

27. FOUR-WAY SWITCH & LIGHT FIXTURE (FIXTURE AT END OF CABLE RUN)

Use this layout variation of circuit map 26 where it is more practical to locate the fixture at the end of the cable run. Requires two three-way switches and one four-way switch and two-wire and three-wire cables.

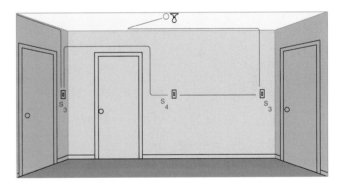

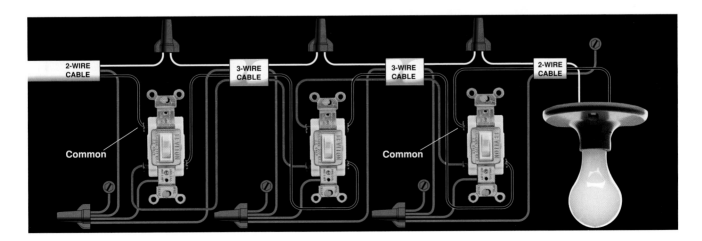

28. MULTIPLE FOUR-WAY SWITCHES CONTROLLING A LIGHT FIXTURE

This alternate variation of the four-way switch layout (circuit map 27) is used where three or more switches will control a single fixture. The outer switches are three-way and the middle are four-way. Requires two three-way switches and two four-way switches and two-wire and three-wire cables.

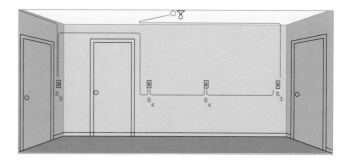

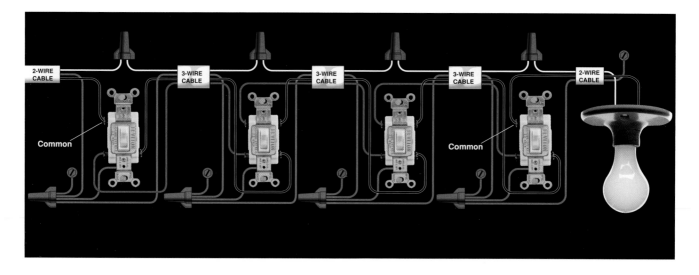

29. FOUR-WAY SWITCHES & MULTIPLE LIGHT FIXTURES

This variation of the four-way switch layout (circuit map 26) is used where two or more fixtures will be controlled from multiple locations in a room. Outer switches are three-way and the middle switch is a four-way. Requires two three-way switches and one four-way switch and two-wire and three-wire cables.

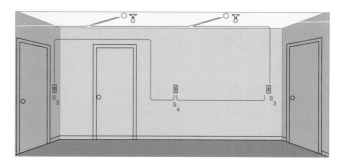

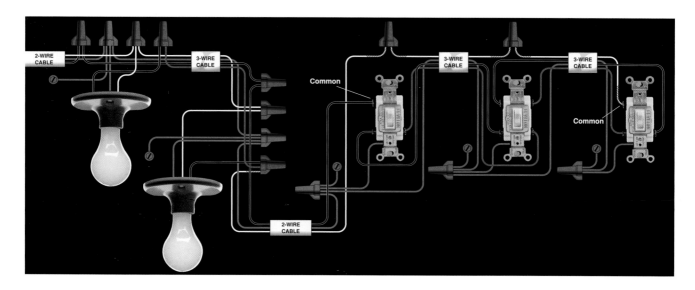

30. CEILING FAN/LIGHT FIXTURE CONTROLLED BY GANGED SWITCHES (FAN AT END OF CABLE RUN)

This layout is for a combination ceiling fan/light fixture controlled by a speed-control switch and dimmer in a double-gang switch box. Requires two-wire and three-wire cables.

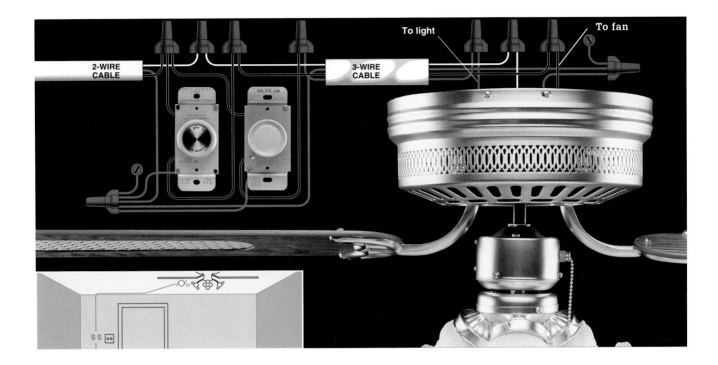

31. CEILING FAN/LIGHT FIXTURE CONTROLLED BY GANGED SWITCHES (SWITCHES AT END OF CABLE RUN)

Use this switch loop layout variation when it is more practical to install the ganged speed control and dimmer switches for the ceiling fan at the end of the cable run. Requires two-wire and three-wire cables.

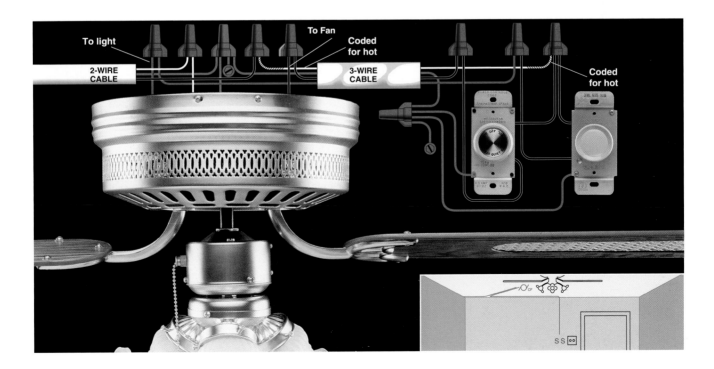

Common Wiring Projects

The instructions that follow show you how to accomplish the most popular home wiring projects. Refer to pertinent sections elsewhere in the book to find background information on tools and skills needed to get the job done.

In this chapter:
- GFCI & AFCI Breakers
- Whole-House Surge Arrestors
- Service Panels
- Subpanels
- 120/240-Volt Dryer Receptacles
- 120/240-Volt Range Receptacles
- Childproofing Your Home
- Ceiling Lights
- Recessed Ceiling Lights
- Track Lights
- Undercabinet Lights
- Vanity Lights
- Low-Voltage Cable Lights
- Hard-wired Smoke & CO Detectors
- Landscape Lights
- Doorbells
- Programmable Thermostats
- Wireless Switches
- Baseboard Heaters
- Wall Heaters
- Radiant Floor Mats
- Ceiling Fans
- Bathroom Vent Fans
- Range Hoods
- Backup Power Supply
- Wiring an Outbuilding
- Motion-Sensing Floodlights

GFCI & AFCI Breakers

ARC-FAULT CIRCUIT-INTERRUPTER BREAKERS

Installing an arc-fault circuit-interrupter (AFCI) breaker is an easy way to protect a circuit against a line-to-neutral electrical arc fault that, if uninterrupted, could cause a fire. AFCIs prevent electrical fires by sensing arcing and instantly disconnecting the damaged circuit before the arc builds enough heat to catch surrounding materials on fire.

The National Electric Code (NEC) requires that an arc-fault circuit-interrupter (AFCI) breaker be installed on all branch circuits that supply outlets or fixtures in bedrooms in newly constructed homes. They're a prudent precaution in any home, especially if it has older wiring. AFCI breakers will not interfere with the operation of GFCI receptacles, so it is safe to install an AFCI breaker on a circuit that contains GFCI receptacles.

GROUND-FAULT CIRCUIT-INTERRUPTER BREAKERS

A GFCI breaker is an important safety device that disconnects a circuit in the event of an overload, short circuit, or line-to-ground fault.

On new construction, GFCI protection is required on outlets located within a 6-ft. radius of laundry, utility, and kitchen or bathroom sinks, and in garages and unfinished basements. In general it is a good practice to protect all receptacle and fixture locations that could encounter damp or wet circumstances. Typically, a GFCI receptacle is installed at each location, but in some cases—outdoor circuits or older homes with boxes too shallow for GFCI receptacles, for instance—it is advisable to protect the entire circuit with a GFCI breaker.

Tools & Materials ›

Insulated screwdriver	Combination tool AFCI or
Circuit tester	GFCI breaker

AFCI breakers (right) are similar in appearance to GFCI breakers (left), but they function differently. AFCI breakers trip when they sense an arc fault between the hot and neutral wires. GFCI breakers trip when they sense circuit overloads, short circuits, or a fault between the hot wire and the ground.

How to Install an AFCI or GFCI Breaker

Locate the breaker for the circuit you'd like to protect. Then turn off the main circuit breaker. Remove the cover from the panel, and test to ensure that power is off (page 80). Remove the breaker you want to replace from the panel. Remove the black wire from the LOAD terminal of the breaker.

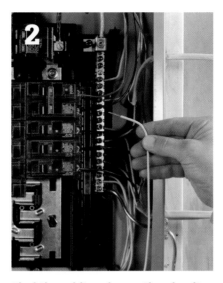

Find the white wire on the circuit you want to protect, and remove it from the neutral bus bar.

Flip the handle of the new AFCI or GFCI breaker to OFF. Loosen both of the breaker's terminal screws. Connect the white circuit wire to the breaker terminal labeled PANEL NEUTRAL. Connect the black circuit wire to the breaker terminal labeled LOAD POWER.

Connect the new breaker's coiled white wire to the neutral bus bar on the service panel.

Make sure all the connections are tight. Snap the new breaker into the bus bar.

Turn the main breaker on. Turn off and unplug all fixtures and appliances on the AFCI or GFCI breaker circuit. Turn the AFCI or GFCI breaker on. Press the test button. If the breaker is wired correctly, the breaker trips open. If it doesn't trip, check all connections or consult an electrician. Replace the panel cover.

Whole-House Surge Arrestors

Electrical surges caused by lighting or utility malfunctions can destroy or seriously damage sensitive electronics. Many homes contain tens of thousands of dollars worth of computers and home entertainment equipment protected by no more than a $10 plug-in surge suppressor. While these devices do afford a modest level of protection, they are no match for the voltage a lightning strike will push through a system. And they offer no protection for the wiring itself. Whole-house surge arrestors provide comprehensive protection for the wiring and devices attached to it.

Whole-house surge arrestors are available in two basic types. One type is wired on the utility side of the panel, normally at the meter. When installed by a licensed electrician, these devices provide the highest level of protection, shielding the panel and all electrical devices in the house. The other type wires directly into the panel and protects all circuits originating at that panel. Manufacturers offer units that are housed in separate boxes (these look like a small subpanel) as well as models that are designed to replace a double-pole breaker in the panel itself. These install like standard breakers. Both types provide protection for the whole house. Freestanding models are also available with separate protection for phone, data, and cable-television lines—a wise addition if you need to protect networked computers or cable-TV receivers.

Whatever style you choose, look for models with the Underwriters Laboratories 1449 rating and indicator lights showing that the system is protected. Most manufacturers also include a warranty against defect that covers a certain amount of property damage.

A whole-house surge arrestor is an inexpensive defense against expensive damage from high-voltage shocks caused by lightning strikes and power surges. Most models install next to the main panel.

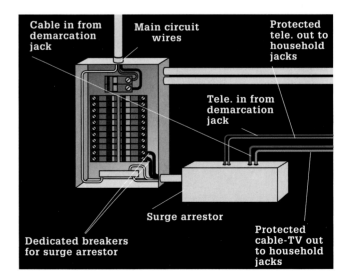

A surge arrestor installed at the panel protects all downstream connected devices and wires.

Tools & Materials ▸

Hammer	Conduit nipple
Combination tool	and locknuts
Screwdrivers	Two 15- or
Cable ripper	20-amp single-
Linesman's pliers	pole breakers
Circuit tester	Coaxial cable
Crimping tools	and terminators
Whole-house	UTP cable
surge arrestor	and terminators

How to Install a Whole-House Surge Arrestor

Turn off power at the main breaker. Remove the cover, and test to make sure the power is off. Mount the arrestor near the service panel following the manufacturer's instructions. Typically, the arrestor mounts on one side of the panel so its knockout lines up with a lower knockout on the panel. Remove the knockout on the panel. Install a conduit nipple on the arrestor, and thread the wires from the arrestor through the nipple and into the panel. Slip the other end of the nipple through the opening in the panel, and tighten the locknut. Secure the box to the wall with screws as directed.

Connect the two black wires to two dedicated 15- or 20-amp breakers. Trim the wires as short as possible without making sharp bends. Connect the white neutral wire to the neutral bar and green grounding wire to grounding bar. Keep wire lengths as short as possible. Snap the new breakers into the bus bar. Restore the power and carefully test that the voltage between the two black arrestor leads is 240 volts. Replace the panel cover and the arrestor cover. If the arrestor has indicator lights, they should glow, showing that the system is now protected.

LINE bar

EQUIPMENT bar

Variation: If the arrestor has separate protection for the telephone circuits, remove the cable that runs from the phone demarcation jack to the junction box. Then remove a knockout in the arrestor and route a new UTP cable from the demarcation jack to the arrestor. Strip insulation from the wires and connect them to the terminals on the LINE bar (labeled IN on some models) on the phone protection module in the arrestor. Run a UTP cable from the EQUIPMENT bar (labeled OUT on some models) to the junction box. Strip and connect the wires from this cable to the appropriate terminals in the arrestor and the junction box.

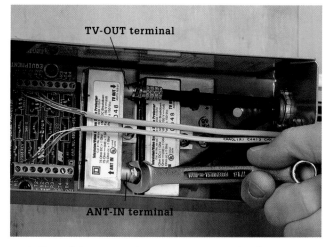

TV-OUT terminal

ANT-IN terminal

Variation: If the arrestor has separate protection for a cable television circuit, remove the appropriate knockout from the arrestor and run a coaxial cable to the arrestor from the cable-TV demarcation jack. Connect the coaxial cable to the ANT-IN terminal on the cable-TV protection module. Run another coaxial cable from the TV-OUT terminal to the cable TV junction box or the distribution panel. Do not overtighten the connections.

Service Panels

Only a generation ago, fuse boxes were commonplace. But as our demands for power increased, homeowners replaced the 60-amp boxes with larger, safer, and more reliable circuit breaker panels. Typical new homes were built with perfectly adequate 100-amp load centers. But today, as average home size has risen to more than 2,500 sg. ft. and the number of home electronics has risen exponentially, 100 amps is adequate service. As a result, many homeowners have upgraded to 200-amp service, and new single-family homes often include 250-amps or even 300-amps of power.

Upgrading your electrical service panel from 100 amps to 200 amps is an ambitious project that requires a lot of forethought. To do the job, you will need to have your utility company disconnect your house from electrical service at the transformer that feeds your house. Not only does this involve working them into your schedule, it means you will have no power during the project. You can rent a portable generator to provide a circuit or two, or you can run a couple extension cords from a friendly neighbor. But unless you are a very fast worker, plan on being without power for at least a day while the project is in process.

Also check with your utility company to make sure you know what equipment is theirs and what belongs to you. In most cases, the electric meter and everything on the street side belongs to the power company, and the meter base and everything on the house side is yours. Be aware that if you tamper with the sealed meter in any way, you likely will be fined.

Upgrading a service panel is a major project. Do not hesitate to call for help at any point if you're unsure what to do.

After

Before

Modern homeowners consume more power than our forebears, and it is often necessary to upgrade the electrical service to keep pace. While homeowners are not allowed to make the final electrical service connections, removing the old panel and installing the new panel and meter base yourself can save you hundreds or even thousands of dollars.

Tools & Materials ▸

200-amp load center (service panel)	Service entry cable
	Circuit wires
200-amp bypass meter base	Plywood backer board
	Screwdrivers
Circuit breakers	Drill/driver
Schedule 80 or IMC conduit and fittings	Tape
	Allen wrench
	Circuit tester
Weatherhead	Multimeter

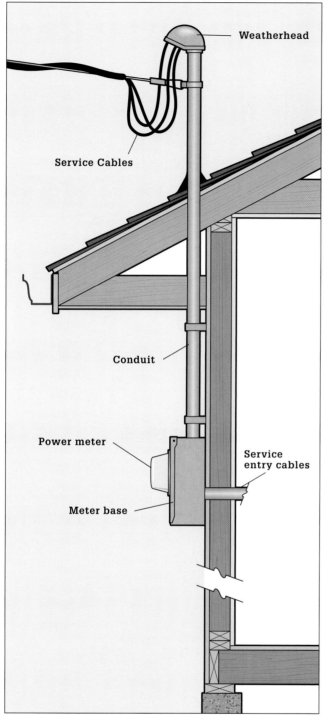

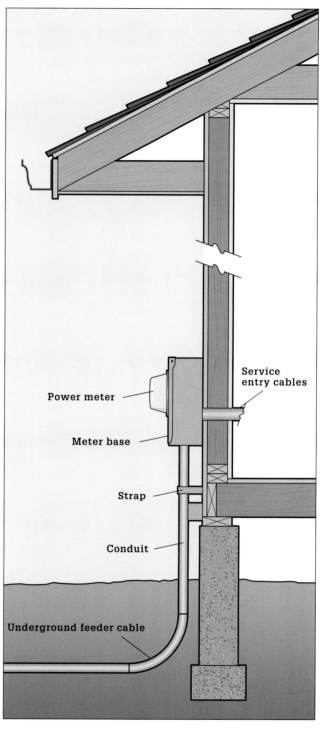

Aboveground meter with riser. In this common configuration, the power cables from the closest transformer (called the service drop) are connected to the power distribution system in your house inside a protective hood called a weatherhead. The service cables from the weatherhead are routed to a power meter that's owned by your utility company but is housed in a base that's considered your property. From the meter the cables (called service entry cables or SECs) enter your house through the wall and are routed to the main service panel, where they are connected to the main circuit breaker.

Underground service feeder. Increasingly, homebuilders are choosing to have power supplied to their new homes through underground feeder cable instead of an overhead service drop. Running the cables in the ground eliminates problems with power outages caused by ice accumulation or fallen trees, but it entails a completely different set of cable and conduit requirements. For the homeowner, however, the differences are minimal because the hookups are identical once the power service reaches the meter.

Locating Your New Panel ▸

Local codes dictate where the main service panel may be placed relative to other parts of your home. Although the codes may vary (and always take precedence), national codes stipulate that a service panel (or any other distribution panel) may not be located near flammable materials, in a bathroom, in an area with a ceiling height less than 78", or directly above a workbench or other permanent work station or appliance. The panel also can't be located in a crawl space or in a partial basement. The panel must be framed with at least 30" of clear space on all sides. If you are installing a new service entry hookup, there are many regulations regarding height of the service drop and the meter (the meter should always be located 66" above grade). Contact your local inspections office for specific regulations.

All the equipment you'll need to upgrade your main panel is sold at most larger building centers. It includes (A) a new 200-amp panel; (B) a 200-amp bypass meter base (also called a socket); (C) individual circuit breakers (if your new panel is the same brand as your old one you may be able to reuse the old breakers); (D) new, usually larger, SE cable (2/0 copper seen here); (E) 2" dia. rigid conduit; (F) weatherhead shroud for mast.

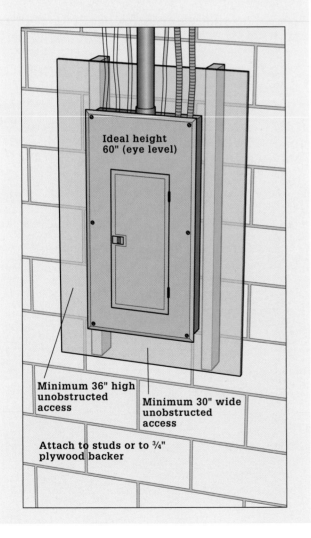

Ideal height 60" (eye level)

Minimum 36" high unobstructed access

Minimum 30" wide unobstructed access

Attach to studs or to ¾" plywood backer

Meter

Shutoff switch

A shutoff switch next to the electric meter is required if your main service panel is too far away from the point where the service cable enters your house. The maximum distance allowed varies widely, from as little as 3 ft. to more than 10 ft. Wiring the service cable through the shutoff has the effect of transforming your main service panel into a subpanel, which will impact how the neutral and ground wires are attached (see Subpanels, pages 184 to 187).

How to Replace a Main Service Panel

Shut off power to the house at the transformer. This must be done by a technician who is certified by your utility company. Also have the utility worker remove the old meter from the base. It is against the law for a homeowner to break the seal on the meter.

Label all incoming circuit wires before disconnecting them. Labels should be written clearly on tape that is attached to the cables outside of the existing service panel.

Disconnect incoming circuit wires from breakers, grounding bar, and neutral bus bar. Also disconnect cable clamps at the knockouts on the panel box. Retract all circuit wires from the service panel and coil up neatly, with the labels clearly visible.

Unscrew the lugs securing the service entry cables at the top of the panel. For 240-volt service you will find two heavy-gauge SE cables, probably with black sheathing. Each cable carries 120 volts of electricity. A neutral service cable, usually of lighter gauge than the SE cables, will be attached to the neutral bus bar. This cable returns current to the source.

(continued)

5

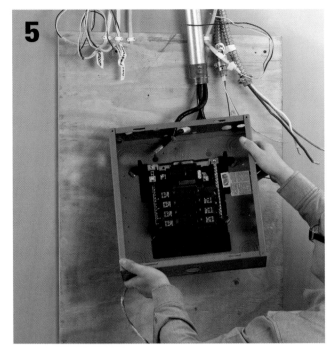

Remove the old service panel box. Boxes are rated for a range of power service; and if you are upgrading, the components in the old box will be undersized for the new service levels. The new box will have a greater number of circuit slots as well.

6

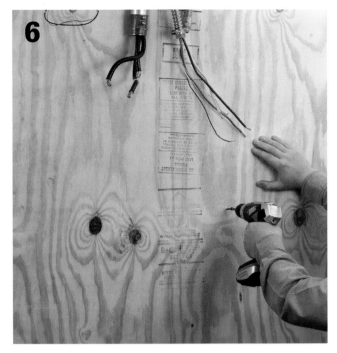

Replace the old panel backer board with a larger board in the installation area (see sidebar, page 178). A piece of ¾" plywood is typical. Make sure the board is well secured at wall framing members.

7

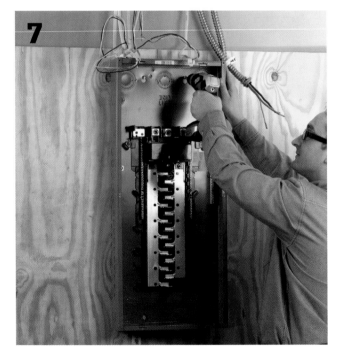

Attach the new service panel box to the backer board, making sure that at least two screws are driven through the backer and into wall studs. Drill clearance holes in the back of the box at stud locations if necessary. Use roundhead screws that do not have tapered shanks so the screwhead seats flat against the panel.

8

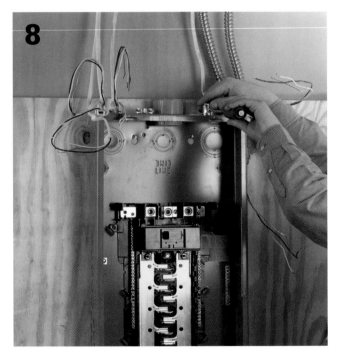

Attach properly sized cable clamps to the box at the knockout holes. Do not crowd multiple lines into a knockout hole, and plan carefully to avoid removing knockouts that you do not need to remove (if you do make a mistake, you can fill the knockout hole with a plug).

Tip ▶

Some wiring codes allow you to make splices inside the service panel box if the circuit wire is too short. Use the correct wire cap and wind electrical tape over the conductors where they enter the cap. If your municipality does not allow splices in the panel box, you'll have to rectify a short cable by splicing it in a junction box before it reaches the panel, and then replacing the cable with a longer section for the end of the run. Make sure each circuit line has at least 12" of slack.

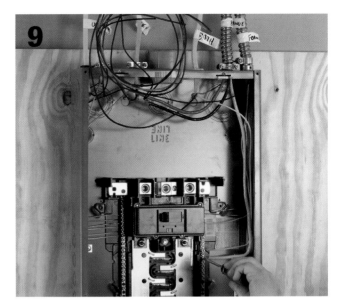

Attach the white neutral from each circuit cable to the neutral bus bar. Most panels have a preinstalled neutral bus bar, but in some cases you may need to purchase the bar separately and attach it to the panel back. The panel should also have a separate grounding bar that you also may need to purchase separately. Attach the grounds as well (it's generally allowed to twist bare ground wires together and attach them to a single screw terminal). Do not attach neutrals and grounding wires to the same bar.

Attach the hot lead wire to the terminal on the circuit breaker and then snap the breaker into an empty slot. When loading slots, start at the top of the panel and work your way downward. It is important that you balance the circuits as you go to equalize the amperage. For example, do not install all the 15 amp circuits on one side and all the 20 amp circuits on the other. Also, if you have multiple larger-capacity circuits, such as a 50-amp dryer and a 50-amp range, do not install them on the same side of the panel in case they will be drawing electricity at the same time.

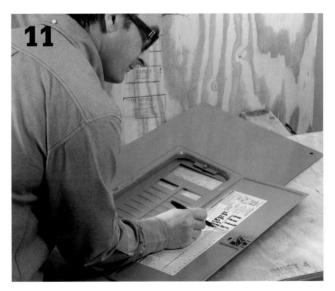

Create an accurate circuit index and affix it to the inside of the service panel door. List all loads that are on the circuit as well as the amperage. Once you have restored power to the new service panel (see step 18), test out each circuit to make sure you don't have any surprises. With the main breakers on, shut off all individual circuit breakers and then flip each one on by itself. Walk through your house and test every switch and receptacle to confirm the loads on that circuit.

(continued)

12

Install grounding conductors. Local codes are very specific about how the grounding needs to be accomplished. For example, some require multiple rods driven at least 6 ft. apart. Discuss your grounding requirements thoroughly with your inspector or an electrician before making your plan.

13

Replace the old meter base (have the utility company remove the meter when they shut off power to the house, step 1). Remove the old meter base, also called a socket, and install a new base that's rated for the amperage of your new power service. Here, a 200-amp bypass meter base is being installed.

14

Update the conduit that runs from your house to the bottom of the meter base. This should be 2" rigid conduit in good repair. Attach the conduit to the base and wall with the correct fittings.

15

Install new service entry wires. Each wire carries 120 volts of current from the meter to the service wire lugs at the top of your service panel. Code is very specific about how these connections are made. In most cases, you'll need to tighten the terminal nuts with a specific amount of torque that requires a torque wrench to measure. Also attach the sheathed neutral wire to the neutral/grounding lug.

16

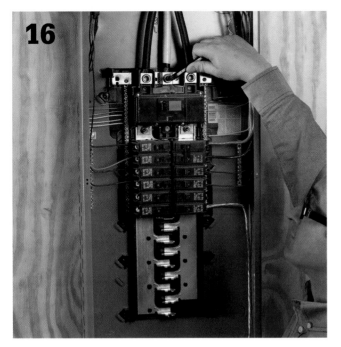

Attach the SE wires to the lugs connected to the main breakers at the top of your service entry panel. Do not remove too much insulation on the wires—leaving the wires exposed is a safety hazard. The neutral service entry wire is attached either directly to the neutral bus bar or to a metal bridge that is connected to the neutral bonding bus bar.

17

Install service entry wires from the meter to the weatherhead, where the connections to the power source are made. Only an agent for your public utility company may make the hookup at the weatherhead.

Tip ▸

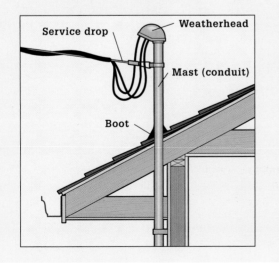

The service drop must occur at least 10 ft. above ground level, and as much as 14 ft. in some cases. Occasionally, this means that you must run the conduit for the service mast up through the eave of your roof and seal the roof penetration with a boot.

18

Have the panel and all connections inspected and approved by your local building department, and then contact the public utility company to make the connections at the power drop. Once the connections are made, turn the main breakers on and test all circuits.

Subpanels

Install a circuit breaker subpanel if the main circuit breaker panel does not have enough open breaker slots for the new circuits you are planning. Called non-service rated panels in most code books, the subpanel serves as a second distribution center for connecting circuits. It receives power from a double-pole feeder circuit breaker you install in the main circuit breaker panel.

If the main service panel is so full that there is no room for the double-pole subpanel feeder breaker, you can reconnect some of the existing 120-volt circuits to special slimline breakers (photos below).

Plan your subpanel installation carefully, making sure your electrical service supplies enough power to support the extra load of the new subpanel circuits. Assuming your main service is adequate, consider installing an oversized subpanel feeder breaker in the main panel to provide enough extra amps to meet the needs of future wiring projects.

Also consider the physical size of the subpanel, and choose one that has enough extra slots to hold circuits you may want to install later. The smallest panels have room for up to six single-pole breakers

(or three double-pole breakers), while the largest models can hold up to 20 single-pole breakers.

Subpanels often are mounted near the main circuit breaker panel. Or, for convenience, they can be installed close to the areas they serve, such as in a new room addition or a garage. In a finished room, a subpanel can be painted or housed in a decorative cabinet so it is less of a visual distraction. If it is covered, make sure the subpanel is easily accessible and clearly identified.

Tools & Materials ▸

Hammer	Cable clamps
Screwdriver	Three-wire NM cable
Circuit tester	Cable staples
Cable ripper	Double-pole circuit breaker
Combination tool	Circuit breaker subpanel
Screws	Slimline circuit breakers

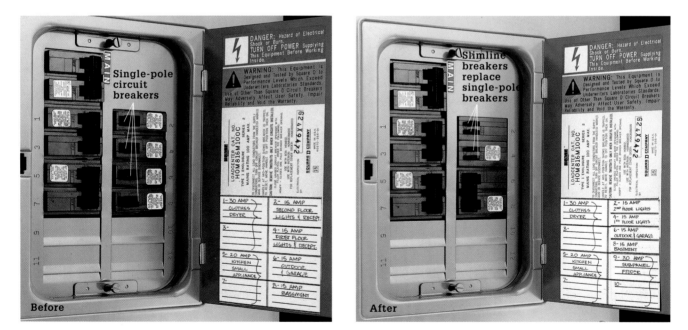

To conserve space in a service panel, you can replace single-pole breakers with slimline breakers. Slimline breakers take up half the space of standard breakers, allowing you to fit two circuits into one single slot on the service panel. In the service panel shown above, four single-pole 120-volt breakers were replaced with slimline breakers to provide the double opening needed for a 30-amp, 240-volt subpanel feeder breaker. Use slimline breakers with the same amp rating as the standard single-pole breakers you are removing, and make sure they are approved for use in your panel.

How to Plan a Subpanel Installation

1. Find the gross electrical load for only those areas that will be served by the subpanel. Refer to Evaluate Electrical Loads (pages 136 to 137). Example: In the 400-sq.-ft. attic room addition shown on pages 144 to 147, the gross load required for the basic lighting/receptacle circuits and electric heating is 5,000 watts.	Gross electrical load:	_5,000_ watts
2. Multiply the gross electrical load times 1.25. This safety adjustment is required by the National Electrical Code. Example: In the attic room addition (gross load 5,000 watts), the adjusted load equals 6,250 watts.	_5,000_ watts × 1.25 =	_6,250_ watts
3. Convert the load into amps by dividing by 230. This gives the required amperage needed to power the subpanel. Example: The attic room addition described above requires about 27 amps of power (6,250 ÷ 230).	_6,250_ watts ÷ 230 =	_27.2_ amps
4. For the subpanel feeder breaker, choose a double-pole circuit breaker with an amp rating equal to or greater than the required subpanel amperage. Example: In a room addition that requires 27 amps, choose a 30-amp double-pole feeder breaker.	[X] 30-amp breaker [ ] 40-amp breaker [ ] 50-amp breaker	
5. For the feeder cable bringing power from the main circuit breaker panel to the subpanel, choose three-wire NM cable with an ampacity equal to the rating of the subpanel feeder breaker. Example: For a 40-amp subpanel feeder breaker, choose 8/3 cable for the feeder.	[ ] 10/3 cable [X] 8/3 cable [ ] 6/3 cable	

How to Install a Subpanel

Mount the subpanel at shoulder height following manufacturer's recommendations. The subpanel can be mounted to the sides of studs or to plywood attached between two studs. Panel shown here extends ½" past the face of studs so it will be flush with the finished wall surface.

Open a knockout in the subpanel using a screwdriver and hammer. Run the feeder cable from the main circuit breaker panel to the subpanel, leaving about 2 ft. of excess cable at each end. See page 40 if you need to run the cable through finished walls.

Attach a cable clamp to the knockout in the subpanel. Insert the cable into the subpanel, then anchor it to framing members within 8" of each panel, and every 4 ft. thereafter.

(continued)

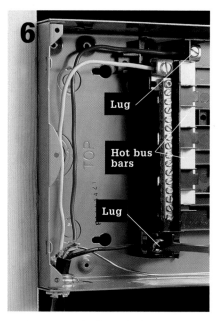

Strip away outer sheathing from the feeder cable using a cable ripper. Leave at least ¼" of sheathing extending into the subpanel. Tighten the cable clamp screws so cable is held securely, but not so tightly that the wire sheathing is crushed.

Strip ½" of insulation from the white neutral feeder wire, and attach it to the main lug on the subpanel neutral bus bar. Connect the grounding wire to a setscrew terminal on the grounding bus bar. Fold excess wire around the inside edge of the subpanel.

Strip away ½" of insulation from the red and the black feeder wires. Attach one wire to the main lug on each of the hot bus bars. Fold excess wire around the inside edge of the subpanel.

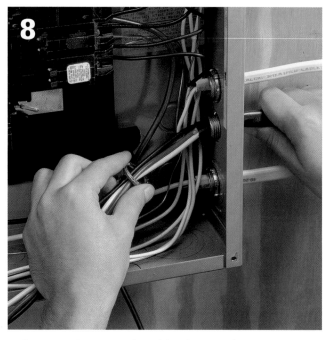

At the main circuit breaker panel, shut off the main circuit breaker, then remove the coverplate and test for power (page 80). If necessary, make room for the double-pole feeder breaker by removing single-pole breakers and reconnecting the wires to slimline circuit breakers. Open a knockout for the feeder cable using a hammer and screwdriver.

Strip away the outer sheathing from the feeder cable so that at least ¼" of sheathing will reach into the main service panel. Attach a cable clamp to the cable, then insert the cable into the knockout, and anchor it by threading a locknut onto the clamp. Tighten the locknut by driving a screwdriver against the lugs. Tighten the clamp screws so the cable is held securely, but not so tightly that the cable sheathing is crushed.

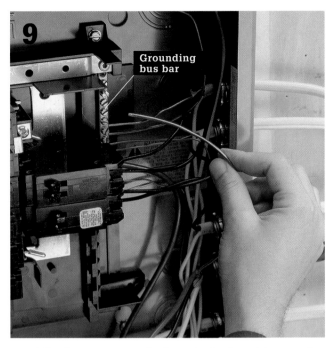

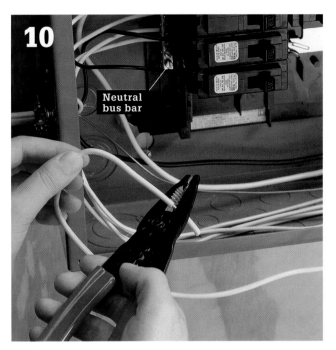

Bend the bare copper wire from the feeder cable around the inside edge of the main circuit breaker panel, and connect it to one of the setscrew terminals on the grounding bus bar.

Strip away ½" of insulation from the white feeder wire. Attach the wire to one of the setscrew terminals on the neutral bus bar. Fold excess wire around the inside edge of the service panel.

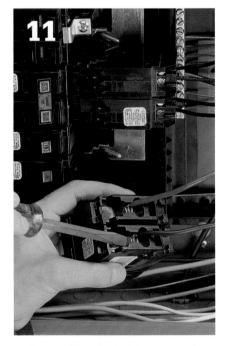

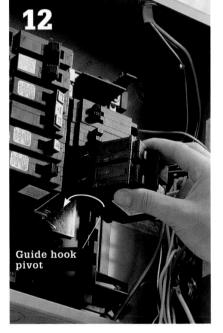

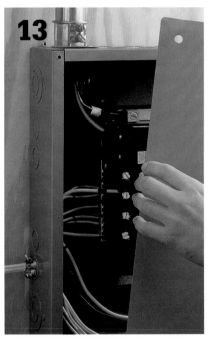

Strip ½" of insulation from the red and the black feeder wires. Attach one wire to each of the setscrew terminals on the double-pole feeder breaker.

Hook the end of the feeder circuit breaker over the guide hooks on the panel, then push the other end forward until the breaker snaps onto the hot bus bars (follow manufacturer's directions). Fold excess wire around the inside edge of the circuit breaker panel.

If necessary, open two knockouts where the double-pole feeder breaker will fit, then reattach the cover plate. Label the feeder breaker on the circuit index. Turn main breaker on, but leave feeder breaker off until all subpanel circuits have been connected and inspected.

120/240-Volt Dryer Receptacles

Many dryers require both 120- and 240-volt power. If you are installing this type of electric dryer, you will need to install a 30-amp, 120/240-volt receptacle that feeds from a dedicated 30-amp double-pole breaker in your service panel. Verify your dryer's electric requirements before wiring a new receptacle.

Begin the installation by identifying a location for the dryer receptacle. Run 10/3 NM cable from the service panel to the new receptacle. If you are mounting the dryer receptacle box on an unfinished masonry wall, run the cable in conduit and secure the box and conduit with masonry screws. If you are mounting the receptacle box in finished drywall, cut a hole, fish the cable through, and mount the receptacle in the wall opening.

Tools & Materials ▸

Combination tool
Drill
Circuit tester
Hammer
Screwdriver
30-amp double-pole breaker

30-amp 120/240-volt dryer receptacle
10/3 NM cable or 10-gauge THHN/THWN
Receptacle box
Conduit (for masonry walls)

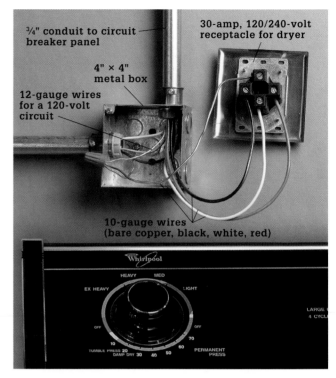

A 240-volt installation is no more complicated than wiring a single-pole breaker and outlet. The main difference is that the dryer circuit's double-pole breaker is designed to contact both 120-volt bus bars in the service panel. Together, these two 120-volt circuits serve the dryer's heating elements with 240 volts of power. The timer, switches, and other dryer electronics utilize the circuit's 120-volt power.

How to Install a 120/240-Volt Dryer Receptacle

1

Connect the white neutral wire to the silver neutral screw terminal. Connect each of the black and the red wires to either of the brass screw terminals (the terminals are interchangeable). Connect the bare copper ground wire to the receptacle grounding screw. Attach the cover plate.

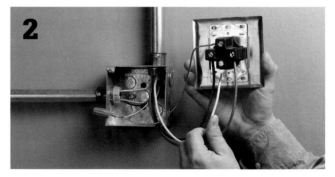

2

With the service panel main breaker shut off, connect the dryer cable to a dedicated 30-amp double-pole breaker. Connect the ground wire to the panel grounding bar. Connect the white neutral wire to the neutral bar. Connect the red and the black wires to the two brass screw terminals on the breaker. Snap the breaker into the bus bar. Attach the panel cover. Turn the breakers on and test the circuit.

120/240-Volt Range Receptacles

Many electric ranges require both 120- and 240-volt power. If you are installing this type of electric range, you will need to install a 50- or 60-amp 120/240-volt receptacle that feeds from a dedicated 50- or 60-amp breaker in the service panel. Breaker amperage depends on the amount of power the range draws. Verify requirements before wiring a receptacle.

A range receptacle and breaker installation is no more complicated than wiring a single-pole breaker and outlet. The main difference is that the range circuit's double-pole breaker is designed to contact both 120-volt bus bars in the service panel. Together these two 120-volt circuits serve the range's heating elements with 240 volts of power. The timer, switches, and other range electronics utilize the circuit's 120-volt power.

Modern range receptacles accept a four-prong plug configuration. The cable required is four-conductor service entrance round (SER) cable, containing three insulated wires and one ground. The two hot wires might be black and red (shown below) or black and black with a red stripe. The neutral wire is generally white or gray. The grounding wire is green or bare. The size used for a kitchen range is usually 6/3 grounded SER copper cable. The receptacle itself is generally surface mounted for easier installation (shown below), though flush-mounted units are also available.

Tools & Materials ▸

Combination tool	Surface-mounted
Circuit tester	range receptacle
Drill	6/3 grounded
Hammer	SER cable
Screwdriver	50- or 60-amp
Drywall saw	double-pole
Fish tape	circuit breaker

How to Install a Kitchen Range Receptacle

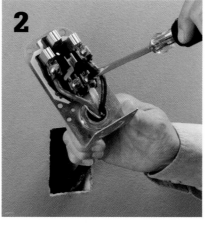

Turn power off. Identify a location for the surface-mounted range receptacle. Cut a small hole in the wall. Fish the SER cable from the service panel into the wall opening. Thread the cable into a surface-mounted receptacle and clamp it. Strip insulation from the individual wires.

Wire the receptacle. Connect the bare copper ground wire to the receptacle grounding screw. Connect the white neutral wire to the silver neutral screw terminal. Connect each of the hot (black and red) wires to either of the brass screw terminals (the terminals are interchangeable). Mount the housing on the wall and attach the cover plate.

Wire the SER cable to a 50- or 60-amp breaker. With the main breaker off, remove the panel cover. Remove a knockout from the panel and feed the cable into the panel. Connect the ground to the grounding bar. Connect the neutral wire from the cable to the neutral bar. Connect the red and the black wires to the two brass screw terminals on the breaker. Snap it into the bus bar. Attach the panel cover. Turn the breakers on and test the circuit.

Childproofing Your Home

Thousands of children are shocked every year when they insert foreign objects in receptacles. Plug-in safety caps are an effective solution, but they make receptacles less convenient. Installing a tamper-resistant receptacle is an easy variation of replacing a bad receptacle. And there are some other simple solutions that will allow you to childproof receptacles in just a few minutes. For more information on receptacle product used in childproofing, see page 107.

Function & Safety ▸

An extension handle for a toggle-style light switch lets small children turn on lights themselves in the event of an emergency.

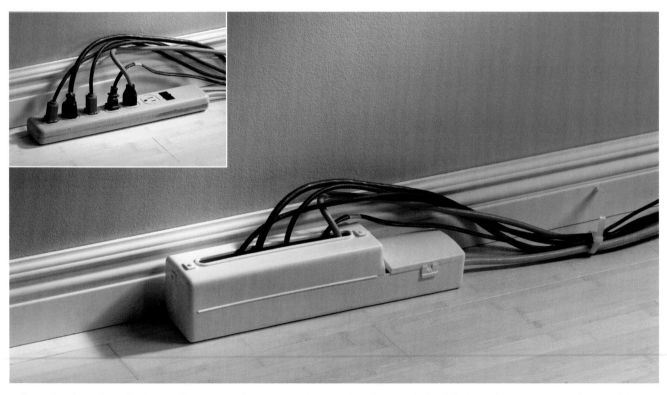

A few simple safety devices will make your home a much safer place for your kids while boosting your peace of mind. This device (see resources, page 347) clamps over a power strip to prevent busy hands from playing with the plugs.

How to Install Safety Receptacle Cover Plates

You can get much of the protection of a tamperproof outlet with a safety cover plate. Adding one takes only minutes and requires no contact with wiring. Remove the old cover plate from the receptacle by unscrewing the screw that holds the plate to the electrical box.

Hold the safety cover plate over the receptacle. Use a small screwdriver to tighten the screws.

To plug a device in, push the slider aside and insert the plug. The shutters automatically snap over the slots when nothing is plugged in.

How to Install a Plug Cover

Plug covers are designed to replace cover plates on receptacles where devices are plugged in more or less permanently to prevent children from unplugging them. After removing the old cover plate, hold the plug cover's base plate over the receptacle and screw it in with a small screwdriver.

Plug in your lamp or other device, and snap the plug cover into the new base plate. Cords should fit through the slots in the plug cover.

How to Install a Tamper-Resistant Receptacle

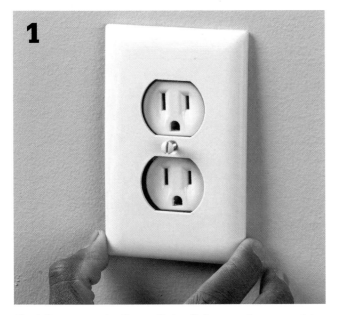

1

Shut the power to the switch off. Remove the cover plate from the receptacle by unscrewing the screw that holds the plate to the electrical box. Set the screw and the plate aside.

2

Use a voltage sensor to double-check that the circuit is dead. Hold your voltage sensor's probe within ½" of the wires on either side of the receptacle. If the sensor beeps or lights up, then the receptacle is still live, and you'll need to trip the correct breaker to disconnect power to the receptacle. If the sensor does not beep or light up, the receptacle is dead and you can proceed safely.

3

Remove the old receptacle from the box by unscrewing the two long screws that hold the receptacle to the box, one at the top and another at the bottom. Once the screws are out, gently pull the receptacle away from the box. Depending on how your receptacle has been wired, there may be two colored wires and a bare wire or four colored wires and a bare wire.

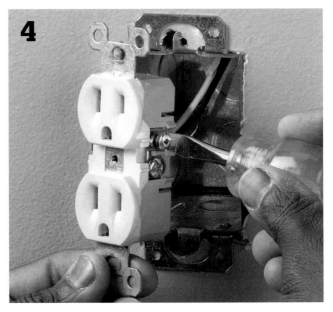

4

Remove the receptacle completely by unscrewing the screws that hold the wires. Disconnect each wire by turning the screws on the sides of the receptacle just enough to free the wires.

5

Tamper-resistant receptacle

6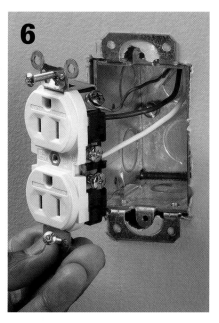

7

Shutters

If you have more than 8" of wire in the box, snip off wire ends and prepare cut ends for connectors. Attach the black wire to the brass (gold) screw terminal on the tamper-resistant receptacle.

Now take one of the white wires and wrap the end of the wire around one of the silver screws. Tighten the screw so it's snug. Do the same for the second white wire, if there is one. Connect the copper wire to the green-colored screw on the receptacle.

Once the connections are made, gently tuck the wires and the receptacle into the box so the holes at top and bottom of the receptacle align with the holes in the box. Use a screwdriver to drive the two long mounting screws that hold the receptacle to the box. Replace the cover plate. Restore the power and test the tamper-resistant receptacle.

Safety Tip ▸

Any receptacle is made safer by installing it upside down with the rounded grounding slot at the top. Three-prong receptacles are almost always installed with the round third prong facing down, but some experts recommend wiring receptacles with the third prong on top. This is because the third prong is the grounding prong and doesn't carry any current under normal operation. In theory, if something were to fall on a partially inserted plug, it would hit the harmless grounding prong and not the current-carrying slot prongs. Either way, you're wiring it right, but upside down may be slightly safer.

Ceiling Lights

Ceiling fixtures don't have any moving parts and their wiring is very simple, so, other than changing bulbs, you're likely to get decades of trouble-free service from a fixture. This sounds like a good thing, but it also means that the fixture probably won't fail and give you an excuse to update a room's look with a new one. Fortunately, you don't need an excuse. Upgrading a fixture is easy and can make a dramatic impact on a room. You can substantially increase the light in a room by replacing a globe-style fixture by one with separate spot lights, or you can simply install a new fixture that matches the room's décor.

Tools & Materials ▸

Replacement light fixture
Wire stripper
Voltage sensor
Insulated screwdrivers
Wire connectors

Installing a new ceiling fixture can provide more light to a space, not to mention an aesthetic lift. It's one of the easiest upgrades you can do.

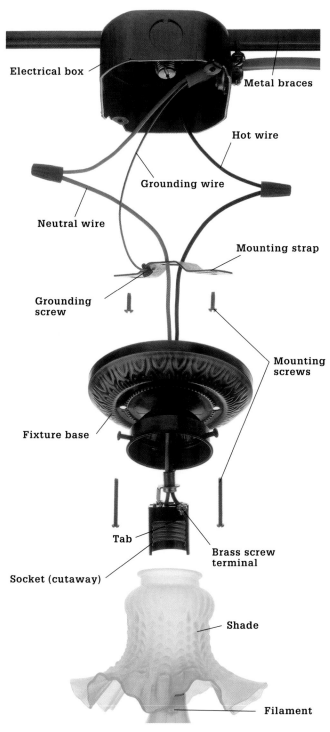

Electrical box

Metal braces

Hot wire

Grounding wire

Neutral wire

Mounting strap

Grounding screw

Mounting screws

Fixture base

Tab

Brass screw terminal

Socket (cutaway)

Shade

Filament

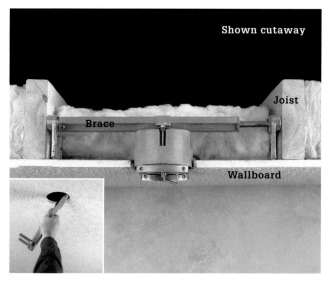

Shown cutaway

Joist

Brace

Wallboard

If the new fixture is much heavier than the original fixture, it will require additional bracing in the ceiling to support the electrical box and the fixture. The manufacturer's instructions should specify the size and type of box. If the ceiling is finished and there is no access from above, you can remove the old box and use an adjustable remodeling brace appropriate for your fixture (shown). The brace fits into a small hole in the ceiling (inset). Once the bracing is in place, install a new electrical box specified for the new fixture.

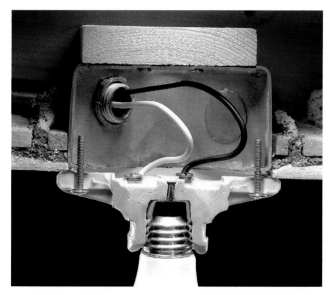

No matter what a ceiling light fixture looks like on the outside, they all attach in basically the same way. An electrical box in the ceiling is fitted with a mounting strap, which holds the fixture in place. The bare wire from the ceiling typically connects to the mounting strap. The two wires coming from the fixture connect to the black and the white wires from the ceiling.

Inexpensive light fixtures have screw terminals mounted directly to the backside of the fixture plate. Often, as seen here, they have no grounding terminal. Some codes do not allow this type of fixture, but even if your hometown does approve them, it is a good idea to replace them with a better quality, safer fixture that is UL-approved.

How to Replace a Ceiling Light

Shut off power to the ceiling light and remove the shade or diffuser. Loosen the mounting screws and carefully lower the fixture, supporting it as you work (do not let light fixtures hang by their electrical wires alone). Test with a voltage sensor to make sure no power is reaching the connections.

Remove the twist connectors from the fixture wires or unscrew the screw terminals and remove the white neutral wire and the black lead wire (inset).

Before you install the new fixture, check the ends of the wires coming from the ceiling electrical box. They should be clean and free of nicks or scorch marks. If they're dirty or worn, clip off the stripped portion with your combination tool. Then strip away about ¾" of insulation from the end of each wire.

Attach a mounting strap to the ceiling fixture box if there is not one already present. Your new light may come equipped with a strap, otherwise you can find one for purchase at any hardware store.

5

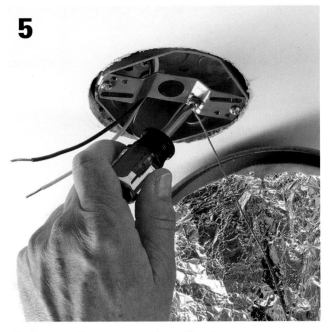

Lift the new fixture up to the ceiling (you may want a helper for this) and attach the bare copper ground wire from the power supply cable to the grounding screw or clip on the mounting strap. Also attach the ground wire from the fixture to the screw or clip.

6

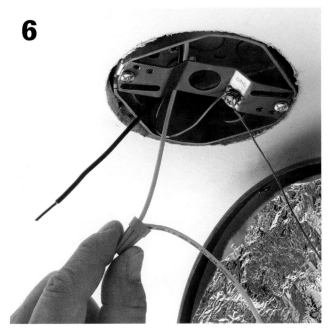

With the fixture supported by a ladder or a helper, join the white wire lead and the white fixture wire with a wire connector (often supplied with the fixture).

7

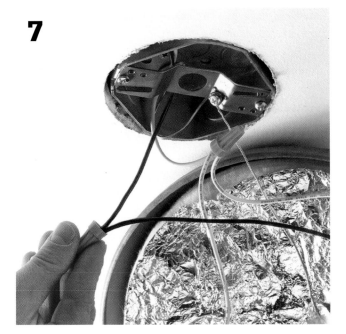

Connect the black power supply wire to the black fixture wire with a wire connector.

8

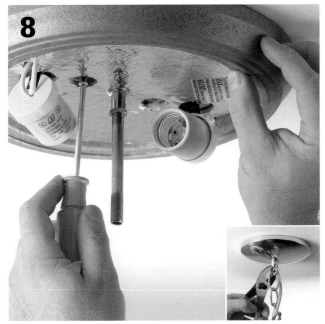

Position the new fixture mounting plate over the box so the mounting screw holes align. Drive the screws until the fixture is secure against the ceiling. *Note: Some fixtures are supported by a threaded rod or nipple in the center that screws into a female threaded opening in the mounting strap (inset).*

Recessed Ceiling Lights

Recessed lights are versatile fixtures suited for a variety of situations. Fixtures rated for outdoor use can also be installed in roof soffits and overhangs for accent and security lighting. Recessed fixtures can also be installed over showers or tubs. Be sure to use fixture cans and trims rated for bathroom use.

There are recessed lighting cans in all shapes and sizes for almost every type of ceiling or cabinet. Cans are sold for unfinished ceilings (new construction) or for finished ceilings (retrofit installation). Cans are also rated as insulation compatible or for uninsulated ceilings. Be sure to use the correct one for your ceiling to prevent creating a fire hazard.

Choose the proper type of recessed light fixture for your project. There are two types of fixtures: those rated for installation within insulation (left), and those which must be kept at least 3" from insulation (right). Self-contained thermal switches shut off power if the unit gets too hot for its rating. A recessed light fixture must be installed at least ½" from combustible materials.

Tools & Materials ▶

Recessed-lighting can for new construction or remodeling and trim	Circuit tester Cable ripper Combination tool	Pliers Fish tape	Drywall saw NM cable

Recessed ceiling lights often are installed in series to provide exacting control over the amount and direction of light. Spacing the canisters in every other ceiling joist bay is a common practice.

Recessed Materials

Recessed ceiling light housings come in many sizes and styles for various purposes and budgets. Some are sold with trim kits (below) included. Some common types are: new construction recessed housing (sold in economical multipacks) (A); airtight recessed housings (for heated rooms below unheated ceilings) (B); shallow recessed housings (for rooms with 2 × 6" ceiling joists) (C); small aperture recessed housing (D); recessed slope ceiling housing (for vaulted ceilings) (E).

Trim kits for recessed ceiling lights may be sold separately. Common types include: recessed open trim (E); baffle trim (C); recessed open trim with baffle (A, F); recessed eyeball trim (B); showerlight trim (D); airtight recessed trim (E).

How to Install Recessed Ceiling Lights

Mark the location for the light canister. If you are installing multiple lights, measure out from the wall at the start and end of the run, and connect them with a chalkline snapped parallel to the wall. If the ceiling is finished with a surface (wallboard), see next page.

Install the housing for the recessed fixture. Housings for new construction (or remodeling installations where the installation area is fully accessible from either above or below) have integral hanger bars that you attach to the each joist in the joist bay.

Run electric cable from the switch to each canister location. Multiple lights are generally installed in series so there is no need to make pigtail connections in the individual boxes. Make sure to leave enough extra cable at each location to feed the wire into the housing and make the connection.

Run the feeder cables into the electrical boxes attached to the canister housings. You'll need to remove knockouts first and make sure to secure the cable with a wire staple within 8" of the entry point to the box.

Connect the feeder wires to the fixture wires inside the junction box. Twist the hot lead together with the black fixture wire, as well as the black lead to other fixtures further downline. Also connect the neutral white wires. Join the ground wires and pigtail them to the grounding screw or clip in the box. Finish the ceiling, as desired.

Attach your trim kit of choice. Normally, these are hung with torsion spring clips from notches or hooks inside the canister. This should be done after the ceiling is installed and finished for new construction projects. With certain types of trim kits, such as eyeball trim, you'll need to install the light bulb before the trim kit.

How to Connect a Recessed Fixture Can in a Finished Ceiling

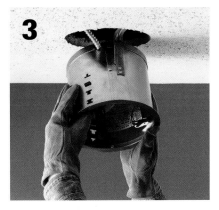

Make the hole for the can. Most fixtures will include a template for sizing the hole. Fish 14/2 cable from the switch location to the hole. Pull about 16" of cable out of the hole for making the connection.

Remove a knockout from the electrical box attached to the can. Thread the cable into the box; secure it with a cable clamp. Remove sheathing insulation. Connect the black fixture wire to the black circuit wire, the white fixture wire to the white circuit wire, and then connect the ground wire to the grounding screw or grounding wire attached to the box.

Retrofit cans secure themselves in the hole with spring-loaded clips. Install the can in the ceiling by depressing the mounting clips so the can will fit into the hole. Insert the can so that its edge is tight to the ceiling. Push the mounting clips back out so they grip the drywall and hold the fixture in place. Install the trim piece.

Track Lights

Track lighting offers a beautiful and functional way to increase the amount of light in a room or simply to update its look. A variety of fixture and lamp options lets you control the shape, color, and intensity of the light. Installing track lighting in place of an existing ceiling-mounted light fixture involves basic wiring and hand-tool skills, but the connections are even easier to make than with traditional light fixtures. Once installed, the system is very easy to upgrade or expand in the future.

Tools & Materials ▸

Drill/driver and bits
Wire stripper
Screwdriver
Voltage sensor
Toggle bolts

Prewired track
   and fittings
Track light heads
Wire connector
Ceiling box

If you currently have a ceiling-mounted light fixture that is not meeting your lighting needs, it's simple to replace it with a track-lighting fixture. With track lighting you can easily change the type and number of lights, their position on the track, and the direction they aim. These fixtures come in many different styles, including short 3-ft. track systems with just one or two lights up to 12-ft. systems with five or more lights.

How to Install Track Lighting

1

Disconnect the old ceiling light fixture (for remodeling projects) after shutting off power to the circuit at the main service panel. The globe or diffuser and the lamps should be removed before the fixture mounting mechanism is detached.

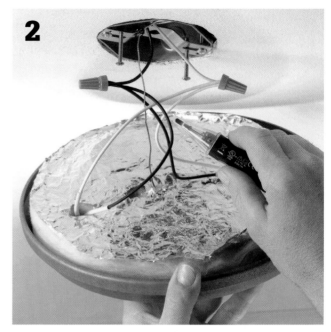

2

Test the fixture wires with a voltage sensor to make sure the circuit is dead. Support the fixture from below while you work—never allow a light fixture to hang by its electrical wires alone. Remove the wire connectors and pull the wires apart. Remove the old light fixture.

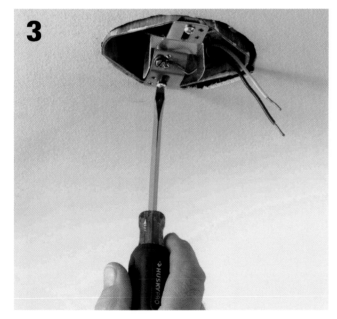

3

Attach the mounting strap for the new track light to the old ceiling box. If the mounting strap has a hole in the center, thread the circuit wires through the hole before screwing the strap to the box. The green or bare copper ground from the circuit should be attached to the grounding screw or clip on the strap or box.

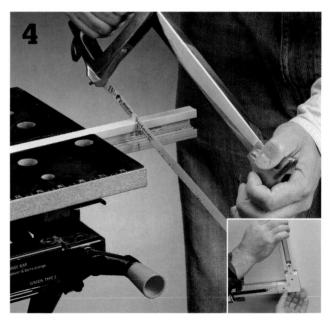

4

Cut the track section to length, if necessary, using a hack saw. Deburr the cut end with a metal file. If you are installing multiple sections of track, assemble the sections with the correct connector fittings (sold separately from your kit). You can also purchase T-fittings or L-fittings (inset photo) if you wish to install tracks in either of these configurations.

(continued)

5

Position the track section in the mounting saddle on the mounting strap and hold it temporarily in place in the location where it will be installed. The track section will have predrilled mounting holes in the back. Draw a marking point on the ceiling at each of these locations. If your track does not have predrilled mounting holes, remove it and drill a ³⁄₁₆" hole in the back every 16".

6

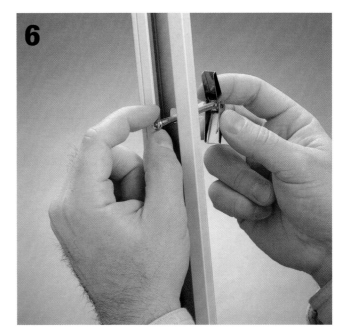

Insert the bolt from a toggle bolt or molly bolt into each predrilled screw location and twist the toggle or molly back onto the free end. These types of hardware have greater holding power than anchor sleeves. Drill a ⅝" dia. access hole in the ceiling at each of the mounting hole locations you marked on the ceiling in step 5.

7

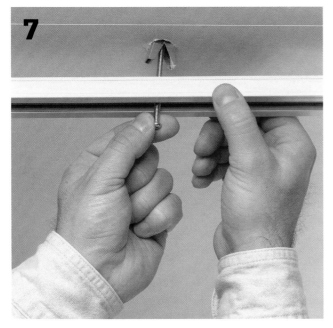

Insert the toggle or molly into the access hole far enough so it clears the top of the hole and the wings snap outward. Then tighten each bolt so the track is snug against the ceiling. If the mounting hole happens to fall over a ceiling joint, simply drive a wallboard screw at that hole location.

8

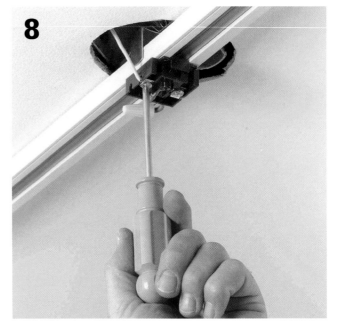

Hook up wires from the track's power supply fitting to the circuit wires. Connect black to black and white to white. The grounding wire from the power supply fitting can either be pigtailed to the circuit ground wire and connected to the grounding screw or clip, or it can be twisted together with the circuit grounding wire at the grounding terminal. Snap the fitting into the track if you have not already done so.

9

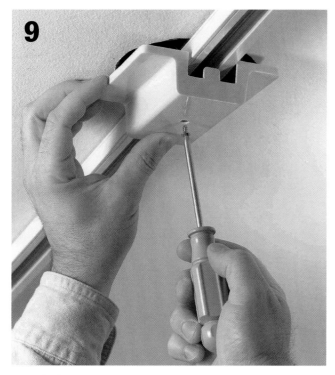

Attach the protective cover that came with your kit to conceal the ceiling box and the electrical connections. Some covers simply snap in place, others require a mounting screw.

10

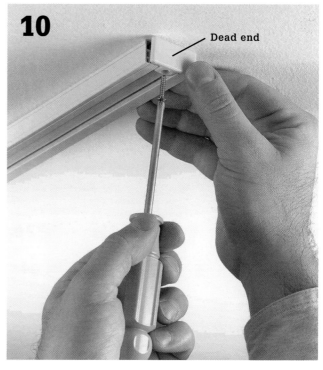

Dead end

Cap the open ends of the track with a dead end cap fitting. These also may require a mounting screw. Leaving track ends open is a safety violation.

11

Insert the light heads into the track by slipping the stem into the track slot and then twisting it so the electrical contact points on the head press against the electrified inner rails of the track slot. Tug lightly on the head to make sure it is secure before releasing it.

12

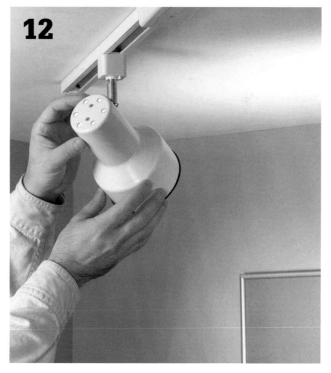

Arrange the track light heads so their light falls in the manner you choose, and then depress the locking tab on each fixture to secure it in position. Restore power and test the lights.

Undercabinet Lights

Hardwired undercabinet lights illuminate the kitchen countertop and sink areas that fall in the shadow of ceiling lights. Most of these light fixtures, which are often called strip lights, utilize fluorescent, halogen, or xenon bulbs that emit very low levels of heat and are therefore very efficient.

If you are doing a kitchen remodel with all-new cabinets, run the new light circuit wiring before the cabinets are installed. For a retrofit, you'll need to find an available power source to tie into. Options for this do not include the dedicated 20-amp small-appliance circuits that are required in kitchens. The best bet is to run new circuit wire from a close-by ceiling light switch box, but this will mean cutting into the walls to run cable. Another option is to locate a receptacle that's on the opposite side of a shared wall, preferably next to a location where a base cabinet is installed in the kitchen. By cutting an access hole in the cabinet back you can tie into the receptacle box and run cable through the wall behind the cabinets, up to the upper cabinet location, and out the wall to supply the fixture that's mounted to the underside of the upper cabinet.

You can purchase undercabinet lights that are controlled by a wall switch, but most products have an integral on/off button so you can control lights individually.

Tools & Materials ▸

Circuit tester	Wire stripper
Utility knife	Undercabinet
Wallboard saw	lighting kit
Hammer	14/2 NM cable
Screwdriver	Wire connectors
Drill and hole saw	Switch box
Jigsaw	Switch

Undercabinet lights provide directed task lighting that bring sinks and countertop work surfaces out from the shadows. Hardwired lights may be controlled either by a wall switch or an onboard on/off switch located on the fixture. *Note: Do not supply power for lights from small-appliance circuit.*

How to Install a Hardwired Undercabinet Light

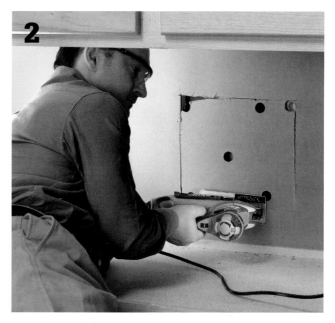

Look in the adjoining room for a usable power source in the form of a receptacle that has a box located in the wall behind your base cabinets. Unlike the small-appliance circuit with outlets in your backsplash area, these typically are not dedicated circuits (which can't be expanded). Make sure that the receptacle's circuit has enough capacity to support another load. Shut the power to the receptacle off at the main service panel and test for power.

Cut a hole in the base cabinet back panel to get access to the wall behind it in roughly the area where you know the next-door receptacle to be. Use a keyhole saw or drywall saw and make very shallow cuts until you have positively identified the locations of the electrical box and cables. Then finish the cuts with a jigsaw.

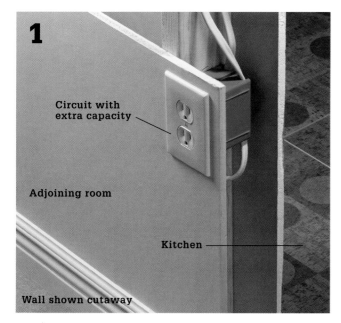

Drill an access hole into the kitchen wall for the cable that will feed the undercabinet light. A ½" dia. hole should be about the right size if you are using 12-ga. or 14-ga. sheathed NM cable.

Cut a small access hole (4 × 4" or so) in the back panel of the base cabinet directly below the undercabinet light location.

(continued)

5

Feed cable into the access hole at the light location until the end reaches the access hole below. Don't cut the cable yet. Reach into the access hole and feel around for the free cable end and then pull it out through the access hole once you've found it. Cut the cable, making sure to leave plenty of extra on both ends.

6

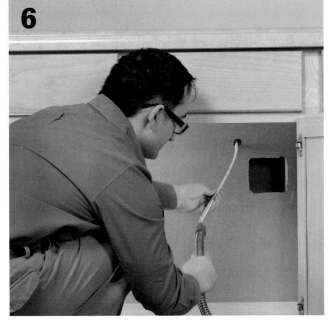

String the cable into a piece of flexible conduit that's long enough to reach between the two access holes in the base cabinets. Attach a connector to each end of the conduit to protect the cable sheathing from the sharp edges of the cut metal. *Tip: To make patching the cabinet back easier, drill a new access hole for the cable near the square access hole.*

7

Hang the conduit with hanger straps attached to the base cabinet frame or back panel, drilling holes in the side walls of the cabinet where necessary to thread the conduit through. On back panels, use small screws to hang the straps instead of brads or nails. Support the conduit near both the entrance and the exit holes (the conduit should extend past the back panels by a couple of inches).

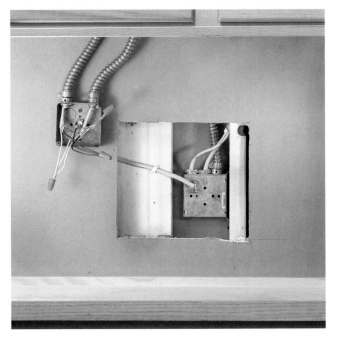

Variation: If you are installing more than one undercabinet light, run cable down from each installation point as you did for the first light. Mount an electrical junction box to the cabinet back near the receptacle providing the power. Run the power cables from each light through flexible conduit and make connections inside the junction box. Be sure to attach the junction box cover once the connections are made.

Remove the receptacle from the box you are tying into and insert the new circuit cable into one of the knockouts using a cable clamp. Check a wire capacity chart (see page 26) to make sure the box is big enough for the new conductors. Replace it with a larger box if necessary. Reinstall the receptacle once the connections are made.

Install the undercabinet light. Some models have a removable diffuser that allows access to the fixture wires, and these should be screwed to the upper cabinet prior to making your wiring hookups. Other models need to be connected to the circuit wires before installation. Check your manufacturer's installations.

Connect wires inside the light fixture according to the light manufacturer's directions. Make sure the incoming cable is stapled just before it enters the light box and that a cable clamp is used at the knockout in the box to protect the cable. Restore power and test the light.

Cut patches of hardboard and fit them over the access holes, overlapping the edges of the cutouts. Adhere them to the cabinet backs with panel adhesive.

Vanity Lights

Many bathrooms have a single fixture positioned above the vanity, but a light source in this position casts shadows on the face and makes grooming more difficult. Light fixtures on either side of the mirror is a better arrangement.

For a remodel, mark the mirror location, run cable, and position boxes before drywall installation. You can also retrofit by installing new boxes and drawing power from the existing fixture.

The light sources should be at eye level; 66" is typical. The size of your mirror and its location on the wall may affect how far apart you can place the sconces, but 36 to 40" apart is a good guideline.

Tools & Materials ▸

Drywall saw
Drill
Combination tool
Circuit tester
Screwdrivers
Hammer
Electrical boxes
  and braces
Vanity light fixtures
NM cable
Wire connectors

Vanity lights on the sides of the mirror provide good lighting.

How to Replace Vanity Lights in a Finished Bathroom

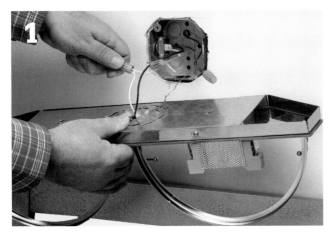

Turn off the power at the service panel. Remove the old fixture from the wall and test to make sure that the power is off. Then remove a strip of drywall from around the old fixture to the first studs beyond the approximate location of the new fixtures. Make the opening large enough that you have room to route cable from the existing fixture to the boxes.

Mark the location for the fixtures and install new boxes. Install the boxes about 66" above the floor and 18 to 20" from the centerline of the mirror (the mounting base of some fixtures is above or below the bulb, so adjust the height of the bracing accordingly). If the correct location is on or next to a stud, you can attach the box directly to the stud, otherwise you'll need to install blocking or use boxes with adjustable braces (shown).

3

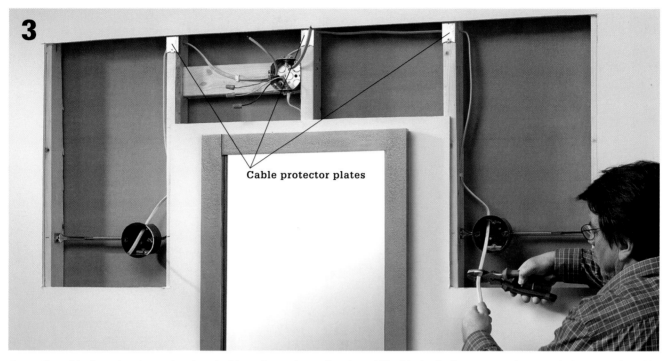

Cable protector plates

Open the side knockouts on the electrical box above the vanity. Then drill ⅝" holes in the centers of any studs between the old fixture and the new ones. Run two NM cables from the new boxes for the fixtures to the box above the vanity. Protect the cable with metal protector plates. Secure the cables with cable clamps, leaving 11" of extra cable for making the connection to the new fixtures. Remove sheathing and strip insulation from the ends of the wires.

4

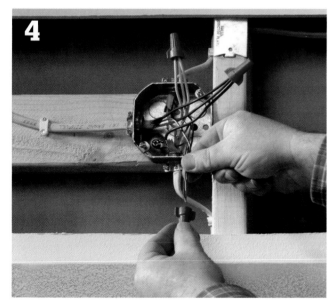

Connect the white wires from the new cables to the white wire from the old cable, and connect the black wires from the new cables to the black wire from the old cable. Connect the ground wires. Cover all open boxes and then replace the drywall, leaving openings for the fixture and the old box. (Cover the old box with a solid junction box cover plate.)

5

Install the fixture mounting braces on the boxes. Attach the fixtures by connecting the black circuit wire to the black fixture wire, and connecting the white circuit wire to the white fixture wire. Connect the ground wires. Position each fixture over each box, and attach with the mounting screws. Restore power and test the circuit.

Low-voltage Cable Lights

This unique fixture system is a mainstay of retail and commercial lighting and is now becoming common in homes. Low-voltage cable systems use two parallel cables to suspend and provide electricity to fixtures mounted anywhere on the cables. A 12-volt transformer feeds low-voltage power to the cables.

The system's ease of installation, flexibility, and the wide variety of individual lights available make it perfect for all kinds of spaces. Low-voltage cable light systems are ideal for retrofits and for situations where surface-mounted track is undesirable or impossible to install.

Tools & Materials ▸

Combination tool
Screwdriver
Drill
Fish tape
Switch

Low-voltage cable light kit
Electrical boxes
NM cable

Low-voltage Cable Lighting Kit ▸

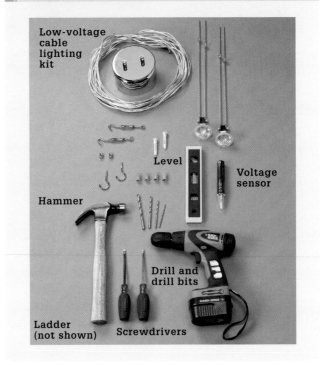

Low-voltage cable lighting kit · Level · Voltage sensor · Hammer · Drill and drill bits · Ladder (not shown) · Screwdrivers

Low-voltage cable lights are low profile and easy to install, but they provide a surprising amount of light.

How to Install Low-voltage Cable Lighting

Cable Light Kits ▶

Low-voltage cable lights typically are sold in kits that contain the hanging lights, the low-voltage cable, and a decorative transformer that can be ceiling mounted or wall mounted.

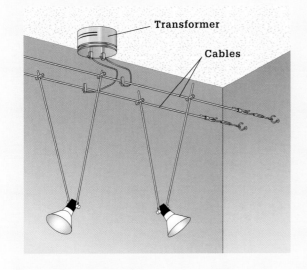

Transformer

Cables

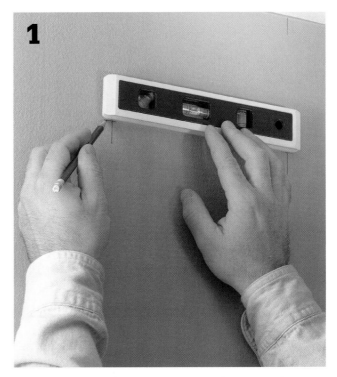

1

Lay out locations for the screw eyes that are used to suspend the cables, which should be in a parallel line. The path should lead the cables within a foot of the existing ceiling fixture box that you are using to provide power.

2

Install wall anchors at the appointed locations for the screw eyes that will suspend the cables. Plastic sleeve anchors are adequate in most cases. Drive the anchors into guide holes with a hammer.

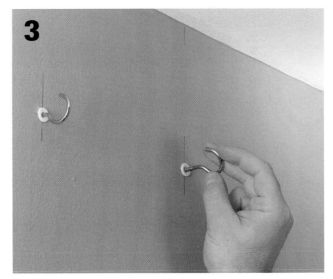

3

Twist the screw eyes into the wall anchor sleeves, taking care to make sure they are driven in equal amounts and are not overdriven. Install a set of screw eyes the same distance apart on each facing wall in the installation area. Cut two pieces of low-voltage cable to span between screw eyes on facing walls. Recommendations may vary— for the product shown here the cable is cut 12" shorter than the distance between the screw eyes.

(continued)

4

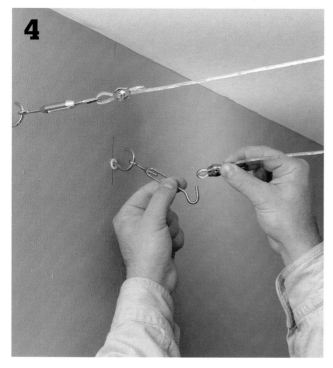

Use the crimping hardware in your kit to form small loops at the ends of each cable. Slip the loops over the screw eyes on one end, and attach them to turnbuckles at the opposite ends. Slide the turnbuckles over the screw eyes and tighten them until the cables are taut.

5

Attach the transformer crossbar to the electrical box containing the circuit leads. Shut off the power at the main service panel and test for power, then remove the old fixture if you have not already done so.

6

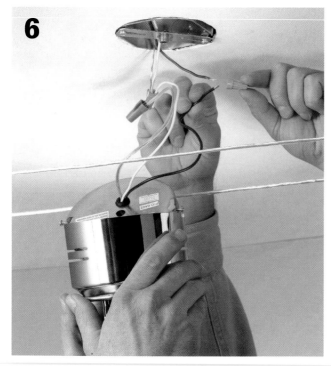

Make wiring connections for the transformer inside the electrical box. Make sure the transformer is supported while you join the wires. Be sure to attach the grounding wires to the grounding screw or clip in the box.

7

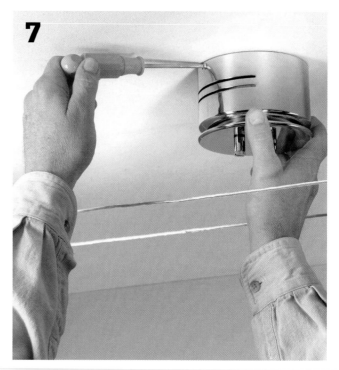

Mount the transformer onto the electrical box according to the manufacturer's instructions. The model shown here has a separate chrome cover that is secured with a setscrew after the transformer is mounted to the crossbar.

8

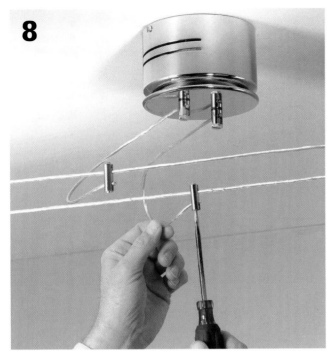

Thread short lengths of cable into the openings on the screw terminals on the transformer. Tighten the screws until the pointed probe in each terminal pierces the cable sheathing and makes contact with the wire inside. Do the same with the other ends of the jumper cables using the provided connector hardware.

Tip ▶

Install the transformer in a wall location if there is a more convenient power source or if you simply prefer the appearance of the wall location.

9

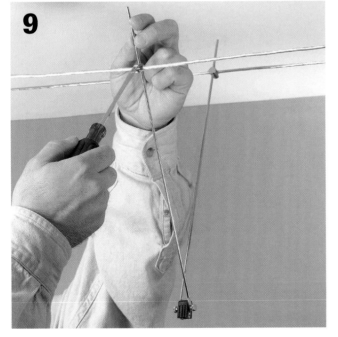

Hang the light fixture holders from the cables, tightening the screws in the hanger ends until their probes pierce the cable sheathing and make contact. It's a good idea to hang all of the fixtures and arrange them to your liking before you begin tightening the screws and piercing the sheathing.

10

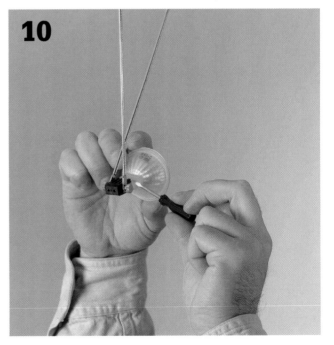

Insert the special low-voltage bulbs into the fixture holders and secure them as instructed (here, we are tightening a setscrew). Turn on the power and test the lights, adjusting the angles and directions of the bulbs.

Hard-wired Smoke & CO Detectors

Smoke and carbon monoxide (CO) alarms are an essential safety component of any living facility. All national fire protection codes require that new homes have a hard-wired smoke alarm in every sleeping room and on every level of a residence, including basements, attics, and attached garages. A smoke alarm needs to be protected with an AFCI circuit if it is installed in a bedroom.

Most authorities also recommend CO detectors on every level of the house and in every sleeping area.

Heat alarms, which detect heat instead of smoke, are often specified for locations like utility rooms, basements, or unfinished attics, where conditions may cause nuisance tripping of smoke alarms.

Hard-wired alarms operate on your household electrical current but have battery backups in case of a power outage. On new homes, all smoke alarms must be wired in a series so that every alarm sounds regardless of the fire's location. When wiring a series of alarms, be sure to use alarms of the same brand to ensure compatibility. Always check local codes before starting the job.

Ceiling-installed alarms should be 4" away from the nearest wall. Don't install smoke alarms near windows, doors, or ducts, where drafts might interfere with their operation.

Tools & Materials ▸

Screwdriver	self-clamping)
Combination tool	Two- and three-wire
Fish tape	14-gauge
Drywall saw	NM cable
Wall or ceiling	Alarms
outlet boxes	Wire connectors
Cable clamps	15-amp single-pole
(if boxes are not	breaker

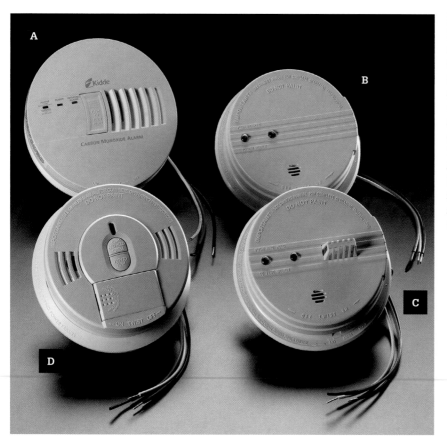

Smoke detectors and carbon monoxide (CO) detectors are required in new construction. Hard-wired carbon monoxide detectors (A) are triggered by the presence of carbon monoxide gas. Smoke detectors are available in photoelectric and ionizing models. In ionizing detectors (B), a small amount of current flows in an ionization chamber. When smoke enters the chamber, it interrupts the current, triggering the alarm. Photoelectric detectors (C) rely on a beam of light, which when interrupted by smoke triggers an alarm. Heat alarms (D) sound an alarm when they detect areas of high heat in the room.

How to Connect a Series of Hard-wired Smoke Alarms

1

Three-wire cable to next detector in series

Two-wire cable from service panel

Pull 14/2 NM cable from the service panel into the first ceiling electrical box in the smoke alarm series. Pull 14/3 NM cable between the remaining alarm outlet boxes. Use cable clamps to secure the cable in each outlet box. Remove sheathing and strip insulation from wires.

2

Ensure power is off and test for power. Wire the first alarm in the series. Use a wire connector to connect the ground wires. Splice the black circuit wire with the alarm's black lead and the black wire going to the next alarm in the series. Splice the white circuit wire with the alarm's white wire and the white (neutral) wire going to the next alarm in the series. Splice the red traveler wire with the odd-colored alarm wire (in this case, also a red wire).

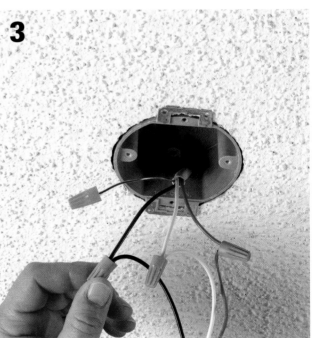

3

Wire the remaining alarms in the series by connecting the like-colored wires in each outlet box. Always connect the red traveler wire to the odd-colored (in this case, red) alarm wire. This red traveler wire connects all the alarms together so that when one alarm sounds, all the alarms sound. If the alarm doesn't have a grounding wire, cap the ground with a wire connector. When all alarms are wired, install and connect the new 15-amp breaker.

Landscape Lights

Some landscape lighting manufacturers pitch their systems as security products. If you keep the outside of your house well lit, the reasoning goes, the thieves will turn elsewhere to find easier pickings. It's possible that the companies are right about this. But probably the stronger arguments are for improved safety and appearance.

It can't be surprising that adding some light to the dark makes going places safer. This idea has been around for a long time—a very long time. But the notion that you can improve the look of your house by adding some nightlights is more recent. In fact, decorating with exterior lights became widespread only in the last 25 years, when low-voltage landscape lighting showed up. The beauty of low-voltage lighting is that it can be installed by anyone without the risk of being shocked.

Low-voltage lights are powered by a transformer that steps 120-volt current down to a safe 12 volts.

Choosing the location for the transformer is an important part of planning. You have two options: inside the house and outside the house. The outside installation is a little easier, but the inside one is a little better, especially from a security standpoint. Also take some time to review your light placement. Once you are happy with the plan, drive a small stake where you want each light to go.

Tools & Materials ▸

Drill/driver & bits
Hammer
Screwdrivers
Hacksaw

Spade
Low-voltage fixture
Wires
Transformer

Low-voltage lights are safe to install and use to beautify your outdoor spaces. Unlike solar landscape lights, they are powered by good old reliable electricity, so they really can stay on all night if you wish them to.

How To Modify Landscape Lights for Deck Installation

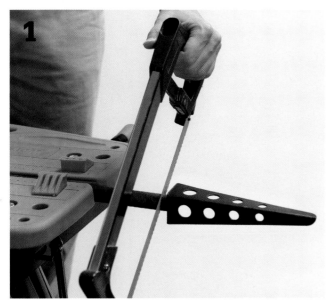

Specialty lights can cost a lot more than the standard plastic spike-base lamps. Because of this, many people modify the cheaper units to serve other purposes. To do this, first cut off the spike-base with a hacksaw.

To install a modified light on a deck, bore a wire-clearance hole through a deck board. Then feed the low-voltage wire through this hole and attach the base to the deck with screws. The same technique can be used to install modified units on planters or railings.

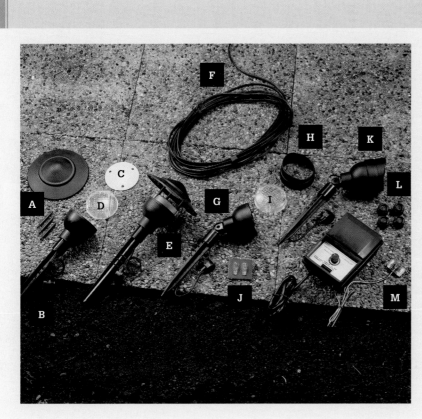

Landscape lighting can be ordered in kit form or as individual pieces. Kits include a few light heads, some wire, and a transformer that changes standard house current into low-voltage power. If you want half a dozen lights along the front walk, for example, then the kit is a good idea. It's cheaper, very easy to install, and will last a long time unless the lights get run over by a lawnmower.

Parts of a complete outdoor low-voltage lighting system include: (F) low-voltage cable; (H) lens hood; (K, G, E, B) low-voltage landscape light fixtures; (L) cable connector caps; (M) transformer/timer; (J) wall light bulbs; (I, D) lens; (C) reflector; (A) lens cap.

How to Install Low-Voltage Landscape Lights

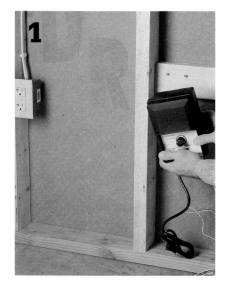

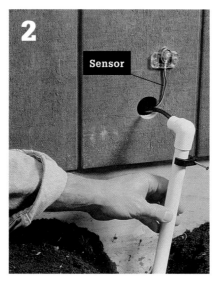

Install the transformers. In a garage, mount one on a wall within 24" of a GFCI receptacle and at least 12" off the floor. On an outdoor receptacle on a wall or a post, mount the transformer on the same post or an adjacent post at least 12" off the ground and not more than 24" from the receptacle.

Drill a hole through the wall or rim joist for the low-voltage cable and any sensors to pass through. If a circuit begins in a high-traffic area, protect the cable by running it through a short piece of PVC pipe or conduit, and then into the shallow trench.

Attach the end of the low-voltage wire to the terminals on the transformer. Make sure that both strands of wire are held tightly by their terminal screws.

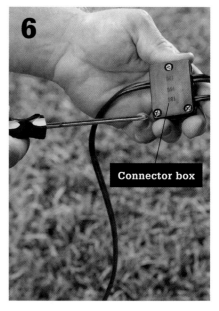

Transformers usually have a simple mechanism that allows you to set times for the lights to come ON and go OFF automatically. Set these times before hanging the transformer.

Many low-voltage light fixtures are modular, consisting of a spiked base, a riser tube, and a lamp. On these units, feed the wires and the wire connector from the light section down through the riser tube and into the base.

Take apart the connector box and insert the ends of the fixture wire and the low-voltage landscape cable into it. Puncture the wire ends with the connector box leads. Reassemble the connector box.

Feed the wire connector back into the light base and attach it to the lampholder according to directions. Install the low-voltage light bulb.

Assemble the fixture parts that cover the bulb, including the lens cap and reflector or the cap.

Lay out the lights, with the wires attached, in the pattern you have chosen. Then cut the sod between fixtures with a spade. Push the blade about 5" deep and pry open a seam by rocking the blade back and forth.

Gently force the cable into the slot formed by the spade; don't tear the wire insulation. A paint stick (or a cedar shingle) is a good tool for this job. Push the wire to the bottom of the slot.

Firmly push the light into the slot in the sod. If the lamp doesn't seat properly, pull it out and cut another slot at a right angle to the first and try again.

Once the lamp is stabilized, tuck any extra wire into the slot using the paint stick. No part of the wire should be exposed when you are done with the job.

Doorbells

Most doorbell problems are caused by loose wire connections or worn-out switches. Reconnecting loose wires or replacing a switch requires only a few minutes. Doorbell problems also can occur if the chime unit becomes dirty or worn, or if the low-voltage transformer burns out. Both parts are easy to replace. Because doorbells operate at low voltage, the switches and the chime unit can be serviced without turning off power to the system. However, when replacing a transformer, always turn off the power at the main service panel.

Most houses have other low-voltage transformers in addition to the doorbell transformer. These transformers control heating and air-conditioning thermostats (page 226 to 229), or other low-voltage systems. When testing and repairing a doorbell system, it is important to identify the correct transformer. A doorbell transformer has a voltage rating of 24 volts or less. This rating is printed on the face of the transformer. A doorbell transformer often is located near the main service panel and in some homes is attached directly to the service panel. The transformer that controls a heating/air-conditioning thermostat system is located near the furnace and has a voltage rating of 24 volts or more.

Occasionally, a doorbell problem is caused by a broken low-voltage wire somewhere in the system. You can test for wire breaks with a battery-operated multitester. If the test indicates a break, new low-voltage wires must be installed between the transformer and the switches, or between the switches and chime unit. Replacing low-voltage wires is not a difficult job, but it can be time-consuming. You may choose to have an electrician do this work.

Tools & Materials ▸

Continuity tester
Screwdriver
Multimeter
Needlenose pliers
Cotton swab
Rubbing alcohol

Replacement
    doorbell switch
    (if needed)
Masking tape
Replacement chime
    unit (if needed)

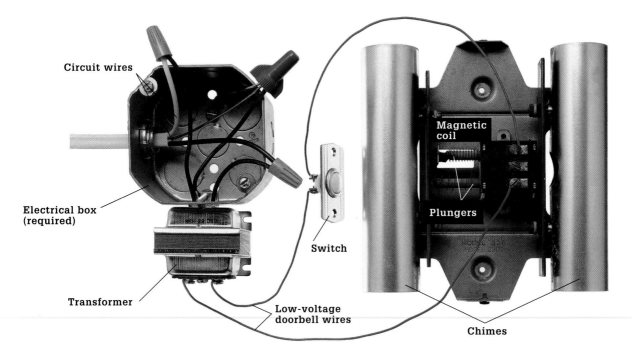

Circuit wires

Magnetic coil

Electrical box (required)

Plungers

Switch

Transformer

Low-voltage doorbell wires

Chimes

A home doorbell system is powered by a transformer that reduces 120-volt current to low-voltage current of 24 volts or less. Current flows from the transformer to one or more push-button switches. When pushed, the switch activates a magnetic coil inside the chime unit, causing a plunger to strike a musical tuning bar.

How to Test a Nonfunctional Doorbell System

1

Remove the mounting screws holding the doorbell switch to the siding.

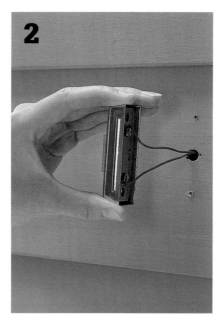

2

Carefully pull the switch away from the wall.

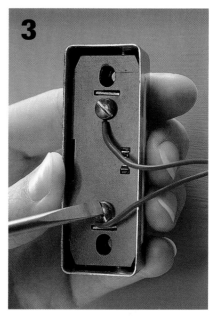

3

Inspect wire connections on the switch. If wires are loose, reconnect them to the screw terminals. Test the doorbell by pressing the button. If the doorbell still does not work, disconnect the switch and test it with a continuity tester.

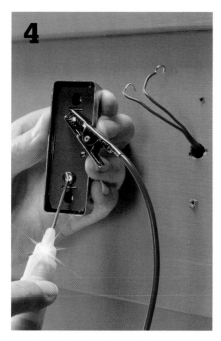

4

Attach the clip of a continuity tester to one screw terminal and touch the probe to the other screw terminal. Press the switch button. Tester should glow. If not, then the switch is faulty and must be replaced.

5

Twist the doorbell switch wires together temporarily to test the other parts of the doorbell system.

6

Transformer

Locate the doorbell transformer, often found near the main service panel. Transformer may be attached to an electrical box, or may be attached directly to the side of the service panel.

(continued)

7

Identify the doorbell transformer by reading its voltage rating. Doorbell transformers have a voltage rating of 24 volts or less. Turn off power to the transformer at main service panel. Remove cover on electrical box, and test wires for power. Reconnect any loose wires. Replace taped connections with wire connectors.

8

Reattach cover plate. Inspect the low-voltage wire connections, and reconnect any loose wires using needlenose pliers or a screwdriver. Turn on power to the transformer at the main service panel.

9

Touch the probes of the multitester to the low-voltage screw terminals on the transformer. If transformer is operating properly, the meter will detect power within 2 volts of transformer's rating. If not, the transformer is faulty and must be replaced.

10

Test the chime unit. Remove the cover plate on the doorbell chime unit. Inspect the low-voltage wire connections, and reconnect any loose wires.

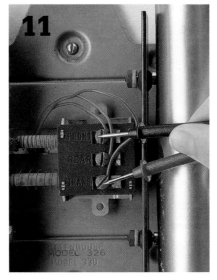

11

Test that the chime unit is receiving current. Touch probes of a multimeter to screw terminals. If the multimeter detects power within 2 volts of the transformer rating, then the unit is receiving proper current. If it detects no power or very low power, there is a break in the low-voltage wiring and new wires must be installed.

12

Clean the chime plungers (some models) with a cotton swab dipped in rubbing alcohol. Reassemble doorbell switches, then test the system by pushing one of the switches. If doorbell still does not work, then the chime unit is faulty and must be replaced (page 225).

How to Replace a Doorbell Switch

Remove the doorbell switch
mounting screws, and carefully pull the switch away from the wall.

Disconnect wires from the switch.
Tape wires to the wall to prevent them from slipping into the wall cavity.

Purchase a new doorbell switch,
and connect wires to screw terminals on new switch. (Wires are interchangeable and can be connected to either terminal.) Anchor the switch to the wall.

How to Replace a Doorbell Chime Unit

Turn off power to the doorbell at the main panel. Remove the cover plate from the old chime. Label the low-voltage wires FRONT, REAR, or TRANS to identify their screw terminal locations. Disconnect the wires. Remove the old chime unit.

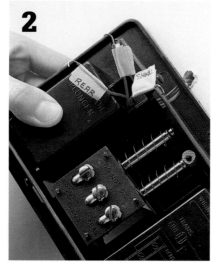

Purchase a new chime unit that matches the voltage rating of the old unit. Thread the low-voltage wires through the base of the new chime unit. Attach the chime unit to the wall using the mounting screws included with the installation kit.

Connect the low-voltage wires to the screw terminals on the new chime unit. Attach the cover plate and turn on the power at the main service panel.

Programmable Thermostats

A thermostat is a temperature-sensitive switch that automatically controls home heating and air-conditioning systems. There are two types of thermostats used to control heating and air-conditioning systems. Low-voltage thermostats control whole-house heating and air conditioning from one central location. Line-voltage thermostats are used in zone heating systems, where each room has its own heating unit and thermostat.

A low-voltage thermostat is powered by a transformer that reduces 120-volt current to about 24 volts. A low-voltage thermostat is very durable, but failures can occur if wire connections become loose or dirty, if thermostat parts become corroded, or if a transformer wears out. Some thermostat systems have two transformers. One transformer controls the heating unit, and the other controls the air-conditioning unit.

Line-voltage thermostats are powered by the same circuit as the heating unit, usually a 240-volt circuit. Always make sure to turn off the power before servicing a line-voltage thermostat.

A thermostat can be replaced in about one hour. Many homeowners choose to replace standard low-voltage or line-voltage thermostats with programmable setback thermostats. These programmable thermostats can cut energy use by up to 35 percent.

When buying a new thermostat, make sure the new unit is compatible with your heating/air-conditioning system. For reference, take along the brand name and model number of the old thermostat and of your heating/air-conditioning units. When buying a new low-voltage transformer, choose a replacement with voltage and amperage ratings that match the old thermostat.

Tools & Materials ▸

Screwdriver
Masking tape
New thermostat

A programmable thermostat allows you to significantly reduce your energy consumption by taking greater control over your heating and cooling system.

Traditional Low-Voltage Thermostats

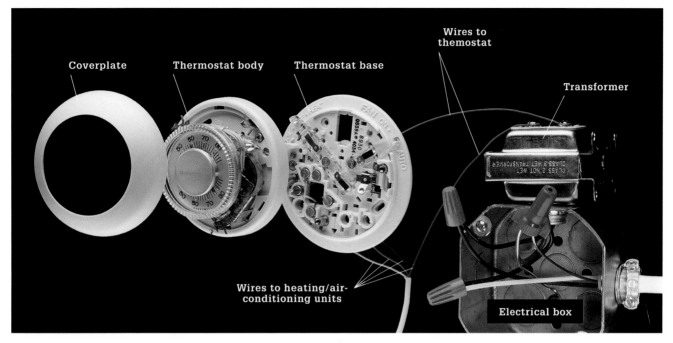

Coverplate   **Thermostat body**   **Thermostat base**

Wires to themostat

Transformer

Wires to heating/air-conditioning units

Electrical box

Low-voltage thermostat system has a transformer that is either connected to an electrical junction box or mounted inside a furnace access panel. Very thin wires (18 to 22 gauge) send current to the thermostat. The thermostat constantly monitors room temperatures and sends electrical signals to the heating/cooling unit through additional wires. The number of wires connected to the thermostat varies from two to six, depending on the type of heating/air-conditioning system. In the common four-wire system shown above, power is supplied to the thermostat through a single wire attached to screw terminal R. Wires attached to other screw terminals relay signals to the furnace heating unit, the air-conditioning unit, and the blower unit. Before removing a thermostat, make sure to label each wire to identify its screw terminal location.

Programmable Thermostats

Programmable thermostats contain sophisticated circuitry that allows you to set the heating and cooling systems in your house to adjust automatically at set times of the day. Replacing a manual thermostat with a programmable model is a relatively simple job that can have big payback on heating and cooling energy savings.

How to Upgrade to a Programmable Thermostat

1

Start by removing the existing thermostat. Turn off the power to the furnace at the main service panel and test for power. Then remove the thermostat cover.

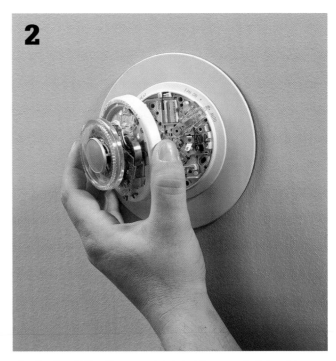

2

The body of the thermostat is held to a wall plate with screws. Remove these screws and pull the body away from the wall plate. Set the body aside.

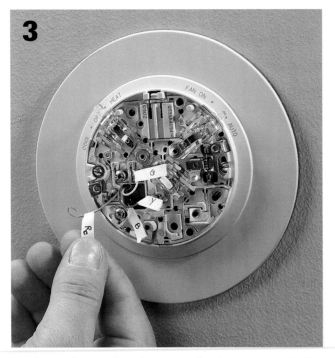

3

The low-voltage wires that power the thermostat are held by screw terminals to the mounting plate. Do not remove the wires until you label them with tape according to the letter printed on the terminal to which each wire is attached.

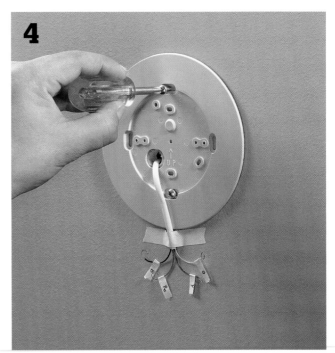

4

Once all the wires are labeled and removed from the mounting plate, tape the cable that holds these wires to the wall to keep it from falling back into the wall. Then unscrew the mounting plate and set it aside.

5

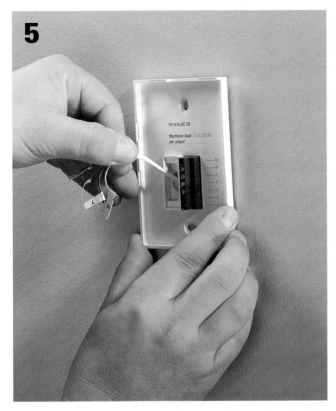

Position the new thermostat base on the wall and guide the wires through the central opening. Screw the base to the wall using wall anchors if necessary.

6

Check the manufacturer's instructions to establish the correct terminal for each low-voltage wire. Then connect the wires to these terminals, making sure each screw is secure.

7

Programmable thermostats require batteries to store the programs so they won't disappear if the power goes out in a storm. Make sure to install batteries before you snap the thermostat cover in place. Program the new unit to fit your needs, and then turn on the power to the furnace.

Mercury Thermostats ▶

Older model thermostats (and even a few still being made today) often contained one or more small vials of mercury totaling 3 to 4 grams in weight. Because mercury is a highly toxic metal that can cause nerve damage in humans, along with other environmental problems, DO NOT dispose of an old mercury thermometer with your household waste. Instead, bring it to a hazardous waste disposal site or a mercury recycling site if your area has one (check with your local solid waste disposal agency). The best way to determine if your old thermostat contains mercury is simply to remove the cover and look for the small glass vials or ampules containing the silverfish mercury substance. If you are unsure, it is always better to be safe and keep the device in question out of the normal waste stream.

Wireless Switches

Sometimes a light switch is just in the wrong place, or it would be more convenient to have two switches controlling a single fixture. Adding a second switch the conventional way generally requires hours of work and big holes in walls. (Electricians call this a three-way switch installation.) Fortunately, wireless switch kits are available to perform basically the same function for a fraction of the cost and effort. There is a bit of real wiring involved here, but it's not nearly as complicated as the traditional method of adding a three-way switch installation.

The kits work by replacing a conventional switch with a unit that has a built-in radio frequency receiver that will read a remote device mounted within a 50-ft. radius. The kits come with a remote, battery-powered switch (it looks like a standard light switch) that you can attach to a wall with double-sided tape.

Two other similar types of wireless switch kits are also available. One allows you to control a plugged-in lamp or appliance with a remote light switch. The second type allows you to control a conventional light fixture remotely, but instead of replacing the switch, the receiver screws in below the light bulb. This is particularly useful if you want to control a pull-chain light from a wall switch.

Tools & Materials ▸

Voltage sensor
Screwdrivers
Wire connectors

Wireless switch
transmitter &
receiver/switch

A wireless switch is a two-part switching system: a wireless switch with a battery-powered transmitter can be attached to any wall surface; an existing switch is then replaced with a new switch containing a receiver that is triggered by signals from the wireless transmitter, effectively creating a three-way switch condition.

Wireless switch with transmitter

Switch with wireless receiver

Wireless Switch Products ▶

Wireless lamp switch

Wireless wall switch kit

Wireless plug-in switch

Wireless kits are available to let you switch lights on and off remotely in a variety of ways: at the switch, at the plug, or at the bulb socket.

The remote switch is a wireless transmitter that requires a battery. The transmitter switch attaches to the wall with adhesive tape or velcro strips.

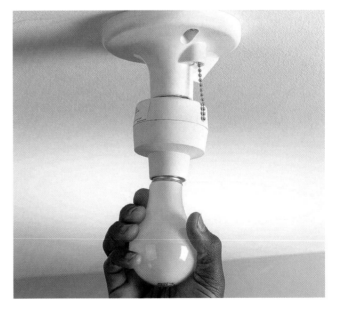

A receiver with a receptacle can be plugged into any receptacle to give it wireless functionality. The switch is operated with a remote control transmitter.

A radio-controlled light fixture can be threaded into the socket of any existing light fixture so it can be turned on and off with a remote control device.

How To Install a Wireless Wall Switch

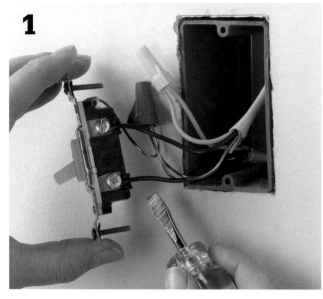

1

Get rid of the old switch. Shut off power to the switch circuit and then disconnect and remove the old switch.

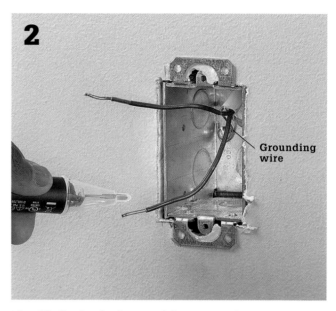

2

Grounding wire

Identify the lead wire. Carefully separate the power supply wires (any color but white or green) in the switch box so they are not contacting each other or any other surface. Restore power and test each lead wire with a sensor to identify which wire carries the power (the LINE) and which is headed for the fixture the switch controls (the LOAD). Shut power back off and then label the wires.

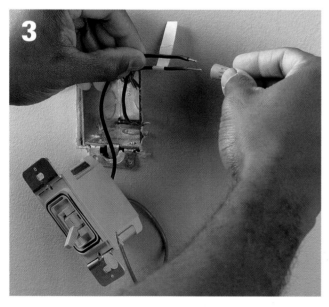

3

Connect the LINE wire to the LINE terminal or wire on the switch. Connect the LOAD wire (or wires) to the LOAD terminal or wire. The neutral whites (if present) and green grounding wires should be twisted together with a connector. The greens should be grounded to the grounding clip or terminal in the box. *Note: Some switch boxes, such as the one above, are wired with NM2 cable that has two blacks and a green wire and no white.*

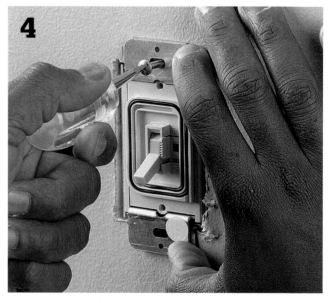

4

Once the wires are firmly connected, you can attach the switch to the box. Tuck the new switch and wires neatly back into the box. Then drive the two long screws that are attached to the new switch into the two holes in the electrical box.

Attach the cover plate to the new wireless switch. Turn the power service back on and test to make sure the switch operates normally.

Remove the backing from the adhesive pads on the back of the wireless switch transmitter box. Install a new 9-volt battery (or other type as required) in the box, and connect it to the switch transmitter terminals.

Stick the transmitter box to the wall at the desired location. The box should be no more than 50 ft. from the receiver switch (see manufacturer's suggestions). The box should be at the same height (usually 48") as the other switch boxes.

Test the operation of both switches. Each switch should successfully turn the light fixture on and off. You've just successfully created a three-way switch installation without running any new wires.

Baseboard Heaters

Baseboard heaters are a popular way to provide additional heating for an existing room or primary heat to a converted attic or basement.

Heaters are generally wired on a dedicated 240-volt circuit controlled by a thermostat. Several heaters can be wired in parallel and controlled by a single thermostat (see circuit map 15, page 161).

Baseboard heaters are generally surface-mounted without boxes, so in a remodeling situation, you only need to run cables before installing wallboard. Be sure to mark cable locations on the floor before installing drywall. Retrofit installations are also not difficult. You can remove existing baseboard and run new cable in the space behind.

(see circuit map 15, page 161).

Tools & Materials ▸

Drill/driver
Wire stripper
Cable ripper
Wallboard saw
Baseboard heater or heaters
240-thermostat (in-heater or in-wall)
12/2 NM cable
Electrical tape
Basic wiring supplies

Baseboard heaters can provide primary or supplemental heat for existing rooms or additions. Install heaters with clear space between the heater and the floor.

Baseboard Thermostats

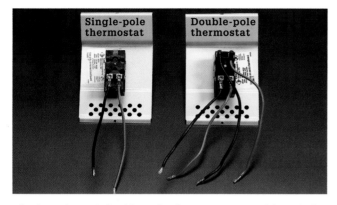

Single-pole and double-pole thermostats work in a similar manner, but double-pole models are safer. The single-pole model will open the circuit (causing shutoff) in only one leg of the power service. Double-pole models have two sets of wires to open both legs, lessening the chance that a person servicing the heater will contact a live wire.

In-heater and wall-mount are the two types of baseboard thermostats you can choose from. If you are installing multiple heaters, a single wall-mount thermostat is more convenient. Individual in-heater thermostats give you more zone control, which can result in energy savings.

How Much Heater Do You Need? ▸

If you don't mind doing a little math, determining how many lineal feet of baseboard heater a room requires is not hard.

1. Measure the area of the room in square feet (length × width): _____
2. Divide the area by 10 to get the baseline minimum wattage: _____
3. Add 5% for each newer window or 10% for each older window: _____
4. Add 10% for each exterior wall in the room: _____
5. Add 10% for each exterior door: _____
6. Add 10% if the space below is not insulated: _____

7. Add 20% if the space above is not well insulated: _____
8. Add 10% if ceiling is more than 8 ft. high: _____
9. Total of the baseline wattage plus all additions: _____
10. Divide this number by 250 (the wattage produced per foot of standard baseboard heater): _____
11. Round up to a whole number. This is the minimum number of feet of heater you need. _____

Note: It is much better to have more feet of heater than is required than fewer. Having more footage of heater does not consume more energy; it does allow the heaters to work more efficiently.

Planning Tips for Baseboard Heaters ▸

- 240-volt heaters are much more energy efficient than 120-volt heaters.
- Baseboard heaters require a dedicated circuit. A 20-amp, 240-volt circuit of 12-gauge copper wire will power up to 16 ft. of heater.
- Do not install a heater beneath a wall receptacle. Cords hanging down from the receptacle are a fire hazard.

- Do not mount heaters directly on the floor. You should maintain at least 1" of clear space between the baseboard heater and the floor covering.
- Installing heaters directly beneath windows is a good practice.
- Locate wall thermostats on interior walls only, and do not install directly above a heat source.

How to Install a 240-volt Baseboard Heater

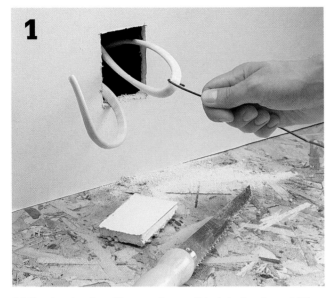

1

At the heater locations, cut a small hole in the drywall 3 to 4" above the floor. Pull 12/2 NM cables through the first hole: one from the thermostat, the other to the next heater. Pull all the cables for subsequent heaters. Middle-of-run heaters will have two cables, while end-of-run heaters have only one cable. (See also circuit map 15, page 161.)

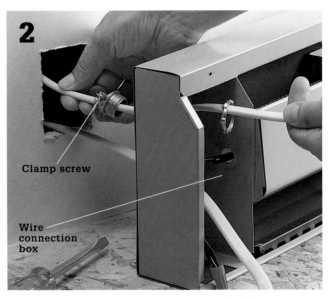

2

Clamp screw

Wire connection box

Remove the cover on the wire connection box. Open a knockout for each cable that will enter the box, then feed the cables through the cable clamps and into the wire connection box. Attach the clamps to the wire connection box, and tighten the clamp screws until the cables are gripped firmly.

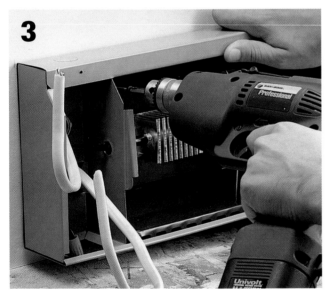

3

Anchor heater against wall about 1" off floor by driving flathead screws through back of housing and into studs. Strip away cable sheathing so at least ½" of sheathing extends into the heater. Strip ¾" of insulation from each wire using a combination tool.

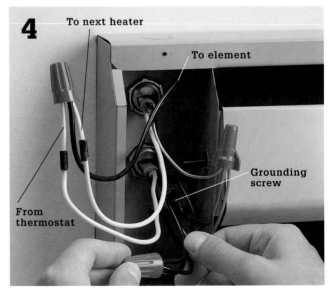

4

To next heater

To element

From thermostat

Grounding screw

Make connections to the heating element if the power wires are coming from a thermostat or another heater controlled by a thermostat. See next page for other wiring schemes. Connect the white circuit wires to one of the wire leads on the heater. Tag white wires with black tape to indicate they are hot. Connect the black circuit wires to the other wire lead. Connect a grounding pigtail to the green grounding screw in the box, then join all grounding wires with a wire connector. Reattach cover.

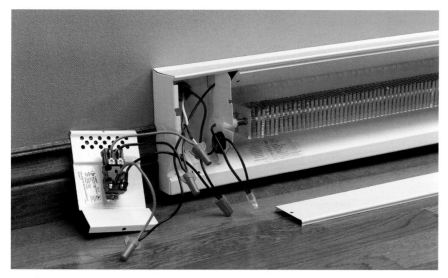

One heater with end-cap thermostat. Run both power leads (black plus tagged neutral) into the connection box at either end of the heater. If installing a single-pole thermostat, connect one power lead to one thermostat wire and connect the other thermostat wire to one of the heater leads. Connect the other hot LINE wire to the other heater lead. If you are installing a double-pole thermostat, make connections with both legs of the power supply.

Multiple heaters. At the first heater, join both hot wires from the thermostat to the wires leading to the second heater in line. Be sure to tag all white neutrals hot. Twist copper ground wires together and pigtail them to the grounding screw in the baseboard heater junction box. This parallel wiring configuration ensures that power flow will not be interrupted to the downstream heaters if an upstream heater fails.

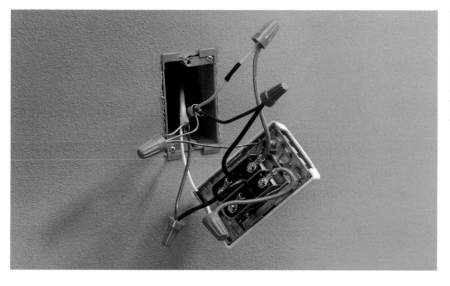

Wall-mounted thermostat. If installing a wall-mounted thermostat, the power leads should enter the thermostat first and then be wired to the individual heaters singly or in series. Hookups at the heater are made as shown in step 4. Be sure to tag the white neutral as hot in the thermostat box as well as in the heater box.

Wall Heaters

Installing a wall heater is an easy way to provide supplemental heat to a converted attic or basement without expanding an existing HVAC system.

Wall heaters are easy to install during a remodel (most have a separate can assembly that you attach to the framing before the drywall is installed). They can also be retrofitted.

Most models available at home centers use 120-volt current (shown below), but 240-volt models are also available.

Tools & Materials ▸

Drywall saw	12/2 NM cable
Drill	Wire connectors
Fish tape	Wall heater
Combination tool	Thermostat (optional)
Screwdrivers	Wallboard saw

Wall heaters are an easy-to-install way to provide supplemental heat. Some models have built-in thermostats, while others can be controlled by a remote thermostat.

How to Install a Wall Heater in a Finished Wall

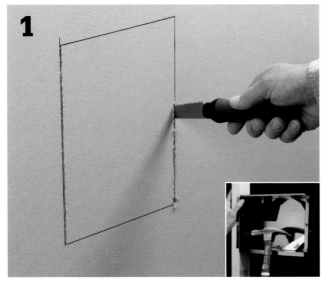

1

Make an opening in the wall for the heater. Use a stud finder to locate a stud in the area where you want to install the heater. Mark the opening for the heater according to the manufacturer's guidelines so that one side of the heater sits flush with a stud. Pay attention to clearance requirements. Cut the opening with a wallboard saw. If the wall is open, install the heater can before hanging drywall (inset).

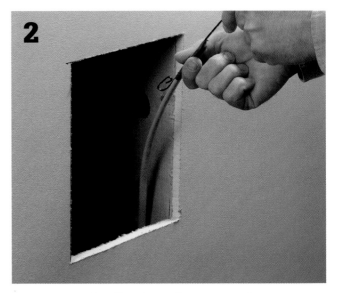

2

Ensure power is off and test for power. Pull 12/2 NM cable from the main panel to the wall opening. If the heater is controlled by a separate thermostat, pull cable to the thermostat and then run another cable from the thermostat to the heater location.

3 **Disconnect and remove** the motor unit from the heater can. Remove a knockout from the can and route the cable into the can.

4 **Install the can in the opening.** Secure the cable with a clamp, leaving 8 to 12" of cable exposed. Attach the can to the framing as directed by the manufacturer.

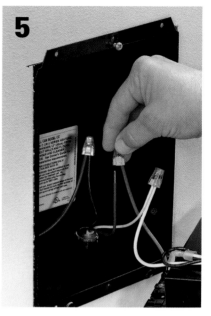

5 **Wire the heater.** Connect the black circuit wire to one of the black heater leads. Connect the white circuit wire to the other lead. Connect the grounds.

6 **Secure the heater unit** in the can as directed by the manufacturer. Reconnect the motor if necessary. Attach the grill and thermostat knob as directed. Connect the new circuit breaker at the main panel.

Variation: Connect a thermostat to control a wall heater. Some wall heaters do not use built-in thermostats. Install a thermostat in the heater circuit before the wall heater. Connect the black and the white wires coming from the main panel to the red leads on the thermostat. Connect the wires going to the heater to the black leads on the thermostat. Connect the grounds.

Radiant Floor Mats

Floor-warming systems require very little energy to run and are designed to heat ceramic tile floors only; they generally are not used as sole heat sources for rooms.

A typical floor-warming system consists of one or more thin mats containing electric resistance wires that heat up when energized like an electric blanket. The mats are installed beneath the tile and are hardwired to a 120-volt GFCI circuit. A thermostat controls the temperature, and a timer turns the system off automatically.

The system shown in this project includes two plastic mesh mats, each with its own power lead that is wired directly to the thermostat. Radiant mats may be installed over a plywood subfloor, but if you plan to install floor tile you should put down a base of cementboard first, and then install the mats on top of the cementboard.

A crucial part of installing this system is to use a multimeter to perform several resistance checks to make sure the heating wires have not been damaged during shipping or installation.

Electrical service required for a floor-warming system is based on size. A smaller system may connect to an existing GFCI circuit, but a larger one will need a dedicated circuit; follow the manufacturer's requirements.

To order a floor-warming system, contact the manufacturer or dealer (see Resouces, page 347). In most cases, you can send them plans and they'll custom-fit a system for your project area.

Tools & Materials ▸

Vacuum cleaner	Electric wire fault
Multimeter	indicator (optional)
Tape measure	Radiant floor mats
Scissors	12/2 NM cable
Router/rotary tool	Conduit
Marker	Wire connectors
Trowel	Thinset mortar
or rubber float	Thermostat with sensor
Notched trowel	Junction box(es)
Staple gun	Tile or stone
Hot glue gun	floorcovering

A radiant floor-warming system employs electric heating mats that are covered with floor tile to create a floor that's cozy under foot.

Installation Tips ▸

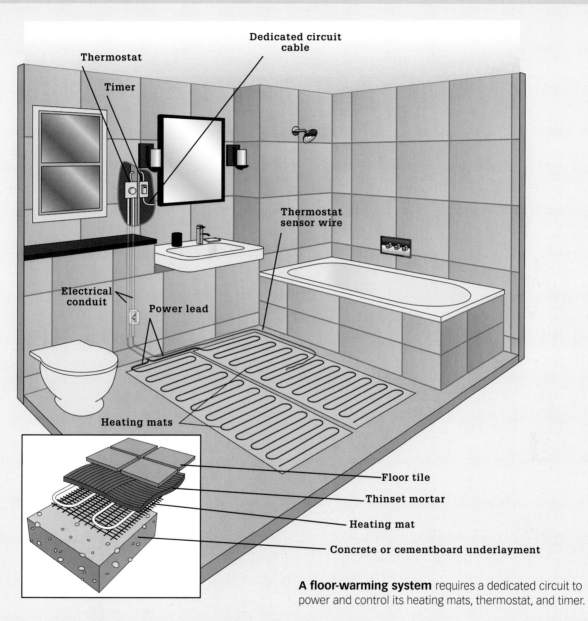

Dedicated circuit cable

Thermostat

Timer

Thermostat sensor wire

Electrical conduit

Power lead

Heating mats

Floor tile

Thinset mortar

Heating mat

Concrete or cementboard underlayment

A floor-warming system requires a dedicated circuit to power and control its heating mats, thermostat, and timer.

- Each radiant mat must have a direct connection to the power lead from the thermostat, with the connection made in a junction box in the wall cavity. Do not install mats in series.
- Do not install radiant floor mats under shower areas.
- Do not overlap maps or let them touch.
- Do not cut heating wire or damage heating wire insulation.
- The distance between wires in adjoining mats should equal the distance between wire loops measured center to center.

Installing a Radiant Floor-Warming System

Floor-warming systems must be installed on a circuit with adequate amperage and a GFCI breaker. Smaller systems may tie into an existing circuit, but larger ones need a dedicated circuit. Follow local building and electrical codes that apply to your project.

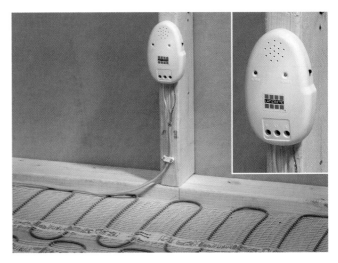

An electric wire fault indicator monitors each floor mat for continuity during the installation process. If there is a break in continuity (for example, if a wire is cut) an alarm sounds. If you choose not to use an installation tool to monitor the mat, test for continuity frequently using a multimeter.

How To Install a Radiant Floor-Warming System

Install electrical boxes to house the thermostat and timer. In most cases, the box should be located 60" above floor level. Use a 4"-deep × 4"-wide double-gang box for the thermostat/timer control if your kit has an integral model. If your timer and thermostat are separate, install a separate single box for the timer.

Drill access holes in the sole plate for the power leads that are preattached to the mats (they should be over 10 ft. long). The leads should be connected to a supply wire from the thermostat in a junction box located in a wall near the floor and below the thermostat box. The access hole for each mat should be located directly beneath the knockout for that cable in the thermostat box. Drill through the sill plate vertically and horizontally so the holes meet in an L-shape.

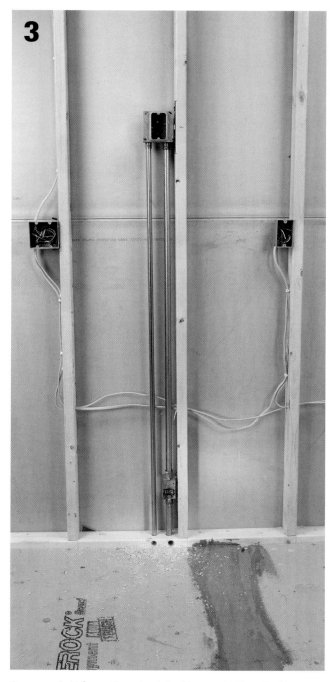

Run conduit from the electrical boxes to the sill plate. The line for the supply cable should be ¾" conduit. If you are installing multiple mats, the supply conduit should feed into a junction box about 6" above the sill plate and then continue into the ¾" hole you drilled for the supply leads. The sensor wire needs only ½" conduit that runs straight from the thermostat box via the thermostat. The mats should be powered by a dedicated 20-amp GFCI circuit of 12/2 NM cable run from your main service panel to the electrical box (this is for 120-volt mats—check your instruction manual for specific circuit recommendations).

Clean the floor surface thoroughly to get rid of any debris that could potentially damage the wire mats. A vacuum cleaner generally does a more effective job than a broom.

Test for resistance using a multimeter set to measure ohms. This is a test you should make frequently during the installation, along with checking for continuity (see page 241). If the resistance is off by more than 10% from the theoretical resistance listing (see manufacturer's chart in installation instructions), contact a technical support operator for the kit manufacturer. For example, the theoretical resistance for the 1 × 50 ft. mat seen here is 19, so the ohms reading should be between 17 and 21.

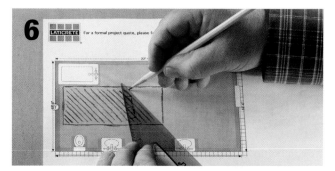

Finalize your mat layout plan. Most radiant floor warming mat manufacturers will provide a layout plan for you at the time of purchase, or they will give you access to an online design tool so you can come up with your own plan. This is an important step to the success of your project, and the assistance is free.

(continued)

7

Unroll the radiant mat or mats and allow them to settle. Arrange the mat or mats according to the plan you created. It's okay to cut the plastic mesh so you can make curves or switchbacks, but do not cut the heating wire under any circumstances, even to shorten it.

8

Finalize the mat layout and then test the resistance again using a multimeter. Also check for continuity in several different spots. If there is a problem with any of the mats, you should identify it and correct it before proceeding with the mortar installation.

9

Run the thermostat sensor wire from the electrical box down the ½" conduit raceway and out the access hole in the sill plate. Select the best location for the thermostat sensor and mark the location onto the flooring. Also mark the locations of the wires that connect to and lead from the sensor.

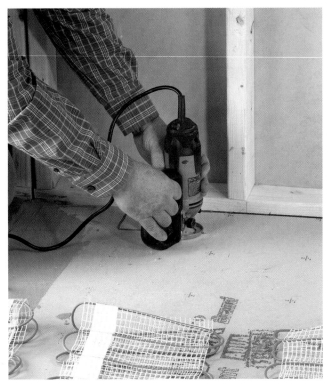

If your local codes require it, roll the mats out of the way and cut a channel for the sensor and the sensor wires into the floor or floor underlayment. For most floor materials, a spiral cutting tool does a quick and neat job of this task. Remove any debris.

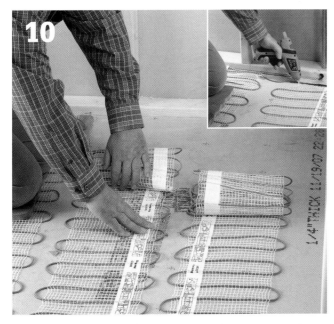

Bond the mats to the floor. If the mats in your system have adhesive strips, peel off the adhesive backing and roll out the mats in the correct position, pressing them against the floor to set the adhesive. If your mats have no adhesive, bind them with strips of double-sided carpet tape. The thermostat sensor and the power supply leads should be attached with hot glue (inset photo) and run up into their respective holes in the sill plate if you have not done this already. Test all mats for resistance and continuity.

Cover the floor installation areas with a layer of thinset mortar that is thick enough to fully encapsulate all the wires and mats (usually around ¼" in thickness). Check the wires for continuity and resistance regularly and stop working immediately if there is a drop in resistance or a failure of continuity. Allow the mortar to dry overnight.

Connect the power supply leads from the mat or mats to the NM cable coming from the thermostat inside the junction box near the sill. Power must be turned off. The power leads should be cut so about 8" of wire feeds into the box. Be sure to use cable clamps to protect the wires.

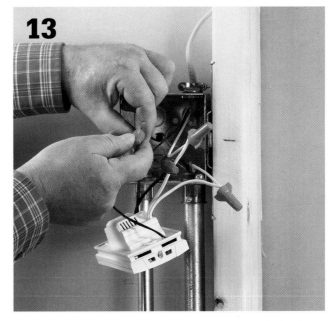

Connect the sensor wire and the power supply lead (from the junction box) to the thermostat/timer according to the manufacturer's directions. Attach the device to the electrical box, restore power, and test the system to make sure it works. Once you are convinced that it is operating properly, install floor tiles and repair the wall surfaces.

Ceiling Fans

Ceiling fans are installed and wired like ceiling fixtures. They always require heavy-duty bracing and electrical boxes rated for ceiling fans.

Most standard ceiling fans work with a wall switch functioning as master power for the unit. Pull chains attached to the unit control the fan and lights. In these installations, it's fairly simple to replace an existing ceiling fixture with a fan and light.

If you will be installing a new circuit for the fan, use three-wire cable so both the light and the motor can be controlled by wall switches (circuit maps 30 and 31, page 169).

Because ceiling fans generally weigh more than ceiling lights and the motion of the blade creates more stress, it is very important that the ceiling box is securely mounted and is rated for ceiling fans. Ceiling boxes rated for ceiling fans are marked with the phrase "For ceiling fan support." If your existing ceiling box is not fan-rated, replace it with one that is. And be sure to inspect the manner in which the box is mounted to make sure it is strong enough (see page 248).

Installation varies from fan to fan, so be sure to follow the manufacturer's instructions.

Tools & Materials ▸

Screwdriver	Ceiling fan light kit
Combination tool	2 × 4 lumber or
Pliers or	adjustable ceiling
adjustable wrench	fan crossbrace
Circuit tester	1½" and 3"
Hammer	wallboard screws

A ceiling fan helps keep living spaces cooler in the summer and warmer in the winter. Replacing an overhead light with a fan/light is an easy project with big payback.

Ceiling Fan Types

Labels: Mounting bracket, Canopy, Motor, Fan blades, Switch housing, Pull chain, Bottom cap

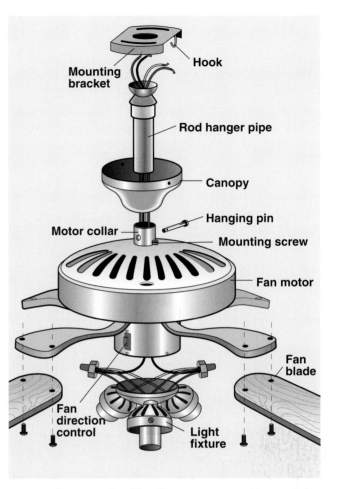

Labels: Mounting bracket, Hook, Rod hanger pipe, Canopy, Hanging pin, Mounting screw, Motor collar, Fan motor, Fan blade, Fan direction control, Light fixture

Bracket-mounted ceiling fans are hung directly from a mounting bracket that is attached to the ceiling box. A canopy conceals the motor and the connections.

Downrod mounted ceiling fans are supported by a metal rod that's hung from the ceiling mounting bracket. The length of the rod determines the height of the fan. Downrod fans are used in rooms with ceilings 8 ft. high or higher.

Fans that Heat ▶

The first generation of ceiling fans did one job: they spun and moved air. As the technology advanced, light kits were added to replace the light source that is lost when a fan-only appliance is installed. Now, some ceiling fans are manufactured with electric heating elements that can produce up to 5,000 BTUs of heat, comparable to a small space heater. Located in the fan canopy, the ceramic heat elements direct heat out the vents and force it down to the living level in the room, along with the heated air that naturally rises.

Fan-mounted heaters are relatively light duty, so they generally do not require a dedicated circuit. In most cases, you can supply power to the heater/fan with any 15-amp room light circuit that has extra capacity.

Supporting Ceiling Boxes

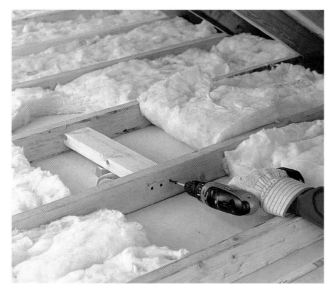

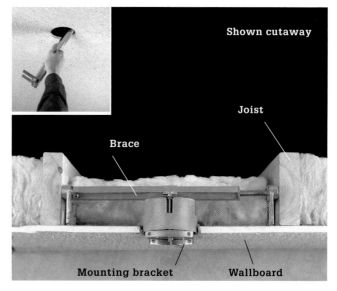

Shown cutaway

Joist

Brace

Mounting bracket   **Wallboard**

Add a wood brace above the ceiling box if you have access from above (as in an attic). Cut a 24" brace to fit and nail it between the ceiling joists. Drive a couple of deck screws through the ceiling box and into the brace. If the box is not fan-rated, replace it with one that is.

Install an adjustable fan brace if the ceiling is closed and you don't want to remove the wallcoverings. Remove the old light and the electrical box and then insert the fan brace into the box opening (inset photo). Twist the brace housing to cause it to telescope outward. The brace should be centered over the opening and at the right height so the ceiling box is flush with the ceiling surface once it is hung from the brace.

Bracket-mounted Fans

Direct-mount fan units have a motor housing with a mounting tab that fits directly into a slot on the mounting bracket. Fans with this mounting approach are secure and easy to install but difficult to adjust.

Ball-and-socket fan units have a downrod, but instead of threading into the mounting bracket, the downrod has an attached ball that fits into a hanger "socket" in the mounting bracket. This installation allows the fan to move in the socket and find its own level for quiet operation.

How to Install Downrod Ceiling Fans

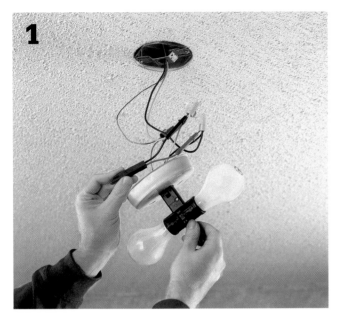

1

Shut off the power to the circuit at the service panel. Unscrew the existing fixture and carefully pull it away from the ceiling. Test for power by inserting the probes of a tester into the wire connectors on the black and the white wires. Disconnect and remove the old fixture.

2

Canopy

Rod hanger pipe

Run the wires from the top of the fan motor through the canopy and then through the rod hanger pipe. Slide the rod hanger pipe through the canopy and attach the pipe to the motor collar using the included hanging pin. Tighten the mounting screws firmly.

3

Hanging pin

Hang the motor assembly by the hook on the mounting bracket. Connect the wires according to manufacturer's directions using wire connectors to join the fixture wires to the circuit wires in the box. Gather the wires together and tuck them inside the fan canopy. Lift the canopy and attach it to the mounting bracket.

4

Fan housing

Attach the fan blades with the included hardware. Connect the wiring for the fan's light fixture according to the manufacturer's directions. Tuck all wires into the switch housing and attach the fixture. Install light bulbs. Restore power and test the fan.

Bathroom Vent Fans

Most vent fans are installed in the center of the bathroom ceiling or over the toilet area. A fan installed over the tub or shower area must be GFCI protected and rated for use in wet areas. You can usually wire a fan that just has a light fixture into a main bathroom electrical circuit, but units with built-in heat lamps or blowers require separate circuits.

If the fan you choose doesn't come with a mounting kit, purchase one separately. A mounting kit should include a vent hose (duct), a vent tailpiece, and an exterior vent cover.

The most common venting options are attic venting and soffit venting. Attic venting routes fan ductwork into the attic and out through the roof. Always insulate ducting in this application to keep condensation from forming and running down into the motor. And carefully install flashing around the outside vent cover to prevent roof leaks.

Soffit venting involves routing the duct to a soffit (roof overhang) instead of through the roof. Check with the vent manufacturer for instructions for soffit venting.

To prevent moisture damage, always terminate the vent outside your home—never into your attic or basement.

You can install a vent fan while the framing is exposed or as a retrofit, as shown in this project.

Tools & Materials ▸

Drill	NM cable (14/2, 14/3)
Jigsaw	Cable clamp
Combination tool	Hose clamps
Screwdrivers	Pipe insulation
Caulk gun	Roofing cement
Reciprocating saw	Self-sealing
Pry bar	roofing nails
Drywall screws	Shingles
Double-gang retrofit	Wire connectors
electrical box	Switch and timer

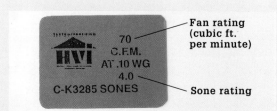

Check the information label attached to each vent fan unit. Choose a unit with a fan rating at least 5 CFM higher than the square footage of your bathroom. The sone rating refers to quietness rated on a scale of 1 to 7; quieter is lower.

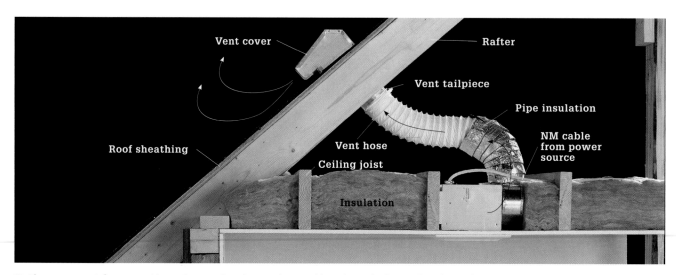

Bathroom vent fans must be exhausted to the outdoors, either through the roof or through a wall. Flexible ductwork is allowed for bath vent fans (but not for clothes dryers).

How to Install a Bathroom Vent Fan

Position the vent fan unit against a ceiling joist. Outline the vent fan onto the ceiling surface. Remove the unit, then drill pilot holes at the corners of the outline and cut out the area with a jigsaw or drywall saw.

Remove the grille from the fan unit, then position the unit against the joist with the edge recessed ¼" from the finished surface of the ceiling (so the grille can be flush mounted). Attach the unit to the joist using drywall screws.

Variation: For vent fans with heaters or light fixtures, some manufacturers recommend using 2× lumber to build dams between the ceiling joists to keep the insulation at least 6" away from the fan unit.

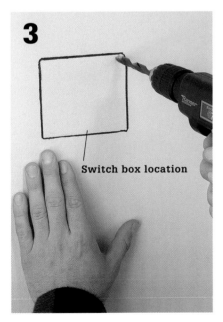

Mark and cut an opening for a double-gang box on the wall next to the latch side of the bathroom door, then run a 14/3 NM cable from the switch cutout to the fan unit. Run a 14/2 NM cable from the power source to the cutout.

Switch box location

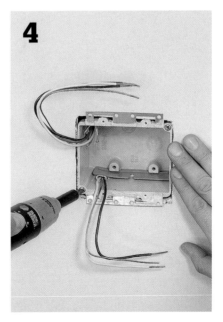

Strip 10" of sheathing from the ends of the cables, then feed the cables into a double-gang retrofit switch box so at least ½" of sheathing extends into the box. Clamp the cables in place. Tighten the mounting screws until the box is secure.

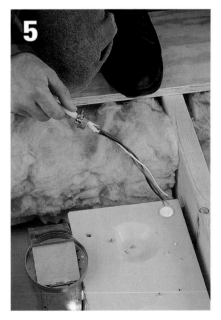

Strip 10" of sheathing from the end of the cable at the vent unit, then attach a cable clamp to the cable. Insert the cable into the fan unit. From the inside of the unit, screw a locknut onto the threaded end of the clamp.

(continued)

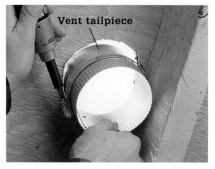

Mark the exit location in the roof next to a rafter for the vent duct. Drill a pilot hole, then saw through the sheathing and roofing material with a reciprocating saw to make the cutout for the vent tailpiece.

Remove a section of shingles from around the cutout, leaving the roofing paper intact. Remove enough shingles to create an exposed area that is at least the size of the vent cover flange.

Attach a hose clamp to the rafter next to the roof cutout about 1" below the roof sheathing (top). Insert the vent tailpiece into the cutout and through the hose clamp, then tighten the clamp screw (bottom).

Slide one end of the vent duct over the tailpiece, and slide the other end over the outlet on the fan unit. Slip hose clamps or straps around each end of the vent duct, and tighten the clamps.

Wrap the vent hose with pipe insulation. Insulation prevents moist air inside the hose from condensing and dripping down into the fan motor.

Apply roofing cement to the bottom of the vent cover flange, then slide the vent cover over the tailpiece. Nail the vent cover flange in place with self-sealing roofing nails, then patch in shingles around the cover.

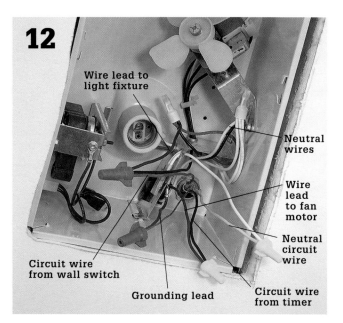

12

Wire lead to light fixture

Neutral wires

Wire lead to fan motor

Neutral circuit wire

Circuit wire from wall switch

Grounding lead

Circuit wire from timer

Ensure power is off and test for power. Make the following wire connections at the fan unit: the black circuit wire from the timer to the wire lead for the fan motor; the red circuit wire from the single-pole switch (see step 14) to the wire lead for the light fixture in the unit; the white neutral circuit wire to the neutral wire lead; the circuit grounding wire to the grounding lead on the fan unit. Make all connections with wire connectors. Attach the cover plate over the unit when the wiring is completed.

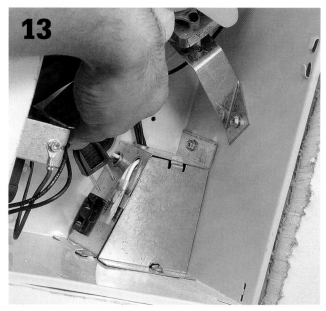

13

Connect the fan motor plug to the built-in receptacle on the wire connection box, and attach the fan grille to the frame using the mounting clips included with the fan kit. *Note: If you removed the wall and ceiling surfaces for the installation, install new surfaces before completing this step.*

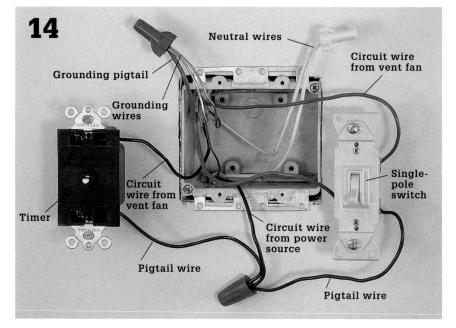

14

Neutral wires

Circuit wire from vent fan

Grounding pigtail

Grounding wires

Circuit wire from vent fan

Single-pole switch

Timer

Pigtail wire

Circuit wire from power source

Pigtail wire

Ensure power is off and test for power. At the switch box, add black pigtail wires to one screw terminal on the timer and to one screw terminal on the single-pole switch; add a green grounding pigtail to the groundling screw on the switch. Make the following wire connections: the black circuit wire from the power source to the black pigtail wires; the black circuit wire from the vent fan to the remaining screw on the timer; the red circuit wire from the vent fan to the remaining screw on the switch. Join the white wires with a wire connector. Join the grounding wires with a green wire connector.

15

Tuck the wires into the switch box, then attach the switch and timer to the box. Attach the cover plate and timer dial. Turn on the power.

Range Hoods

Range hoods do more than just get rid of cooking odors. Their most important job is to reduce the amount of water vapor in the air that's generated by routine cooking. The pot of water that boils for 30 minutes before you remember to drop in the pasta adds a lot of water vapor into your house. Usually the results are innocent enough. But prolonged periods of high moisture can lead to mildew and other molds that can stain your walls and ceilings and possibly make family members sick.

The hardest part of adding a range hood is installing the ductwork between the hood and the outside of your house. If the range is located on an outside wall, the best choice is to run the duct from the back of the hood straight through the wall. If you have wood siding, this job is not difficult. But if you have brick or stone, plan on spending several hours to cut this hole.

If the range is on an interior wall, the preferred route is usually from the top of the hood through the roof. It's also possible to put the duct into the attic, then across the ceiling (between two rafters or trusses) and out through an overhanging soffit.

Tools & Materials ▸

Hammer	Vent hood and ductwork
Jigsaw	Vent cover
Screwdrivers	Wire connectors
Drill/driver & bits	Sheet metal screws
Utility knife	Duct tape
Circular saw	Plastic roof cement
Caulk gun	Caulk

A range hood captures steam and airborne food particles and draws them directly out of your house through a vent pipe. For slide-in stoves, the hood usually is installed under a short cabinet that contains the ductwork connection.

Range Hoods & Vents

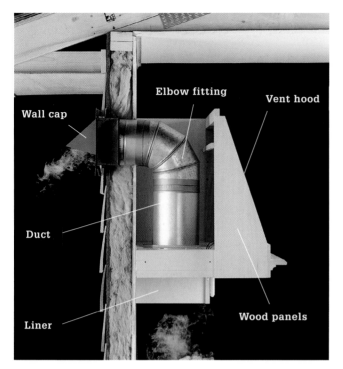

Cabinet-mounted range hoods draw steam upward and out of the house through a wall-mounted or roof-mounted vent.

Wall-mounted range hoods function in the same manner as cabinet mounted but they are not integrated into the kitchen cabinet system.

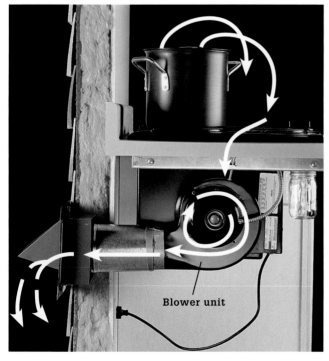

Downdraft vents pull steam downward and vent it out though a wall vent. While leaving the space above the stovetop uncluttered, these vents are much less efficient (in large part because steam naturally rises).

Island vents hang down from ceiling-mounted ductwork and draw steam and odors up from stovetops that are installed in kitchen islands. They typically have a very contemporary appearance.

How to Install a Range Hood

Install the vent duct in the wall first, then cut a hole in the back of the range hood cabinet and mount the cabinet over the duct. Cut a vent hole in the bottom of the cabinet to match the opening on the top of the hood.

Make sure the circuit power is turned off at the service panel and test for power. Then join the power cable wires to the lead wires inside the range hood. Use wire connectors for this job.

Get someone to help lift the range hood into place and hold it there while you attach it. Drive two screws through both sides and into the adjacent cabinets. If the hood is slightly small for the opening, slip a shim between the hood and the walls, trying to keep the gaps even.

Run ductwork from the cabinet to the exhaust exit point. Use two 45° adjustable elbows to join the duct in the wall to the top of the range hood. Use sheet metal screws and duct tape to hold all parts together and keep them from moving.

Venting Choices

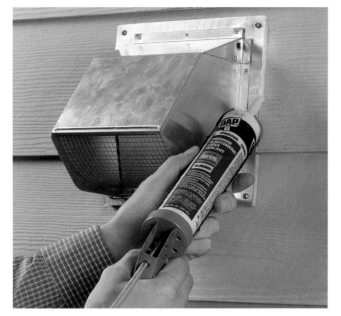

Wall vent: If the duct comes out through the sidewall of the house, install a vertical duct cap. Make sure to seal around the perimeter of the cap with exterior caulk.

Masonry wall vent: You can run ductwork out through an exterior wall made of brick or stucco, but it is a lot of work. You need to cut an opening in the wall with a masonry saw or chip one with a cold chisel and then attach the vent cover with masonry nails.

Soffit vent: If the duct goes through an overhang soffit, you'll need a transition fitting to connect the round duct to a short piece of rectangular duct. Once these parts are installed, add a protective grille to keep animals and insects from getting into the duct.

Roof vent: For ducts that pass through the roof, cut an access hole through the roofing and sheathing, then install a weatherproof cap on top of the duct and under the roofing shingles. Make a waterproof seal by caulking the cap with plastic roof cement. If you don't have much roofing experience, consult a roofing manual for some more information on this step. Also see page 252.

Backup Power Supply

Installing a backup generator is an invaluable way to prepare your family for emergencies. The simplest backup power system is a portable gas-powered generator and an extension cord or two. A big benefit of this approach is that you can run a refrigerator and a few worklights during a power outage with a tool that can also be transported to remote job sites or on camping trips when it's not doing emergency backup duty. This is also the least expensive way to provide some backup power for your home. You can purchase a generator at most home centers and be up and running in a matter of hours. If you take this approach, it is critically important that you make certain any loads being run by your generator are disconnected from the utility power source.

The next step up is to incorporate a manual transfer switch for your portable generator. Transfer switches are permanently hardwired to your service panel. They are mounted on either the interior or the exterior of your house between the generator and the service panel. You provide a power feed from the generator into the switch. The switch is wired to selected essential circuits in your house, allowing you to power lights, furnace blowers, and other loads that

can't easily be run with an extension cord. But perhaps the most important job a transfer switch performs is to disconnect the utility power. If the inactive utility power line is attached to the service panel, "backfeed" of power from your generator to the utility line can occur when the generator kicks in. This condition could be fatal to line workers who are trying to restore power. The potential for backfeed is the main reason many municipalities insist that only a licensed electrician hook up a transfer switch. Using a transfer switch not installed by a professional may also void the warranty of the switch and the generator.

Automatic transfer switches turn on the generator and switch off the utility supply when they detect a significant drop in line voltage. They may be installed with portable generators, provided the generator is equipped with an electric starter.

Large standby generators that resemble central air conditioners are the top of the line in backup power supply systems. Often fueled by home natural gas lines or propane tanks that offer a bottomless fuel source, standby generators are made in sizes with as much as 20 to 40 kilowatts of output—enough to supply all of the power needs of a 5,000-sq.-ft. home.

Generators have a range of uses. Large hard-wired models can provide instant emergency power for a whole house. Smaller models (below) are convenient for occasional short-term backup as well as job sites or camping trips.

Choosing a Backup Generator

A 2,000- to 5,000-watt gas-powered generator and a few extension cords can power lamps and an appliance or two during shorter-term power outages. Appliances must not be connected to household wiring and the generator simultaneously. Never plug a generator into an outlet. Never operate a generator indoors. Run extension cords through a garage door.

A permanent transfer switch patches electricity from a large portable generator through to selected household circuits via an inlet at your service panel (inset), allowing you to power hardwired fixtures and appliances with the generator.

For full, on-demand backup service, install a large standby generator wired through to an automatic transfer panel. In the event of a power outage, the household system instantly switches to the generator.

A Typical Backup System

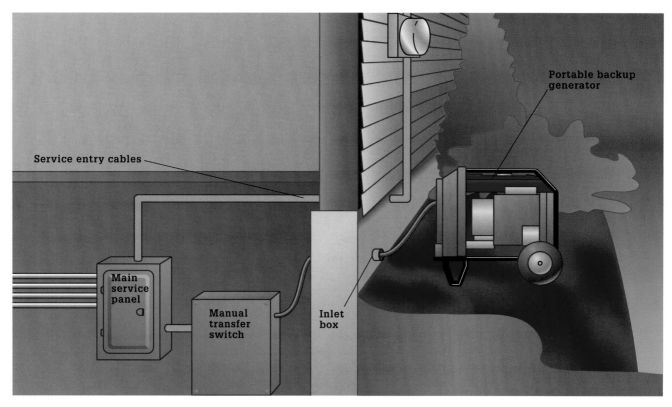

Backup generators supply power to a manual transfer switch, which disconnects the house from the main service wires and routes power from the generator through selected household circuits.

Choosing a Generator

Choosing a generator for your home's needs requires a few calculations. The chart below gives an estimate of the size of generator typically recommended for a house of a certain size. You can get a more accurate number by adding up the power consumption (the watts) of all the circuits or devices to be powered by a generator. It's also important to keep in mind that, for most electrical appliances, the amount of power required at the moment you flip the ON switch is greater than the number of watts required to keep the device running. For instance, though an air conditioner may run on 15,000 watts of power, it will require a surge of 30,000 watts at startup (the power range required to operate an appliance is usually listed somewhere on the device itself). These two numbers are called run watts and surge watts. Generators are typically sold according to run watts (a 5,000-watt generator can sustain 5,000 watts). They are also rated for a certain number of surge watts (a 5,000-watt generator may be able to produce

a surge of 10,000 watts). If the surge watts aren't listed, ask or check the manual. Some generators can't develop many more surge watts than run watts; others can produce twice as much surge as run wattage.

It's not necessary to buy a generator large enough to match the surge potential of all your circuits (you won't be turning everything on simultaneously), but surge watts should factor in your purchasing decision. If you will be operating the generator at or near capacity, it is also a wise practice to stagger startups for appliances.

Size of house (in square feet)	Recommended generator size (in kilowatts)
Up to 2,700	5–11
2,700–3,700	14–16
3,700–4,700	20
4,700–7,000	42–47

Types of Transfer Switches

Cord-connected transfer switches (shown above) are hard-wired to the service panel (in some cases they're installed after the service panel and operate only selected circuits). These switches contain a male receptacle for a power supply cord connected to the generator. Automatic transfer switches (not shown) detect voltage drop-off in the main power line and switch over to the emergency power source.

When using a cord-connected switch, consider mounting an inlet box to the exterior wall. This will allow you to connect a generator without running a cord into the house.

Generator Tips ▸

If you'll need to run sensitive electronics such as computers or home theater equipment, look for a generator with power inverter technology that dispenses "clean power" with a stable sine wave pattern.

A generator that will output 240-volt service is required to run most central air conditioners. If your generator has variable output (120/240) make sure the switch is set to the correct output voltage.

Running & Maintaining a Backup System

Even with a fully automatic standby generator system fueled by natural gas or propane, you will need to conduct some regular maintenance and testing to make sure all systems are ready in the event of power loss. If you're depending on a portable generator and extension cords or a standby generator with a manual transfer switch, you'll also need to know the correct sequence of steps to follow in a power emergency. Switches and panels also need to be tested on a regular basis, as directed in your owner's manual. And be sure that all switches (both interior and exterior) are housed in an approved enclosure box.

Pull-cord starter

Smaller portable generators often use pull-cords instead of electric starters.

ANATOMY OF A PORTABLE BACKUP GENERATOR

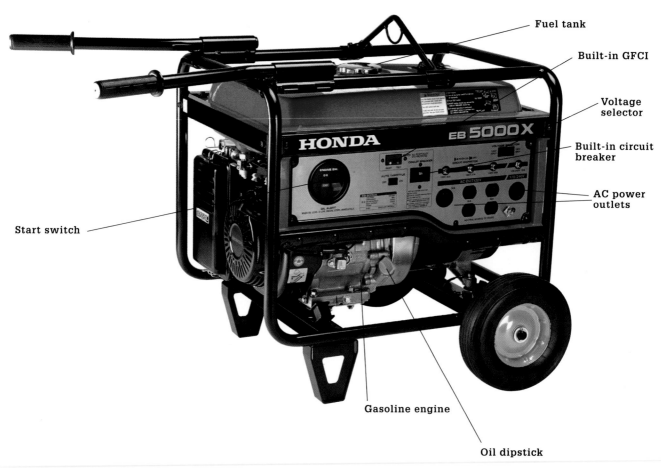

Fuel tank

Built-in GFCI

Voltage selector

Built-in circuit breaker

AC power outlets

Start switch

Gasoline engine

Oil dipstick

Portable generators use small gasoline engines to generate power. A built-in electronics panel sets current to AC or DC and the correct voltage. Most models will also include a built-in circuit breaker to protect the generator from damage in the event it is connected to too many loads. Better models include features like built-in GFCI protection. Larger portable generators may also feature electric starter motors and batteries for push-button starts.

Operating a Manual System During an Outage

Plug the generator in at the inlet box. Make sure the other end of the generator's outlet cord is plugged into the appropriate outlet on the generator (120-volt or 120/240-volt AC) and the generator is switched to the appropriate voltage setting.

Start the generator with the pull-cord or electric starter (if your generator has one). Let the generator run for several minutes before flipping the transfer switch.

Flip the manual transfer switch. Begin turning on loads one at a time by flipping breakers on, starting with the ones that power essential equipment. Do not overload the generator or the switch and do not run the generator at or near full capacity for more than 30 minutes at a time.

Maintaining and Operating an Automatic Standby Generator

If you choose to spend the money and install a dedicated standby generator of 10,000 watts or more and operate it through an automatic transfer switch or panel, you won't need to lift a hand when your utility power goes out. The system kicks in by itself. However, you should follow the manufacturer's suggestions for testing the system, changing the oil, and running the motor periodically.

Outbuildings

Nothing improves the convenience and usefulness of an outbuilding more than electrifying it. Running a new underground circuit from your house to an outbuilding lets you add receptacles and light fixtures both inside the outbuilding and on its exterior.

Adding an outdoor circuit is not complicated, but every aspect of the project is strictly governed by local building codes. Therefore, once you've mapped out the job and have a good idea of what's involved, visit your local building department to discuss your plans and obtain a permit for the work.

This project demonstrates standard techniques for running a circuit cable from the house exterior to a shed, plus the wiring and installation of devices inside the shed. To add a new breaker and make the final circuit connections to your home's main service panel, see page 176. The building department may recommend or require using a GFCI breaker to protect the entire circuit. Alternatively, you may be allowed to provide GFCI protection to the circuit devices via the receptacle inside the shed. GFCI protection is required on all outdoor circuits.

For basic electrical needs, such as powering a standard light fixture and small appliances or power tools, a 15-amp circuit should be sufficient. However, if you plan to run power-hungry equipment like stationary woodworking or welding tools, you may need one or more dedicated 20-amp circuits. Also, if the shed is more than 50 ft. away from the house, you may need heavier-gauge cable to account for voltage drop.

Most importantly, don't forget to call before you dig. Have all utility and service lines on your property marked even before you make serious project plans. This is critical for your safety, of course, and it may affect where you can run the circuit cable.

Adding an electrical circuit to an outbuilding like this shed greatly expands the activities the building will support and is also a great benefit for home security.

Spray paint
Trenching shovel
    (4" wide blade)
4" Metal junction box
Metal L-fittings (2)
    and conduit nipple
    for IMC conduit
Wood screws
IMC conduit
    with watertight
    threaded and
    compression fittings
Wrenches

Hacksaw
90° sweeps for IMC
    conduit (2)
Plastic conduit
    bushings (2)
Pipe straps
Silicone caulk
    and caulk gun
Double-gang
    boxes, metal (2)
One exterior
    receptacle box
    (with cover)

Single-pole switches (2)
Interior ceiling light
    fixture and metal
    fixture box
Exterior motion
    detector fixture and
    plastic fixture box
EMT metal conduit
    and fittings for
    inside the shed
Utility knife
UF two-wire cable
    (12 gauge)

NM two-wire cable
    (12 gauge)
15 amp GFI protected
    circuit breaker
Wire stripper
Pliers
Screwdrivers
Wire connectors
Hand tamper

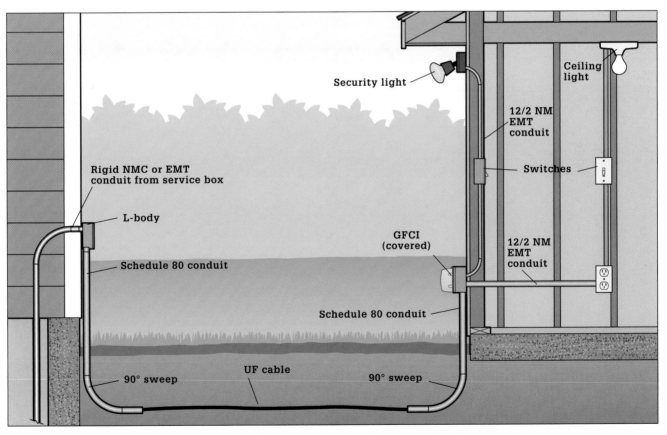

A basic outdoor circuit starts with a waterproof fitting at the house wall connected to a junction box inside. The underground circuit cable—rated UF (underground feeder)—runs in an 18"- to 24"-deep trench and is protected from exposure at both ends by metal or PVC conduit. Inside the shed, standard NM cable runs through metal conduit to protect it from damage (not necessary if you will be adding interior wallcoverings). All receptacles and devices in the shed must be GFCI protected.

How to Wire an Outbuilding

Identify the circuit's exit point at the house and entry point at the shed and mark them. Mark the path of the trench between the exit and entry points using spray paint. Make the route as direct as possible. Dig the trench to the depth required by local code using a narrow trenching shovel.

From outside, drill a hole through the exterior wall and the rim joist at the exit point for the cable (you'll probably need to install a bit extender or an extralong bit in your drill). Make the hole just large enough to accommodate the L-body conduit fitting and conduit nipple.

Assemble the conduit and junction box fittings that will penetrate the wall. Here, we attached a 12" piece of ¾" IMC (intermediate metallic conduit) and a sweep to a metal junction box with a compression fitting, and then inserted the conduit into the hole drilled in the rim joist. The junction box is attached to the floor joist.

From outside, seal the hole around the conduit with expandable spray foam or caulk, and then attach the free end of the conduit to the back of a waterproof L-body fitting. Mount the L-body fitting to the house exterior with the open end facing downward.

5

Cut a length of IMC to extend from the L-fitting down into the trench using a hacksaw. Deburr the cut edges of the conduit. Secure the conduit to the L-fitting, then attach a 90° sweep to the bottom end of the conduit using compression fittings. Add a bushing to the end of the sweep to protect the circuit cable. Anchor the conduit to the wall with a corrosion-resistant pipe strap.

6

Inside the shed, drill a ¾" dia. hole in the shed wall. On the interior of the shed, mount a junction box with an open back to allow the cable to enter through the hole. On the exterior side directly above the end of the UF trench, mount an exterior-rated receptacle box with cover. The plan (and your plan likely will differ) is to bring power into the shed through the hole in the wall behind the exterior receptacle.

7

Run IMC from the exterior box down into the trench. Fasten the conduit to the building with a strap. Add a 90° sweep and bushing, as before. Secure the conduit to the box with an offset fitting. Anchor the conduit with pipe straps, and seal the entry hole with caulk.

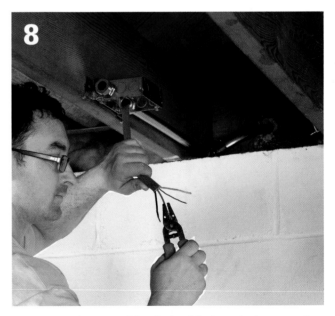

8

Run UF (underground feeder) cable from the house to the outbuilding. Feed one end of the UF circuit cable up through the sweep and conduit and into the L-fitting at the house (the back or side of the fitting is removable to facilitate cabling). Run the cable through the wall and into the junction box, leaving at least 12" of extra cable at the end.

(continued)

Lay the UF cable into the trench, making sure it is not twisted and will not contact any sharp objects. Roll out the cable and then feed the other end of the cable up through the conduit and into the receptacle box in the shed, leaving 12" of slack.

Inside the outbuilding, install the remaining boxes for the other switches, receptacles, and lights. With the exception of plastic receptacle boxes for exterior exposure, use metal boxes if you will be connecting the boxes with metal conduit.

Connect the electrical boxes with conduit and fittings. Inside the outbuilding, you may use inexpensive EMT to connect receptacle, switch, and fixture boxes. Once you've planned your circuit routes, start by attaching couplings to all of the boxes.

Cut a length of conduit to fit between the coupling and the next box or fitting in the run. If necessary, drill holes for the conduit through the centers of the wall studs. Attach the conduit to the fitting that you attached to the first box.

13

If you are surface-mounting the conduit or running it up or down next to wall studs, secure it with straps no more than 3 ft. apart. Use elbow fittings for 90° turns and setscrew couplings for joining straight lengths as needed. Make holes through the wall studs only as large as necessary to feed the conduit through.

14

Measure to find how much NM cable you'll need for each run, and cut a piece that's a foot or two longer. Before making L-turns with the conduit, feed the cable through the first conduit run.

15

Feed the other end of the cable into the next box or fitting in line. It is much easier to feed cable into 45° and 90° elbows if they have not been attached to the conduit yet. Continue feeding cable into the conduit and fitting until you have reached the next box in line.

16

Once you've reached the next box in line, coil the end of the cable and repeat the process with new cable for the next run. Keep working until all of the cable is run and all of the conduit and fittings are installed and secured. If you are running multiple cables into a single box, write the origin or destination on a piece of masking tape and stick it to each cable end.

(continued)

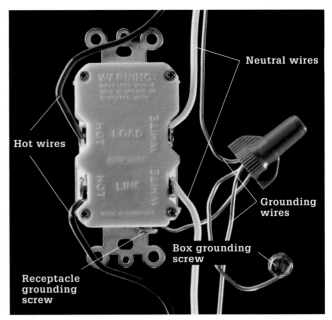

Hot wires

Neutral wires

Grounding wires

Box grounding screw

Receptacle grounding screw

Make the wiring connections at the receptacles. Strip ¾" of insulation from the circuit wires using a wire stripper. Connect the white (neutral) wire and black (hot) wire of the UF cable to the LINE screw terminals on the receptacle. Connect the white (neutral) and black (hot) wires from the NM cable to the LOAD terminals. Pigtail the bare copper ground wires and connect them to the receptacle ground terminal and the metal box. Install the receptacle and cover plate.

Variation: Installing a GFCI-protected breaker for the new circuit at the main service panel is the best way to protect the circuit and allows you to use regular receptacles in the building, but an alternative that is allowed in many areas is to run the service into a GFCI-protected receptacle and then wire the other devices on the circuit in series. If you use this approach, only the initial receptacle needs to be GFCI protected.

Continue installing receptacles in the circuit run, and then run service from the last receptacle to the switch box for the light fixture or fixtures. (If you anticipate a lot of load on the circuit, you should probably run a separate circuit for the lights). Twist the white neutral leads and grounding leads together and cap them. Attach the black wires to the appropriate switches. Install the switches and cover plate.

Install the light fixtures. For this shed, we installed a caged ceiling light inside the shed and a motion-detector security light on the exterior side (see pages 272 to 275).

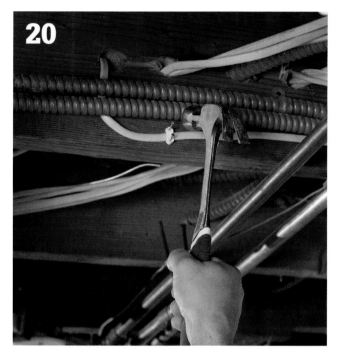

Run NM cable from the electrical box in the house at the start of the new circuit to the main service panel. Use cable staples if you are running the cable in floor joist cavities. If the cable is mounted to the bottom of the floor joists or will be exposed, run it through conduit.

At the service panel, feed the NM cable in through a cable clamp. Arrange for your final electrical inspection before you install the breaker. Then attach the wires to a new circuit breaker and install the breaker in an empty slot. Label the new circuit on the circuit map.

Turn on the new circuit and test all of the receptacles and fixtures. Depress the Test button and then the Reset button if you installed a GFCI receptacle. If any of the fixtures or receptacles is not getting power, check the connections first and then test the receptacle or switch for continuity with a multimeter.

Lay narrow scraps of lumber over the cable in the trench as an extra layer of protection from digging and then backfill with dirt to cover. Replace the sod in the trench if you saved it.

Motion-Sensing Floodlights

Most houses and garages have floodlights on their exteriors. You can easily upgrade these fixtures so that they provide additional security by replacing them with motion-sensing floodlights. Motion-sensing floods can be set up to detect motion in a specific area—like a walkway or driveway—and then cast light into that area. And there are few things intruders like less than the spotlight. These lights typically have timers that allow you to control how long the light stays on and photosensors that prevent the light from coming on during the day.

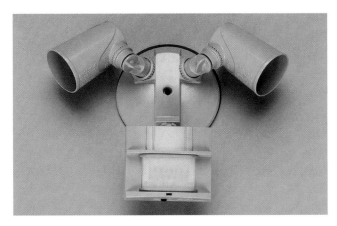

A motion-sensing light fixture provides inexpensive and effective protection against intruders. It has an infrared eye that triggers the light fixture when a moving object crosses its path. Choose a light fixture with: a photo cell to prevent the light from turning on in daylight; an adjustable timer to control how long the light stays on; and range control to adjust the reach of the motion-sensor eye.

An exterior floodlight with a motion sensor is an effective security measure. Keep the motion sensor adjusted to cover only the area you wish to secure—if the coverage area is too large the light will turn on frequently.

How to Install a New Exterior Fixture Box

On the outside of the house, make the cutout for the motion-sensor light fixture in the same stud cavity with the GFCI cutout. Outline the light fixture box on the wall, then drill a pilot hole and complete the cutout with a wallboard saw or jigsaw.

Estimate the distance between the indoor switch box and the outdoor motion-sensor box, and cut a length of NM cable about 2 ft. longer than this distance. Use a fish tape to pull the cable from the switch box to the motion-sensor box. See page 40 for tips on running cable through finished walls.

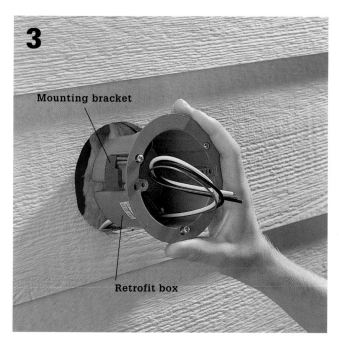

Mounting bracket

Retrofit box

Strip about 10" of outer insulation from the end of the cable using a cable ripper. Open a knockout in the retrofit light fixture box with a screwdriver. Insert the cable into the box so that at least ¼" of outer sheathing reaches into the box.

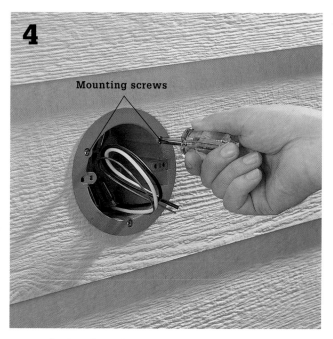

Mounting screws

Insert the box into the cutout opening, and tighten the mounting screws until the brackets draw the outside flange firmly against the siding.

How to Replace a Floodlight with a Motion-Sensor Light

1

Turn off power to the old fixture. To remove it, unscrew the mounting screws on the part of the fixture attached to the wall. There will probably be four of them. Carefully pull the fixture away from the wall, exposing the wires. Don't touch the wires yet.

2

Before you touch any wires, use a voltage sensor to verify that the circuit is dead. With the light switch turned on, insert the sensor's probe into the electrical box and hold the probe within ½" of the wires inside to confirm that there is no voltage flow. Disconnect the wire connectors and remove the old fixture.

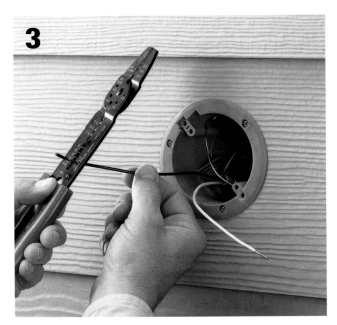

3

Examine the ends of the three wires coming from the box (one white, one black, and one bare copper). They should be clean and free of corrosion. If the ends are in poor condition, clip them off and then strip ¾" of wire insulation with a combination tool.

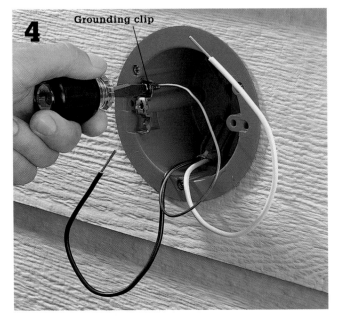

4

Grounding clip

If the electrical box is nonmetallic and does not have a metal grounding clip install a grounding clip or replace the box with one that does have a clip, and make sure the ground wire is attached to it securely. Some light fixtures have a grounding terminal on the base. If yours has one, attach the grounding wire from the house directly to the terminal.

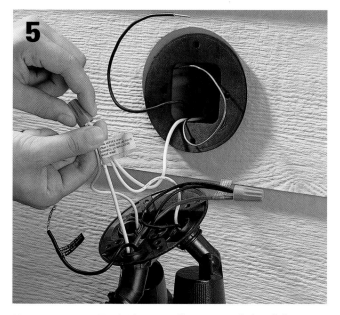

Now you can attach the new fixture. Begin by sliding a rubber or foam gasket (usually provided with the fixture) over the wires and onto the flange of the electrical box. Set the new fixture on top of a ladder or have a helper hold it while you make the wiring connections. There may be as many as three white wires coming from the fixture. Join all white wires, including the feed wire from the house using a wire connector.

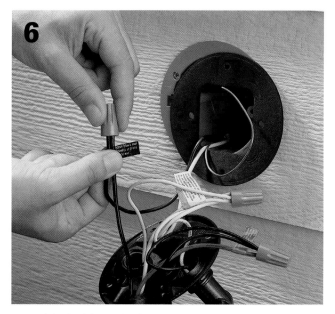

Next, join the black wire from the box and the single black wire from the fixture with a wire connector. You may see a couple of black wires and a red wire already joined on the fixture. You can ignore these in your installation.

Neatly tuck all the wires into the box so they are behind the gasket. Align the holes in the gasket with the holes in the box, and then position the fixture over the gasket so its mounting holes are also aligned with the gasket. Press the fixture against the gasket and drive the four mounting screws into the box. Install floodlights (exterior rated) and restore power.

Test the fixture. You will still be able to turn it on and off with the light switch inside. Flip the switch on and pass your hand in front of the motion sensor. The light should come on. Adjust the motion sensor to cover the traffic areas and pivot the light head to illuminate the intended area.

Repair Projects

"Repair" and "wiring" are two words you don't see together too much anymore. In most cases of an electrical failure, the repair is to replace the failed device. But it may also be reconnected to a bad splice or a loose connection.

The electrical items that most frequently require actual repairs are light fixtures. If you include lamps and cords in this category, you've pretty much covered it. Most electrical failures result from poorly made connections in the original installation. Exceptions are switches, which tend to wear out over time and require replacement, and ceiling fans. Ceiling fans are unique in that, like switches, they contain moving parts—and rapidly moving parts at that. Catching a switch pull chain on a moving blade is the cause of many ceiling fan problems, along with blades that have fallen out of balance and have begun to wobble.

When replacing part of an electrical fixture, the rule of thumb for finding the replacement part is to remove the broken part and bring it with you to a lighting or electrical supply store. Failing that, take down the make and serial number of the fixture so the clerk can look up part information for you.

In this chapter:

- Repairing Light Fixtures
- Repairing Chandeliers
- Repairing Ceiling Fans
- Repairing Fluorescent Lights
- Replacing Plugs & Cords
- Replacing a Lamp Socket

Repairing Light Fixtures

Light fixtures are attached permanently to ceilings or walls. They include wall-hung sconces, ceiling-hung globe fixtures, recessed light fixtures, and chandeliers. Most light fixtures are easy to repair using basic tools and inexpensive parts.

If a light fixture fails, always make sure the light bulb is screwed in tightly and is not burned out. A faulty light bulb is the most common cause of light fixture failure. If the light fixture is controlled by a wall switch, also check the switch as a possible source of problems.

Light fixtures can fail because the sockets or built-in switches wear out. Some fixtures have sockets and switches that can be removed for minor repairs. These parts are held to the base of the fixture with mounting screws or clips. Other fixtures have sockets and switches that are joined permanently to the base. If this type of fixture fails, purchase and install a new light fixture.

Damage to light fixtures often occurs because homeowners install light bulbs with wattage ratings that are too high. Prevent overheating and light fixture failures by using only light bulbs that match the wattage ratings printed on the fixtures.

Techniques for repairing fluorescent lights are different from those for incandescent lights. Refer to pages 288 to 293 to repair or replace a fluorescent light fixture.

Tools & Materials ▶

Circuit tester
Screwdriver
Continuity tester

Combination tool
Replacement parts,
    as needed

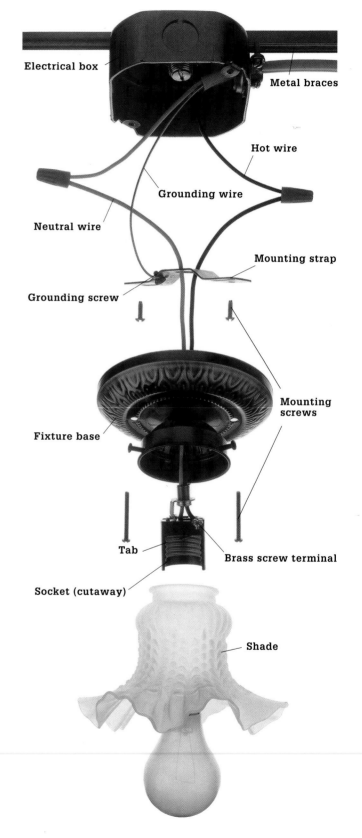

In a typical incandescent light fixture, a black hot wire is connected to a brass screw terminal on the socket. Power flows to a small tab at the bottom of the metal socket and through a metal filament inside the bulb. The power heats the filament and causes it to glow. The current then flows through the threaded portion of the socket and through the white neutral wire back to the main service panel.

Electrical box
Metal braces
Hot wire
Grounding wire
Neutral wire
Mounting strap
Grounding screw
Mounting screws
Fixture base
Tab
Brass screw terminal
Socket (cutaway)
Shade

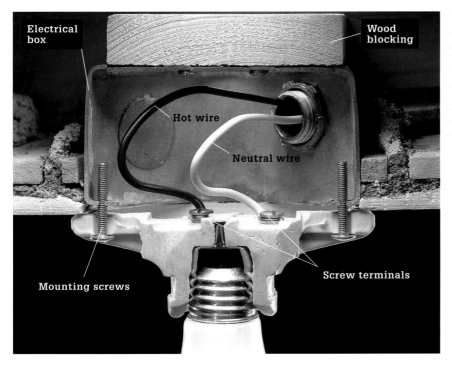

Electrical box

Wood blocking

Hot wire

Neutral wire

Mounting screws

Screw terminals

Before 1959, incandescent light fixtures (shown cutaway) often were mounted directly to an electrical box or to plaster lath. Electrical codes now require that fixtures be attached to mounting straps that are anchored to the electrical boxes. If you have a light fixture attached to plaster lath, install an approved electrical box with a mounting strap to support the fixture.

Problem	Repair
Wall- or ceiling-mounted fixture flickers or does not light.	1. Check for faulty light bulb. 2. Check wall switch and repair or replace, if needed. 3. Check for loose wire connections in electrical box. 4. Test socket and replace, if needed (pages 280 to 281). 5. Replace light fixture.
Built-in switch on fixture does not work.	1. Check for faulty light bulb. 2. Check for loose wire connections on switch. 3. Replace switch. 4. Replace light fixture.
Chandelier flickers or does not light.	1. Check for faulty light bulb. 2. Check wall switch and repair or replace, if needed. 3. Check for loose wire connections in electrical box. 4. Test sockets and fixture wires, and replace, if needed.
Recessed fixture flickers or does not light.	1. Check for faulty light bulb. 2. Check wall switch and repair or replace, if needed. 3. Check for loose wire connections in electrical box. 4. Test fixture and replace, if needed.

How to Remove a Light Fixture & Test a Socket

Turn off the power to the light fixture at the main service panel. Remove the light bulb and any shade or globe, then remove the mounting screws holding the fixture base to the electrical box or mounting strap. Carefully pull the fixture base away from the box.

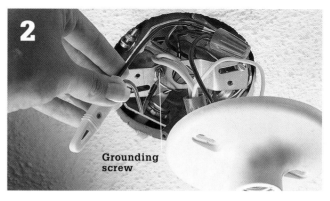

Grounding screw

Test for power by touching one probe of a circuit tester to the green grounding screw, then inserting the other probe into each wire connector. Tester should not glow. If it does, there is still power entering the box. Return to the service panel and turn off power to the correct circuit.

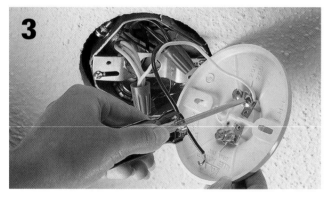

Disconnect the light fixture base by loosening the screw terminals. If fixture has wire leads instead of screw terminals, remove the light fixture base by unscrewing the wire connectors.

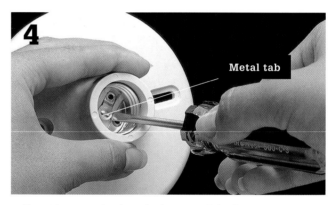

Metal tab

Adjust the metal tab at the bottom of the fixture socket by prying it up slightly with a small screwdriver. This adjustment will improve the contact between the socket and the light bulb.

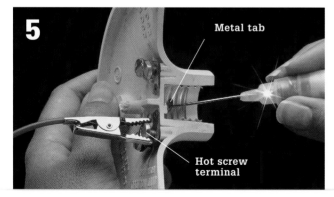

Metal tab

Hot screw terminal

Test the socket (shown cutaway) by attaching the clip of a continuity tester to the hot screw terminal (or black wire lead) and touching probe of tester to metal tab in bottom of socket. Tester should glow. If not, socket is faulty and must be replaced.

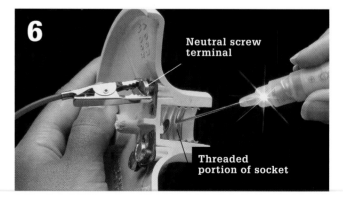

Neutral screw terminal

Threaded portion of socket

Attach tester clip to neutral screw terminal (or white wire lead), and touch probe to threaded portion of socket. Tester should glow. If not, socket is faulty and must be replaced. If socket is permanently attached, replace the fixture.

How to Replace a Socket

Remove the old light fixture. Remove the socket from the fixture. The socket may be held by a screw, clip, or retaining ring. Disconnect wires attached to the socket.

Purchase an identical replacement socket. Connect the white wire to the silver screw terminal on the socket, and connect the black wire to the brass screw terminal. Attach the socket to the fixture base, and reinstall the fixture.

How to Test & Replace a Built-in Light Switch

Retaining ring

Remove the light fixture. Unscrew the retaining ring holding the switch.

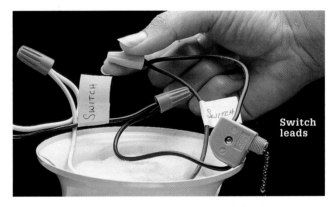

Switch leads

Label the wires connected to the switch leads. Disconnect the switch leads and remove the switch.

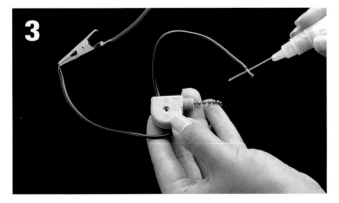

Test the switch by attaching the clip of the continuity tester to one of the switch leads and holding the tester probe to the other lead. Operate the switch control. If the switch is good, the tester will glow when the switch is in one position, but not both.

If the switch is faulty, purchase and install an exact duplicate switch. Remount the light fixture, and turn on the power at the main service panel.

Repairing Chandeliers

Repairing a chandelier requires special care. Because chandeliers are heavy, it is a good idea to work with a helper when removing a chandelier. Support the fixture to prevent its weight from pulling against the wires.

Chandeliers have two fixture wires that are threaded through the support chain from the electrical box to the hollow base of the chandelier. The socket wires connect to the fixture wires inside this base.

Fixture wires are identified as hot and neutral. Look closely for a raised stripe on one of the wires. This is the neutral wire that is connected to the white circuit wire and white socket wire. The other smooth fixture wire is hot and is connected to the black wires.

If you have a new chandelier, it may have a grounding wire that runs through the support chain to the electrical box. If this wire is present, make sure it is connected to the grounding wires in the electrical box.

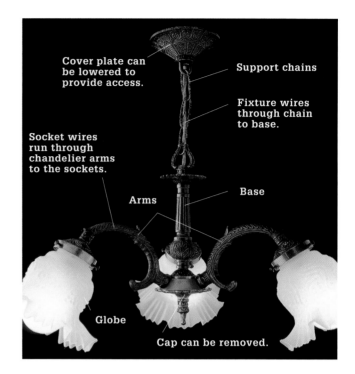

Cover plate can be lowered to provide access.

Support chains

Fixture wires through chain to base.

Socket wires run through chandelier arms to the sockets.

Arms

Base

Globe

Cap can be removed.

How to Repair a Chandelier

Label any lights that are not working using masking tape. Turn off power to the fixture at the main service panel. Remove light bulbs and all shades or globes.

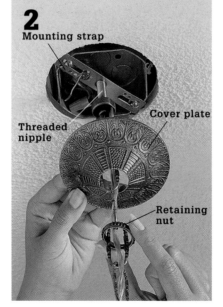

Mounting strap

Cover plate

Threaded nipple

Retaining nut

Unscrew the retaining nut and lower the decorative coverplate away from the electrical box. Most chandeliers are supported by a threaded nipple attached to a mounting strap.

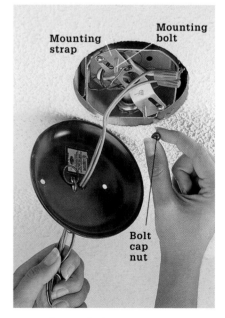

Mounting strap

Mounting bolt

Bolt cap nut

Mounting variation: Some chandeliers are supported only by the cover plate that is bolted to the electrical box mounting strap. These types do not have a threaded nipple.

3

Grounding screw

Test for power with a circuit tester. Tester should not glow. If it does, turn off power to the correct circuit at the panel.

4

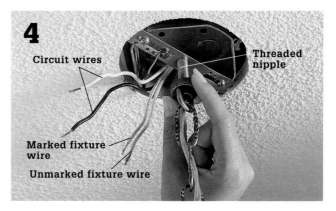

Circuit wires

Threaded nipple

Marked fixture wire

Unmarked fixture wire

Disconnect fixture wires by removing the wire connectors. Unscrew threaded nipple and carefully place chandelier on a flat surface.

5

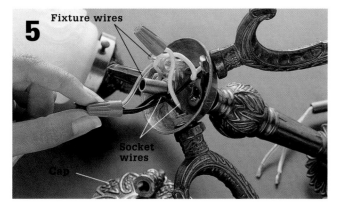

Fixture wires

Socket wires

Cap

Remove the cap from the bottom of the chandelier, exposing the wire connections inside the hollow base. Disconnect the socket wires and fixture wires.

6

Test socket by attaching clip of continuity tester to black socket wire and touching probe to tab in socket. Repeat with socket threads and white socket wire. If tester does not glow, the socket must be replaced.

7

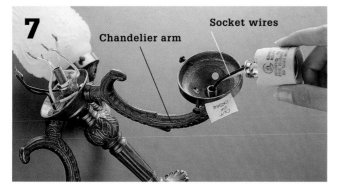

Chandelier arm

Socket wires

Remove a faulty socket by loosening any mounting screws or clips and pulling the socket and socket wires out of the fixture arm. Purchase and install a new chandelier socket, threading the socket wires through the fixture arm.

8

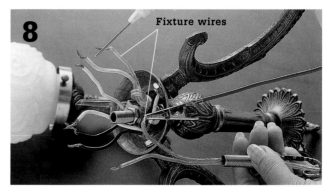

Fixture wires

Test each fixture wire by attaching clip of continuity tester to one end of wire and touching probe to other end. If tester does not glow, wire must be replaced. Install new wires, if needed, then reassemble and rehang the chandelier.

Repairing Ceiling Fans

Ceiling fans contain rapidly moving parts, making them more susceptible to trouble than many other electrical fixtures. Installation is a relatively simple matter, but repairing a ceiling fan can be very frustrating. The most common problems you'll encounter are balance and noise issues and switch failure, usually precipitated by the pull chain breaking. In most cases, both problems can be corrected without removing the fan from the ceiling. But if you have difficulty on ladders or simply don't care to work overhead, consider removing the fan when replacing the switch.

Ceiling fans are subject to a great deal of vibration and stress, so it's not uncommon for switches and motors to fail. Minimize wear and tear by making sure blades are in balance so the fan doesn't wobble.

Tools & Materials ▸

Screwdriver
Combination tool

Replacement switch
Voltage Sensor

How to Troubleshoot Blade Wobble

Start by checking and tightening all hardware used to attach the blades to the mounting arms and the mounting arms to the motor. Hardware tends to loosen over time, and this is frequently the cause of wobble.

If wobble persists, try switching around two of the blades. Often, this is all it takes to get the fan back into balance. If a blade is damaged or warped, replace it.

If the blades are tight and you still have wobble, turn the power off at the panel, remove the fan canopy, and inspect the mounting brace and the connection between the mounting pole and the fan motor. If any connections are loose, tighten them and then replace the canopy.

How to Fix a Loose Wire Connection

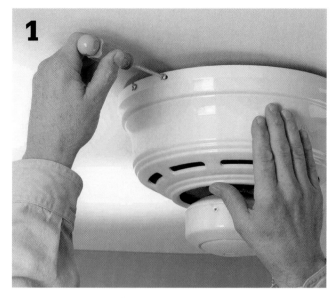

1

A leading cause of fan failure is loose wire connections. To inspect these connections, first shut off the power to the fan. Remove the fan blades to gain access, then remove the canopy that covers the ceiling box and fan mounting bracket. Most canopies are secured with screws on the outside shell. Have a helper hold the fan while you remove the screws so it won't fall.

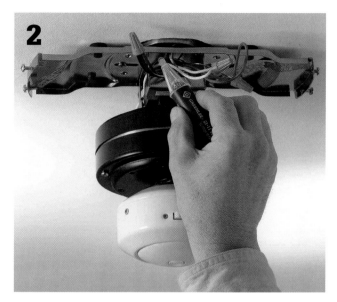

2

Once the canopy is lowered, you'll see black, white, green, copper, and possibly blue wires. Hold a voltage sensor within ½" of these wires with the wall switch that controls the fan in the ON position. The black and blue wires should cause the sensor to beep if power is present.

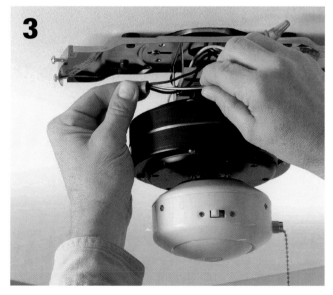

3

When you have confirmed that there is no power, check all the wire connections to make certain each is tight and making good contact. You may be able to see that a connection has come apart and needs to be remade. But even if you see one bad connection, check them all by gently tugging on the wire connectors. If the wires pull out of the wire connector or the connection feels loose, unscrew the wire connector from the wires.

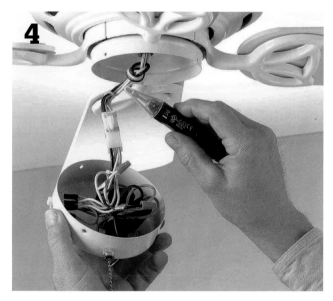

4

Test the wires by placing a voltage sensor within ½" of the wires. If the sensor beeps or lights up, then the circuit is still live and is not safe to work. When the sensor does not beep or light up, the circuit is dead and may be worked upon. If everything works, reinstall the canopy by replacing the screws that were holding it in place. Reattach the fan blades and then restore power.

How to Replace a Ceiling Fan Pull-Chain Switch

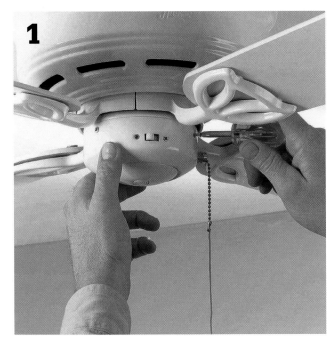

Turn off the power at the main service panel. Use a screwdriver to remove the three to four screws that secure the bottom cap on the fan switch housing. Lower the cap to expose the wires that supply power to the pull-chain switch.

Test the wires by placing a voltage sensor within ½" of the wires. If the sensor beeps or lights up, then the circuit is still live and is not safe to work. When the sensor does not beep or light up, the circuit is dead and may be worked upon.

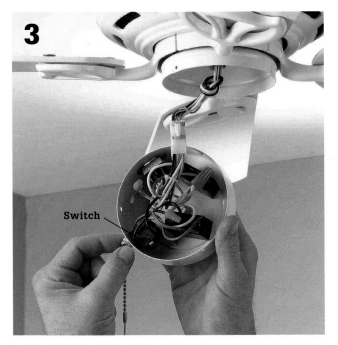

Switch

Locate the switch unit (the part that the pull chain used to be attached to if it broke off); it's probably made of plastic. You'll need to replace the whole switch. Fan switches are connected with from three to eight wires, depending on the number of speed settings.

Attach a small piece of tape to each wire that enters the switch and write an identifying number on the tape. Start at one side of the switch and label the wires in the order they're attached.

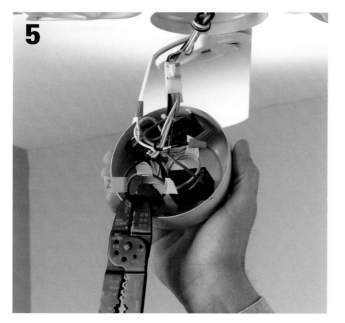

5

Disconnect the old switch wires, in most cases by cutting the wires off as close to the old switch as possible. Unscrew the retaining nut that secures the switch to the switch housing.

Buyer's Tip ▸

Here's how to buy a new switch. Bring the old switch to the hardware store or home center, and find an identical new switch—one with the same number and color of wires. It should also attach to the fan motor wires in the same way (slots or screw terminals or with integral wires and wire connectors) and attach to the fan in the same way. If you are unable to locate an identical switch, find the owners manual for your ceiling fan and contact the manufacturer. Or, find the brand and model number of the fan and order a switch from a ceiling fan dealer or electronics supply store.

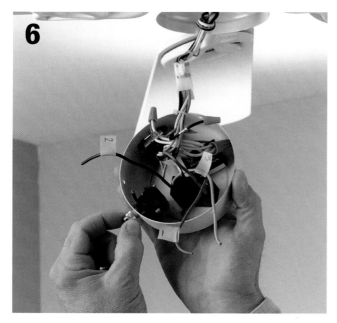

6

Remove the switch. There may be one or two screws that hold it in place or it may be secured to the outside of the fan with a small knurled nut, which you can loosen with needlenose pliers. Purchase an identical new switch.

7

Connect the new switch using the same wiring configuration as on the old model. To make connections, first use a wire stripper to strip ¾" of insulation from the ends of each of the wires coming from the fan motor (the ones you cut in step 5). Attach the wires to the new switch in the same order and configuraion as they were attached to the old switch. Secure the new switch in the housing and make sure all wires are tucked neatly inside. Reattach the bottom cap. Test all the fan's speeds to make sure all the connections are good.

Repairing Fluorescent Lights

Fluorescent lights are relatively trouble free and use less energy than incandescent lights. A typical fluorescent tube lasts about three years and produces two to four times as much light per watt as a standard incandescent light bulb.

The most frequent problem with a fluorescent light fixture is a worn-out tube. If a fluorescent light fixture begins to flicker or does not light fully, remove and examine the tube. If the tube has bent or broken pins or black discoloration near the ends, replace it. Light gray discoloration is normal in working fluorescent tubes. When replacing an old tube, read the wattage rating printed on the glass surface, and buy a new tube with a matching rating. Never dispose of old tubes by breaking them. Fluorescent tubes contain a small amount of hazardous mercury. Check with your local environmental control agency or health department for disposal guidelines.

Fluorescent light fixtures also can malfunction if the sockets are cracked or worn. Inexpensive replacement sockets are available at any hardware store and can be installed in a few minutes.

If a fixture does not work even after the tube and sockets have been serviced, the ballast probably is defective. Faulty ballasts may leak a black, oily substance and can cause a fluorescent light fixture to make a loud humming sound. Although ballasts can be replaced, always check prices before buying a new ballast. It may be cheaper to purchase and install a new fluorescent fixture rather than to replace the ballast in an old fluorescent light fixture.

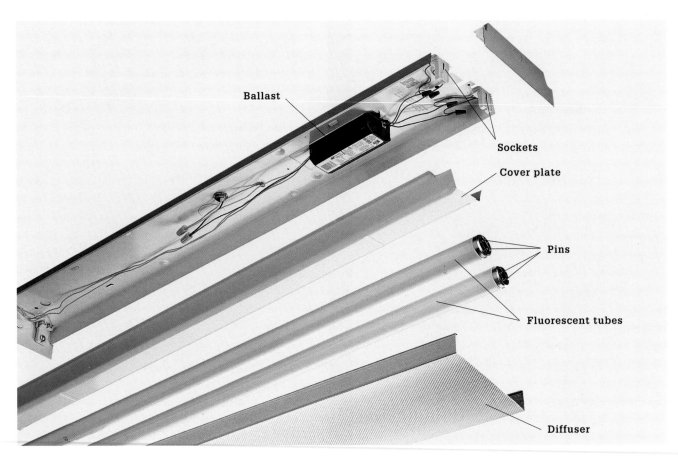

Ballast

Sockets

Cover plate

Pins

Fluorescent tubes

Diffuser

A fluorescent light works by directing electrical current through a special gas-filled tube that glows when energized. A white translucent diffuser protects the fluorescent tube and softens the light. A cover plate protects a special transformer, called a ballast. The ballast regulates the flow of 120-volt household current to the sockets. The sockets transfer power to metal pins that extend into the tube.

Problem	Repair
Tube flickers, or lights partially.	1. Rotate tube to make sure it is seated properly in the sockets. 2. Replace tube and the starter (where present) if tube is discolored or if pins are bent or broken. 3. Replace the ballast if replacement cost is reasonable. Otherwise, replace the entire fixture.
Tube does not light.	1. Check wall switch and repair or replace, if needed. 2. Rotate the tube to make sure it is seated properly in sockets. 3. Replace tube and the starter (where present) if tube is discolored or if pins are bent or broken. 4. Replace sockets if they are chipped or if tube does not seat properly. 5. Replace the ballast or the entire fixture.
Noticeable black substance around ballast.	Replace ballast if replacement cost is reasonable. Otherwise, replace the entire fixture.
Fixture hums.	Replace ballast if replacement cost is reasonable. Otherwise, replace the entire fixture.

Tools & Materials ▸

Screwdriver
Ratchet wrench
Combination tool
Circuit tester
Replacement tubes
Starters, or ballast
 (if needed)
Replacement fluorescent light fixture
 (if needed)

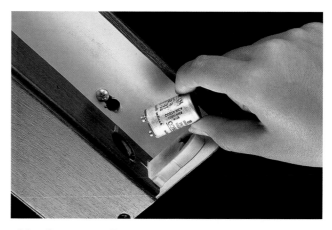

Older fluorescent lights may have a small cylindrical device, called a starter, located near one of the sockets. When a tube begins to flicker, replace both the tube and the starter. Turn off the power, then remove the starter by pushing it slightly and turning counterclockwise. Install a replacement that matches the old starter.

How to Replace a Fluorescent Tube

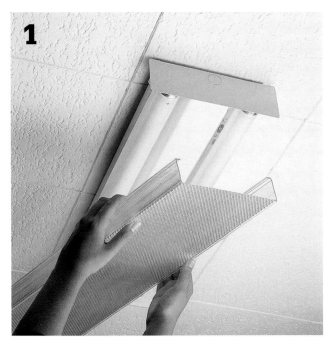

1

Turn off power to the light fixture at the switch. Remove the diffuser to expose the fluorescent tube.

2

Remove the fluorescent tube by rotating it ¼ turn in either direction and sliding the tube out of the sockets. Inspect the pins at the end of the tube. Tubes with bent or broken pins should be replaced.

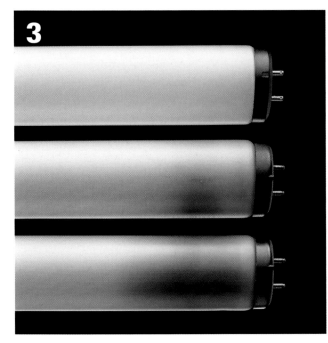

3

Inspect the ends of the fluorescent tube for discoloration. New tube in good working order (top) shows no discoloration. Normal, working tube (middle) may have gray color. A worn-out tube (bottom) shows black discoloration.

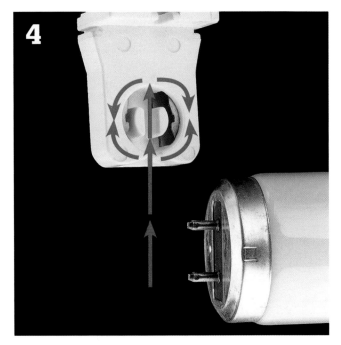

4

Install a new tube with the same wattage rating as the old tube. Insert the tube so that pins slide fully into sockets, then twist tube ¼ turn in either direction until it is locked securely. Reattach the diffuser, and turn on the power at the main service panel.

How to Replace a Socket

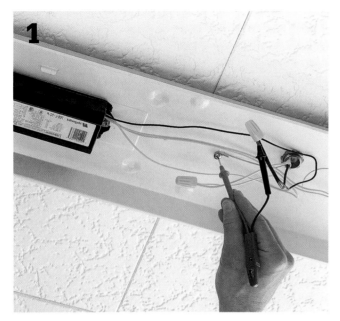

Turn off the power at the main service panel. Remove the diffuser, fluorescent tube, and the cover plate. Test for power by touching one probe of a neon circuit tester to the grounding screw and inserting the other probe into the hot wire connector. If tester glows, return to the service panel and turn off correct circuit.

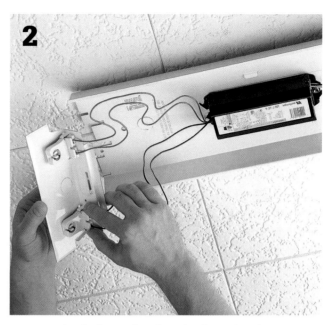

Remove the faulty socket from the fixture housing. Some sockets slide out, while others must be unscrewed.

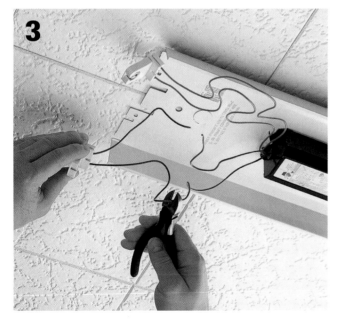

Disconnect wires attached to socket. For push-in fittings (above) remove the wires by inserting a small screwdriver into the release openings. Some sockets have screw terminal connections, while others have preattached wires that must be cut before the socket can be removed.

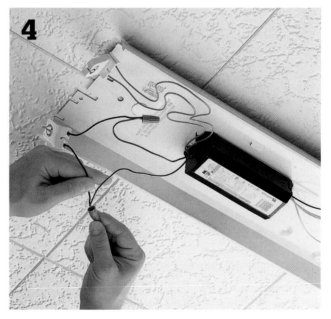

Purchase and install a new socket. If socket has preattached wire leads, connect the leads to the ballast wires using wire connectors. Replace cover plate, and then the fluorescent tube, making sure that it seats properly. Replace the diffuser. Restore power to the fixture at the main service panel and test.

How to Replace a Ballast

1

Turn off the power at the main service panel, then remove the diffuser, fluorescent tube, and cover plate. Test for power using a circuit tester (page 291, step 1).

2

Remove the sockets from the fixture housing by sliding them out, or by removing the mounting screws and lifting the sockets out.

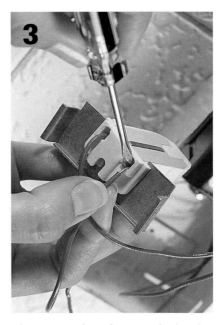

3

Disconnect the wires attached to the sockets by pushing a small screwdriver into the release openings (above), by loosening the screw terminals, or by cutting wires to within 2" of sockets.

4

Remove the old ballast using a ratchet wrench or screwdriver. Make sure to support the ballast so it does not fall.

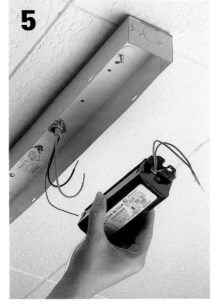

5

Install a new ballast that has the same ratings as the old ballast.

6

Attach the ballast wires to the socket wires using wire connectors, screw terminal connections, or push-in fittings. Reinstall the cover plate, fluorescent tube, and diffuser. Turn on power to the light fixture at the main service panel.

How to Replace a Fluorescent Light Fixture

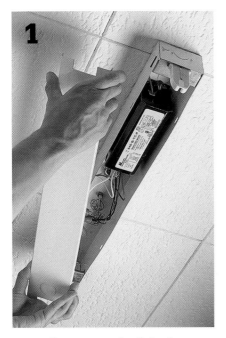

1

Turn off power to the light fixture at the main service panel. Remove the diffuser, tube, and cover plate. Test for power using a circuit tester.

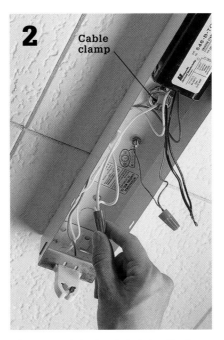

2

Cable clamp

Disconnect the insulated circuit wires and the bare copper grounding wire from the light fixture. Loosen the cable clamp holding the circuit wires.

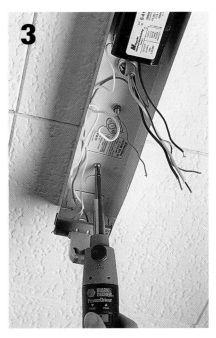

3

Unscrew the fixture from the wall or ceiling and carefully remove it. Make sure to support the fixture so it does not fall.

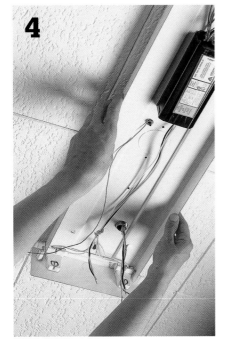

4

Position the new fixture, threading the circuit wires through the knockout opening in the back of the fixture. Screw the fixture in place so it is firmly anchored to framing members.

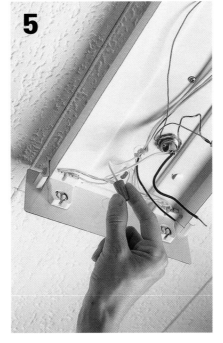

5

Connect the circuit wires to the fixture wires using wire connectors. Follow the wiring diagram included with the new fixture. Tighten the cable clamp holding the circuit wires.

6

Attach the fixture cover plate, then install the fluorescent tubes and attach the diffuser. Turn on power to the fixture at the main service panel and test.

Replacing Plugs & Cords

Replace an electrical plug whenever you notice bent or loose prongs, a cracked or damaged casing, or a missing insulating faceplate. A damaged plug poses a shock and fire hazard.

Replacement plugs are available in different styles to match common appliance cords. Always choose a replacement that is similar to the original plug. Flat-cord and quick-connect plugs are used with light-duty appliances, like lamps and radios. Round-cord plugs are used with larger appliances, including those that have three-prong grounding plugs.

Some tools and appliances use polarized plugs. A polarized plug has one wide prong and one narrow prong, corresponding to the hot and neutral slots found in a standard receptacle.

If there is room in the plug body, tie the individual wires in an underwriter's knot to secure the plug to the cord.

Tools & Materials ▸

Combination tool
Needlenose pliers
Screwdriver
Replacement plug

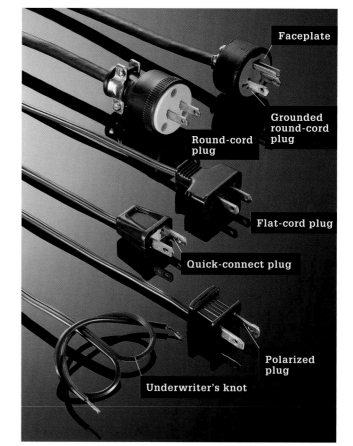

Faceplate
Round-cord plug
Grounded round-cord plug
Flat-cord plug
Quick-connect plug
Underwriter's knot
Polarized plug

How to Install a Quick-connect Plug

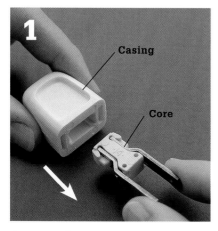

1

Casing
Core

Squeeze the prongs of the new quick-connect plug together slightly and pull the plug core from the casing. Cut the old plug from the flat-cord wire with a combination tool, leaving a clean cut end.

2

Feed unstripped wire through rear of plug casing. Spread prongs, then insert wire into opening in rear of core. Squeeze prongs together; spikes inside core penetrate cord. Slide casing over core until it snaps into place.

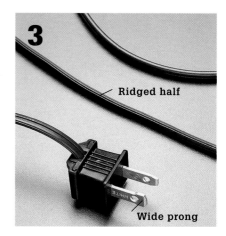

3

Ridged half
Wide prong

When replacing a polarized plug, make sure that the ridged half of the cord lines up with the wider (neutral) prong of the plug.

How to Replace a Round-cord Plug

Cut off round cord near the old plug using a combination tool. Remove the insulating faceplate on the new plug and feed cord through rear of plug. Strip about 3" of outer insulation from the round cord. Strip ¾" insulation from the individual wires.

Tie an underwriter's knot with the black and the white wires. Make sure the knot is located close to the edge of the stripped outer insulation. Pull the cord so that the knot slides into the plug body.

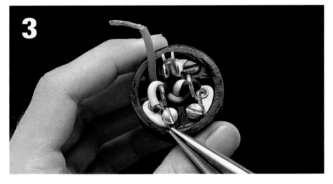

Hook end of black wire clockwise around brass screw and white wire around silver screw. On a three-prong plug, attach third wire to grounding screw. If necessary, excess grounding wire can be cut away.

Tighten the screws securely, making sure the copper wires do not touch each other. Replace the insulating faceplate.

How to Replace a Flat-cord Plug

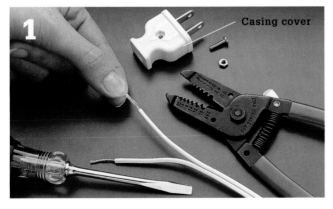

Cut old plug from cord using a combination tool. Pull apart the two halves of the flat cord so that about 2" of wire are separated. Strip ¾" insulation from each half. Remove casing cover on new plug.

Hook ends of wires clockwise around the screw terminals, and tighten the screw terminals securely. Reassemble the plug casing. Some plugs may have an insulating faceplate that must be installed.

How to Replace a Lamp Cord

1

With the lamp unplugged, the shade off, and the bulb out, you can remove the socket. Squeeze the outer shell of the socket just above the base and pull the shell out of the base. The shell is often marked Press at some point along its perimeter. Press there and then pull.

2

Under the outer shell there is a cardboard insulating sleeve. Pull this off and you'll reveal the socket attached to the end of the cord.

3

With the shell and insulation set aside, pull the socket away from the lamp (it will still be connected to the cord). Unscrew the two screws to completely disconnect the socket from the cord. Set the socket aside with its shell (you'll need them to reassemble the lamp)

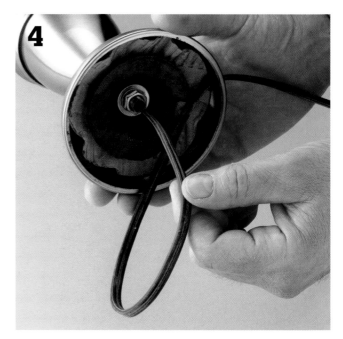

4

Remove the old cord from the lamp by grasping the cord near the base and pulling the cord though the lamp.

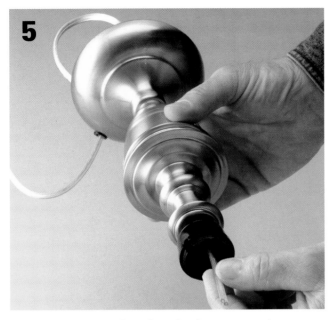

Bring your damaged cord to a hardware store or home center and purchase a similar cord set. (A cord set is simply a replacement cord with a plug already attached.) Snake the end of the cord up from the base of the lamp through the top so that about 3" of cord is visible above the top.

Carefully separate the two halves of the cord. If the halves won't pull apart, you can carefully make a cut in the middle with a knife. Strip away about ¾" of insulation from the end of each wire.

Connect the ends of the new cord to the two screws on the side of the socket (one of which will be silver in color, the other brass-colored). One half of the cord will have ribbing or markings along its length; wrap that wire clockwise around the silver screw and tighten the screw. The other half of the cord will be smooth; wrap it around the copper screw and tighten the screw.

Set the socket on the base. Make sure the switch isn't blocked by the harp—the part that holds the shade on some lamps. Slide the cardboard insulating sleeve over the socket so the sleeve's notch aligns with the switch. Now slide the outer sleeve over the socket, aligning the notch with the switch. It should snap into the base securely. Screw in a light bulb, plug the lamp in, and test it.

Replacing a Lamp Socket

Next to the cord plug, the most common source of trouble in a lamp is a worn light bulb socket. When a lamp socket assembly fails, the problem is usually with the socket-switch unit, although replacement sockets may include other parts you do not need.

Lamp failure is not always caused by a bad socket. You can avoid unnecessary repairs by checking the lamp cord, plug, and light bulb before replacing the socket.

Tools & Materials ▸

Replacement socket
Continuity tester
Screwdriver

Socket-mounted switch types are usually interchangeable: choose a replacement you prefer. Clockwise from top left: twist knob, remote switch, pull chain, push lever.

Tip ▸

When replacing a lamp socket, you can improve a standard ON-OFF lamp by installing a three-way socket.

How to Repair or Replace a Lamp Socket

1

Contact tab

Unplug lamp. Remove shade, light bulb, and harp (shade bracket). Scrape contact tab clean with a small screwdriver. Pry contact tab up slightly if flattened inside socket. Replace bulb, plug in lamp, and test. If lamp does not work, unplug, remove bulb, and continue with next step.

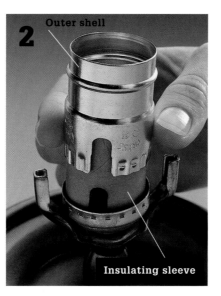

2

Outer shell

Insulating sleeve

Squeeze outer shell of socket near Press marking, and lift it off. On older lamps, socket may be held by screws found at the base of the screw socket. Slip off cardboard insulating sleeve. If sleeve is damaged, replace entire socket.

3

Check for loose wire connections on screw terminals. Refasten any loose connections, then reassemble lamp, and test. If connections are not loose, remove the wires, lift out the socket, and continue with the next step.

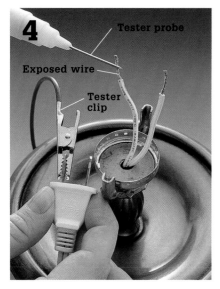

4

Tester probe

Exposed wire

Tester clip

Test for lamp cord problems with continuity tester. Place clip of tester on one prong of plug. Touch probe to one exposed wire, then to the other wire. Repeat test with other prong of plug. If tester fails to light for either prong, then replace the cord and plug. Retest the lamp.

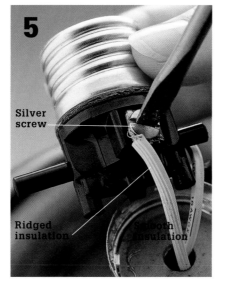

5

Silver screw

Ridged insulation

Smooth insulation

If cord and plug are functional, then choose a replacement socket marked with the same amp and volt ratings as the old socket. One half of flat-cord lamp wire is covered by insulation that is ridged or marked: attach this wire to the silver screw terminal. Connect other wire to brass screw.

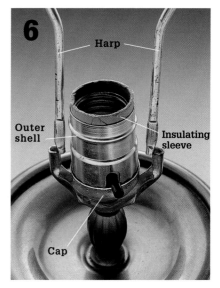

6

Harp

Outer shell

Insulating sleeve

Cap

Slide insulating sleeve and outer shell over socket so that socket and screw terminals are fully covered and switch fits into sleeve slot. Press socket assembly down into cap until socket locks into place. Replace harp, light bulb, and shade.

APPENDIX: Home Automation

An automated home can add security, peace of mind, and convenience to day-to-day activities like adjusting your home's lighting, temperature, and security systems. Home-automation components can also enable you to fully maximize the capabilities of your existing home's products and systems, and helps them run more efficiently together. Comprehensive systems have the capability to control lighting, HVAC, irrigation, entertainment components, video surveillance, and pool and spa equipment, just to mention a few. The applications are endless.

Most systems can be upgraded in segments. You can start off with a small, standalone system. That will allow you to turn your lights on and off remotely. Or you can dive in and use your home computer as a command center, where you monitor and control everything from your home's temperature and lighting. With some systems, you can configure alerts that call preprogrammed telephone numbers to warn you of a water leak or that an intruder has gained entry. These PC controllers can be software or hardware interfaces or a standalone PC-like device built for home automation.

All home-automation systems start with a backbone that carries commands, a main controller that issues commands, and device controllers that translate the command to a compatible device. The backbone of a system is the wiring that carries the commands. Many new homes are hard-wired with high-performance fiber optic, Category 5 (for telephone and data), and coaxial audio and video cable for the ultimate in home control and capability. With sufficient basement or attic access, remodeling a home network can be achieved by running new cables in walls and installing outputs for Internet, satellite, or digital TV data.

Wireless automation systems, like X10, use your home's existing electrical circuit wiring to carry bursts of RF (radio frequency) to command-compatible electric devices that understand the language. These "wireless" systems—sometimes called powerline carrier systems—allow ease of installation in places where hard-wiring is not practical.

Wireless home-automation systems all use a protocol—a common language—that all the devices in the automated home network understand to communicate with compatible remote devices.

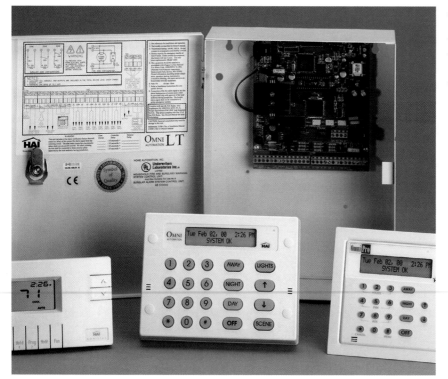

An automation system that uses a network wiring system to route signals throughout the home can be accessed through control panels or key pads mounted in convenient locations around your home.

Today, X10 is the predominant protocol in home automation, but other common systems include CEBus, LonWorks, and Smart House. The main obstacle to any home automation is integration. When planning an automation system, take care to purchase components that are compatible with your data transmission system.

Many home-automation components now offer two-way communication, meaning that they not only send out signals to control your home's lighting, heaters, home stereo equipment, or other electric devices, they also have the capability to receive information from external sensors, report on that information (by telephone), and intervene if necessary.

For example, sensors can be installed to shut off water in the event of a leak. When the sensor senses the leak, it will automatically shut off the water main and call several preprogrammed phone numbers to alert you to the situation. Other sensors can be programmed to report by phone on temperature and other indoor and outdoor home conditions to keep you informed while you are away from home. These systems are especially useful for vacation homes or second homes.

Do-it-yourself home-automation systems are readily available at home centers, retail outlets, and online retailers. Cost and complexity varies, depending on the scale, control, and complexity of the system. Almost all systems are upgradeable for future expansion. Command and control products have existed for years. To remain competitive, today's manufacturers are increasingly developing specifications for very low-cost command and control applications.

The market for automation devices is increasing as consumers become more technically savvy, and demand higher performance from their household devices. Many businesses now use a home-office as their main command center, and as such, they require high-speed data transmission and computer networking capabilities, not to mention increased security to protect their investment. Whether you are outfitting a single-family home, commercial property, or home-office, home-automation products increase the value of your property. They can also offer you increased home convenience, capability, safety, and energy efficiency that can save valuable time and money over time.

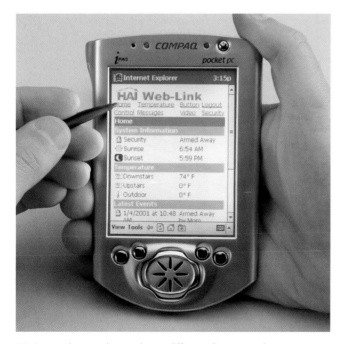

PDAs can be used to activate different features of your home-automation system from outside the house via the Internet.

X10 is the simplest and most affordable retrofit automation system. It uses existing wiring to control everything from lighting to appliances from a variety of controllers.

Installing an X10 System

An X10 system uses your home's existing electric wiring to remotely control most electric devices in your home. Because X10 technology does not require cutting holes in drywall and running new wiring, the systems are popular additions to existing homes seeking home automation.

The X10 system works by using your home's existing electrical wiring as a communication conduit to transmit radio-frequency (RF) control signals to every outlet in your house, allowing you to plug in X10 modules (devices that receive and translate X10 signals) to turn individual lights, appliances, or other devices on and off.

Basic X10 modules understand six actions: on, off, all on, all off, dim, and brighten. More sophisticated modules can perform additional functions like controlling the speed of a ceiling fan or turning off a high-load appliance like a hot tub.

Because each X10 module in your home receives all the RF control signals sent from the X10 controller, the system is coded with addresses that identify which module is which. Otherwise it would be impossible to direct a command to only one light or one group of lights in a home full of X10 modules. For this reason, the X10 system identifies modules with 16 different house codes (letters A to P) and 16 different unit codes (numbers 1 to 16), for a total of 256 pieces of unique controllable equipment.

For example, program all your home's exterior lighting as house code "E." To turn all the exterior lights on at once, have your controller send a signal that commands all "E" lights to come on. If you would like only the front porch light to come on, then code that light as 1 of 16 possible outdoor lights on the "E" section of your home. Then send a signal that commands light "E-1" to come on.

Controllers vary from handheld models like TV remotes to key-fob remotes to desktop keypads. Most X10 modules are similar in size to a small, square AC adaptor. To minimize visibility of the system, you can install in-wall X10 receptacles that look similar to a typical 120-volt power outlet. X10 wall switches are a simple, discreet way to control hard-wired lights, ceiling fans, heaters, and other devices.

X10 remote-control technology does not require additional wiring—so the chore and expense of cutting holes in wallboard and running new cable is eliminated. Devices can be switched on and off and dimmed from control panels or wireless remotes (inset).

How to Install an X10 System

1

Plug the lamp or appliance receiver module into a standard 120-volt outlet.

2

Plug the lamp or appliances you would like to control into the receiver module.

3

Program the unit. Some units program by pressing a reset button, after which they retain the first code received from a transmitter (shown). Others have a dial for house and unit codes. Use a small screwdriver to turn the code dials to set a unique house and unit code that identifies the module's address.

4

Plug a system transmitter, such as the desktop controller (shown) or wireless remote transceiver, into another three-pin (grounded) or two-pin (nongrounded) outlet.

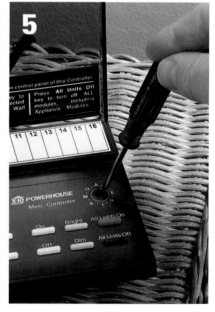

5

Set the system transmitter's code to match the house and unit codes you selected for your receiver modules. To test operation, use the controller to send a specific on or off command to a specific lamp or appliance module address.

Adding Key-chain Remote Control to Home Lighting

A basic wireless key-chain remote controller can be used to control two or more home lighting devices. More elaborate systems can control several devices and appliances. Key-chain remotes allow you to turn on your home's interior or exterior lighting to brighten a dark sidewalk or entryway. Never walk into a dark house again.

Installation of the system is simple, just plug a receiver module into a 120-volt outlet, and then plug a light or other device into the outlet on the bottom of the receiver module. Program the key-chain remote to identify each individual transceiver's "address" (a house code and a unit code), and installation is complete.

Remote kits include a plug-in receiver unit (left) and a key-chain remote (right). Some models include multiple transceivers that let you connect several lamps or other plug-in appliances.

How to Add a Key-chain Remote to Home Lighting

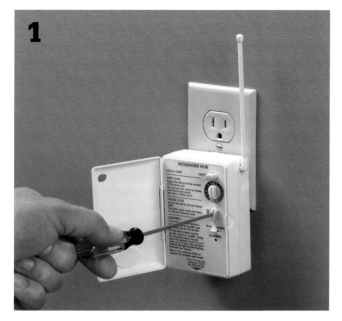

1

Select an address code on the receiver module. Lift the cover on the receiver module and use a screwdriver to choose a unique address for the lamp you wish to operate. If this is your only device, any address will do.

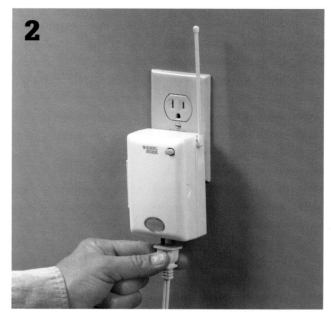

2

Plug the lamp you would like to control into the receiver module. Plug the module into a 120-volt receptacle. If the hard-wired outlet you are utilizing is controlled by a wall switch, make sure the switch remains in the on position.

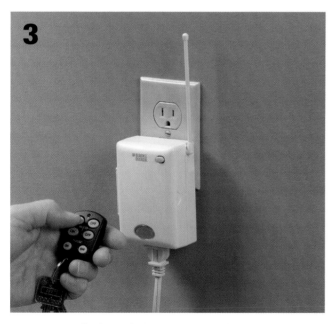

3

To program the key-chain remote with the address of the light you would like to control, hold the remote near the receiver module and press down one of the the remote's on buttons for five to six seconds. The LED light will flash, signaling that the remote is programming itself with the address of the nearest module. Repeat this process to program the second on button for another module. Programming methods may vary. Follow manufacturer's instructions.

Tip ▶

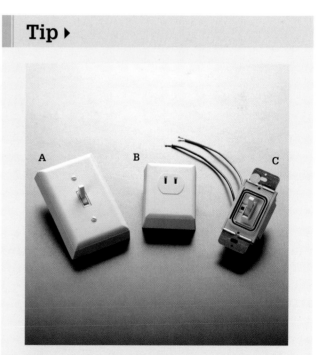

With a wireless wall switch kit, you can add a switch to control a hard-wired light fixture in minutes, without any additional wiring. Kits include a transmitter switch (A) and a plug-in receiver base (B) or a receiver switch (C).

Installing a Remote Thermostat Control

Many thermostats that offer remote control from a computer or phone require professional installation, but others are easy to install, allowing you to use a telephone to monitor your home or cabin while you are away. They allow telephone command of a thermostat, ensuring that your house is warm from the moment you walk in the door. And if you forget to turn the thermostat down before you leave, you can easily command that function by telephone. The thermostat can also be controlled locally, using the manual controls on the thermostat.

The monitoring system shown here is simple to install, program, and operate, and requires no changes to your standard electrical or telephone service. It can work with an existing three- or four-wire, low-voltage thermostat, but you will need to install a secondary thermostat wired in parallel by passing the low-voltage supply through the unit. Set the primary thermostat to an "at-home" temperature. Set the secondary thermostat to an "away" temperature to keep your home at minimal heat when you are away. You can choose which thermostat will control your furnace from any touch-tone phone.

An easier option is to replace the existing thermostat with a compatible setback thermostat that is preprogrammed with an away and a home temperature setting. The advantage of this option is that it requires only one thermostat for all heating and air conditioning tasks. One pair of wires connects the setback thermostat to the monitoring system.

In addition to controlling thermostats, the monitor will give you temperature updates, and depending on the sensors you install, it can alert you to water leaks, power failures, broken glass, and a host of others. The unit can be programmed to dial up to eight phone numbers until it gets an answer.

Tools & Materials ▸

Screwdriver
Circuit tester
Setback thermostat

Remote monitoring
system

Remote monitoring systems can be programmed to dial up to eight phone numbers when abnormal conditions occur, such as temperature dips or spikes, water leaks, or forced entry/intrusions. The system will continue dialing your programmed alarm phone numbers in sequence until the call is answered. It can also control a thermostat.

How to Install a Remote Monitoring System

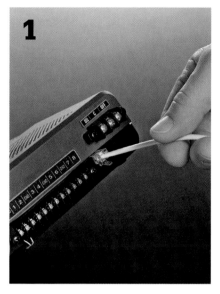

Open the battery compartment and install the recommended batteries for power backup. Use a phone cord to connect the transceiver to any standard phone jack. Plug the transceiver's electric cord into a 120-volt outlet.

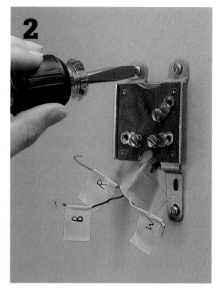

At the main panel, shut off power to the furnace. Remove the cover plate on your existing thermostat, and pull it out of the wall just enough to view wire connections. Write down the terminal location (R, W, G, Y) of each colored wire connected on the existing thermostat. Disconnect the wires on the old thermostat and remove.

Attach the base plate of the new thermostat to the wall. Connect each of the wires that were connected to the old thermostat to the same terminal labels on the new setback thermostat. Using the provided cable, connect the CLK1 wire to the remote terminal; connect the CLK2 wire to the C (common) terminal. Snap the thermostat onto the base plate. Terminal labels may vary.

Connect the CLK1 wire from the setback thermostat to the on terminal on the back of the monitor. Connect the CLK2 wire to the C terminal. Turn on the power to the furnace and check the thermostat for proper operation.

Program the transceiver according to your needs and the manufacturer's specifications. Programming consists of setting high and low temperature limits, configuring any additional sensor inputs as normally open or normally closed (according to sensor type), and setting dial-out telephone numbers for emergency notification. Before programming, it is very important to check that the sensors you have wired to the unit are set in their normal, nonalarm positions. Mount the transceiver on a wall or set it on a table near the thermostat.

Installing Automatic Water Shutoff Valves

An automatic water shutoff valve can protect your home or vacation property from costly water damage caused by leaking washing machines, dishwashers, toilets, or refrigerator ice machines. The system uses a water sensor placed on the floor in the vicinity of the appliance. If a leak does occur, the sensor sends an electrical signal to a control unit, which then activates a magnetic shutoff valve that stops the flow of water to the appliance. Installation of the system is simple, requires no plumber or specialized tools, and typically can be up and running in under an hour.

More elaborate whole-house systems are also available. These install at the main shutoff valve. Wireless sensors placed near appliances and pipes sense leaks and tell the valve to shutoff water to the whole house.

Tools & Materials ▸

Drill
Screwdriver
Adjustable wrench
  or pliers

Teflon tape
Automatic shutoff
  valve kit

How to Install Automatic Water Shutoff Valves on a Washer

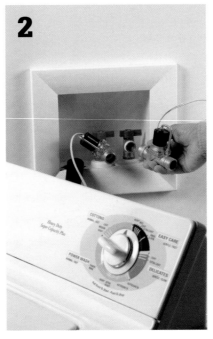

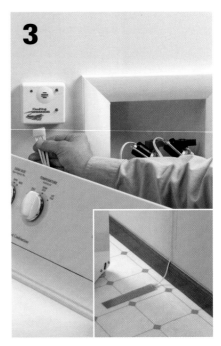

Turn your home's main water supply off. Locate the flexible supply hoses that supply the washer, and turn the shutoff valves off. Use a wrench or pliers to disconnect the water supply hoses from the existing shutoff valves.

Connect one automatic shutoff valve to each of the existing hot and cold shutoff valves that serve the washer (wrap all threads with Teflon plumber's tape before installing). Reconnect the water supply hoses to the automatic shutoff valve outlets. Turn the water main on and check for leaks.

Mount the control unit in a location convenient for periodic testing. Plug the valve and sensor wiring harness into the control unit. Connect the water sensor by attaching the supplied two-conductor wire to the terminals on the back of the control unit. Place the water sensor on the floor immediately under the supply pipes (inset). Connect the transformer to the control unit and plug in the transformer. Look for an indicator light that signals the system is operational.

Installing a Wireless Phone Jack

A wireless phone jack system will allow you to quickly convert any 120-volt outlet into a working phone jack. A typical kit includes one base unit transmitter, one receiver module, and a 6-ft. phone cord. The system works by sending a signal from an existing phone jack (via 120-volt transmitter) to a 120-volt jack receiver module in another room. Change the location of the added phone jack at any time by moving it to a different 120-volt outlet. The entire system can be installed in minutes and requires no tools, drilling, or wiring.

Each wireless phone jack system can be used to add one phone jack anywhere in the house. This system is ideal for quickly installing a phone in a bathroom or guest room. To prevent interference, locate the receiver module away from TV or radio equipment.

How to Add a Wireless Phone Jack

Plug the telephone cable from an existing telephone jack into either jack on the right side of the base unit. (It is important to plug in the base unit before the receiver unit. In the event of a problem, unplug both units and start again.)

Plug the base unit transmitter into a nearby 120-volt outlet. To use a phone at the existing jack location, plug that phone into the extra jack on the side of the base unit transmitter.

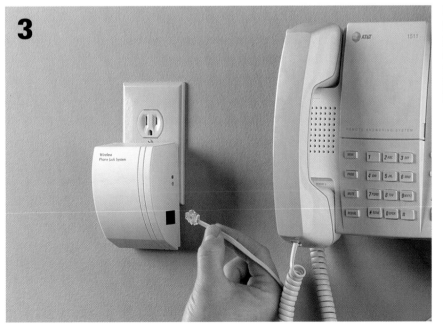

Plug the wireless phone jack receiver module into a 120-volt outlet near where you would like your new phone jack. Plug a telephone, modem, fax, or other telephone-operated equipment into the jack on the receiver unit. There should now be a dial tone on the added phone line.

Multimedia outlets use modular jacks, connectors, and terminals to allow homeowners to customize outlets according to the network needs of each room.

Voice/data jacks can accommodate any pin-size telecommunication jack to allow for standard phone and data lines, or the ability to create multiline phone, data, and computer networks for the home office. Reassigning any line is quick and easy.

Accessories, such as closed-circuit cameras, allow homeowners to tailor the system to their specific needs.

Video F-connectors provide every room in your house with the ability to receive and redistribute antenna, cable TV, and satellite signals, as well as internal transmission signals from DVD, VCR, and closed-circuit cameras.

Audio terminals or a recessed speaker system can be installed for a home theater system or to create an internal audio system with localized volume control.

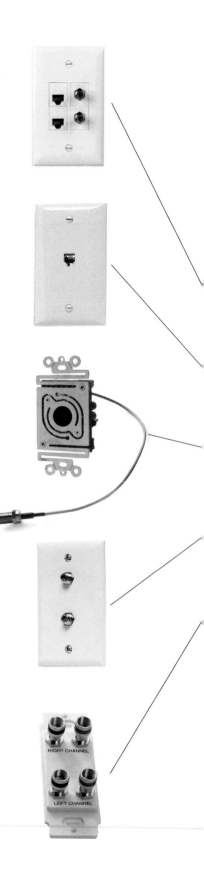

Home Network Wiring Systems

The ability to send and receive information electronically has become an important part of our lives. Internet access, multiple phone lines, cable television, satellites, wired and wireless home computer networks, and security systems are commonplace in many homes. And as our telecommunications needs grow, a better, faster, and more convenient way to manage these separate systems will be necessary.

A home network system brings all these single systems together at one central location. It provides a transmission path for electronic information rather than for electricity. Electronic information can be voice, video, audio, or computer data. Network wiring is about moving this electronic information to wherever you need it.

Older phone and cable TV wiring use a continuous loop wiring method. With this method, various jacks and connectors are installed along a single loop of cable or wire running throughout the house. Though easier to install, this method is unreliable, especially with the large demands placed upon the lines by computers and other electronic devices.

In this traditional method, the cable or wire that is split runs from the demarcation point, Network Interface Device (NID), or service entrance—the point where the service providers transfer ownership of the lines to the homeowner. The transmission signals are strongest at the point they enter the home. But repeatedly splitting cables and wires throughout the run degrades the strength of the signal. Also, if there is a problem in the line, all the jacks and connectors in the run are affected.

New home network wiring systems resolve this problem. The system employs a star topology in which all cables and wires are distributed from a central point. All inputs are brought to a centralized distribution center that contains modules designed to maintain the strength of voice, data, and video (VDV) transmission signals. High-performance cable and wires are routed to any room in the house where VDV capability is necessary. Plug-and-play multimedia outlets provide easy access to a variety of signals.

The system can be used to create home computer networks, multiroom audio systems, multiple phone lines for home offices, and distribution for DVD, DVR, VCR, or closed-circuit television signals to any room of the house.

Installing a system is a project that any homeowner can accomplish. Many home centers carry all the components and materials necessary for installation.

It is much easier to run cables and wires in unfinished walls, but retrofit installations are quite manageable if you carefully plan the system needs, determine the optimal location for each unit, and map out the cable routes.

Though installation methods and techniques for network wiring systems are generally the same, there are some differences between the different manufacturers' systems. Always carefully read and follow both the instruction and operation manuals provided by the manufacturer of your specific network wiring system.

Installing a Home Network System

With the increasing need for networking capabilities in the home for work and entertainment, standards have been developed by the Telecommunications Industry Association (TIA) and the Electronic Industry Alliance (EIA) in accordance with the Federal Communications Commission (FCC). These standards are becoming the code requirements for home network wiring installation across the country. Make sure to check with your local building inspector for the current codes in this new and changing area of home wiring.

There are four components to a network wiring system: the distribution center, the distribution modules, cables and wires, and the multimedia outlets. Each component serves a particular function in the distribution of voice, data, and video signals throughout your home network system.

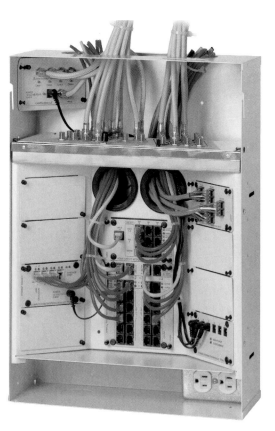

The distribution center houses all of the primary controls for your voice, data, and video signals.

Distribution Center

The distribution center is the central hub of the network wiring system, housing the distribution modules and the cable and wire connections that link the entire network. All service cables from outside your home (antenna, cable TV, telecommunication lines, etc.) are routed from the service entrance to the distribution center, where their signals are then distributed to every room in your house. In addition, signals generated within your home (such as DVD, VCR, audio, or computer networks) can be routed back to the center and redistributed to the multimedia outlets in the rooms of your choice.

Distribution centers are designed to allow easy access to the modules and cable connections. This makes reconfiguring outlets in any room quick and simple. Most distribution centers are heavy-gauge steel boxes with plastic covers sized to fit between

standard stud spans of 16" on-center. These enclosure-style centers have open tops or holes to accommodate the many cables and wires routed to and from the modules contained inside. Smaller distribution centers that hold only a few of the most basic modules are also available. These centers are generally not enclosed, so care must be taken to keep all cables and wires together.

Typically, the lower portion of the distribution center houses the electrical transformer that supplies power to the system. A dedicated 15-amp, 120-volt, nonswitchable duplex receptacle must be installed, either in the enclosure itself or within 60" of the distribution center.

The upper portion of the center is reserved for video distribution modules, while a mounting bracket or brackets are fastened at the middle section to hold various home network modules.

Distribution Modules

The distribution modules are the interface devices used to maintain and strengthen the signal for further routing throughout the system. Each module contains at least one input port for receiving the incoming signal to be distributed (or redistributed), and a series of output ports for routing the desired signal to the desired locations. Each module is designed to serve a particular function:

Video distribution modules receive and distribute cable, satellite, UHF, VHF, and other coaxial signals throughout the network. Video modules are also used to create internal video networks through the use of a modulator, a device that receives signals from a source (DVD, VCR, or video camera) and assigns those signals to the unused channels in the cable or satellite system.

Telecommunication modules distribute voice and data signals received from various RJ45 jacks throughout the home network and out to the world.

Computer network modules are used to create home computer networks when used with, and properly configured to, Ethernet network cards and software. Many home-office modules are available that combine the best attributes of the telecommunication and computer network modules for convenient transference of information.

Camera modules distribute video and audio signals received from closed-circuit monitoring cameras to all external TV outlets for viewing. This module typically works in conjunction with a video distribution module.

Audio distribution modules route audio signals received from your stereo receiver or amplifier to speakers or terminals mounted in various locations.

Power distribution modules supply power for all internal DC power patch cords to the amplifier or panel, as well as to those modules requiring a source of electricity.

Manufacturers continually develop new interface modules to support a greater range of systems, from security to internal intercom. Modules compatible with home-automation systems will receive and distribute the signals for lighting control or localized climate control options.

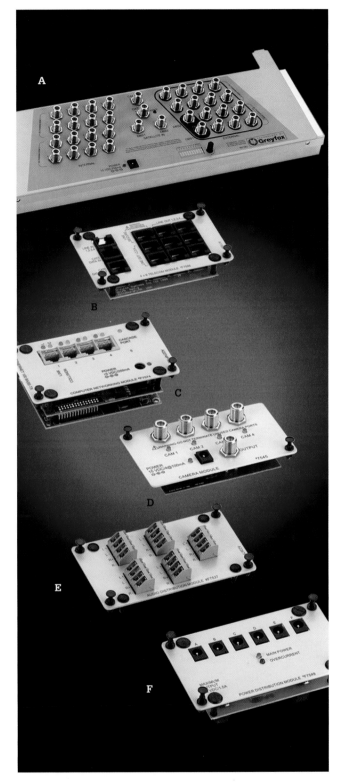

Video distribution module (A), telecommunication module (B), computer network module (C), camera module (D), audio distribution module (E), power distribution module (F).

Cables & Wires

Cables and wires carry signals dispatched from a source to their intended location. The growing need to transfer larger amounts of data faster requires that cables and wires be capable of carrying a high volume of data.

Cables and wires are rated based on their bandwidth, the amount of data that can flow through the cable or wire in a specified unit of time. The greater the bandwidth, the faster data can be transferred.

There are four basic types of cable: Coaxial cable is used for the distribution of audio/video signals throughout the system. Series 6 cable (or RG-6) is a higher-grade coaxial cable and is preferred for home network systems.

Unshielded twisted-pair (UTP) cables are used to carry phone and data signals throughout the system. The most common UTP cable in use is category 5. It is a higher-grade cable with a large bandwidth and meets all standards requirements.

Audio speaker wire is used to route audio signals throughout the system to create a home theater or a multiroom audio system.

Fiber-optic cable (not pictured) uses a transducer that converts the electrical signal into light to pass through the glass or plastic optical fiber wires. At the other end, another transducer converts the light back to an electrical signal. It is less common in residential applications, but it holds tremendous potential for delivering massive amounts of data, video, and audio at unprecedented speeds. Some homeowners choose to "future-proof" their homes and run fiber optic cable even before they have devices to take advantage of it. That way, the cables will be in place when the technology becomes widely available.

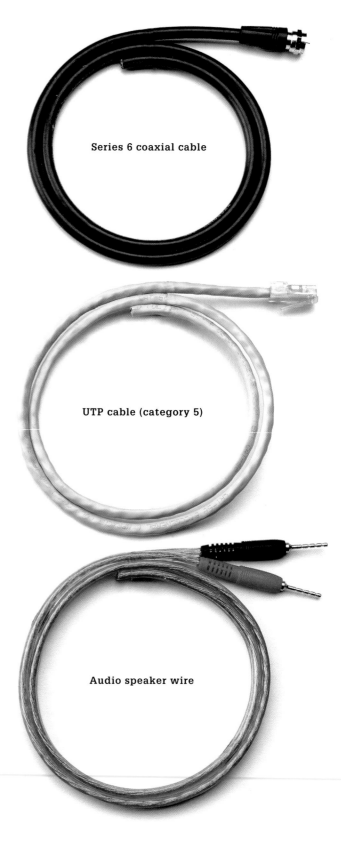

Series 6 coaxial cable

UTP cable (category 5)

Audio speaker wire

Multimedia Outlets & Accessories

The network is accessed at various multimedia outlets installed throughout the home. Each outlet contains a series of jacks and connectors for plug-and-play connection of phones, computers, TVs, VCRs, DVDs, and stereo systems.

RJ45 jacks are the ports for connecting phone and data devices to the network system. RJ45 jacks are wired to a universal pin/pair assignment standard (standard T568A). This configuration allows any size telecommunication plug to be used with the jack. For example, your 4-pin phone plug can be inserted (and will fit) into the 8-pin RJ45 jack. That phone jack can then be removed and an 8-pin Ethernet data line plug can be inserted once the jack has been reconfigured at the distribution box.

F-connectors are threaded terminals for connecting video equipment to the system. F-connector fittings on coaxial cable ends simply screw onto the terminal.

Binding posts are the terminals for tying an audio system into the network. The posts are color coded for polarity. Red or "+" is used to signify positive terminals, and black or "−" for negative terminals. Crossing polarity may cause the speakers to be out of phase, in which case the sound will lack some of its bass.

Multimedia outlets can be tailored to the specific needs of the room in which they are located. Outlets in a home office could contain a dedicated RJ45 jack for each phone, fax, and modem line to allow each device to send and receive data more efficiently.

Accessory options are available with all network wiring systems, though most will require a specialized distribution module. The most common are video cameras sized to fit in 4 × 4 gang boxes for a closed-circuit television system and recess-mounted stereo speaker systems for multiroom audio systems with volume control in each room.

Audio speaker with bracket for recess mounting (A), multimedia outlet with bracket for mounting to electrical receptacles (B), audio system volume control (C), video camera (D), multimedia outlet with audio binding posts (E), F-connectors (F), module jacks and connectors for multimedia outlets (G), RJ45 jack plug (H).

Assessing Needs

When assessing your network system needs, it is always a good idea to install more than you currently think you will use. Routing extra cables and wires to large appliances, such as furnaces and refrigerators, will make it easier to add future home-automation features. Extra outlets in rooms will let you connect new telecommunication devices to the network.

Two standard grades of residential cabling installation currently exist. Grade 1 is a generic cabling system that meets only the minimum requirements for telecommunication services. Each multimedia outlet is provided with one 4-pair UTP cable (minimum category 3, category 5 recommended) as a voice/data line, and one 75-ohm coaxial cable as a video line.

Grade 2 installation meets the requirements for basic, advanced, and multimedia telecommunication services. Two 4-pair UTP cables (minimum category 5, category 5e recommended) are routed to outlets for one voice line and one data line, as well as two 75-ohm coaxial cables (one input and one output) for video lines. Grade 2 installation standards also suggest two-fiber optical fiber cabling for future applications, though this is entirely optional.

Installing multiple Grade 2 outlets in various locations of a room is recommended, especially in entertainment areas and the home office.

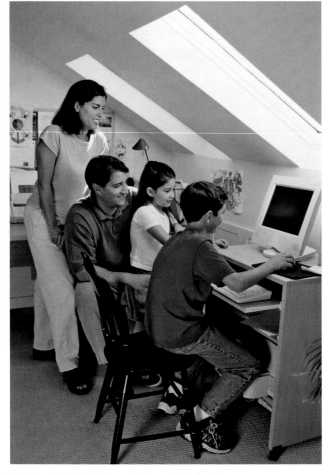

A home office will greatly benefit from the many networking capabilities of a home network system. Installing Grade 2 multimedia outlets next to electrical receptacles will provide a centralized location for all your telecommunication connections.

Home entertainment systems can also use many of the networks in the system. Installing Grade 2 multimedia outlets on each wall of the room will help ease future remodeling or redecorating projects, or the addition of new components to the system.

Determining Locations

A home network system is designed to be installed in a star topology, where all cables and wires are distributed from one central point, the distribution center. The center should be installed in an accessible, central location (such as a basement or utility room) and near the demarcation point, NID, or service entrance. Easy access to the distribution center will not only simplify the current installation, but also simplify future alterations to the system. The central location will make cable lengths less likely to extend past their recommended routing length (295 ft.).

Low-voltage cable and wire routes should be carefully planned. Making sketches and routing maps will save time and help determine the best possible path with the least number of turns and bends. Refer to pages 322 to 323 for other cable and wire needs and restrictions.

The living room, home office, bedroom, entertainment room, recreation or game room, and den are all obvious places for multimedia outlets. But outlets in rooms such as the kitchen, bathroom, laundry and utility room, or at large appliances, will help ready your home for future conveniences.

When determining outlet locations within a room, consider the needs of that particular room. Home offices will benefit from multiple phone and data lines for Internet access on the computer. Plan for these outlets to be mounted alongside a 120-volt receptacle to centralize computer connections.

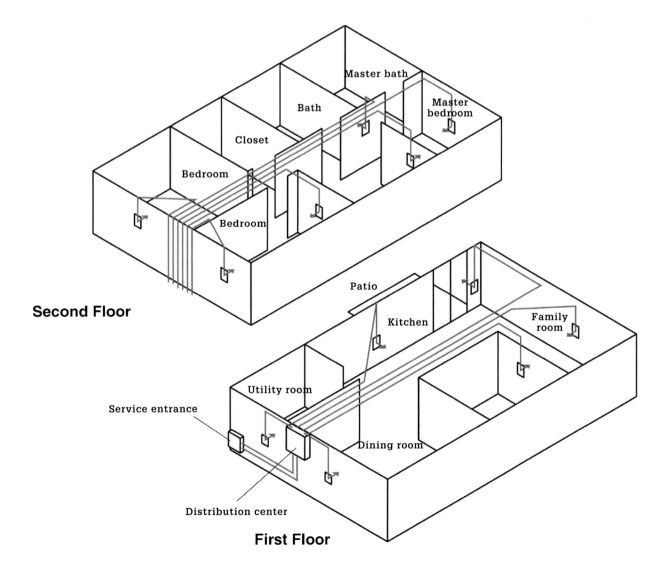

Second Floor

Master bath

Bath

Master bedroom

Closet

Bedroom

Bedroom

Patio

Kitchen

Family room

Utility room

Service entrance

Dining room

Distribution center

First Floor

Preparing Multimedia Outlets

Multimedia outlets are installed much like electrical receptacles, though the connections do not need to be contained in a box. The outlets should be mounted at the same height as receptacles, according to local code.

Extension brackets allow multimedia outlets and electrical receptacles to be placed side by side. The location of the 120-volt receptacle/switch box will always determine the height and location of the bracket. Make sure to choose the correct bracket for the outlet type to be installed. Some manufacturers offer specialized alignment tools for lining up the extension brackets with the existing electrical boxes.

For retrofit installations, hollow-backed gang boxes or 4 × 4" gang boxes are used to prevent damage to cables and wires due to bending or twisting.

Tools & Materials ▸

Level
Screwdriver
Wallboard saw

Extension brackets
Hollow-back boxes
Wallboard screws

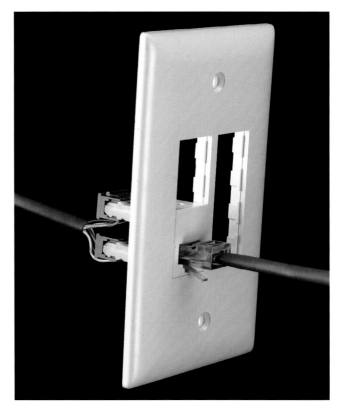

Multimedia outlets can be installed next to electrical outlets in an expanded box, or installed in their own box.

How to Expand a Receptacle Box

Fit the extension bracket over the existing electrical receptacle box. Align the bracket so that it is level and square and properly spaced from the existing box. Use an aligning tool, if provided, or a faceplate as a guide.

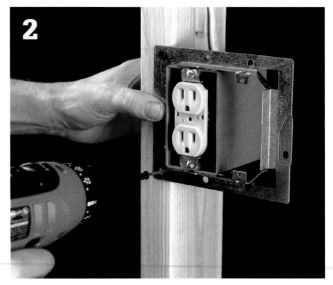

Fasten the bracket to the stud with two screws. The multimedia outlet box is then attached to the mounting ears on the extension bracket.

How to Retrofit a Single Multimedia Outlet Box

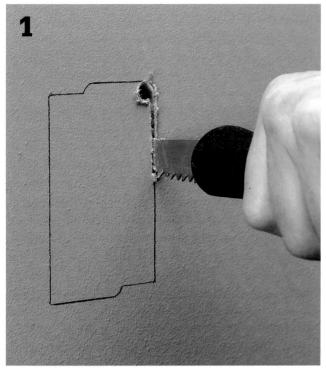

1

Use a wallboard saw to cut a hole at the outlet location that will accommodate the box size, a 4 × 4" gang box or hollow-back box, for a single outlet.

2

Route all the desired cables and wires to the distribution center location. Leave 12 to 18" of slack at each outlet location.

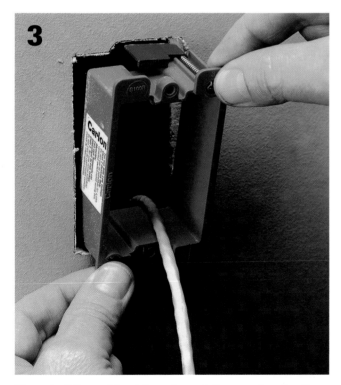

3

Thread all the cables into or through the gang box. Position the box in the hole.

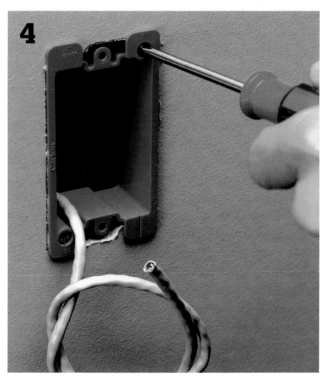

4

Tighten the mounting screws until snug to the wall. Avoid overtightening the screws to avoid damaging the wallboard.

Mounting the Distribution Center

Most distribution centers are designed to fit between standard stud spans of 16" on-center. For stud bays of different dimensions, you need to install blocking to support the distribution center. Retrofit installations require that you remove a large portion of finished wall and then refinish it once installation of the entire system is complete.

The bottom of the enclosure should be installed at least 48" above the floor. Most models require a ¼" gap behind the enclosure to accommodate the modules and fastening hardware. The front should protrude $1^{11}\!/_{16}$" plus the thickness of the drywall from the studs to allow the cover to fit (depends on model).

A dedicated 15-amp, 120-volt electrical receptacle is suggested and may be required, depending on the grade of installation.

Tools & Materials ▸

Screwdriver	Wood shims
Level	Cable clamp
Wood screws	15-amp,
Distribution center	120-volt receptacle

A distribution center organizes all the network controls in one spot.

How to Recess Mount a Distribution Center

Install the distribution center at least 48" above the floor. Position between two studs with a standard span of 16" on-center.

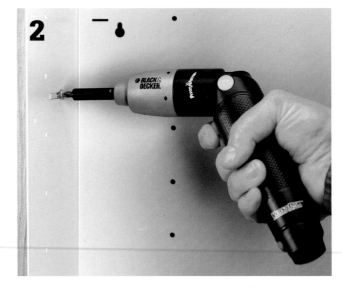

Use wood screws, one for each of the mounting slots located on the sides of the distribution center, to fasten to the studs. Do not fully tighten the screws.

3 1¹¹⁄₁₆" minimum

Use wood shims to create a minimum ¼" gap between the back of the distribution center and the wall. The front edge of the center should protrude at least 1¹¹⁄₁₆" from the finished wall face. Adjust the shims for proper spacing, check for level, and tighten the screws to secure the center in position.

Alternative Method: Surface-mount the distribution center. Leave a ¼" gap between the back of the center and the wall. Use wall anchors where needed, with spacers or shims as necessary.

How to Install the Power Supply

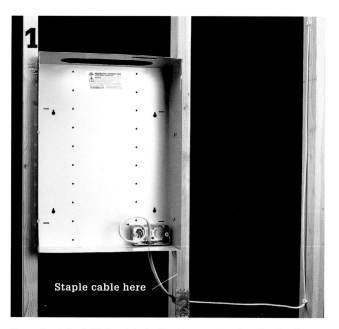

1

Staple cable here

Run electrical NM cable in the bay next to the distribution center using cable staples to affix the cable to the stud. Drill a 1" hole through the stud into the adjoining bay 4" below the distribution center.

2

Feed the NM cable through the hole and into the gang box of the distribution center. Attach the cable with a cable clamp. Install a grounded 15-amp, 120-volt receptacle before completing the rest of the installation.

Routing Cables & Wires

Routing cable and wire of any kind requires drilling holes through framing members throughout the home. Drill holes no closer than 2" from the top or bottom edge of joists. Use nail plates to protect holes in studs within 2" of the edge. Always check your local building codes for requirements in your area.

Low-voltage cable can run a maximum of 295 ft. from the distribution center without any significant signal loss. The cable cannot run within 6" of electrical wires and can cross only from a 90 degree angle, 6" from them.

To route cables and wires, begin at the outlet bracket or box locations, and feed to the distribution center. The maximum allowable pulling tension for UTP cable is 25 pounds. Use electrical tape to hold the tips of all cables and wires together as they are fed, and avoid knots and kinks. Leave at least 12" of slack at bracket or box locations for making connections.

If your service connections are outside the home, drill 1" holes through to the outside near the service entrance location. Insert a 1" PVC conduit, and feed cables and wires through it. Leave 36" of slack, and attach notice tags to the ends for utility workers.

At the distribution center, mark each cable and wire according to its routing location. Feed each through the top of the enclosure, and cut the lead ends so they hang even with the bottom of the distribution center. When routing is complete, tuck all cables and wires neatly inside the distribution center and finish wall construction. For tips on routing cables and wires in finished walls, refer to page 40.

Tools & Materials ▶

Drill	Tape
RJ45 crimp tool	Cables
F-connector	RJ45 plugs
Crimp tool	F-connectors

Drill 1" holes through the top plate above the distribution center. Drill holes in floor joists for running cable along the underside of house levels and from the service entrance to the distribution center.

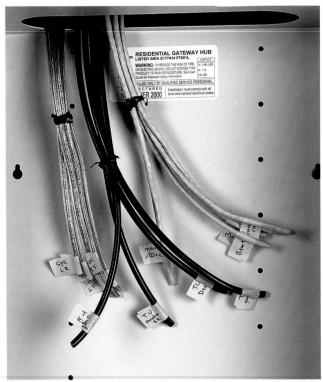

Label each run of cable and wire at the distribution center with the room and location within the room. All cables should hang even with the bottom of the distribution center.

How to Attach RJ45 Plugs to a UTP Cable

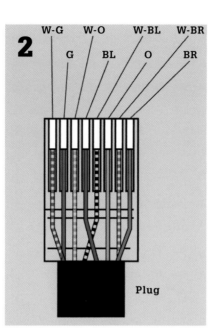

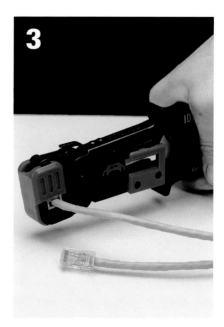

Strip 1 to 2" of outer insulation from the UTP cable. Separate the twisted pairs of individual wires.

Straighten and arrange each of the wires in order, according to the wiring assignment chart. Trim the ends evenly to ½" from the outer insulation. Insert the wires into the grooves of an RJ45 plug.

Make sure each wire is under the proper IDC (the conductor ends of the RJ45 plug) and that the outer insulation is ½" inside the plug. Crimp the plug with an RJ45 crimp tool.

How to Attach F-connectors to Coaxial Cable

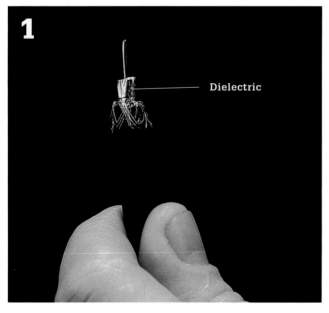

Strip the jacket and dielectric ⅜" from the center conductor. Strip the jacket ¼" from the foil and braid.

Slide the metal F-connector on until the dielectric is flush with center barrel. The center conductor should extend ¹⁄₁₆" past the end of the F-connector. Crimp the outer barrel of the connector to the cable jacket using an F-connector crimp tool.

How to Install a Recessed Speaker System

A home audio system routes speaker wire from a central receiver or amplifier, through the network distribution center, and back through to any room in the house. Each room can then be outfitted with either binding posts for an external speaker system or a recessed speaker system that is wired directly.

A volume control knob can be installed, typically at or near a light switch, to control the input level to the speakers in rooms wired to an external stereo system. Use a standard 4 × 4" gang box to house the module, and install as for an electrical switch.

Tools & Materials ▸

Screwdriver
Speaker mounting
   brackets

Screws
Volume control box
Speakers

Loosely fasten the speaker mounting brackets to the rails with the provided screws or ¼" sheet-metal screws. Attach the assembled brackets to the studs with 1½" screws. Align the loose bracket in the rails so that the outer edge of the bracket will be flush with the outside face of the wallboard. Fully tighten the screws.

An installed audio system is essentially a built-in network of speakers and speaker wire.

2

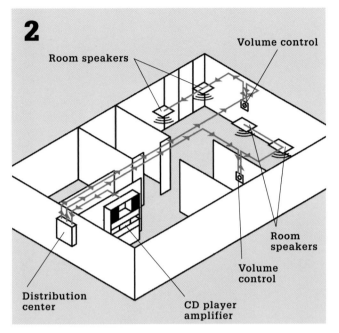

Run stereo speaker wire from each speaker location to the volume control box location. From the volume control box, run wire to the distribution center. Leave 8 to 12" of slack at each location.

3

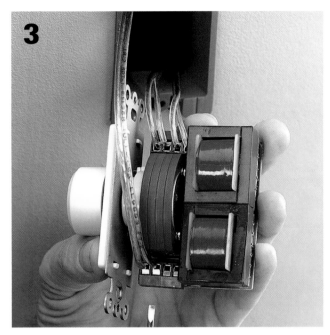

Connect the wires at the volume control with positive to positive (+ or red) and negative to negative (– or black). Position the module in the gang box and screw into place. Attach the cover plate.

4

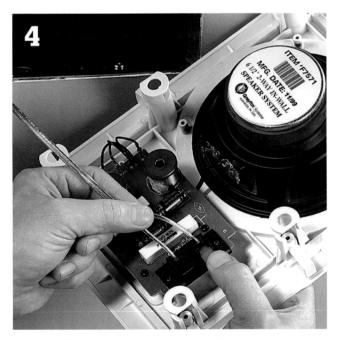

Connect the wires at each speaker. Keep positive to positive (+ or red) and negative to negative (– or black). Attach the speaker to the bracket. Some recessed speakers have plastic mounting arms that swing into place and clamp to the bracket when the front screws are tightened. Follow the manufacturer's directions.

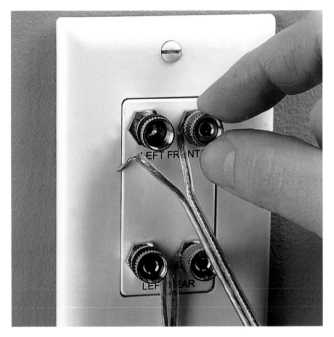

Alternative Method: If not installing a recessed speaker system, install speaker binding posts. The network speaker wire is connected to the back of the binding posts. Run positive to positive (+ or red) and negative to negative (– or black).

Terminating Connectors

With the distribution center and multimedia outlets placed, and all the cables and wires routed, finish the walls in each room before terminating the connectors. Most connectors and jacks are designed to snap into the cover plate.

Any style of telecommunication plug will fit in an RJ45 jack. UTP cable is terminated to the eight pins of the jack in an industry standard configuration referred to as the T568A wiring standard. A 110-punchdown tool is used to terminate the wires to the corresponding terminals.

To terminate video connectors, crimp an F-connector to the coaxial cable end (page 323), and screw it to the backside of the self-terminating F-connector at the cover plate.

Tools & Materials ▸

Wire stripper
Screwdriver
110-punchdown tool

RJ45 jacks
F-connector
  terminals

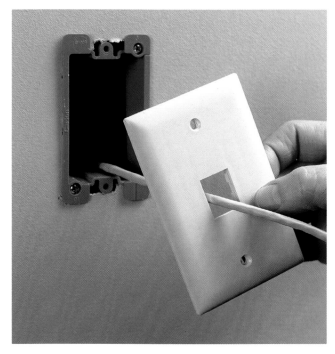

Before terminating a connector, pull all cables and wires for all multimedia outlets through the cover plate, leaving 8 to 12" of slack for termination. Attach the cover plate in place with the screws provided.

How to Terminate an RJ45 Jack

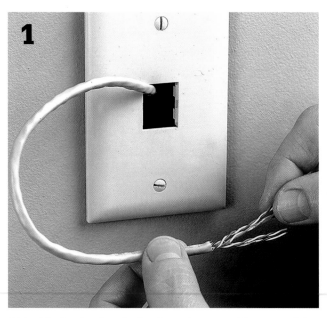

1

Strip 2" of outer insulation from the UTP cable. Be careful not to cut through the twisted pairs within. Untwist each pair of individual wires.

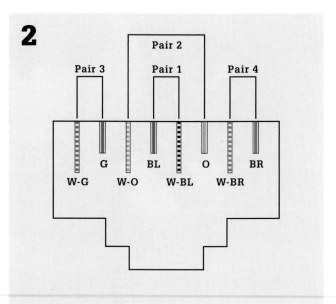

2

The backside of most RJ45 jacks are color-coded in the T568A wiring standard, so the proper colored wire from the UTP cable can be easily terminated to the proper terminal of the jack.

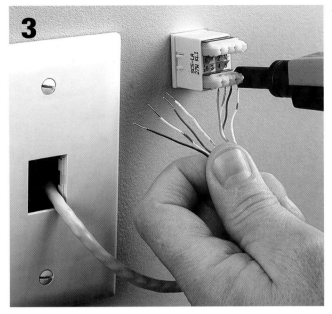

3

4

Terminal cap

Place each wire into the groove of the appropriate terminal on the RJ45 jack, then use a 110-punchdown tool to seat the wire completely. The tool has a spring-tension head that forces the wire down and trims off the end. There should be no more than ½" of wire from the terminal to the outer cable insulation.

Fit a terminal cap over the ends of the jack terminals, then snap the jack into the cover plate.

How to Terminate Video Connectors

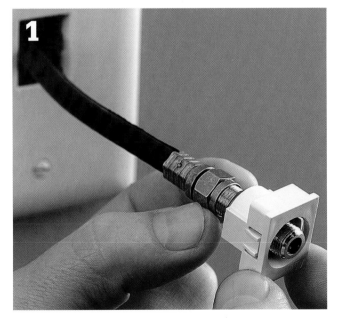

1

2

All coaxial video cables have plug-and-play connectors. The F-connector cable end is simply screwed to the back of the self-terminating F-connector terminal, and then snapped into the cover plate.

Video cameras also have plug-and-play self-terminating F-connector connections. Consult the manufacturer's installation guide for setup and playback of your particular camera.

Making Final Connections

To house the distribution modules, mounting brackets are installed within the distribution center. Some brackets and modules will require screws for installation, while others use plastic pushpin grommets.

For easy connection to modules, RJ45 plugs are attached to UTP cable ends and F-connectors to coaxial cable ends (page 323). All cables and wires should be clearly marked for easy identification and installation. It is best to keep all cables and wires routed to the same modules in neat, organized groupings. Bind the groupings with tie wraps where appropriate.

Once all the connections are made and the system is in working order, a cover is attached to protect the electronic modules and cable connections.

Tools & Materials ▸

Screwdriver
Modules
RJ45 plugs
F-connectors

Screws or pushpin
grommets
(as required)

How to Install Distribution Center Brackets

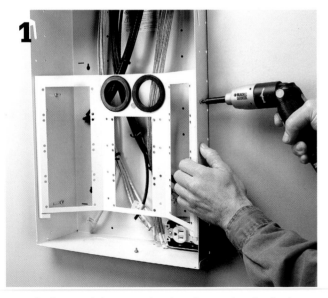

Attach the module mounting bracket to the distribution center. Align the mounting holes of the bracket panel with the prerouted holes in the sides of the distribution center and attach using the screws provided.

Attach any additional single brackets that may be necessary for specialized modules or for keeping power transformers separate. Some brackets require screws for installation, while others use pushpin grommets.

How to Mount & Connect Modules

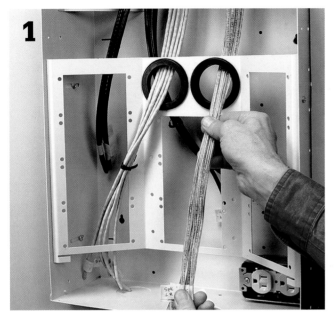

Determine where each module will be placed in the mounting brackets. Route any cables and wires through the mounting brackets to their corresponding module.

Plug the power transformer into the power distribution module, then snap the power module in place. The methods for module installation differ among network wiring manufacturers. Some require screws, while others use convenient pushpin grommets. Plug the power transformer into the 120-volt receptacle of the distribution center.

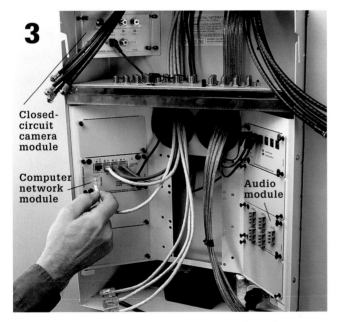

Use patch cords to connect the power module to those modules that require power, such as the video distribution, computer network, and video camera modules. Then install the remaining modules in their chosen locations.

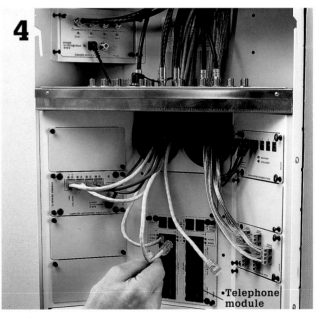

Trim the ends of all cables and wires, and attach the appropriate plugs or connectors. Refer to the labels to connect the proper cable to the proper module output port in order to route the desired function to the desired location. Make sure all cables and wires from the service entrance are connected to an input port.

Testing the System & Troubleshooting Problems

Before connecting to the home network system, do a quick recheck of the connections at the distribution center. Make sure that every module requiring power is patched to the power distribution module. Make sure the service lines from the service entrance are connected to the proper module input port. Check that each cable and wire from the room outlets are hooked up to the proper module output ports.

Cables and wires that are intended for future use should be gathered and loosely tied together. Run the grouping down one side of the distribution center, out of the way of the other connections. The system is now installed. Attach the cover and plug in the power distribution transformer to the receptacle for power.

To check the quality of signals at multimedia outlets, use a standard two-way phone and phone cord for RJ45 jacks, and a small television and short length of coaxial cable for F-connectors. The signals should be clear and strong.

Network system problems can be traced to one of a few simple causes: a bad connection, a bad cable or wire, a problem with a module, or a bad signal routed to the outlet.

Connectors: First, check that plugs and connection ends, and jack and connector terminations are correct. A visual inspection of pin/pair alignment on an RJ45 jack or plug will quickly tell you whether it is in working order. If any of the wires of the UTP cable are terminated to the wrong posts, trim the cable ½" from the base and reterminate the jack or plug. The center conductor of coaxial cables should be straight and extend ¹⁄₁₆" from the F-connector end. Coaxial cables should be tightly attached to the outlet

F-connector: recheck the connections at the distribution center to make sure the desired signal is routed to the proper outlet.

If an RJ45 jack does not work, remove the jack from the cover plate and check the pin/pair assignments on the back of the jack. If any wires are terminated to the wrong post, trim the wire ½" from the base and re-terminate the jack.

A variety of handheld testers can be used to check cables and wires in the network system for continuity, network capabilities, and pin/pair assignments. If a cable or wire is bad, it will have to be replaced.

Cables and wires: damage to cables and wires can easily occur during installation if the proper routing techniques are not observed.

A variety of handheld testers can be used to check cables and wires for continuity, network and performance capabilities, and pin/pair assignments. However, these testers are quite expensive and are not readily available at rental centers. For this reason, if a cable or wire is suspected to be faulty, it may be more economical to forgo testing and just replace the cable.

Modules: If none of the outlets in a particular network are functioning, check the power distribution module to see if there has been a power surge. The module contains a fuse that automatically resets, protecting the system against power trouble. If the LED light appears red, there has been an abnormal and significant electrical surge in the system. Disconnect all the modules from the power module. Begin reconnecting the modules one at a time, until

the LED light on the power module appears red again, indicating the problem module. Disconnect the module, and replace it. Modules for video distribution and computer networks are typically power surge–protected to keep your sensitive and expensive computer and entertainment equipment from damage.

Signals: If, after replacing any damaged modules, there still is no signal or only a very poor signal, test the incoming cables from the service entrance on the interior of the house only. If they are good and problems persist, contact your telecommunication and service providers to check the exterior lines and connections.

Another resource is the growing number of electrical contractors who work with and install network wiring systems. Call around or stop by a home center—many home centers that sell network wiring systems can also help you find a reputable contractor in your area.

Most modules contain built-in surge protection to protect electronic equipment and devices connected to the network. An illuminated indicator light alerts that a power surge has occurred in the system, and the problem module will need to be identified and replaced.

An NID box is located on the outside of the home. It is where the service providers transfer the lines to the homeowner. Test the incoming cable lines on the interior of the house only. If they are good and problems persist, contact your telecommunication providers to have them check the exterior lines and connections from the NID back to the source.

APPENDIX: Common Mistakes

An electrical inspector visiting your home might identify a number of situations that are not up to code. These situations may not be immediate problems. In fact, it is possible that the wiring in your home has remained trouble free for many years.

Nevertheless, any wiring or device that is not up to code carries the potential for problems, often at risk to your home and your family. In addition, you may have trouble selling your home if it is not wired according to accepted methods.

Most local electrical codes are based on the National Electrical Code (NEC), a book updated and published every three years by the National Fire Protection Agency. This code book contains rules and regulations for the proper installation of electrical wiring and devices. Most public libraries carry reference copies of the NEC.

All electrical inspectors are required to be well versed in the NEC. Their job is to know the NEC regulations and to make sure these rules are followed in order to prevent fires and ensure safety. If you have questions regarding your home wiring system, your local inspector will be happy to answer them.

While a book cannot possibly identify all potential wiring problems in your house, we have identified some of the most common wiring defects here and will show you how to correct them. When working on home wiring repair or replacement projects, refer to this section to help identify any conditions that may be hazardous.

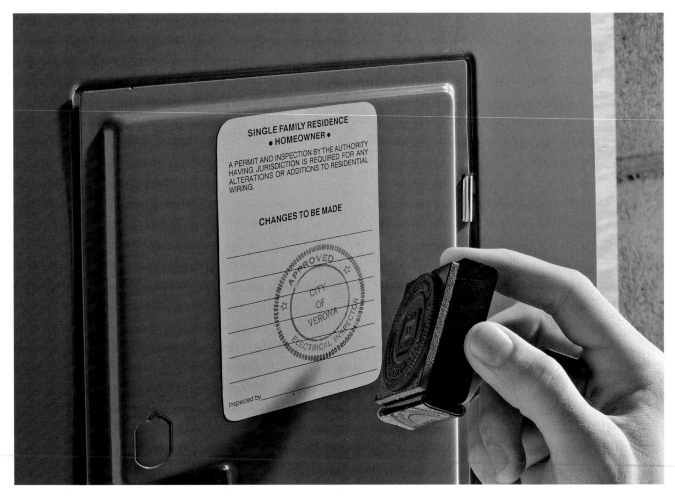

Electrical inspectors are on the lookout for common mistakes. The following pages detail problems to avoid so you will pass inspection on the first try.

Service Panel Inspection

Problem: Rust stains are found inside the main service panel. This problem occurs because water seeps into the service head outside the house and drips down into the service panel.

Solution: Have an electrician examine the service head and the main service panel. If the panel or service wires have been damaged, new electrical service must be installed.

Problem: This problem is actually a very old and very dangerous solution. A penny or a knockout behind a fuse effectively bypasses the fuse, preventing an overloaded circuit from blowing the fuse. This is very dangerous and can lead to overheated wiring.

Solution: Remove the penny and replace the fuse. Have a licensed electrician examine the panel and circuit wiring. If the fuse has been bypassed for years, wiring may be dangerously compromised, and the circuit may need to be replaced.

(continued)

Problem: Two wires connected to one single-pole breaker is a sign of an overcrowded panel and also a dangerous code violation unless the breaker is approved for such a connection.

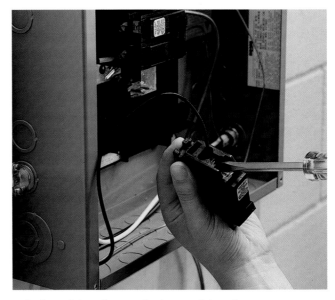

Solution: If there is room in the panel, install a separate breaker for the extra wire. If the panel is overcrowded, have an electrician upgrade the panel or install a subpanel.

Recognizing Aluminum Wire ▸

Inexpensive aluminum wire was used in place of copper in many wiring systems installed during the late 1960s and early 1970s, when copper prices were high. Aluminum wire is identified by its silver color and by the AL stamp on the cable sheathing. A variation, copper-clad aluminum wire, has a thin coating of copper bonded to a solid aluminum core.

By the early 1970s, all-aluminum wire was found to pose a safety hazard if connected to a switch or receptacle with brass or copper screw terminals. Because aluminum expands and contracts at a different rate than copper or brass, the wire connections could become loose. In some instances, fires resulted.

Existing aluminum wiring in homes is considered safe if proper installation methods have been followed, and if the wires are connected to special switches and receptacles designed to be used with aluminum wire. If you have aluminum wire in your home, have a qualified electrical inspector review the system. Copper-coated aluminum wire is not a hazard.

For a short while, switches and receptacles with an Underwriters Laboratories (UL) wire compatibility rating of AL-CU were used with both aluminum and copper wiring. However, these devices proved to be hazardous when connected to aluminum wire. AL-CU devices should not be used with aluminum wiring.

In 1971, switches and receptacles designed for use with aluminum wiring were introduced. They are marked CO/ALR. This mark is now the only approved rating for aluminum wires. If your home has aluminum wires connected to a switch or receptacle without a CO/ALR rating stamp, replace the device with a switch or receptacle rated CO/ALR.

A switch or receptacle that has no wire compatibility rating printed on the mounting strap or casing should not be used with aluminum wires. These devices are designed for use with copper wires only.

Inspecting the Bonding Jumper Wire

Problem: Bonding system jumper wire is missing or is disconnected. In most homes the grounding jumper wire attaches to water pipes on either side of the water meter. Because the ground pathway is broken, this is a dangerous situation that should be fixed immediately.

Solution: Attach a jumper wire to the water pipes on either side of the water meter using pipe clamps. Use #8-gauge bare copper wire for services that are 150 amps or smaller. Use #4 bare copper wire for 200 amp service.

Common Cable Problems

Problem: Cable running across joists or studs is attached to the edge of framing members. Electrical codes forbid this type of installation in exposed areas like unfinished basements or walk-up attics.

Solution: Protect cable by drilling holes in framing members at least 2" from exposed edges and threading the cable through the holes.

(continued)

Problem: Cable running along joists or studs hangs loosely. Loose cables can be pulled accidentally, causing damage to wires.

Solution: Anchor the cable to the side of the framing members at least 1¼" from the edge using plastic staples. NM (nonmetallic) cable should be stapled every 4½ ft. and within 8" of each electrical box.

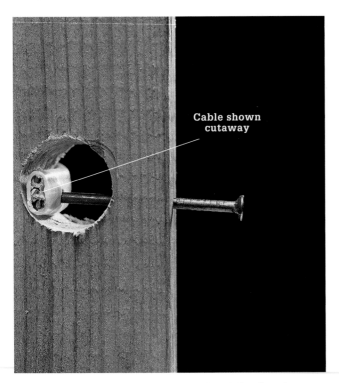

Cable shown cutaway

Problem: Cable threaded through studs or joists lies close to the edge of the framing members. NM (nonmetallic) cable (shown cutaway) can be damaged easily if nails or screws are driven into the framing members during remodeling projects.

Solution: Install metal nail guards to protect cable from damage. Nail guards are available at hardware stores and home centers.

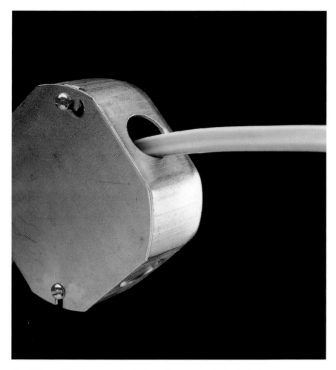

Problem: Unclamped cable enters a metal electrical box. Edges of the knockout can rub against the cable sheathing and damage the wires. *(Note: With plastic boxes, clamps are not required if cables are anchored to framing members within 12" of box.)*

Solution: Anchor the cable to the electrical box with a cable clamp. Several types of cable clamps are available at hardware stores and home centers.

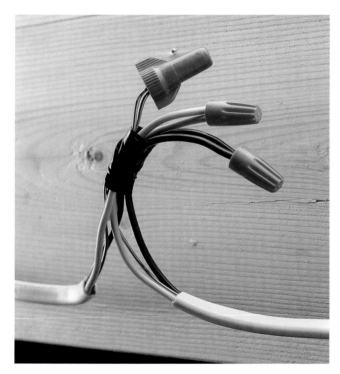

Problem: Cables are spliced outside an electrical box. Exposed splices can spark and create a risk of shock or fire.

Solution: Bring installation up to code by enclosing the splice inside a metal or plastic electrical box. Make sure the box is large enough to accommodate the number of wires it contains.

Checking Wire Connections

Problem: Two or more wires are attached to a single-screw terminal. This type of connection is seen in older wiring but is now prohibited by the National Electrical Code.

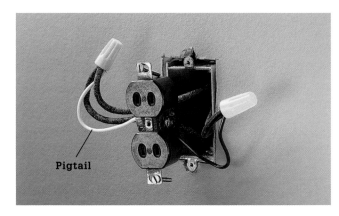

Pigtail

Solution: Disconnect the wires from the screw terminal, then join them to a short length of wire (called a pigtail) using a wire connector. Connect the other end of the pigtail to the screw terminal.

Exposed wire

Problem: Bare wire extends past a screw terminal. Exposed wire can cause a short circuit if it touches the metal box or another circuit wire.

Solution: Clip the wire and reconnect it to the screw terminal. In a proper connection, the bare wire wraps completely around the screw terminal, and the plastic insulation just touches the screw head.

Problem: Wires are connected with electrical tape. Electrical tape was used frequently in older installations, but it can deteriorate over time, leaving bare wires exposed inside the electrical box.

Solution: Replace electrical tape with wire connectors. You may need to clip away a small portion of the wire so the bare end will be covered completely by the connector.

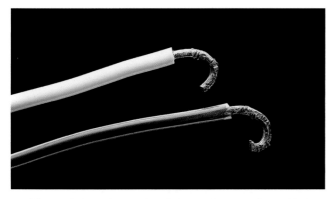

Problem: Nicks and scratches in bare wires interfere with the flow of current. This can cause the wires to overheat.

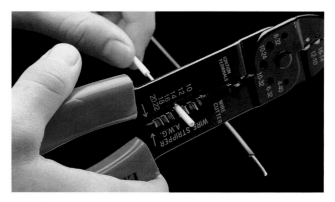

Solution: Clip away damaged portion of wire, then restrip about ¾" of insulation and reconnect the wire to the screw terminal.

Electrical Box Inspection

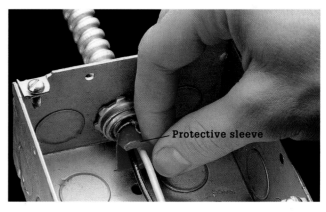

Armored cable

Sharp edges

Problem: No protective sleeve on armored cable. Sharp edges of the cable can damage the wire insulation, creating a shock hazard and fire risk.

Protective sleeve

Solution: Protect the wire insulation by installing a plastic sleeve around the wires. Sleeves are available at hardware stores. Wires that are damaged must be replaced.

Problem: Insulation on wires is cracked or damaged. If damaged insulation exposes bare wire, a short circuit can occur, posing a shock hazard and fire risk.

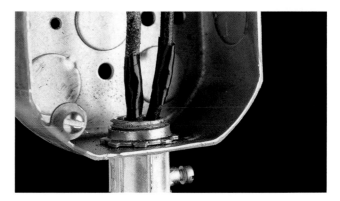

Solution: Wrap damaged insulation temporarily with plastic electrical tape. Damaged circuit wires should be replaced by an electrician.

(continued)

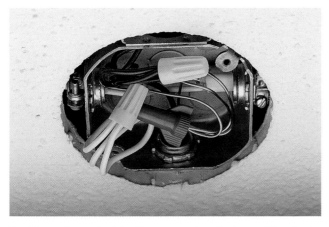

Problem: Open electrical boxes create a fire hazard if a short circuit causes sparks (arcing) inside the box.

Solution: Cover the open box with a solid metal cover plate, available at any hardware store. Electrical boxes must remain accessible and cannot be sealed inside ceilings or walls.

Problem: Short wires are difficult to handle. The National Electrical Code (NEC) requires that each wire in an electrical box have at least 6" of workable length.

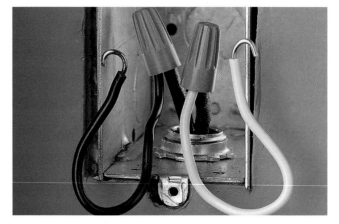

Solution: Lengthen circuit wires by connecting them to short pigtail wires using wire connectors. Pigtails can be cut from scrap wire but should be the same gauge and color as the circuit wires and at least 6" long.

Problem: A recessed electrical box is hazardous, especially if the wall or ceiling surface is made from a flammable material, like wood paneling. The National Electrical Code prohibits this type of installation.

Solution: Add an extension ring to bring the face of the electrical box flush with the surface. Extension rings come in several sizes and are available at hardware stores.

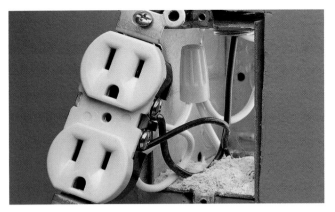

Problem: Open electrical boxes create a fire hazard if a short circuit causes sparks (dust and dirt in electrical box can cause hazardous high-resistance short circuits). When making routine electrical repairs, always check the electrical boxes for dust and dirt buildup.

Solution: Vacuum the electrical box clean using a narrow nozzle attachment. Make sure power to the box is turned off at main service panel before vacuuming.

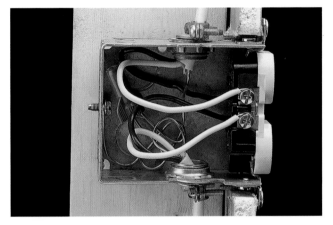

Problem: Crowded electrical box (shown cutaway) makes electrical repairs difficult. This type of installation is prohibited because wires can be damaged easily when a receptacle or switch is installed.

Solution: Replace the electrical box with a deeper electrical box.

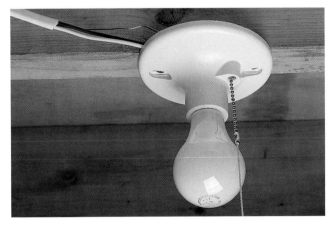

Problem: Light fixture is installed without an electrical box. This installation exposes the wiring connections and provides no support for the light fixture.

Solution: Install an approved electrical box to enclose the wire connections and support the light fixture.

Common Electrical Cord Problems

Problem: Lamp or appliance cord runs underneath a rug. Foot traffic can wear off insulation, creating a short circuit that can cause fire or shock.

Solution: Reposition the lamp or appliance so that cord is visible. Replace worn cords.

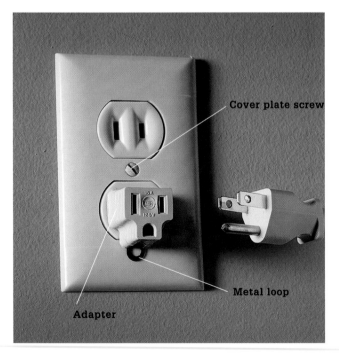

Cover plate screw

Adapter

Metal loop

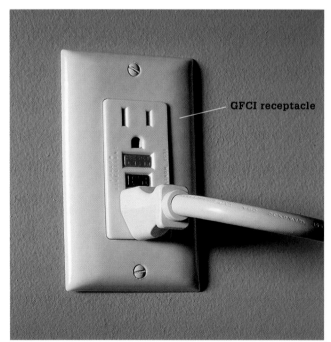

GFCI receptacle

Problem: Three-prong appliance plugs do not fit two slot receptacle. Do not use three-prong adapters unless the metal loop on the adapter is tightly connected to the cover plate screw on receptacle.

Solution: Install a three-prong grounded receptacle if a means of grounding exists at the box. Install a GFCI (ground-fault circuit-interrupter) receptacle in kitchens and bathrooms, or if the electrical box is not grounded.

Problem: Lamp or appliance plug is cracked, or electrical cord is frayed near plug. Worn cords and plugs create a fire and shock hazard.

Solution: Cut away damaged portion of wire and install a new plug (pages 294 to 295). Replacement plugs are available at appliance stores and home centers.

Problem: Extension cord is too small for the power load drawn by a tool or appliance. Undersized extension cords can overheat, melting the insulation and leaving bare wires exposed.

Solution: Use an extension cord with wattage and amperage ratings that meet or exceed the rating of the tool or appliance. Extension cords are for temporary use only. Never use an extension cord for a permanent installation.

Inspecting Receptacles & Switches

Problem: Octopus receptacle attachments used permanently can overload a circuit and cause overheating of the receptacle.

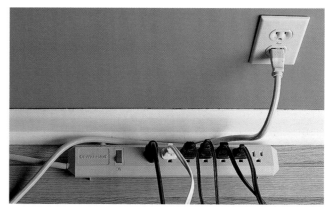

Solution: Use a multi-receptacle power strip with built-in overload protection. This is for temporary use only. If the need for extra receptacles is frequent, upgrade the wiring system.

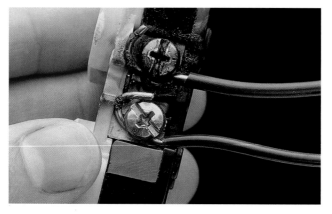

Problem: Scorch marks near screw terminals indicate that electrical arcing has occurred. Arcing usually is caused by loose wire connections.

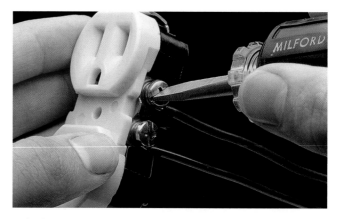

Solution: Clean wires with fine sandpaper, and replace the receptacle if it is badly damaged. Make sure wires are connected securely to screw terminals.

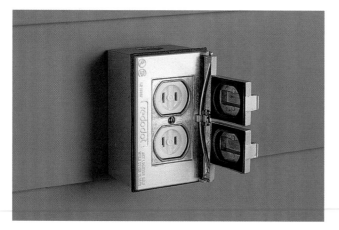

Problem: Exterior receptacle box allows water to enter box when receptacle slots are in use.

Solution: Replace the old receptacle box (no longer code compliant) with an in-use box that has a bubble cover to protect plugs from water while they are in the slots.

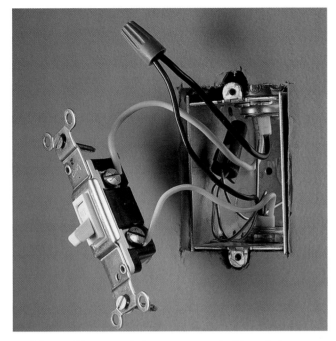

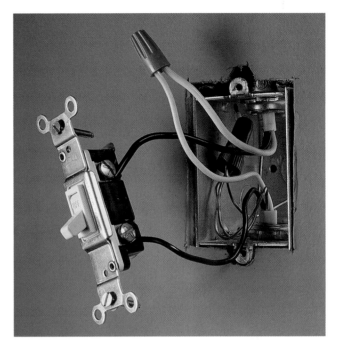

Problem: White neutral wires are connected to switch. Although the switch appears to work correctly in this installation, it is dangerous because the light fixture carries voltage when the switch is off.

Solution: Connect the black hot wires to the switch, and join the white wires together with a wire connector.

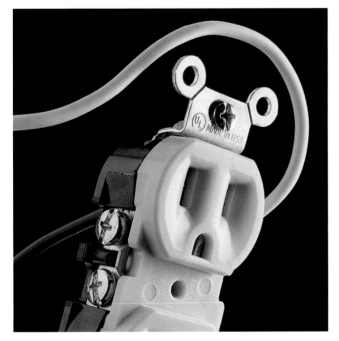

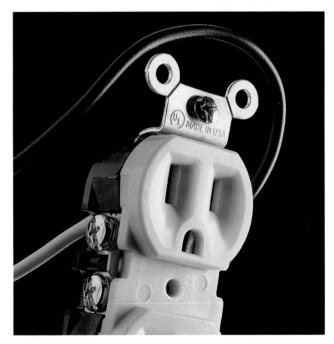

Problem: White neutral wires are connected to the brass screw terminals on the receptacle, and black hot wires are attached to silver screw terminals. This installation is hazardous because live voltage flows into the long neutral slot on the receptacle.

Solution: Reverse the wire connections so that the black hot wires are attached to brass screw terminals and white neutral wires are attached to silver screw terminals. Live voltage now flows into the short slot on the receptacle.

Conversions & Resources

Metric Equivalent

Inches (in.)	1/64	1/32	1/25	1/16	1/8	1/4	3/8	2/5	1/2	5/8	3/4	7/8	1	2	3	4	5	6	7	8	9	10	11	12	36	39.4
Feet (ft.)																								1	3	3 1/12
Yards (yd.)																									1	1 1/12
Millimeters (mm)	0.40	0.79	1	1.59	3.18	6.35	9.53	10	12.7	15.9	19.1	22.2	25.4	50.8	76.2	101.6	127	152	178	203	229	254	279	305	914	1,000
Centimeters (cm)							0.95	1	1.27	1.59	1.91	2.22	2.54	5.08	7.62	10.16	12.7	15.2	17.8	20.3	22.9	25.4	27.9	30.5	91.4	100
Meters (m)																								.30	.91	1.00

Converting Measurements

To Convert:	To:	Multiply by:
Inches	Millimeters	25.4
Inches	Centimeters	25.4
Feet	Meters	0.305
Yards	Meters	0.914
Miles	Kilometers	1.609
Square inches	Square centimeters	6.45
Square feet	Square meters	0.093
Square yards	Square meters	0.836
Cubic inches	Cubic centimeters	16.4
Cubic feet	Cubic meters	0.0283
Cubic yards	Cubic meters	0.765
Pints (U.S.)	Liters	0.473 (Imp. 0.568)
Quarts (U.S.)	Liters	0.946 (Imp. 1.136)
Gallons (U.S.)	Liters	3.785 (Imp. 4.546)
Ounces	Grams	28.4
Pounds	Kilograms	0.454
Tons	Metric tons	0.907

To Convert:	To:	Multiply by:
Millimeters	Inches	0.039
Centimeters	Inches	0.394
Meters	Feet	3.28
Meters	Yards	1.09
Kilometers	Miles	0.621
Square centimeters	Square inches	0.155
Square meters	Square feet	10.8
Square meters	Square yards	1.2
Cubic centimeters	Cubic inches	0.061
Cubic meters	Cubic feet	35.3
Cubic meters	Cubic yards	1.31
Liters	Pints (U.S.)	2.114 (Imp. 1.76)
Liters	Quarts (U.S.)	1.057 (Imp. 0.88)
Liters	Gallons (U.S.)	0.264 (Imp. 0.22)
Grams	Ounces	0.035
Kilograms	Pounds	2.2
Metric tons	Tons	1.1

Converting Temperatures

Convert degrees Fahrenheit (F) to degrees Celsius (C) by following this simple formula: Subtract 32 from the Fahrenheit temperature reading. Then mulitply that number by 5/9. For example, 77°F - 32 = 45. 45 × 5/9 = 25°C.

To convert degrees Celsius to degrees Fahrenheit, multiply the Celsius temperature reading by 9/5, then add 32. For example, 25°C × 9/5 = 45. 45 + 32 = 77°F.

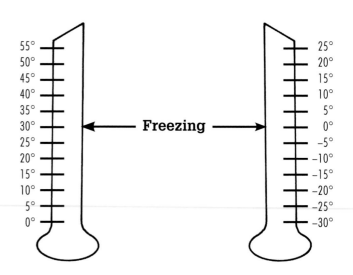

Fahrenheit **Celsius**

Freezing

Briggs & Stratton Power
800 743 4155
www.briggsandstratton.com

Broan-NuTone, LLC
800 558 1711
www.broan.com

Crossville, Inc.
931 484 2110
www.crossvilleinc.com

Cabin Fever
Cabins built in Miami, Florida
www.metroshed.com

Generac Power Systems
www.generac.com
www.guardiangenerators.com

Hakatai Enterprises, Inc.
Glass mosaic tile
www.hakatai.com
shown on pages 254, 256

Home Automation, Inc.
800 229 7256
www.homeauto.com

**Honda Power Equipment/
American Honda Motor Company, Inc.**
678 339 2600
www.hondapowerequipment.com

Hubbardton Forge
802 468 5516
www.vtforge.com

Ideal Industries, Inc.
800 435 0705
www.idealindustries.com

Ikea Home Furnishings
610 834 0180
www.Ikea-USA.com

Insinkerator
800 558 5700
www.insinkerator.com

Kohler
800 4 Kohler
www.kohlerco.com

LATICRETE
Floor warming mats and supplies
800 243 4788
www.laticrete.com
shown on page 241

Pass & Seymour Legrand
800 223 4185
www.passandseymour.com

SieMatic Möbelwerke USA
215 604 1350
www.siematic.com

Westinghouse
Ceiling fans, decorative lighting, solar outdoor lighting,
  & other lighting fixtures and bulbs
800 245 5874
Purchase here: www.budgetlighting.com
www.westinghouse.com

Photo Credits

p. 179 photo © Mike Clarke / www.istock.com
p. 194 photo © George Peters / www.istock.com
p. 198 photo courtesy of Broan NuTone
p. 210 photo (top right) courtesy of Kohler
p. 212 photo courtesy of Ikea
p. 246 photo © George Peters / www.istock.com
p. 247 photo © David Ross / www.istock.com
p. 255 (top right) photo © Steve Harmon / istock.com,
  (lower right) photo courtesy of SieMatic

p. 258 photo © Jeff Chevrier / www.istock.com
p. 259 photos (top right & lower) courtesy of Generac
  Power Systems, Inc.
p. 264 photo courtesy of Cabin Fever, featuring McMaster
  Carr vapor-tight light fixtures
p. 284 (upper right) photo courtesy of Westinghouse
p. 287 (upper right) photo courtesy of Westinghouse

Index

Also From CREATIVE PUBLISHING international

Complete Guide to A Green Home

Complete Guide to Attics & Basements

Complete Guide to Basic Woodworking

Complete Guide Build Your Kids a Treehouse

Complete Guide to Contemporary Sheds

Complete Guide to Creative Landscapes

Complete Guide to Custom Shelves & Built-Ins

Complete Guide to Decorating with Ceramic Tile

Complete Guide to Decks

Complete Guide to DIY Projects for Luxurious Living

Complete Guide to Dream Bathrooms

Complete Guide to Dream Kitchens

Complete Guide to Finishing Walls & Ceilings

Complete Guide to Floor Décor

Complete Guide to Gazebos & Arbors

Complete Guide to Home Carpentry

Complete Guide to Landscape Construction

Complete Guide Maintain Your Pool & Spa

Complete Guide to Masonry & Stonework

Complete Guide to Outdoor Wood Projects

Complete Guide to Painting & Decorating

Complete Guide to Patios

Complete Guide to Plumbing

Complete Guide to Roofing & Siding

Complete Guide to Trim & Finish Carpentry

Complete Guide to Windows & Entryways

Complete Guide to Wiring

Complete Guide to Wood Storage Projects

Complete Guide to Yard & Garden Features

Complete Outdoor Builder

Complete Photo Guide to Home Repair

Complete Photo Guide to Home Improvement

Complete Photo Guide to Homeowner Basics

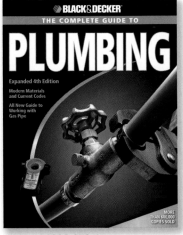

ISBN 1-58923-378-6

ISBN 1-58923-355-7

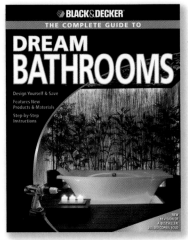

ISBN 1-58923-377-8

Creative Publishing international

400 First Avenue North • Suite 300 • Minneapolis, MN 55401 • www.creativepub.com